The Collected Papers

OF

OTTO FENICHEL

SECOND SERIES

Books by Otto Fenichel

The Psychoanalytic Theory of Neurosis

The Collected Papers of Otto Fenichel: First Series
With an Introduction by Bertram D. Lewin, M.D.

The Collected Papers of Otto Fenichel: Second Series

THE *Collected Papers*

OF

OTTO FENICHEL

SECOND SERIES

———★★———

W · W · NORTON & COMPANY · INC · *New York*

PRINTED IN THE UNITED STATES OF AMERICA

FOR THE PUBLISHERS BY THE VAIL-BALLOU PRESS

2 3 4 5 6 7 8 9

Contents

Preface

THE publication of the two series of Otto Fenichel's *Collected Papers* is the result of the concerted efforts made by those who felt that this book would at once be a memorial to Otto Fenichel and the fulfillment of a public need. My sincere appreciation goes to all those who have contributed to the completion of this project.

This new collection will now make easily available all those papers written in English which had previously appeared in many different periodicals, and besides it will make accessible those papers which had not been translated before.

These papers were written over a period of 24 years and though changing views are expressed in them no attempts at unification were made, as it seemed essential to me to preserve their original form.

In all references to Freud's work the latest editions are given. This procedure makes for easy recourse for those interested in the context of the quotation but inevitably obscures the actual chronological sequence of Freud's writings.

There are a few papers of Otto Fenichel which are not included in the two volumes: early publications of his which deal with Jewish, youth movement, and social problems and which seemed to me not to belong to his strictly psychoanalytic writings.

These two volumes, however, together with his previous books, represent Otto Fenichel's life work, his contribution to psychoanalysis.

HANNA FENICHEL

Acknowledgments

GRATEFUL acknowledgment is made to the publishers of the following periodicals for permission to print those papers of which they control the copyrights: *The Psychoanalytic Quarterly, The International Journal of Psycho-analysis, The Psychoanalytic Review, The American Imago, Psychosomatic Medicine,* and the former *Zeitschrift fuer Paedagogik*.

I am greatly indebted to Dr. David Rapaport for doing the rough translations of the previously not translated papers and to Mrs. Alix Strachey, who took the responsibility of the final English form; to Miss Suzette Annin, who with Dr. Rapaport's help is responsible for the completion and unification of the bibliographic footnotes; to Miss Annin and Mrs. Ruth Shippey, secretaries of the Austen Riggs Center, Stockbridge, Mass., who did the work of typing and assembling through all its phases with the help of Miss Sarah Austin, librarian of the Riggs Center for the bibliographic work; to Drs. Alfred Goldberg and Milton Wexler for assistance with the index.

I also wish to thank the publishers for their patience and continuous support during the many months of preparation.

Most of all, however, I want to express my deep gratitude to my friend David Rapaport, without whose unending and devoted help and efforts this publication could not have been achieved.

HANNA FENICHEL

The Collected Papers

OF

OTTO FENICHEL

SECOND SERIES

❀ ❀ ❀ ❀ ❀ ❀ ❀ ❀ ❀ ❀ ❀ ❀ ❀ ❀ ❀ ❀ ❀

O N E

The Symbolic Equation: Girl = Phallus*

I

IN MY article on the analysis of a transvestite,[1] I established the fact that at the root of this perversion there lay the patient's unconscious fantasy of being a girl with a phallus. If—schematically speaking—the homosexual has identified himself with his mother, and the fetishist has not relinquished the belief in the woman's possession of a penis, both of these formulations are valid for the male transvestite: he identifies himself with a woman in whose possession of a penis, furthermore, he wishes to believe.

My patient acted out this rôle of a phallic girl in order to be able to yield to feminine wishes which were opposed by intense castration anxiety. The perversion purportedly counteracted this anxiety, for its purpose, as I stated, was to say to the object: "Love me like the mother (or like the sister); it is not true that I thereby endanger my penis." I was able to demonstrate the probability that this is, in a general sense, the meaning of the transvestite act. It is a compromise between feminine wishes and an opposing fear of castration, or, since the fear of castration is the result of a heightened narcissistic evaluation of one's own penis, between the feminine wish and the narcissistic pride in one's penis. The exhibitionistic behavior of such patients has therefore the double meaning: "I want to be seen and admired for my penis," and "I want to be seen and admired as a beautiful girl." In the earlier paper referred to, I described as the most important incidental factor in transvestitism the fact that usually the identification with the mother is at the same time, on a more superficial level, an identification with

* First published in *Int. Z. Psa.,* Vol. 22, 1936, pp. 299–314.
[1] O. Fenichel, "The Psychology of Transvestitism," No. 20, *The Collected Papers of Otto Fenichel: First Series,* New York, Norton, 1953.

3

a little girl. These objectively contradictory tendencies are supposed to find expression simultaneously; of their relationship to each other, thus far nothing is conveyed. The situation might parallel that of the "Wolf-man," in that a relatively primary feminine longing is opposed by the realization that "the gratification of this desire would cost the penis," [2] as it might be that an originally strong penis pride and a phallic tendency to exhibitionism were inhibited by castration anxiety, and then became replaced by a feminine tendency to exhibitionism. In any case, phallic and feminine pleasure in exhibiting coalesce to form the leading fantasy of such patients: "I show myself as a girl with a penis." My patient, for example, was the recipient in his childhood of both phallic and feminine admiration, in that adults called his penis by pet names and also—because of his long hair—extolled him as a "beautiful girl."

In his perverse practices this patient represented not only a phallic girl but also a phallus pure and simple. I wrote: "The patient combined his femininity with a naïve narcissistic love for his own penis, which as a child he had called pet names; indeed, the girl's name which he wanted to have as a girl bore a striking resemblance to the pet name for his penis. Thus came about the symbolic equation: patient in woman's clothes = mother with penis = penis in general." The strength of the castration anxiety corresponds to the original penis narcissism, on account of which he could only indulge his later narcissistic longing to be admired as a girl by both equipping this girl with a penis and fantasying her as a penis directly. The equations, "I am a girl" and "my whole body is a penis" are here condensed into the idea: "I = my whole body = a girl = the little one = the penis."

Here we see for the first time that the frequently valid symbolic equation "penis = child" (the little one) can also assume the special form "penis = girl."

II

That girls, in their unconscious fantasies, frequently identify themselves with a penis has often been set forth. We also understand how such an identification comes about. It is one way among others of overcoming the original narcissistic penis envy. We know that frequently the aim, "I also want to have a penis"—when oral wishes are in the foreground, or oral fixations exist which in connection with the narcissistic injury occasioned by the discovery of the penis give rise to regressions—passes over into the aim, "I want to incorporate a penis orally"; and again we know that such tendencies, by reactivating old oral-sadistic wishes which once were directed against the mother, result in identification. "I

[2] S. Freud, "From the History of an Infantile Neurosis," *Coll. Pap.*, Vol. III, London, Hogarth, 1948, pp. 555–556.

have seized the penis and eaten it and have now myself become a penis" is the formula of identification of this kind. The prerequisite for a reaction of this description is thus the persistence of "tendencies to incorporation." Lewin [3] has collected material germane to this. According to him, one often finds in women simultaneously the fantasy of possessing a penis and the fantasy of being one. They identify themselves, i.e., their whole body, with a penis, via the pathway of oral introjection. The idea of having bitten off a penis or of having otherwise incorporated it is the continuation of the unconscious equation "body = penis." This equation, the aim of which is in fact that of a *totem* being taken into the body of the object, may therefore be regarded as a passive complement to the fantasy of swallowing a penis. We are dealing, hence, with a postphallic partial regression to oral conceptions.

I myself was able recently to publish the case of a patient in whose sexual life voyeurism played a particularly important rôle. The wish to see a penis covered the deeper one of eating it. This oral-sadistic possessing of the "seen" was meant as a genuine introjection and hence resulted also in identifications.

I have written elsewhere: [4]

"As is usual with oral characters, all her object relations were shot through with identifications. This invariably became particularly evident in sexual relations. Once when a friend of the patient proved to be impotent, her reaction to this was masculine to such a degree that we found for it the following formulation: 'We are impotent.' *Affaires à trois* played an important rôle in her fantasies as well as in her actual love life. She liked her friend to be with another woman in her presence, enjoying this in empathy with him. She found it unthinkable and quite unbearable that her friend might visit another woman in her absence. She had the feeling: 'Without me he can't do it at all!' Her expressions of affection always resulted in her snuggling up to the man's body like a small part of the latter. When her friend left her she experienced a 'sore feeling' in her back, as though her back had grown onto him and had now been torn loose. When, finally, she produced dreams of men who instead of a penis had a child pendent from the abdomen, there was no longer any doubt as to her identification with a penis. In the fantasy of hanging like a penis from the man's abdomen, we had a kind of father's body fantasy, the opposite of the fantasy of eating the father's penis: herself to be eaten as a penis by the father. For the man who had a child hanging from his abdomen instead of a penis appeared once again; now he had many such children; he had placed them inside his belt, or perhaps he held one of them up high in order to harm it, like the great St. Nicholas in *Struwwelpeter;* it was the *'Kindlifresser'* of Bern.

[3] B. D. Lewin, "The Body as Phallus," *Psa. Quart.,* Vol. 2, 1933.
[4] O. Fenichel, "Further Light upon the Pre-oedipal Phase in Girls," No. 24, *First Series.*

"Gradually the oral-sadistic impulses and tendencies toward identification with the penis increasingly manifested characteristics which it was not possible to explain via the penis but necessarily originated in an earlier period."

The father's body fantasy then turned out to be the continuation of a mother's body fantasy, the idea of the penis a continuation of the idea of the inside of the mother's body. To the identification with the penis, the pendent part of the father, there corresponded an identification with the embryo, the dependent of the mother (the *Anhängsel* of the father, the *Inhängsel* of the mother). The intention of disproving oral-sadistic tendencies against the penis by the fantasy of harmonious unity with it—"I am myself the penis"—seems in typical fashion a continuation of the intention of disproving oral-sadistic tendencies against the mother's body by means of the fantasy of harmonious unity with it—"I am myself within the mother's body." We must agree here with Lewin,[5] whose paper on the body as phallus was soon followed by one on claustrophobia—that is, on the body as embryo. But this origin of our fantasy from a longing for the mother's body is of less interest in the present connection than the fantasy of the father's body (*Vaterleibsphantasie*): a little girl hangs from the father's abdomen like a penis. Thus she is inseparably united with him, only a part of him, but his most important part; the father is powerless when she does not function for him as his magic wand, in the manner of Samson's hair.

I have since had the opportunity of analyzing another woman patient who, between striving to be a man and to be able to love as a woman, had found a compromise in loving a man whose penis she unconsciously fantasied herself to be—a form of love which is of necessity strongly marked by identifying features. Let us say a few words about this, since it takes us back to the fantasies of the male patient first discussed.

A gifted and very ambitious young girl was inhibited not only intellectually but in her whole development to such an extent that she sought analysis. She presented, in the first place, the familiar picture of a woman with "sexualization of the intellect." She wanted to shine by means of her intellectual gifts, but was prevented from this by her fear of disgrace. Analysis showed that the exhibitionistic achievement she really craved was basically that of urination, and the disgrace she feared was the discovery of her penisless state. The fear of this "disgrace" was unconsciously intensified by a fear of bloody injury to her genital. This fear manifested itself as a fear of retaliation for corresponding oral-sadistic tendencies, primarily against the penis. For instance, in order to escape the sadomasochistic temptation [6] involved in defloration by a man, she had deflorated

---

[5] B. D. Lewin, "Claustrophobia," *Psa. Quart.,* Vol. 4, 1935.

[6] S. Freud, "Contributions to the Psychology of Love. The Taboo of Virginity," *Coll. Pap.,* Vol. IV, London, Hogarth, 1948.

herself, and was filled with a great longing for "peaceful" sexuality. This longing for harmonious union of man and woman was intended to refute the unconscious impulse to steal the penis and to ward off the consequent fear of retaliation. She made the acquaintance of a man who impressed her as a "ravisher" and of whom she was therefore greatly afraid before she entered into sexual relations with him. To her surprise the actual sexual union with him was quite different from what she had imagined. Tenderness dominated over sensuality; she felt united with him in perfect harmony, clung tenderly to him, free of any anxiety; that she did not achieve orgasm did not seem bad to her at the time; they talked little, and the patient thought this was so because the harmony between them was so perfect that they understood each other without words, since they had become so completely one. During their union she felt so fascinated by the man that she thought she could do nothing that he did not want her to do. To the interpretation that she had behaved as though she were a part of the man's body, the patient responded with a very thinly disguised oedipus dream in which the man was clearly recognizable as a father image. And it was only in relation to the analysis of this dream that the various examples of the many oedipal daydreams of the patient came to be discussed. Her father had traveled much and far, and upon his return from his journeyings used to tell of his adventures. The patient—in the latency period, and, even more clearly, in and after puberty— would then fantasy herself as his companion. Secretly and invisibly, she fantasied she was always with him and experienced all his adventures jointly with him. These fantasies once took concrete form in the patient's giving her father the figure of a little bear which he took with him on his travels. He fell in with these fantasies of his daughter by making it his habit upon his return to take the bear out of his pocket and to assure her that he had kept it sacred and that it was his talisman. The meaning of the fantasy thus was that the patient, as the great father's little companion, protected him to such effect that he would be powerless without that protection. In analysis the patient fantasied herself as this bear which, carried in her father's pocket, took part in his travels. She peeped out of the pocket; she had a fantasy of kangaroos which peeped out of their mother's pouch, and realized that in that night of love's harmony she had snuggled her small body against the big body of her friend as though she were just such a young kangaroo. Thus we have a father's body fantasy, quite after the pattern of the earlier case discussed.

Further analysis revealed unequivocally that here too the *Vaterleibsphantasie* covered a *Mutterliebsphantasie* on a deeper level; that the penis corresponded to the idea of the inside of the mother's body, of the embryo, in whose place she had fantasied herself. The harmonious love scene repeated early experiences with the *mother,* and the whole power of the oral sadism which so disturbed her life appeared only after the patient, speaking of the summer of her fourth year, at which time a sister had been born, said: "My mother couldn't have lain in a hammock then." "But why not?" "Because one would have seen her pregnancy too clearly." And to the remark that her thought suggested that her mother had lain in such a way that she had noticed the pregnancy, the patient replied: "But I clearly remember that she didn't lie in a hammock!" Wherewith the way was opened to the analysis of the patient's anger, stemming from that time. But this is of relatively little interest to us. For us the recognition is sufficient that here too, the fantasy "I am a penis" represents a way out of the two conflicting tendencies, "I want to have a penis" and "I want to love a man as a woman." The fantasy of being a man's penis (and therefore united with him in an inseparable harmony) subserves the overcompensating repression of the other idea: "I am robbing a man and therefore must fear him." For in that case nothing is taken away, and there exists only an indivisible oneness. This, however, is brought about through identification with the penis, which on a deeper level means once again: through the seizing of the penis.

III

The oedipus fantasies of this patient have numerous points of contact with many often recurrent motives of legend and fairy tale; for example, little girl rescuers who protect great men in all their adventures occur not infrequently. Miracle-performing little companions (who do not necessarily have to be female), such as dwarfs, mandrakes, talisman figures of all kinds, have often been analyzed, and the "little double" has been recognized as a phallic figure.[7] The associations of the patient, however, first drew attention to the connections existing between such phallic figures and the "little girl rescuers," by pointing, for example, to Ottogebe, who in her spirit of sacrifice rescued poor Henry, or to Mignon, or to King Lear's youngest daughter, Cordelia, or to King Nicolo —drawn after Lear's image—to whom in his adversity only his youngest daughter remained faithful. The usual interpretation of these girl figures is that they represent a reversal of the "rescue fantasy." As is well known, the fantasy of men rescuing women or girls has been interpreted by Freud in the sense that the rescued women represents the mother.[8] But a female figure who rescues a man must likewise have mother significance. We do not doubt such an interpretation, and would merely note that it leaves many traits of this "girl rescuer" unexplained: her smallness, her outward weakness which stands in such contrast to her magic strength, and all the characteristics which these figures share with

[7] Cf. O. Rank, "Der Doppelgaenger," *Imago*, Vol. 3, 1914.
[8] S. Freud, "Contributions to the Psychology of Love. A Special Type of Choice of Object Made by Men," *Coll. Pap.*, Vol. IV.

the above-mentioned phallic "little double." Might not the interpretation be justified that all these female figures too have a penis significance? Freud's interpretation of Lear's Cordelia, that she represents the death-goddess,[9] does not run counter to such a conception. The death-goddess is at all events a magically omnipotent being, holding the far greater, far stronger father completely in her power; she is connected with those phallic figures by the concept of "magic omnipotence." From the feminine point of view this fantasy can likewise be understood as a compensation for the narcissistic injury of their penislessness, of their being inferior and smaller. "Even though I am little, my father must love me, since without me he can do nothing at all." The infantile omnipotence of the girl, threatened anew through the discovery of the penis, is restored through identification with the penis. I recall the *däumelinchen* fantasies by means of which one of Annie Reich's patients was able to compensate the numerous severe traumata of her early childhood by dominating her male admirers through her enactment in unmistakable fashion of the rôle of a phallus.[10]

IV

In psychoanalytic literature Mignon figures have often been a subject of investigation, but always from the male point of view. Noteworthy in particular in this connection is Sarasin's great work on Mignon herself,[11] who loved Wilhelm in so unhappy and dependent a manner and also had Harfner beside her as a father figure to whom she belonged and together with whom she first formed the "strange family." Sarasin recognized her as a figure in which the poet idealized his sister Cornelia; the poet developed an ambivalent father identification toward her, with mutual rescue (and destruction) fantasies. Sarasin noted that Mignon has various male characteristics, and he cites *inter alia* two quotations from Goethe which may be quoted here: "These two remained to him— Harfner whom he needed, and Mignon whom he could not do without"; in the second passage referred to, Mignon is called a "silly, bisexual creature." Such passages as these have caused other, preanalytic interpreters of Mignon (e.g., Wolff) to emphasize Mignon's hermaphroditic nature; but Sarasin explains these male traces in Mignon simply by reference to the fact that in her there occurs a condensation of the memory of Goethe's sister Cornelia and that of his dead brother Herman Jacob and of his other brothers and sisters. This is certainly correct but does not seem to us sufficient. The poet feels empathy not only for the Harfner-father (grandfather) who kills and rescues children, in order thus

[9] S. Freud, "The Theme of the Three Caskets," *Coll. Pap.*, Vol. IV.
[10] A. Reich, "Zur Genese einer praegenital fixierten Neurose," *Int. Z. Psa.*, Vol. 18, 1932.
[11] P. Sarasin, "Goethes Mignon," *Imago*, Vol. 15, 1929.

to play the role of father toward his brothers and sisters (to love them and threaten them), but he also feels empathy for Mignon—the intensity of Mignon's longing for Italy leaves no doubt of this—in whom he would thus be loved or threatened in passive-homosexual fashion. Mignon's male characteristics stem from the fact that she represents the poet himself, that she gives expression to the fantasy: "How would my father act toward me if I were a girl like Cornelia?" It is interesting that Sarasin, who did not recognize this, nevertheless came close to this interpretation when he wrote: "Here, probably, we are made privy to a state of mind which borders on madness, where the longing for the beloved object obliterates the boundary between the 'I' and the 'you,' and initiates the psyhic process known to us by the name of identification." That Mignon moreover represents not only a boy, but specifically his penis, cannot be maintained with certainty on the ground of her hermaphroditic characteristics, but becomes probable on the basis of the total context, and also if one takes into account, for example, the symbolism of her dancing.

Other available analyses of little girls like these, needful of help, yet in the sense of a talisman, rendering it—infantile women—leave from the masculine standpoint no doubt that in such cases we are dealing invariably with a narcissistic object choice. Such objects always represent the man himself who fantasies himself as a girl. "I want to be loved as a girl in the same way as I now love this infantile woman." The same mechanism of object choice here involved, as Freud has described, pertains to a certain type of male homosexuality,[12] and it is now established that it also occurs in the heterosexual. In my volume, *Perversionen, Psychosen, und Charakterstörungen*,[13] I wrote in this connection: "In feminine men who during childhood or puberty liked to fantasy themselves as girls, the same mechanism is present as in heterosexuals. They fall in love with little girls in whom they see themselves embodied, and to whom they give what their mothers denied them. Very probably this mechanism is also the decisive one in pedophilia." To this we will now add: Basically this object choice in heterosexual persons also represents a homosexual type, in which the woman, chosen in accordance with narcissistic object choice, is usually fantasied together with a great man, a father figure (whom the person himself represents); in empathy with the woman the man thus unconsciously is loved homosexually. Always such fantasies are combined with the idea of mutual protection: the little woman is rescued by the great man in actuality, the latter by the former in magical fashion.

[12] S. Freud, *Three Essays on the Theory of Sexuality*, London, Imago, 1949.
[13] O. Fenichel, *Perversionen, Psychosen, und Charakterstoerungen*, Vienna, Int. Psa. Verlag, 1931, p. 21.

A paper by Spitz on the infantile woman [14] likewise explains the choice of small love objects in need of help on the basis of a narcissistic type of object choice. We are here concerned, he writes, with men who in their childhood were brought up by their mothers more or less openly as girls; such a tendency toward feminization in boys is strengthened by the later and very sudden inhibition of aggressive tendencies; if there is an older sister with whom the boy can identify himself, the eventuation in the narcissistic object choice described is facilitated. Thus Spitz explains the hermaphroditic nature of the "child-woman," and believes that it is connected with socially conditioned changes in educational norms, that this type of choice of love object is currently more prevalent than formerly; he does not recognize, however, that these women represent not only the man himself who loves them but, in particular, his penis. In the way in which the charm of such figures is generally described one invariably finds a suggestion of their phallic nature. They are *phallus girls,* as in the fantasy of the transvestites described above.

V

Recently, in the analysis of a male patient, I was given the opportunity of a glimpse into the genesis of a totally different region of fantasy which at the same time seems to me to facilitate the understanding of the phallus girl—namely, the nature of the clown and of slapstick comedy.

This was a patient with a distinct predilection for clowning, for grotesque humor of the American kind, and so on. Although he had a totally different profession, his favorite fantasy was that of appearing as a cabaret comic or even outright as a clown. There was no doubt that these fantasies were a matter of "wooing exhibitionism"; he wanted to impress by his appearance, and wanted to be loved for his clowning ability. The problem was: What gave this specific form to his exhibitionism?

It seems to us that with this question we approach the problem of a certain specific neurosis of childhood. There is a type of child who invariably seeks to entertain his playmates or adults by jokes of the most varied kind, and who continually plays the clown, the Punchinello. Such children are apparently those whose self-esteem is threatened, whose self-awareness is only restored when they can make others laugh at them. While such children at first are usually successful in this attempt because they are frequently very funny, one gradually realizes that we are concerned here with a neurosis, and that these children could in no wise act differently.

[14] R. A. Spitz, "Ein Beitrag zum Problem der Wandlung der Neurosenform (Die infantile Frau und ihre Gegenspieler)," *Imago,* Vol. 19, 1933.

The exhibiting of one's comic qualities gives the impression of being a *substitute*. It looks as though (and the analysis of the patient mentioned above confirmed this) the children wished originally to exhibit something else, something more serious, and as though their clowning were saying: "As long as I am not taken seriously anyway, I want to have *at least* this success, of making people laugh at me." Instead of a great exhibiting—one is tempted to say, instead of the exhibiting of an erected penis—they "at least" exhibit something else. Since the substitute success which they achieve consists of their being laughed at, it seems as though they were striving to make a virtue of necessity, as though what prevented the original "more serious" exhibiting were the fear of being ridiculed. The formula is roughly as follows: "I want to exhibit— I am afraid of being laughed at for doing so. Therefore I shall exhibit in such a way that you will laugh, that I shall impress you in spite thereof, so that being laughed at is in itself a success. You who laugh at me shall see that he whom you laugh at possesses nevertheless a secret greatness." Of what does this greatness consist? When one analyzes the words and acts of clowns and slapstick comedians, two seemingly contradictory features emerge:

(a) Phallic features: The traditional garb of clowns itself contains many phallic features. The relationships between clown and dwarf are manifold, but the phallic symbolism of the dwarf hardly needs amplification. I will remind you only of the analysis of Gulliver by Ferenczi, who emphasized the phallic symbolism of all those figures who utilize the equation body $=$ penis, and are associated with the fantasy of eating and being eaten.[15]

(b) Pregenital features of various kinds: one has only to witness a clown act in any circus or to attend the performance of a great clown such as Grock, for example, to perceive that a large part of the effect of clowns consists of their more or less disguised expression of the otherwise forbidden tendencies characterizing infantile sexuality. The more these actually projected pregenital tendencies are covered by an aesthetic façade which tempts us to the "premium of laughter," the more we attribute to such slapstick comics the character of real art.[16] The anal-sadistic element seems herein to play an especially prominent role. It would seem that slapstick belongs under the rubric of sadomasochism: beatings are constantly administered. In such sadism, concealed as it is by clowning, one must take cognizance of two things: first, the striving of the clown, whose original wish it was to exhibit "seriously," to revenge himself secretly for the ridicule to which he is exposed (and one may here recall the numerous legends and stories in which court jesters, dwarfs, and similar figures who are

---

[15] S. Ferenczi, "Gulliver Phantasies," *Int. J. Psa.*, Vol. 9, 1928.
[16] Cf. S. Freud, "Wit and Its Relation to the Unconscious," *The Basic Writings*, New York, Modern Library, 1938.

the object of laughter unexpectedly obtain a frightful revenge—as for example in the story "The Hop-Frog" of E. A. Poe); and second, one justifiably thinks of a regression engendered by the circumstance that an original piece of ridicule has disabused the hero with regard to his phallicism. With this second point we arrive at the following general interpretation: Exhibition is here invoked in a specific manner in which phallic and pregenital features are combined with each other. This is apparently to be understood as follows. A phallic exhibiting which must be repressed is replaced by a pregenital exhibiting (which due to its genesis still retains phallic features), going hand in hand with fantasies of omnipotence: "I am small, it is true; you laugh but in spite of my small size I am omnipotent. If my penis is too small, well then, I am in my whole person a penis which you must still respect!"

The pleasure of the child prodigy in exhibiting is apparently related to this. The patient discussed above, who gave her father the bear talisman, was admired in her childhood as a child prodigy. The motive in common is the "greatness of the little one." Here clown and prodigy completely merge in the tradition of the dwarf. The small child, who because of its small size feels despised or castrated, fantasies itself *in toto* as a penis, in order to compensate in this way for the narcissistic injury involved.

We return to our specific theme with the attempt to demonstrate that such phallic figures as clowns, prodigies, and dwarfs are frequently fantasied specifically as a "girl."

The patient with the predilection for slapstick had a remarkably inconsistent attitude toward women. Either he despised them as relatively insignificant compared to the significance of the psychological problems discussed among men; or else he defended the rights of women in a suffragette spirit. These two alternating attitudes (the motives of this alternation were analytically most interesting) were mutually contradictory, and yet had something in common: the "differentness" of women is denied in both cases; in the one case in the attempt to repress women altogether, in the other in denying their individuality. As an advocate of women's rights the patient was ever concerned with showing in an exhibitionistic way how well informed he was on matters feminine, how little different girls really were from him, etc. Thus his feminine identification became clear, "I am myself a girl," an identification which found expression also in woman-despising homosexuality, and which in early childhood had provided an escape from his castration anxiety: "In order not to become like a woman, I act as though I were myself a woman, and furthermore act as though women were no different from men."

If in him the wish, "I want to exhibit my penis," was inhibited by a fear of humiliation, on a deeper level by castration anxiety, it found a substitute in the idea: "I want to exhibit myself as a slapstick comedian (as the pregenital phallus)," and likewise in the idea: "I want to exhibit myself as a girl (as the female phallus)." He fantasied himself not only as a cabaret artist but occasionally also as a female cabaret singer, and in this respect is reminiscent of the transvestite (observed by Hirschfeld) who initiated his transvestite practices by appearing as a female trick shooter—thus a phallic woman—in vaudeville.[17] As such a pregenital, or female, phallus he wanted to be admired—above all, certainly by men. His competitive relationship to other men was outspokenly libidinized: he liked to attack them in various ways, yet always needed their reassurance that they did not take the attack seriously but regarded it in a "sporting" manner, as a sort of love act, somewhat in the manner in which the competitive urinating of little boys—wherein similarly one participant tries to outdo the other—has a homosexual character. Thus all the details described had as their purpose the eliminating of a deep castration fear. To such a purpose was also to be ascribed the feminine identification: "I am a girl, let me be loved as one, but let me not need to be afraid." As in the case of the transvestite mentioned at the beginning, the phallic woman whom the patient enacted was here too regarded as a phallic figure as a whole (slapstick comedian), but here it was possible to recognize that this fantasy of the phallus girl was preceded by an injury to phallic exhibitionism, on the occasion of which the patient developed his deep castration fear. Of this injury to phallic exhibitionism we were given in the analysis a few screen memories, without our being able to ascertain their specific historical character. The fantasy of the phallus girl is a substitute for the phallic exhibition which is inhibited by castration anxiety, and is composed of the two kinds of "castration denial": "I keep my penis by acting as though I were in fact a girl," and "girls are really no different from myself."

VI

Finally, before discussing the general significance of the figure of the phallus girl, I should like to cite a fragment from the analysis of another male patient in order to emphasize still another trait characterizing this figure.

It is the case of a man who through an unhappy marriage saved himself in masochistic fashion from a neurosis, but at the same time had left many of his possibilities and gifts unutilized. It was not difficult to see that he atoned with his whole life for an unknown guilt. This guilt, stemming from his infantile sexuality, was concentrated in shame over an enuresis of some years' duration which persisted past his tenth year. His (inhibited) ambition pointed to the strength of his urethral erotism; his exhibitionistic joy over small achievements (he denied himself large ones) had the unconscious meaning: "Look, today I can actually use the chamber pot!" The bringing into consciousness of his guilt feelings gave

[17] M. Hirschfeld, *Die Transvestiten*, Berlin, Pulvermacher, 1910 (Case 5).

rise at first to a depression during which the patient wept a good deal. After holding himself in check and keeping his eyes closed to his lot in life over the space of many years, this relaxation was greatly welcomed, and the analyst repeatedly urged the patient not to be ashamed, but to allow himself to weep whenever he felt like doing so. After a time, however, it became obvious that the patient was beginning to abuse this invitation. He wept in the analyst's presence in a masochistic manner. What was the meaning of this sudden abundant flood of tears? The patient now no longer wept solely over his fate, but became sentimental and allowed the tears to flow whenever he thought of something "touching," whenever a "good" deed or the like was the subject mentioned. His moral masochism had much of the character of the "rescue fantasy." His unhappy marriage he continued for the sake of his poor wife; he had a vocation in which he was able to "help the poor"; in short, the "good" man, over whose "goodness" he shed tears, was himself. His main fantasy ran thus: the poor little Cinderella that is himself must suffer much and is never understood, but at last comes one who understands him and therewith releases his tears. Dreams and fantasies then showed further that "understanding" really meant "caressing." The patient had been rachitic as a child, had been obliged to rest a good deal, and had been made to feel that he was a burden to his humbly situated family. The neurosis consisted in his attempts to work out the aggressions thus aroused, to make a redeeming Christ out of the persecuted Cinderella. His longing was: "If I suffer much, someone will come at last who will caress me, and then I must weep," and he sought in the environment a person whom he would caress and allow to weep, in the same way as he wanted it done for him. When he had reached this point in the analysis, he began a new affair with a poor girl for whom he felt pity, and developed ejaculatio praecox. The analysis of this new symptom now brought certainty regarding something already suspected: the weeping corresponded to urinating. A poor child (a poor girl) was to be caressed until it wet itself—this a beneficial release with no guilt. There now remained no doubt about who the poor child was to whom this was supposed to happen, and a dream expressed this clearly: his own penis. The urethral fixation of the patient was passive-phallic: "I want to be touched passively on the genitals. Let someone caress my poor little penis, so that it gets wet and is allowed to get wet!" This episode seems worth narrating because it is purely typical that the love which the man directs toward the phallus girl is passive-phallic and urethral.

VII

In connection with the phallic figures which Ferenczi described in his paper on Gulliver,[18] he overlooked the fact that a remarkable number of these at the same time represent girls. He writes: "One of my male patients recalls having

18 S. Ferenczi, op. cit.

used a small female creation of fantasy in his youthful masturbation fantasies, which he always carried in his pocket and took out from time to time in order to play with it." This was the *phallus fantasied as a girl*. Furthermore, Gulliver encounters the giant women who despite their feminine nature manifest clear evidences of the symbolism of erection—and one recalls too the frequent fairy tales of giant girls. Naturally one does not overlook the fact that giant women also represent the adult mother, by comparison with whom the little child feels so small; but it is Ferenczi himself who describes why in all these fantasies the giant, or the dwarf, represents *also* a penis.

Once one has become aware of the fantasy of the phallus girl, one finds in literature the most varied representations of it. Steff Bornstein has called my attention to the fact that it would be worth while in this regard, for example, to investigate the creation of Bettina von Arnim and her relation to Goethe. The fantasy of being given over femininely to a person great and powerful, at the same time to be united with him so indissolubly as to be a very part of him, together with the idea that one is moreover the most important part without which the mighty one would be powerless—this is certainly to be found also as characterizing a particular type of religious devotee. One thinks, for example, of Rilke's lines:

> What will you do, God, when I die,
> When I, your pitcher, broken, lie?
> When I, your drink, go stale or dry?
> I am your garb, the trade you ply,
> You lose your meaning, losing me. †

Or of the lines of Angelus Silesius:

> I am as great as God: He is as I as small;
> He over me or I under Him can never be at all.

And:

> I know that without me God cannot live a moment;
> Were I to perish, He could but give up the ghost.

This reference to the "feminine" lyrics produced by men engenders the thought that other frequently occurring fantasy figures might also be connected with the phallus girl. One thinks, for example, of the figure of the "female soldier" which appears in so many variants in literature. It may be objected that such girlish soldiers or soldierly girls represent "the woman with the penis," and that this by no means necessarily implies that they must represent the penis itself. In the first place one is obliged to perceive in them simply objects of the

† Translated by Babette Deutsch, in *Poems from the Book of Hours*, New York, New Directions, 1941.—Trans. note.

latent homosexuality of all men, regarding whose object choice Freud with justice wrote: "There can be no doubt that a large proportion of male inverts retain the mental quality of masculinity . . . and that what they look for in their sexual object are in fact feminine mental traits. If this were not so, how would it be possible to explain the fact that male prostitutes who offer themselves to inverts—today just as they did in ancient times—imitate women in all externals of their clothing and behavior? . . . In this instance . . . the sexual object is not someone of the same sex but someone who combines the characters of both sexes; there is, as it were, a compromise between an impulse that seeks for a man and one that seeks for a woman, while it remains a paramount condition that the object's body (i.e., genitals) shall be masculine."[19] Moreover, we have frequently found that alleged inverts have been by no means insusceptible to the charms of women, but have continually transposed the excitation aroused by women onto a male object.[20] Correct as this is, it does not explain the circumstance that our "female soldier" so often appears as a "page," i.e., as primarily a helpless little fellow inseparably devoted to a great person, in order in magical fashion to help or to save him. Such girl or half-girl figures are no different from other phallic symbols, which, despised at first on account of their smallness, turn out later to be powerful, and become the most important helper of the hero, much like the small helping animals in fairy tales or like dwarfs.

If these phallus girls are omnipotent in consequence of their phallic nature, it is also true that they can misuse their omnipotence. The "fear of retaliation" felt by some fathers toward their narcissistically (as phallus) loved daughters certainly belongs here.

Thus, what we encounter here is a fantasy in which male and female narcissism, male and female pleasure in exhibiting, are condensed. In such fantasies, penis envy is condensed with her femininity in the woman, penis pride with his castration anxiety in the man.

VIII

Let us emphasize, finally, that the fantasy of phallus girls bears a close relationship to two hitherto little understood forms of perversion. It will already have been noticed that many of the examples cited here are closely related to masochistic fantasies, in particular to masochistic fantasies of the type usually designated as those of complete sexual dependence. This sexual dependence consists of the dependent person's feeling indissolubly united with the person on whom he is dependent, able to do nothing against, or indeed without, his will—representing, as it were, a part of him. One thinks of the type of religious devotee men-

[19] S. Freud, *Three Essays on the Theory of Sexuality*, pp. 22–23.
[20] *Ibid.*, p. 23 footnote.

tioned above, whose devotion is associated with the fantasy that even God would be helpless without him. It would still have to be inquired whether the fantasy is not likewise present in all cases of such sexual dependence; that one has not only become a weak, helpless part of the person one is dependent on, but also the reverse: his most important part; that the person in question is now at the same time in (magical) dependence on the one dependent on him.

Frances Deri has expressed the opinion that this is in fact the pathognomonic mechanism of sexual dependence, and we can only find ourselves in agreement with this opinion.[21]

That which is termed "sodomy," the sexual love for animals, is probably something of a very different kind. One type thereof, however, according to analytic experience seems to stem from the fact that the person concerned has remained fixated at the stage of *partial love*, and sees in animals penis symbols. The unconscious fantasies of "infantile totemism" which magically unite a human being with an animal species [22] are certainly not entirely based on the fact that the animal is fantasied as a part of one's own body, as oneself in phallic form. But there are forms of the love of animals in which the attitude to the loved animal representing the penis is so completely identical with the love of a man for a "child wife," chosen according to the narcissistic type of object choice, that we should like to include this type of animal love here.

One concluding remark may anticipate possible misunderstandings: in cases in which in relation to the penis introjection and eating fantasies play a particular role, or in other words, wherever the symbolic equation body = penis holds, this relation to the penis stems from *pregenital* antecedents. Likewise, the phallus girl is, generally speaking, not only a penis but also a child, feces (content of the mother's body), and milk. It is the *introject,* and one which is again projected. The penis thus is only the final member of the series of introjects. It was primarily my intention at this time to lay emphasis upon this final member of the series.

[21] Josine Mueller, describing a case of dependence, wrote as early as 1925: "She imagined that she herself was the penis of this august father, i.e. his dearest and most important part" ("Atheism in Childhood and Faulty Character Development") *Int. J. Psa.,* Vol. 8, 1927, pp. 521–522.

[22] S. Freud, "Totem and Taboo," Chapter IV, *The Basic Writings,* New York, Modern Library, 1938.

T W O

Symposium on the Theory of the Therapeutic Results of Psychoanalysis[*]

In a short contribution to a discussion the utmost that one can do is to set out one's main thesis schematically.

A neurosis is a discharge of dammed-up instinctual energies, occurring in defiance of the wishes of the ego. In the cases which concern us, namely, the psychoneuroses, this damming up has come about through the ego's constant warding off of the instincts. Since it is only the ego which is accessible to our therapeutic intervention, there are, in principle, two modes of attack. We may try to strengthen the ego with a view to enabling it to put up a more successful defense against the instincts. Or we may induce it to desist from its defense or to replace that defense by one better adapted to the purpose. I need not enlarge on the fact that the first method may sometimes be adopted in the course of a psychoanalytical treatment, but that, fundamentally, analytical therapy employs the second. Two questions arise. First, by what means can we influence the ego to desist from or to modify its defense against the instincts? Secondly, how are we to explain dynamically and economically the changes which take place when the defense has been thus discontinued or modified?

The ego's ill-adapted defense against the instincts is at bottom always prompted by its conviction that instinctual excitation is dangerous and its dread of the unpleasure which might result if it yielded to its impulses. Whether this danger threatens from the external world or has already been introjected is in principle a

* First published in *Int. Z. Psa.*, Vol. 23, 1937, pp. 37–42.

matter of secondary importance. Thus Freud, in *The Problem of Anxiety,* says that the fundamental characteristic of neurosis is the retention of anxiety contents beyond the period at which they are physiologically appropriate. The retaining of a belief in a danger which has no objective existence is, however, itself the result of an instinctual defense set up in childhood under the influence of that anxiety. The instinctual components which have been repelled have become unconscious, and with them the anxiety which prompted the defense; and this anxiety has lost its connection with the personality as a whole. The anxiety does not share in the development of the rest of the ego, nor is it corrected by subsequent experience.

By means of the anti-cathexes of the ego certain mental contents are withheld from consciousness and kept apart from the whole personality, some of these contents being instinctual components and others the ego's unconscious anxiety ideas. It is our task to restore these to the conscious ego and to render the anti-cathexes inoperative.

What makes this possible is the fact that the instinctual components which are warded off produce derivatives. If we follow the fundamental rule of psychoanalysis and exclude as far as possible the purposive ideas of the ego, these derivatives, which are always to be observed in the impulses of human beings, become still clearer. Every interpretation, whether it be that of a resistance or of an id impulse, consists of demonstrating the nature of a derivative as such to that part of the ego which exercises the faculty of judgment. It is no interpretation simply to name unconscious components before they are represented by a preconscious derivative which the patient can recognize as such by merely turning his attention to it. In my paper on psychoanalytic technique [1] I showed that, when we demonstrate to a patient the fact that he is setting up a defense, what its nature is and why, how, and against what he is employing it, we are really training his ego to tolerate instinctual derivatives, which are being made less and less distorted. Sterba, speaking of what is in practice the most useful kind of interpretation, namely, interpretation of the transference resistance, shows that this takes place through a kind of dissociation of the ego into a part which judges reasonably and a part which experiences, the former recognizing that the latter is not appropriate to the real situation but is a legacy from the past. The result is a relative diminution in anxiety, and this assists in the production of fresh and less distorted derivatives. (It would be interesting to inquire how this "ego dissociation" and "self-observation," which we welcome, differ from pathological dissociation and self-observation, the aim of which is to keep certain mental contents in isolation and which actually prevent the production of derivatives.) To bring about this result we make use of the positive trans-

[1] "Concerning the Theory of Psychoanalytic Technique," No. 30, *First Series.*

ference and of transitory identifications with the analyst. Certain fundamental rules of technique, such as that "analysis always starts from the surface presented at the moment" or "interpretation of resistance precedes interpretation of mental contents," and so forth, follow of themselves. I may therefore be excused from touching here, where I must confine myself to my main theme, upon such important questions as "interpretation of resistance and interpretation of psychic contents," and "analysis of the ego and analysis of the id."

In the same way, unconscious resistances are put out of action by demonstrating their conscious derivatives and manifestations to the patient; and, if we seize the right moment to name the id impulses which he has warded off and of which "the ego, grown more tolerant, has already become aware," we shall put a stop to its defensive activities. The "analytical atmosphere," which convinces the patient that he has nothing to fear from toleration of impulses which he generally repels, seems to be not only an indispensable condition for every transference interpretation (for, if the analyst were in any way to join the patient in acting out the situation, it would be impossible to demonstrate the fact that the patient's emotions were determined by situations in the past) but, further, a valuable means of persuading the ego to admit tentatively impulses which it normally repels. Kaiser fears that this may lead to the analysis being isolated from real life, because the patient feels that here he is only playing with his impulses, whereas, in life, where they are serious, it is his duty to go on putting up a defense against them. His fear, I think, is justified in some cases (and where this is so this resistance must be analyzed); but that is not an adequate reason for throwing overboard the advantages of the atmosphere of "tolerance." A technique which employs "action" makes it difficult to confront the ego with its unconscious impulses, and, although it often reveals so much, I think this method is dangerous because it represents only the present and the patient cannot become conscious that he is governed by the past. It is, *au fond*, analogous to the equally dangerous opposite method of analysis, the "theoretical" method, which deals with the past without observing that it is still present.

Freud has said that in analysis we employ every means of suggestion to persuade the ego to desist from the manufacture of defenses. In practice this is certainly still true and the utilization of the transference in this sense is nothing but suggestion. It must, however, be said that the effect which we desire to produce upon the ego will be lasting and profound in proportion as we succeed in using no other means of overcoming resistances than that of confronting the reasonable ego with the fact of its resistances and the history of their origin. This enables the ego to recognize the unconscious element in them and at the same time renders them superfluous. We find too, of course, that in a transitory manner "the analyst insinuates himself into the patient's superego." (This is what takes place in hypnosis, and Strachey holds that it is also characteristic of analytic therapy.) Temporarily, also, we find all the "effects of inexact interpretation" which Glover has investigated. By this I mean that, as the patient gradually abandons his neurotic modes of discharging instinctual energy, he may succeed in finding substitutes for them in transference actions or in some other phenomena which the treatment has made possible.

If we succeed thus in putting an end to the pathogenic defensive activities of the ego, what is the result? Neurotics are people who in their unconscious instinctual life have either remained on an infantile level or have regressed to it—people, that is to say, whose sexuality (or aggressiveness) has retained infantile forms. Theoretically, therefore, we may anticipate that this therapy would result in perversions. Anna Freud holds that with children analytical influence must be combined with educational training; that otherwise, for instance, when the repression against anal erotism is lifted, the child may take to smearing objects with feces. She thinks too that in the case of some adults, whose defenses are motivated by the fear of the amount of their own instinctual energy, the removal of those defenses may result in the instinctual energy breaking out and overwhelming the whole ego. In my opinion practical experience shows that there is no such danger. Moreover, the instinctual components which have been warded off have only retained their infantile character *because* they have been warded off, and have lost connection with the whole personality, which meanwhile has gone on developing. If the energy which was bound in the defensive conflict is readmitted to the whole personality, it will find its proper place there and adapt itself to the genital primacy which has been established. Pregenital sexuality, when it ceases to be bound in the defensive conflict, is by that very fact transformed into genital sexuality with the capacity for orgasm. The experiences of gratification which now become possible are those that contribute most of all to the final removal of the pathogenic damming up of instinctual energy. Isolated "abreactions" cannot accomplish this; they give momentary relief, but they do not bring the defensive conflict to an end, nor do they liberate the libido which it binds. The therapeutic importance of "abreaction" and of "the fizzling-out of repressed instinctual excitation on entering consciousness" is relatively little as compared with the achievement of a well-ordered sexual economy. This is why we rate the curative value of single outbreaks of affect comparatively low, however welcome they may be in some analytic situations, while we think very highly of the process of "working through" which follows. This process, which Rado compares to the work of mourning, means that an unconscious impulse, once recognized, must be demonstrated over and over again, every time that it makes its appearance in one of its manifold forms and connections. Thus, and thus only, can the pathogenic defense against instinct be really abolished. Other modes of discharge, which were previously impossible for the patient, of course become possible when his defense is abandoned. I refer to sublimations. There is no doubt that the latter play a lesser part quantitatively in setting to rights the sexual processes of a personality which has been neurotic than does appropriate sexual gratification.

I propose to employ the few minutes which remain to me in making certain observations on the contributions to our symposium which have so far been read.

Bergler seems to me principally to have brought out particular *ways* in which the patient's ego can be trained to tolerate more readily the derivatives of impulses which it has repelled. There can be no doubt that analysis represents a refutation of the magical equation "thought = act." Certainly, too, it does happen that some patients feel analysis to be a "sexual secret which yet has no harm in it." This does not simply assist the analysis, but it is also a special resistance which must be uncovered as such and got rid of. The notion that, as analysis proceeds, less demon and more superego is progressively projected onto the analyst stands or falls with the demon-ego-ideal theory, which I cannot discuss here. But to my mind the most doubtful of Bergler's points was his argument about "the unconscious sense of guilt as the *vis a tergo*." He states that the superego becomes more tolerant on the basis of a renunciation of infantile sexuality. But how difficult is it for a patient who has been cured to make this renunciation? When genital primacy has been established the infantile sexual impulses as such can simply disappear. Again, I think that patients can be cured by psychoanalysis and become really well without cherishing any resentment.

With Bibring's views I am largely in accordance, but I should like to express one or two slight doubts in connection with three of his points.

(1) It seems to me already perfectly possible to formulate a theory of our therapy. Bibring himself has put one forward. There are many gaps in the details of our knowledge, and we have not yet found the solution of problems arising precisely out of the theory we hold today, but the theory itself is there.

(2) It must not be supposed that fixation through frustration is always *only* a fixation of the ego. The ego, which fears a repetition of the frustration, in the process of defending itself holds down the id, the instinct, to some particular level.

(3) The "pedagogic" importance of the fact that the analyst supports the patient's reason against his archaic ego is, I think, slight, though in some cases we have to make great use of it. For we always work with the "normal remainder of the personality." It must be our ally against resistance and, in spite of our utilization of the transference, without it we shall not succeed.

I am unable to assent to Nunberg's remarks about the repetition compulsion, because my conception of it differs from his. That there is such a compulsion on *this* side of the pleasure principle is, I think, indisputable. *Beyond* the pleasure principle what happens seems to be that quantities of undischarged, dammed-up excitation seek to be mastered retrospectively. The unpleasurable repetition of an unpleasurable experience is at any rate less unpleasurable than having to tolerate unresolved tensions. In principle—though in practice we may not always really succeed in this—a genuine breaking down of the defense should involve the overcoming of the repetition compulsion. If I can induce a patient to exchange autoplastic for alloplastic modes of behavior and enable him to react suitably to reality, this surely means that the repetition compulsion is abolished, not merely transferred from the id to the ego. The old formula, "We cure by making the unconscious conscious" is *topographically* conceived, and there is a danger that in our technique we may do too scant justice to the *dynamic* and *economic* standpoints. In my view it is not simply the function of reality testing that depends on the superego: *all* the ego functions are accessible to the superego's influence.

I am largely in agreement with Strachey; but I think he uses the concept of "introjection" in a wider sense than is legitimate. When I recognize that what someone says is right it does not necessarily mean that I have introjected him.

THREE

Early Stages of Ego Development*

WITHIN the last few years, there has been added to the older field of investigation of psychoanalysis, namely, the instincts, a newer study, that of the ego—a study which is far from being completed. The basic discovery with which Freud introduced the "dynamic" way of thinking, and so, in effect, founded psychoanalysis, was this: the experiences which hysterics did not complete, so that their affects remained "blocked" and sought discharge in symptoms, were experiences which were rejected by a part of their personality. The neurosis was preceded by a "neurotic conflict." [1] This is the model which psychoanalysis set up for psychic processes in general. The situation always is that relatively primary, biological needs—"instincts" or "drives"—are pressing for discharge, while opposing trends develop and make themselves felt under the influence of the external world, and check the discharge or put it off. In this constant interplay between the instincts and the instinct-inhibiting or instinct-modifying institution which develops under the influence of the external world—viz., the ego—the instincts (the repressed) were the first to be studied. Ego psychology proper was not inaugurated until Freud's book *The Ego and the Id* [2] opened the way by introducing the so-called structural point of view, i.e., the recognition that, under the influence of the external world, an organ—the ego—is gradually differentiated out and, like a cortex, envelops the core of the unconscious instinctual reservoir of the id. The ego subserves the interaction between the organism and the external world, i.e., on the one hand the intake of stimulation (perception), and, on the other, the discharge of excitation (motility and sifting of impulses striving toward motility).

* First published in *Imago*, Vol. 23, 1937, pp. 243–269.
[1] J. Breuer and S. Freud, *Studies in Hysteria*, New York, Nerv. Ment. Dis. Pub. Co., 1937.
[2] S. Freud, *The Ego and the Id*, London, Hogarth, 1947.

In keeping with the traditions of psychoanalysis, which was from the beginning a *genetic* psychology, attempting to understand existing structures through their developmental history, the developmental history of the ego (both normal and pathological) soon became the central field of ego psychology. But the farther we reach back into the developmental history of the ego, and the earlier are the ego phases which we try to understand, the more formidable factual and methodological difficulties do we encounter. These might be responsible for the many unclarities which surround the subject and for the, in part, quite contradictory views held by analysts about it; and they would seem to make an attempt to summarize our knowledge of it worth while, however incomplete such a brief review of this still very new and unexplored field must remain.

Our insight into the basic outlines of the psychic development of man has been obtained through observation of adults. The realization that in neurotic phenomena unresolved residues of the past continue to operate in the present made it necessary to study that past and to deduce retrospectively the instinctual conflicts of childhood. It was only much later that our knowledge about infantile sexuality was confirmed by direct observation of children. For obvious reasons the earliest stages of development remained the most obscure; in the first place, it is not always necessary for the comprehension of a neurosis to reach back to such early prehistory; and in the second place, the apprehension of psychic processes becomes more difficult the more we reach back into times in which there was as yet no verbal communication, and in which what we later recognize as differentiated achievements which make our orientation possible, were still integrated in a unity. The attempt to offset the difficulties of retrospective deduction by direct observation of children does not easily succeed for the period preceding the development of language either, since observations on infants are not psychologically unequivocal. The temptation is great to apply concepts and ideas which are fully valid for later stages of development to the behavior of the small child in an unjustified manner—that is, to indulge, as Spitz expresses it, in "adultomorph" thinking in child observation. Indeed, this is a judgment which we cannot avoid passing on various psychoanalytic efforts that have been made in regard to early phases of the ego. Words suited to later stages are all too readily smuggled into the word-disparate forms of experience which belong to undifferentiated archaisms. If the psychoanalytic concept is correct in regarding the psyche as an apparatus for mastering stimuli which is continually increasing in complexity, then in considering the earliest stages we must obviously make do with the terms "excitation" and "discharge," until we can grasp how, from their interplay, more complex apparatuses, progressively less vague and more accessible to words, are differentiated for the reception, conduction, and discharge of stimuli. Psychoanalysts have not yet undertaken systematic observations of infants. Those carried out by experimental psychology certainly help a lot, especially when they are carefully combined with retrospective deductions from analyses of adults and older children. But their point of departure is usually a problem foreign to our way of thinking; and, if they are to be of any use for psychoanalytic ego psychology, they must first be "transposed."

Mental disorders which go with regressions to primitive phases of the ego facilitate our understanding of these primitive phases to an extraordinary degree. In this field they render the same service as the neuroses, as being relapses into infantile sexuality, did in their day for the understanding of infantile sexuality. They are, however, not the only regressions which overtake the ego. There are also physiological situations in healthy people in which functions of the archaic ego reappear: states of intoxication and fatigue, and especially the situations of going to sleep and waking up. Isakower's fine study [3] has recently shown that the observation of these things, too, may be used systematically for the understanding of primitive ego functions.

We are accustomed to regard the ego as an organ which is differentiated only under the influence of the external world. Accordingly, we are accustomed to regard the newborn baby as having as yet no ego. What is meant by that?

The human infant is much more helpless at birth than most other mammals. It cannot survive unless it is cared for. A welter of external stimuli rush in on it, which it cannot master. It cannot move of its own volition, nor can it perceive differentially the stimuli which press in on it. If it could, it would be able to co-ordinate its excitations with stimuli coming from external sources and it could, for a while at least, hold in suspension the urge toward discharge with which every excitation is accompanied. But this is just what it cannot do. It knows no objectual world, and cannot yet "bind" tensions by "anti-cathexes." It may be surmised, therefore, that it does not as yet have a consciousness in the sense in which the adult has, but at most an undifferentiated sensation of pleasure or unpleasure, or "release" and "increase" of tension. But it is precisely these as yet undeveloped functions—namely, reception of the external world (perception), mastery of the motor apparatus (motility), and ability to bind by anti-cathecting, and with them consciousness—which are by definition the essence of the ego. This is what we mean when we speak of the ego-less state of the newborn baby.

To be sure, there is from birth on, and probably even before, a reacting to stimuli. Therefore, there is, in an absolute sense, a sort of pre-ego; or rather, the functions which are later on fulfilled by the ego are accomplished, before it has

[3] O. Isakower, "A Contribution to the Patho-Psychology of Phenomena Associated with Falling Asleep," *Int. J. Psa.*, Vol. 19, 1938.

come into existence, in a completely undifferentiated embryonic manner by the organism as a whole.

The formation of the ego from the ego-less primal state is not a single process. It begins with (or perhaps even before) birth, and probably does not end until the oedipus complex passes away. Strictly speaking, it actually never ends. The term "birth trauma" implies that at birth the organism which is deficient in protective barriers against stimuli, emerges from a relatively stimulus-free environment into an overabundance of stimuli. The inundation of excitations which thus occurs, in view of the insufficiency of the apparatuses of discharge is, according to Freud, the model for all later anxiety.[4]

We may assume that such an inundation by masses of excitation is most unpleasurable and elicits the first psychic tendency, namely, that of eliminating the tension due to excitation. If this tendency succeeds eventually in mastering the externa stimuli fairly well, the infant falls asleep. But a new stimulus, that of hunger, awakens it. The first traces of consciousness obviously do not as yet differentiate between ego and non-ego, but only between tension and relaxation; and most probably with the experience of relaxation those traces of consciousness are once more lost as well (dozing off). If every need could be instantly assuaged, representation of reality would probably never develop.

It is evident that the missing of an already known "something" which removes a need is what goes to form the first "object."[5]

It is true that before the establishment of this "first object" the infant is, in fact, dependent upon others, whose supplies alone keep him alive. From a biological point of view, he is passively at the mercy of objects. But in a psychological sense these are not yet his "objects," since he experiences only tension and relaxation and has no possibility of perceiving objects of the external world. (Is it so difficult to distinguish the objective world which appears before the adult observer from the subjective world we assume in the infant?) For this reason I consider it misleading to speak in this situation of "passive object love."[6] We shall return to this point below.

Bernfeld[7] has pointed out how and why the infant's life alternates between sleep and hunger. Hunger introduces into the organism a state of tension from somatic sources and a tendency to remove this. The hunger being satisfied, tension ceases and the relatively stimulus-free state of sleep is reinstated. The first

[4] S. Freud, *The Problem of Anxiety*, New York, Psa. Quart. Press and Norton, 1936.

[5] S. Ferenczi, "The Problem of Acceptance of Unpleasant Ideas—Advances in Knowledge of the Sense of Reality," *Further Contributions to the Theory and Technique of Psycho-Analysis*, London, Hogarth, 1950.

[6] Cf. M. Balint, "Zur Kritik der Lehre von den praegenitalen Libidoorganisationen," *Int. Z. Psa.*, Vol. 21, 1935.

[7] S. Bernfeld, *The Psychology of the Infant*, New York, Brentano's, 1929.

traces of object representations and of consciousness mentioned above must therefore arise in the state of hunger. We can suppose that later on, when the beginnings of subsequent ego functions are more clearly developed, the infant's realization of the fact that it takes an intervention by the external world to eliminate his hunger, leads to his first cathexis of longing in regard to the external objects in question. The earliest object cathexes would then persist only as long as the object is absent; once the object intervenes, the cathexis vanishes and sleep sets in. The first "affirmation" of the world is an intermediate aim on the way to its "negation." Perhaps this is the point which provides a common origin for the antithesis that plays such a fundamental role in human life, viz., the longing for absence of stimulation (Nirvana principle) on the one hand and the craving for stimulus (longing for objects) on the other—that is, between a "death-instinct" which strives for freedom from stimulation, and Eros which strives for an increase of tension by merging with other objects.[8]

In any case, "arising of the ego" and "arising of reality" are identical. An ego exists in so far as there exist ideas of objects. This is already implied in the definition of the ego, as "that part of the psychic apparatus which represents reality." It is thus that in describing the nature of schizophrenia, for instance, we can just as well say that the organism "has broken with reality" as that "the ego is disrupted"; or we can just as well say that the schizophrenic has regressed to the time "before reality testing arose," as to the time "before ego differentiation began." We are persons inasmuch as we experience ourselves in contrast to others. Owing to this relation of the ego to reality, it is only a difference in terminology whether we speak of "stages in the development of the ego" or of "stages in the development of the sense of reality." [9] In the subject's discovery of reality, as Freud has pointed out,[10] the discovery of his own body plays a very special role. While at first he only has a perception of tensions and only the "internal" exists for him, and while, later on, with his discovery of an object which intervenes to eliminate these tensions, the "external" also comes to exist, his body is both at the same time. By virtue of this characteristic it stands out for him from the rest of the external world, and thus enables him to work out the distinction between ego and non-ego. The sum of representations of his own body and its organs which arises in this process, the so-called "body image," is of fundamental importance for the further development of the ego. It does not coincide with the objective body, since, for instance, clothing or amputated limbs may belong to it.

The first reactions to objects which are recognized as such still contain, in-

[8] Cf. O. Fenichel, "A Critique of the Death Instinct," No. 32, *First Series*.

[9] S. Ferenczi, "Stages in the Development of the Sense of Reality," *Sex in Psychoanalysis*, New York, Brunner, 1950.

[10] S. Freud, *The Ego and the Id*.

tegrated into a unity, much that becomes differentiated later on. At first the reactions are reflex-like, i.e., every stimulus demands—in accordance with the Nirvana principle—an immediate reaction. Reception and discharge of stimulus, perception and motor reaction, are still extraordinarily close to each other, are inseparably intertwined. Primitive perception is precisely characterized by its intimate tie with motor reaction. The subject *perceives,* in that he alters his body under the influence of the perceived object (and possibly only in that he notices this alteration of his body). Investigations like those of Spielrein,[11] which show that many perceptions that are considered visual are based on kinesthetic sensations, are pertinent here; so are eidetic investigations proving that primitive visual perceptions go hand in hand with motor reactions or readiness for such reactions; [12] and so, too, are observations of motor attitudes in hypnagogic and hypnopompic hallucinations.[13]

The original connection between perception and motor attitude also emerges from Freud's exposition of the activity of the perceptual apparatus.[14] As long as we speak of intensive external stimuli streaming in upon the organism which is still without any stimulus barrier, so that "traumatic situations" arise, our conception is that the external world with its stimuli rushes upon the organism and is experienced by it passively. The construction of a specific perceptual system (an ego), coinciding with the construction of a barrier system against stimuli, "changes passivity into activity"; perceptions become rhythmic, evidently under the influence of centrifugal ("motor") pulsations of cathexes, which we may consider as the first attempt at "mastering" external stimuli. Here probably lies the basis for the differentiation between "Cs" and "Mem-Systems," [15] and with it the basis of a differentiated consciousness. *After* this differentiation has been fashioned the organism is capable of protecting itself against an excess of stimulation by completely suspending the perceptual functions.[16] The newly arisen ego can again recede into the id. This capacity can still be observed in fainting spells, and in some symptoms of traumatic neuroses. It is obviously the model for all defense, both against external unpleasure and against the subject's own instincts, since repression may be considered as a partial suspension of perceiving (that is, a suspension of perceiving specific instinctual impulses).[17]

[11] S. Spielrein, "Kinderzeichnungen bei offenen und geschlossenen Augen," *Imago,* Vol. 17, 1931.
[12] G. Bally, "Die Wahrnehmungslehre Jaenschs und ihre Beziehung zu psychoanalytischen Problemen," *Imago,* Vol. 17, 1931.
[13] O. Isakower, *op. cit.*
[14] S. Freud, "A Note upon the 'Mystic Writing-Pad,' " *Coll. Pap.,* Vol. V, London, Hogarth, 1950.
[15] S. Freud, "The Interpretation of Dreams," Chapter VII in *The Basic Writings,* New York, Modern Library, 1938.
[16] For details see A. Kardiner, "The Bio-Analysis of the Epileptic Reaction," *Psa. Quart.,* Vol. 1, 1932.
[17] Cf. O. Fenichel, "Organ Libidinization Accompanying the Defense against Drives," No. 14, *First Series.*

A somewhat similar recession of the ego into the id occurs in the state of sleep.

The phenomenon which Bernfeld has described as "fascination" [18] is evidently also a function of the ego in response to traumatic stimuli. A primitive attempt to master perceptual stimuli consists in the primitive ego's motor imitation of the percept. For clearly, perception and change of one's own organism in accordance with the percept are originally identical. Patients of Goldstein with brain injuries could, as is known, compensate their alexia by following with movements of the head the forms of the letters they saw, so that they could read them kinesthetically by means of their head movements. [19] This is a primitive reaction to perception, or rather an assimilation to the percept, a sort of identification, by means of which alone perception can take place. Even though later on what we call "perception" and "identification" are very different, primitive perception is the common matrix of both.

Another primitive reaction to the first external objects sounds simpler and is easier to empathize: one wants to put them into one's mouth. It was hunger, after all, which, by repeatedly interrupting the relatively stimulus-free state of sleep, compelled recognition of an external world. The experience of satiety which eliminated this tension (and at first, no doubt, with it the external world) became the model for the mastery of external stimuli in general. The first reality is the edible. Thus, to "cognize" reality originally meant to judge whether it leads to satisfaction or increases tension, whether it can be swallowed or should be spat out. [20] Taking-in-the-mouth or spitting-out of objects is the basis of all perception, and in regressive states we can observe that for the unconscious all sensory organs are actually mouthlike. [21]

The primitive reactions of assimilation to, and oral introjection of, what is perceived, are obviously closely related. Freud had always stressed that what is recognized by normal psychology and pathopsychology in later periods as "identification" gives the impression of a regression, of a "secondary" identification, which was preceded by a "primary identification" as the first attempt at coming to terms with the world of objects. In this primary identification, instinctual behavior and ego behavior are not yet differentiated; it is at one and the same time the first oral object love, the first perception (involving assimilation and introjection), and the first motor reaction to external stimuli. Assimilation to the external world by oral incorporation of it is also the basis of that primitive coming to terms in thought with the environment which we call "magic."

[18] S. Bernfeld, "Ueber Faszination," *Imago*, Vol. 14, 1928.
[19] Cf. J. Steinfeld, "Ein Beitrag zur Analyse der Sexualfunktion," *Z. Neur. Psychiat.*, Vol. 107, 1927.
[20] Cf. S. Freud, "Negation," *Coll. Pap.*, Vol. V.
[21] Cf. O. Fenichel, "Respiratory Introjection" and "The Scoptophilic Instinct and Identification," Nos. 23 and 33, *First Series*.

I should like here to look ahead and make a small digression, though it takes us away from the theory of perception: This incorporation, which is the first reaction of all to objects, and the precursor of many subsequent libidinal destructive and narcissistic attitudes—this incorporation, when carried out, undoubtedly once more abolishes the object. And the attitude that the object exists only to satisfy the ego and may disappear once it has satisfied it, does indeed remain the criterion of archaic "love." [22] The question is: Can the aim of such an incorporation, which actually annihilates the object—and can the aim of its prefigurative presentation, the striving to swallow an object—can these be called *ambivalent?* We know that analytic research has confirmed Abraham's supposition that incorporative aims are not restricted to oral trends, but obtain in all erotogenic zones from which object-directed trends arise; and he did not hesitate to describe as "ambivalent" those stages of development whose objectual trends are characterized by the aim of incorporation.[23] But it is perhaps important to emphasize that a subjective will to annihilate or ruin—a wild destructive tendency—directed against the object, such as is demonstrable in the unconscious of manic-depressives, need not necessarily be implied by the aim of incorporation. This incorporation is only the matrix of both subsequent love and subsequent destructiveness, but not yet either of these. An explicit pleasure in destruction, which we undoubtedly see in some small children (and which is not simply projected back into childhood subsequently) must by no means be attributed to every infant sucking at its mother's breast.[24] Since orally fixated people—those who later become depressives, addicts, oral characters, etc., and in whom oral sadism and the related retributive anxiety, as described by Melanie Klein, are so clearly manifest—have so often had early childhood experiences (frustrations) which have become decisive for their fixation on such fantasies, it becomes probable that such experiences, or at least a special constitution, are responsible for the specifically sadistic character of their incorporative wishes, i.e., for their subjective wishes to destroy. Just because such cases always confirm anew Klein's findings, we must ask ourselves whether these findings are not merely products of pathology, and whether it is not the case that oral-sadistic drives of the normal infant do not contain such a high degree of will to destroy and of a corresponding fear of retribution. We must remember also that incorporation clearly attains its subjective destructive tone only secondarily, by making use of its objectively destructive nature; because the first, object-inimical reaction against objects which bring displeasure or deny pleasure, is not swallow-

---

[22] A. Balint, "Die Psychoanalyse des Kinderzimmers," *Z. psa. Paed.*, Vol. 6, 1932.

[23] K. Abraham, "A Short Study of the Development of the Libido, Viewed in the Light of Mental Disorders," *Selected Papers*, London, Hogarth, 1948.

[24] As is done by Melanie Klein (cf. *The Psychoanalysis of Children*, New York, Norton, 1932) and her circle.

ing them but spitting them out. It is also questionable whether the primitive ego recognizes the object, which at one time gives satisfaction, and at another denies it, *as* one and the same, so that it *can* be ambivalent toward it—whether there do not rather exist side by side separate representations of a good object which is to be acquired by incorporation, and of a bad object which is to be spat out, and which is only subsequently also to be annihilated by devouring. It is a matter of definition whether we wish to designate primitive incorporation as ambivalent and so consider the ambivalence of emotions as inborn, or not. Primitive incorporation is ambivalent in so far as it contains simultaneously characteristics of subsequent love and characteristics of subsequent hate; it is not ambivalent in so far as love and hate as opposites are not yet developed, and it cannot be said that they are simultaneously present. The striving to attain satisfaction without regard for the object (and thereby objectively destroying the object) and the striving to annihilate the object in hate, are not the same.

Let us return to the theory of perception. The differences in the perceiving of small children and adults must result in their experiencing the world differently. Observations on mentally ill persons who have regressed to primitive types of perception confirm that the archaic world appears vaguer and less differentiated, that its objects flow into one another and into the ego, or into ego constituents, and that the first representations are large in size, inclusive, and inexact. They consist, not of elements which are only later on put together, but of wholes which are only later on recognized as multiple. Not only can perception and motility—i.e., stimulation and reaction to it—not be separated from each other, but sensations belonging to different sensory fields cannot be separated either. Moreover, the data of the so-called "lower senses" and of kinesthesia predominate, as regressive phenomena of all kinds confirm; and it is these elements, too, which give magic character to the beginnings of thought (a subject to which we shall come later).

Not only the *form* of the perceptions, but their *contents* too are different. Hermann called the perceptions "to which the small child is exposed, but which disappear later on for internal or external reasons," "primary perceptions." [25] A part of these primary perceptions arises from the biological circumstances of the child (from the perspective of the small body the world appears different to each sense),[26] or from the different spatial experience.

Hermann calls special attention to two primary perceptions: "glowing of eyes" and "internal sounds." The small child's anxiety with respect to the latter

[25] I. Hermann, "Urwarnehmungen, insbesondere Augenleuchten und Lautwerden des Inneren," *Int. Z. Psa.*, Vol. 20, 1934.
[26] A. Meyer, "Das Kleinkind und seine Umwelt," *Z. psa. Paed.*, Vol. 10, 1936.

arises in the final analysis, he thinks, from its responding to disturbing stimuli with the Moro reflex, which causes a quick tensing of the arms lying near its head and results in the becoming audible of an internal sound which probably stems from tensing the eardrum. According to analytic clinical experience, which does not reach back so deeply into the reflexive life of the infant, its frequent fear at "internal sounds" proves, it is true, to be nothing but fear at the sensations of its own sexual excitement in general.

When we call the primitive ego a "weak" ego, we use an equivocal term. The primitive ego is "weak" in that it is more powerless both toward the external world and toward its own drives than the differentiated ego. But since the separation of ego and non-ego is not yet definitively accomplished, and it regards the external world or parts of it as part of itself, it feels powerful, "omnipotent." The much-quoted "omnipotence of thought" is—according to Ferenczi [27]—merely a special case of this "primitive omnipotence," and a relatively late one, which only arises after the development of the (motor) ability to think. Ferenczi has spoken of a first "unconditional omnipotence" which obtains as long as there exists no representation of objects as yet; it becomes "conditional" in the course of experiencing excitations which cannot be mastered and which elicit all sorts of un-co-ordinated movements of discharge in the undeveloped motor apparatus. Inasmuch as these movements, or this crying, is understood by the external world as a signal to eliminate the tensions, the child experiences such discharge reactions as magic powers and as an "omnipotence of movements."

The separation of ego and objectual world is no sudden process; it takes place slowly and gradually. A longing for the original objectless state probably always remains ("oceanic feeling").[28] Introjections can always make parts of the external world disappear; and projections, by which unpleasurable parts of the ego are relegated to the external world, also rest on the still reversible character of the separation between ego and non-ego as far as it has gone. When experience forces the child to give up the belief in his own omnipotence, he regards the adults of his environment, who are now becoming independent objects, as almighty, and he attempts to re-acquire a share in this omnipotence by introjecting them (or parts of them). A large part of certain "narcissistic feelings of well-being" of later times has the characteristic content of reunion with an almighty being of the external world (as we see in religious ecstasy, patriotism, etc.—impulses which are always marked by the ego's participating through them in something unattainably high).

The point of departure for this constant alternation of the external and the

[27] S. Ferenczi, op. cit.
[28] S. Freud, Civilization and Its Discontents, London, Hogarth, 1946.

internal world is to be found in the stage which Freud calls "the purified pleasure-ego."[29] The most primitive means employed against unpleasure, its hallucinatory elimination, is soon shipwrecked on reality; the young organism then attempts to allocate to the ego, by introjection, whatever is pleasurable, and to allocate to the external world, by projection, whatever is unpleasurable. It is not certain whether all projection, in the psychiatric sense, is really founded upon an unconscious representation of the elimination of a bodily substance; but in any case, projection belongs to a world in which ego and objectual world are not as yet definitely separated. Traces of this "transitivistic" world persist for a long time. The child who, in playing hide-and-seek, closes its eyes and then thinks that it cannot be seen, is one example. Here, as in the "animistic" view of the world, we have a sort of "inverted identification," which is related to primitive identification. In it there is a (fancied) assimilation of the external world to the ego, just as in primitive identification there is an assimilation of the ego to the external world.[30] Many characteristics of the primitive ego must be discussed and understood from this standpoint.

From these insights into primitive "omnipotence" we may derive, as Rado has most clearly shown,[31] an understanding of a need which is very important in the psychology of human beings in general. The memory of past stages of omnipotence (and of their having always been interrupted by unpleasurable states of hunger, and restored by satiation) persists in the form of an eternal longing to recover them. The need to feel once more this state of indestructible narcissistic wholeness may be called a "narcissistic need." By "self-regard" can then be meant a person's perception of this state, and of how near or how far he is from it. We cannot discuss here the significance of self-regard and of its forms of regulation for character formation and for the psychology of psychoses. For the primitive stages of ego development only the following is important:

If the assumption is correct that the most primitive stage is wholly objectless (has no ego as yet), that the first object representations arise in the state of lack of gratification, that the first longing for the object is a longing for the disappearance of a disturbing unpleasure, and that the first gratifications by the object eliminate the object itself and restore the narcissistic state—if this is correct, then it follows that in such stages the "longing for the restoration of omnipotence" cannot yet be distinguished from the longing for the elimination of instinctual tension and with it of the object world. "Narcissistic needing" and

---

[29] S. Freud, "Instincts and Their Vicissitudes," *Coll. Pap.*, Vol. IV, London, Hogarth, 1948.

[30] Cf. E. P. Hoffmann, "Projektion und Ich-Entwicklung," *Int. Z. Psa.*, Vol. 21, 1935.

[31] First in S. Rado, "The Psychic Effects of Intoxicants," *Int. J. Psa.*, Vol. 7, 1926; further developed in several later papers.

"erotic needing" are not yet differentiated from each other. From this, however, arises the original method of regulation of self-regard: success in bringing about an intervention of the external world to eliminate unpleasure restores high self-regard. The first supply of gratification from the external world, the supply of nourishment, is simultaneously the first regulator of self-regard. We have discussed how, after the renunciation of one's own omnipotence, there persists a belief in the omnipotence of adults, and a tendency to share it again by means of reintrojection. Thus, all love received from a more powerful being fulfills the same function as the supply of milk does in infancy. The primitive means of gratification of narcissistic neediness is the feeling of being loved. The small child's self-regard is lowered if it suffers a loss of love, and is increased if it receives love. Later on, narcissistic and erotic needs become differentiated. The latter develops in relationships to real objects, the former in those between ego and superego. Every guilt feeling lowers self-regard, every fulfillment of an ideal heightens it. But as in all psychic developments, the old is still demonstrable behind the new: part of the relationships to real objects also remains under the rule of self-regard. The primitive regulation of self-regard can best be studied in people who have remained fixated at this stage. They need "external narcissistic supplies" to maintain their self-regard. It goes without saying that there are the most varied subtypes among such people. First of all there are "instinct-ridden" individuals who want to acquire by force what is indispensable to them and is being withheld by the bad external world; in contrast to them are the masochists, who try to defend themselves against this inclination to violence, and who plead for the indispensable supplies by means of their suffering. It is this need, with its corresponding fear of loss of love, which makes children "educable," i.e., which, in their dependence on the love supplies of the external world, makes them ready to undertake that renunciation of other instincts which the external world demands.[32]

The fact that in this phase erotic and narcissistic needing alike impels the child to long for love, and the fact that the longing at this time must be more than longing, namely, a drive just as crucial to life as hunger or the need to breathe, and finally, the fact that traces of this kind of object relationship somewhere or other underlie all its subsequent forms, including "active" love— all this permits us to regard this as a "passive object love" on the part of the small child. One must realize that this "passive object love" has still many archaic features, which have been overcome in the "passive object love" of, say, a normal adult woman. These are the features which Alice Balint has pointed out and which find their explanation in the various characteristics of early ego phases,

[32] Cf. O. Fenichel, "A Contribution to the Psychology of Jealousy," No. 31, First Series.

and particularly in their insufficient differentiation between erotic and narcissistic needs: the subject wishes only to get something from the object, and when that wish is fulfilled, the object loses all interest for him and fuses once more with his ego.

Should this archaic "passive object love" be called a "primary passive object love"? [33] I think not. It is not primary; for we saw that it was preceded by an objectless stage in which, although *objectively* the infant was dependent upon supplies from an object, *subjectively* this fact had as yet no representations in his mind, since there were no object cathexes, but only states of disturbing tension or gratifying relaxation of tension.

In order that this secondary passive object love, following upon a primary objectless stage, may lead to love of a tertiary sort, a further step in development must be made. This corresponds to the advance from incorporative aims and partial objects to genital aims and total objects, described by Abraham.[34] Certain prerequisites for the achievement of this step are necessary, and these are not easy to survey. I agree with Ferenczi that it is first and foremost experiences in real life which oblige the child to have regard for the object [35] and turn *pre-love* into love. Contrary to Jekels and Bergler,[36] we believe that intrapsychic conflicts between the ego and the later established superego play a minor role here—and, indeed, that where such conflicts dominate objectional relationships, we get, not love, but pathological caricatures of it. What mechanisms the "erotic sense of reality" uses to enforce empathic regard for the object is not quite clear, but they must be identificatory processes of a certain kind. "Identification," however, means many things, and in this particular case it must be of a specific kind which should be more exactly apprehendable; at this point the problem of empathy arises.

We have digressed very far from the topic of the development of perception and must return to it; and we must now also investigate the development of the ego functions at the opposite pole of the relationships between subject and external world. The control of the "motor apparatus," too, is a task which the human infant must learn bit by bit and in constant connection with the development of his "feeling" and sensory apparatus. The gradual gaining of mastery over motility is, from the psychological point of view, a gradual replacement of mere reactions of discharge by actions, that is, the interpolation of a time interest between stimulus and reaction, the acquisition of a certain tolerance of tension, a "binding" of primitive reactive impulses by means of "anti-

[33] Cf. A. Balint, *op. cit.*
[34] K. Abraham, *op. cit.*
[35] S. Ferenczi, *Thalassa, A Theory of Genitality*, Albany, Psa. Quart. Press, 1938.
[36] L. Jekels and E. Bergler, "Uebertragung und Liebe," *Imago*, Vol. 20, 1934.

cathexes." [37] Another prerequisite of all action, besides the mastery of the somatic apparatuses, is the development of the *function of judgment,* i.e., the ability to anticipate the future in thought, to "sample" it—behavior which is altogether characteristic of the ego. This can, for instance, be observed in the so-called "anxiety signal," which, in circumstances of danger, anticipates the threatening traumatic situation, and also in "thinking" ("thinking is experimental action") which appears later in verbal form. The main stations along the developmental road of motor mastery of the body are learning to walk, becoming clean, and learning to talk. This road of development in turn coincides with what Freud has called the "reality principle," with whose development perception also loses its primitive character. In discussing primitive ego functions the interdependence of the sensory and the motor sphere cannot be overstated. The ability to act, to judge reality, and to tolerate tension ("stimulus barrier erected through deployment of anti-cathectic quantities") are identical. It is evident that these abilities are developed around the emergence of the concept of "danger." We must first, therefore, say something about anxiety.[38]

The biological inability to master instinctual tensions without help is the cause of the first "anxiety." *Originally* the ego—or rather the psychic apparatus which, not yet differentiated into ego and id, fulfills, among other things, functions which are later those of the ego—experiences anxiety passively as something which occurs automatically whenever the excitation in the id is excessive, because, owing to the relative insufficiency of the apparatuses of discharge, there is a damming up of need. Anxiety can, in that case, be conceived of as being a discharge of this dammed-up excitation which is effected, *in spite* of the insufficiency of the apparatus, by the path of the vegetative nervous system, or rather, as the ego's manner of experiencing that alternative, that "nevertheless" † discharge, it might be termed. Freud, assuming, in analogy to hysterical attacks, that a specific syndrome of somatic processes of discharge with definite experiential quality (an affect) must be *historically* derived from a situation in which the innervations in question were expedient, has suggested that we should regard the act of birth as the experience in which was first shaped the syndrome "anxiety," which appears again with every subsequent high need-tension "analogous to birth." This anxiety appertaining to a "traumatic state" which the ego originally experienced only passively, may later on still be observed in the anxiety of the traumatic and actual neuroses. In traumatic neuroses there is, in fact, an excess of afflux of excitation. In actual neuroses the damming

---

[37] S. Freud, "Formulations Regarding the Two Principles in Mental Functioning," *Coll. Pap.,* Vol. IV.

[38] Cf. for this and the following, S. Freud, *The Problem of Anxiety.*

† Fenichel calls it a *"dennoch" Abfuhr.*—Trans. note.

up corresponds to a deficit in the discharge of excitation; external or internal conditions prevent normal discharge of excitation, and this leads to a vegetative "nevertheless" break-through, which the ego experiences passively.

In other forms which anxiety assumes in older children and adults the case is different. We have seen that the gradual development of the ego as an apparatus differentiated to receive stimuli serves to build a stimulus barrier, in that the ego, by evolving a function of judgment, develops the ability to anticipate the future in thought, and to direct its subsequent actions accordingly. The expression "danger" means that the judging ego, anticipating the future in fantasy, pronounces of a situation which is not yet "traumatic," that it may become "traumatic." Such a judgment obviously establishes in the id conditions analogous to those which the occurrence of the traumatic situation itself would, except that these are less in degree; and therefore they, too, must be experienced by the ego as anxiety. Thus, by passing the judgment of danger, the ego itself produces a bit of anxiety, or rather, with the development of the ability to judge, the ego has acquired a means by which to "tame" anxiety and to use it for its own purposes, in that the experiencing of the "anticipated" small anxiety serves as signal for the defensive parts of the ego to set the defense in motion. The useful and expedient component of an anxiety which arises in danger, the introduction of defensive measures, is due to the judging ego; its inexpedient component which, under certain circumstances, may render vain the defensive measures—e.g., by paralysis—is due to the circumstance that the ego does not produce, but only uses anxiety, and that it has no means which are more expedient at its disposal.

One complication which is frequently found in neurotic anxiety need not interest us any further here. This is that the ego, judging that there is danger, has wanted to establish conditions analogous to a trauma in the id, and so create a "little anxiety" as "signal," but that it comes too close, as it were, with the match it has lit to a store of dynamite. The ego's aim at procuring a "small dose" fails because of the presence of dammed-up libido; the judgment of "danger" acts exactly like the full occurrence of the traumatic situation itself, and a major anxiety attack sets in, against which the ego is helpless.[39]

The "animistic misunderstanding," which ascribes to the outer world one's own uninhibited drives with incorporative aims, is responsible for the anxiety *contents* of the primitive ego. In this misunderstanding we see the primitive "talion principle" in action, according to which like can and should be undone by like.

The earliest anxiety confronting the instincts is clearly the consequence of

[39] Cf. O. Fenichel, "Defense Against Anxiety, Particularly by Libidinization," No. 27, *First Series*.

the infant's physiological inability to gratify his drives; in other words, it is anxiety that external aid in gratification may not be forthcoming. The "fear concerning loss of love" gains additional importance from the fact that the primitive regulation of self-regard, too, occurs by means of supplies of love from without. An ego that is loved, therefore, feels strong and an ego that is abandoned feels weak and exposed to all dangers; and an ego that is still loved has every reason to fear abandonment. The tendency to project drives that are considered dangerous onto the outer world and to assume that one's own characteristics exist in other people as well, complicate the state of affairs. When a child devours his surroundings in fantasy and meets with frustration, *in any way*, it will fantasy that it might be devoured by its parents. (It is well known that later on the superego, too, is not only as severe toward his ego as his parents were toward him, but also as violent against it as he wanted to be violent against them.) In this way there arise those fears of imaginary injuries to the body, whose final and most important representative is the fear of genital castration which later supplies the ego with the principal motive for its defensive activity against drives.

The primitive ego's learning to cognize, love, and fear reality are functions whose basic development precedes even the learning of speech. But the latter function seems to bring with it for the first time the "reality principle" in the strict sense of the word, and to complete the building up of a true "ego." Words not only make possible communication with the objects, but also refine "experimental action," which anticipates the future, into "thinking" proper and lead to the final consolidation of a consciousness (to make a representation conscious means to connect it with verbal images).[40] Of course consciousness already exists without words, as is shown by regressive states and "preconscious fantasy thinking."[41] But this is only the undifferentiated "primal form" of thinking, which displays all the characteristics of the primitive ego (large compass of the concepts, formation of concepts through reactive identity, etc.). Schilder has demonstrated that every single thought still passes through such a wordless "primal form" before it is formulated in words.[42] That the connection with a verbal image, the naming, thus facilitates thinking and thereby provides the ego with a better weapon against excitations of all kinds, explains the ancient magical belief that knowing the name of something gives one command over it (cf. the story of Rumpelstiltskin). There is no doubt that the striving to master instinctual excitations in this way contributes considerably to the development of the intellect. There is a "flight" from fantasy into sober

[40] S. Freud, "The Unconscious," *Coll. Pap.*, Vol. IV.

[41] J. Varendonck, "The Psychology of Daydreams," *Organization and Pathology of Thought*, D. Rapaport, ed., New York, Columbia University Press, 1951.

[42] P. Schilder, "On the Development of Thoughts."

reality, which serves the purpose of disproving anxiety. A pathological caricature of this is the flight of compulsive characters from emotionally rich experience to the shadow world of words and concepts—a flight which, it is true, is usually unsuccessful, in that after the instincts that have been fended off have made their way into the defense itself, the concepts and words are once more treated as the instincts formerly were. Anna Freud has recently shown that the jump in the development of intelligence which occurs during puberty also assists the endeavor to master instinctual excitations.[43]

The omnipotence of thoughts moves on to an omnipotence of words. The gradual discovery of the meaning of sounds (which has as yet been little studied by psychoanalysis) [44] is obviously the last definitive step in the evolution of the ego. The theory of aphasia—which has so far been little regarded by psychoanalysts—will, moreover, have decisive contributions to make about the way in which this evolution proceeds from the integrated to the differentiated, from the whole to the part, from a broad compass to a narrow one.

Thinking is in general a further elaboration and differentiation of the function of judgment. Reaction does not follow upon stimulation but is postponed till it assumes the character of aim-directed action. The postponement is accomplished by means of the familiar "experimental action," through using small innervations in the sense of the actions that are planned, so that the planned action and the consequences that are to be expected from it are "tasted"; it is obvious how much such anticipation is facilitated by the development of verbal images. Thinking establishes the reality principle. This assertion is contradicted by the fact that at first thinking is obviously *not* in line with reality but magical; i.e., it is influenced by the belief in one's own and other people's omnipotence, by the equation of the object and its representation, by an insufficient differentiation of ego and non-ego, especially in projective misapprehension, by an insufficiently sharp delineation of representations and concepts, so that part and whole appear equal and similar things identical, and, finally, by symbolism. Nevertheless, this unadaptedness of thinking to external reality does not alter the fact that even such judgments of reality are also in the nature of anticipation of the future which delay immediate reaction.

"Preconscious imaginative thinking" thus appears to us to be in the first place a *preparation* for reality. Its development, however, is undoubtedly carried on in the interests of another function as well. It becomes a *substitute* for reality where this is too ungratifying, making use for this purpose of the residues of the original phase of "hallucinatory wish fulfillment." While thinking which *pre-*

[43] A. Freud, *The Ego and the Mechanisms of Defence,* New York, Int. Univ. Press, 1946.
[44] Cf. M. Chadwick, "The Child's Early Discrimination between Sound and Speech," *Psyche,* Vol. 32, 1928.

pares for reality tends later to take verbal form and assumes a "logical" character (even though traces of magic remain everywhere in evidence in it), thinking which *replaces* reality tends to remain on a tangible, wordless, and magical level (as we see in daydreams). It would be an enticing task to work out the differences between imagination which prepares for reality and imagination which replaces reality. The differences probably depend on whether the innervations involved in such thinking are by their nature able to discharge tensions to a considerable extent, or whether they only augment them by increasing the longing for discharge on actual objects.

In this way the entire development of the primitive ego is best described from the angle of a development from the pleasure principle to the reality principle, occurring under the constant influence of the external world (which creates a representative of itself in the ego) as it plays upon the organism which, to begin with, followed the Nirvana principle. But the external world as a source of stimulation is not experienced only as a disturber; for there also exists the phenomenon of "a craving for stimulus" which seemingly contradicts the Nirvana principle. Reality does not only disturb, but also contains in its objects the possibility of gratification. We have asserted that to our mind the acceptance of the external world, which emerges in the craving for stimulus, is not from the start the antithesis of the Nirvana principle which wants to destroy the external world as a source of excitation, but that it must be genetically-dialectically derived from the Nirvana principle. When the sleeping infant is awakened by somatically determined hunger, in wishing to pacify the hunger and to continue sleeping, it first follows its Nirvana principle. When later on it recognizes that an intervention of the external world is necessary for this progress, it strives to induce such intervention and reaches out toward the external world. The first craving for stimulus occurs not in contradiction to, but in the service of, the Nirvana principle. The contradictions only appear later on. The infant's primitive interest in the external world is in any case solely and entirely due to the circumstance that the external world is a source of gratification for it. This interest is first determined by hunger, later by the other erotogenic zones. The instinctual interest engaged in the external world determines what is primarily of interest there; but here "animistic misapprehension" and symbolic thinking must always be taken into account, for these induce the child to be interested not only in real but also in symbolic possibilities of gratification.

A knowledge of the primitive types of reality perception is necessary in order to understand the pathological behavior of children and adults. Conversely, these primitive types of perception—the pregenital world with its introjections and projections, with its primitive fears and defensive measures against those fears—can be inferred only from this pathological behavior. The objects of the external world emanate, as Glover has described, from the instincts.[45]

So far we have spoken of the reality principle as a postponement of the final reaction, a saving up of discharge until certain opportunities present themselves in reality. But this also involves refraining, temporarily or permanently, from inexpedient discharges. At the same time as the mastery of motility increases, i.e., as an apparatus of discharge develops, there develops too an apparatus of non-discharge, a defensive apparatus. By this I mean an apparatus which wards off internal instinctual impulses which seem unsuitable or dangerous to the ego. But this apparatus does no more than set in motion against the *instinctual* impulses something which has already been at work previously against unpleasant *external* experiences. As we know, the organism, subjected to the pleasure principle, has sought from the very beginning to escape from the unpleasure forced upon it by the external world. The earliest defensive reaction of all, in which the ego had least to do in an active and critical way, was the complete reactive suspension of ego functions; the next is the partial and elective suspension of ego functions, as for instance, in negative hallucination, the not-noticing of unpleasant external circumstances. This latter behavior is the core of what is later met with as denial; and still later, after the reality principle has reached a certain stage, i.e., after regard for reality has begun, it is replaced by *phobic* avoidance. Other defensive mechanisms too, as we know, are archaic; e.g., projection, a direct descendant of "spitting out" of bad-tasting objects, and introjection, the intention to annihilate disliked objects by devouring them.

Anna Freud has discussed in her book how these and other defensive mechanisms change when the ego proceeds to use them not only against the external world, but also in its struggle against drives which appear dangerous to it.[46] We should like to add that after the apparatus for instinctual defense has been elaborated in the ego the defensive attitudes which are directed against the external world and those which are directed against the instincts can by no means be sharply separated. Repression, which does not come into being till relatively later, is not sharply distinguished from the various forms of denial: external impressions are forgotten or left unnoticed, because they constitute a situation of temptation for the proscribed drive, and the drive is defended against from fear of a punitive intervention by the external world.

The later defensive attitudes are in part characterized by the establishment of an expenditure of anti-cathectic energy in the ego, in order to safeguard forever

---

[45] Cf. E. Glover, "The Relation of Perversion-Formation to the Development of Reality-Sense," *Int. J. Psa.*, Vol. 14, 1933.

[46] A. Freud, *op. cit.*

the defensive action which has been carried out on one occasion (as we see in reaction formation, active inhibition by means of ego restriction, etc.). They are also in part characterized by the ego having learned to intervene in a process in order to alter it, without hindering its course (e.g., turning the drive into its opposite or against the ego, or alloplastic behavior toward the outer world). But these defensive attitudes no longer belong to the "early" developmental stages of the ego.

Let us repeat the reasons which can prompt an ego interested in the pleasurable gratification of its instincts to turn, paradoxically, against those instincts: (1) The biological circumstance that the infant does not control its motor apparatus and needs the help of the external world to get gratification, has the consequence that—since the external world cannot always immediately come to its aid automatically—the child is placed in "traumatic situations." This experience brings the first realization that drives can become dangerous. (2) Threats and prohibitions about its instincts by the external world create in the infant a fear of the consequences of instinctual action or even fear at the mere noticing of instinctual tension, which condenses into a prophylactic defense against "traumatic situations." Such interventions on the part of the external world are again of two kinds: (a) Objective—the fire burns the child who, following his drive, reaches with his hand for it. (b) Educational measures—deliberately or unwittingly, adults give the child to understand that they disapprove of his drive, and impose renunciations on him. They can do this not only because of their physical power, but also by virtue of the nature of the child's self-regard which is dependent upon supplies of love. (3) This external world, inimical to instinct, is "projectively misapprehended," and this explains, as indicated above, the intensity and content of the anxieties which motivate the defense against drives.

Later on a fourth circumstance is added to these. This is the dependence of the ego upon the superego, which is an endopsychic representative of the objective, educating, and projectively misunderstood external world.

These motives, then, prompt the judging ego to protest against certain instinctual excitations and to ward them off. In this way conflicts arise and the failure of the defensive activity of the ego leads to neuroses. Most of the neuroses of small children seem to rest, as far as the literature on the subject reports, on such a conflict between drive on the one hand and fear of the reaction of the (misunderstood) anti-instinctual external world on the other. The fact that this external world is not as yet internalized seems to make these neuroses more easily amenable to therapeutic influence. For even when the child's projective misapprehension is most excessive, and when, despite having the best of parents, he expects to be devoured and chopped up, he nevertheless fears those evil consequences of his instinctual gratification as coming from *without*. Combating such neuroses before the internalization of the conflict is completed seems therefore prophylactically very important.

To what extent the "development of the sense of reality" succeeds normally, to what extent what was vague becomes definite, what was magical becomes logical, what was anxiety-laden becomes the object of one's own alloplastic activity, and to what extent the old forms persist—all this depends as much on constitution and fate-fraught experience, as do the analogous phenomena belonging to the more familiar field of libido development. The causes of the persistence of ego fixations, which, in later disturbances, make ego regressions possible, are studied by the psychoanalysis of the ego just as much as libido fixations are studied by psychoanalysis of the id. Clearly the developments of ego and id do not proceed side by side separately, but exert a manifold influence upon each other. Freud already wrote years ago: "We know that the understanding of the developmental disposition to a neurosis is complete only if it takes into account the phase of ego-development in which the fixation occurs just as much as that of libido-development." [47] But research seems only recently to have reached the point where the concepts "ego fixation" and "ego regression" assume fairly definite forms. They may encompass the entire ego—constitution and experience again forming a complementary series—in which case we have to do with "infantile types," in whom the described characteristics of the archaic ego can, to a greater or lesser extent, be studied, or they may be partial, and that again may mean various things:

Single ego functions may prolong, or reassume, the possession of certain characteristics belonging to the primitive phases; in this sense we may designate "eidetic" types as perceptual fixations. Or the form of thinking may retain more of its magical character than it does in normal persons; this is the case, for instance, in every obsessional neurosis where a very precociously and strongly developed intellect is in sharp contrast to the belief in omnipotence and talion held by the unconscious parts of the ego. (The defensive work of obsessional neurosis is a far more active achievement of the ego than is that of hysteria. It is based, as Freud has said, on the fact that the development of the ego has "hurried ahead" of the development of the libido; but the early demands made on the ego at a time when it still has some of its archaic characteristics evidently gives occasion for a fixation on precisely this stage, despite the precocious flowering of the intellect.) Or else, again, the manner of dealing with objects shows primitive characteristics; there are fixations at pre-stages of love, at incorporative aims, at the regulation of self-regard as it obtains in small children. These types

[47] S. Freud, "The Predisposition to Obsessional Neurosis," *Coll. Pap.*, Vol. II, London, Hogarth, 1948.

especially are often designated as "oral," and rightly, in so far as their ego has retained a characteristic which it had at the time of the oral stage of libido organization. One must note, however, that there may be a discrepancy between ego development and instinctual development; while the "oral" type of regulation of self-regard persists, the oral zone need not likewise remain libidinally dominant. Or, finally—and this was noticed only in recent years, despite its fundamental importance—the ego fixation may be limited to certain kinds of defense, which are always used by the ego whenever it turns against any instinct. Such habitual defenses can be divided into special ones, which are applied in certain situations or toward certain objects, and general ones, which are rigid, and are applied automatically without regard for the situation or object. These latter belong to the character of the person, and are to be regarded as dead rudiments of a once live instinctual conflict; their treatment in analysis is not pertinent here. Their special quality, i.e., the ego fixation, depends on several circumstances. It depends partly on the nature of the drives against which the defense is principally directed, partly on the age at which the child was exposed to the underlying instinctual conflict. But its main explanation is historical—i.e., analysis succeeds in showing that the special form of defense was either the most useful in a past situation, or was enforced on the subject (identification) by the external world in a past situation.[48]

A crucial role in the establishment of ego fixations is played by yet another factor. This factor does not, in the main, belong any more to the "early" stages of ego development, which are our only concern here; but it is already preparing during this period. This is the superego.

We have mentioned that the mechanism of introjection may be employed against dreaded powers of the external world. In analysis—particularly in that of manic-depressives and other cases in whose genesis conflicts pivoting on oral sadism play the main role—we find that this defense often misfires in the sense that later on the child fears the introjects just as much as it formerly feared the objects. This anxiety becomes condensed with the "projective misunderstanding" of the external world. It seems to me, however, that our comprehension of the pregenital world, remote as it is from the child's later world of thought, is made more difficult if we speak of a particularly strict "early-infantile superego," [49] since this is a term which pertains only to later stages of development.

Conflicts between drives and the drive-frustrating external world have a quite general tendency to become internalized. This is easy to understand. When a child, afraid of losing his mother's love because of a certain instinctual activity, unintermittently wards off that drive in order not to anger his mother, and

---

[48] These issues are discussed by Anna Freud, *op. cit.*
[49] Melanie Klein.

finally erects inside himself a constant watcher to prevent the instinctual activity under any circumstances, even when the mother is absent—then what has happened is, at bottom, nothing else than that a part of his ego, in accordance with its function of representing the external world, has adapted itself to reality. In view of all we have heard about primitive object relations, this adaptation can only occur through identification. Thus arise the pre-stages of the superego, Ferenczi's "sphincter morality." [50] Are these pre-stages especially strong or especially weak? They are strong in that they threaten the most gruesome punishments, but they are weak in that they can easily be circumvented and deceived, when nobody is watching or when another person of authority in the external world gives permission for the prohibited action. Thus introjection is readily canceled by projection, and the functions of the superego pre-stages are once again attributed to persons in the external world. The emphasis of the personality fluctuates between drive and prohibition of drive, and as a whole it has no unitary organized character as yet. Yet here already a part of the instinctual energy is used, under the influence of the external world, to suppress the rest of instinctual energy, and this change in the direction of operation of instinctual energy is brought about by identification. Only after this does the decline of the oedipus complex erect that clearly delineated "grade in the ego" which becomes crucial for the further development of the ego. This further development, and the means the ego uses in its struggle against the superego, do not belong to our present theme.

It is not possible to present in these pages a bibliography characterizing one by one all writings on which my survey of our knowledge of the early stages of ego development is based. The foundation stone of the study of the ego was laid by Ferenczi in his paper on "Stages in the Development of the Sense of Reality" [51] and his later investigations have continued to be decisive for our knowledge of the ego. Melanie Klein,[52] and following her, Ernest Jones,[53] Joan Riviere,[54] Susan Isaacs [55] and other English authors have dealt with our subject in great

[50] S. Ferenczi, "Psycho-Analysis of Sexual Habits," *Further Contributions to the Theory and Technique of Psycho-Analysis.*

[51] S. Ferenczi, "Stages in the Development of the Sense of Reality," *Sex in Psychoanalysis.* Cf. also *Thalassa, A Theory of Genitality.* See "Psycho-Analysis of Sexual Habits" and "The Problem of Acceptance of Unpleasant Ideas—Advances in Knowledge of the Sense of Reality," both in *Further Contributions to the Theory and Technique of Psycho-Analysis;* "The Principle of Relaxation and Neocatharsis," *Int. J. Psa.,* Vol. 11, 1930; "Gedanken ueber das Trauma," *Int. Z. Psa.,* Vol. 20, 1934.

[52] For the summary of M. Klein's views see *The Psychoanalysis of Children.* Since then she has published "A Contribution to the Psychogenesis of Manic-Depressive States," *Int. J. Psa.,* Vol. 16, 1935.

[53] E. Jones, "The Early Development of Female Sexuality," "Fear, Guilt and Hate," "The Phallic Phase," all in *Papers on Psycho-Analysis,* 5th ed., Baltimore, Williams and Wilkins, 1948.

[54] J. Riviere, "Womanliness as a Masquerade," *Int. J. Psa.,* Vol. 10, 1929; "Jealousy as a Mechanism of Defence," *Int. J. Psa.,* Vol. 13, 1932.

[55] S. Isaac, "Privation and Guilt," *Int. J. Psa.,* Vol. 10, 1929; "Bad Habits," *Int. J. Psa.,* Vol. 16, 1935.

detail. I have incorporated the positive findings of the British school in my pragmatic presentation of the early ego phases, just as I have the contributions of other authors. Unfortunately, some of the views expressed in those studies, and the theoretical conception to which they subject the results of their practical research, give rise to serious doubts; in addition, they are in part written in a nomenclature which is completely different from ours. Some of the criticisms I have mentioned, others must be discussed in other places. A detailed comparison of the British school's view and the critical objections raised against them by other psychoanalysts, may be found in the recently published discussion between Riviere and Waelder [56] on the psychic conflicts of the early years of life. Of the multitude of papers considered in my lecture I would like to single out a few for special mention: Federn's detailed investigations of the *empirical* nature of what we call "ego feeling," its composite nature and the manifold changes in the "boundaries" of this empirical ego; [57] Sabine Spielrein's demonstration of the kinesthetic nature of many sensations which we are wont to consider visual; [58] Bally's presentation of the relation of eidetic findings to psychoanalysis; [59] Anna Freud's book, which is fundamental for the exploration of defenses; [60] E. P. Hoffmann's work on the characteristics of the primitive ego and of primary identification; [61] M. Balint's views on "primary passive object love"; [62] and finally Isakower's fine study concerning phenomena in states of ego regression.[63] Many authors remain unmentioned in this short list.

[56] J. Riviere, "On the Genesis of Psychical Conflict in Earliest Infancy," *Int. J. Psa.*, Vol. 17, 1936; R. Waelder, "The Problem of the Genesis of Psychical Conflict in Earliest Infancy," *Int. J. Psa.*, Vol. 18, 1937.

[57] P. Federn, "Narcissism in the Structure of the Ego," *Int. J. Psa.*, Vol. 9, 1928; "Das Ich als Subjekt und Objekt im Narzissmus," *Int. Z. Psa.*, Vol. 15, 1929; "Ego Feeling in Dreams," *Psa. Quart.*, Vol. 1, 1932; "Die Ichbesetzung bei den Fehlleistungen," *Imago*, Vol. 19, 1933; "Zur Unterscheidung des gesunden und krankhaften Narzissmus," *Imago*, Vol. 22, 1936.

[58] S. Spielrein, *op. cit.*

[59] G. Bally, *op. cit.*

[60] A. Freud, *op. cit.*

[61] E. P. Hoffmann, *op. cit.*

[62] M. Balint, *op. cit.*

[63] O. Isakower, *op. cit.*

FOUR

The Concept of Trauma in Contemporary Psychoanalytical Theory*

By way of introduction I shall go over some familiar ground and briefly summarize a number of fundamental facts from the general theory of the neuroses.

Neurosis is in the first place a motor irruption, unrecognized and undesired by the ego, of quantities of dammed-up excitation. The damming up may be caused by an increase in influx during a given unit of time, as is the case in traumatic neuroses, or by a decrease in discharge (whether this is inhibited by fear of the external world or at the bidding of the superego), as is the case in the psychoneuroses.

Hence arises a peculiar relation between neurosis and anxiety. Anxiety too, according to Freud,[1] is in the first instance a mode in which an increase in the tension arising from urgent needs is experienced. Later, however, it is "harnessed" and turned to account by the ego when it judges a situation to be "dangerous." Thus both in the case of neurosis in general and of anxiety in particular the situation of origin is the same—namely a damming up of excitation, with a relatively inadequate apparatus of discharge. This is in accordance with the important part played by anxiety in the psychology of the neuroses and with the fact that neuroses that are free from anxiety produce anxiety as soon as they are prevented from making use of their symptoms; so that the latter can be regarded as a kind of defense against, or as a secondary and further modifica-

---

* First published in *Int. Z. Psa.*, Vol. 23, 1937, pp. 339–359.
[1] S. Freud, *The Problem of Anxiety*, New York, Psa. Quart. Press and Norton, 1936.

tion of, anxiety. This will become clearer if we recall to our mind Freud's description [2] of anxiety in traumatic states and of the way in which it is subsequently "harnessed" by the ego.

It is only by the ego that anxiety can be felt as a quality of experience accompanied by a particular syndrome of somatic processes of discharge: "the ego is the seat of anxiety." [3] But originally the ego—or rather the mental apparatus which is not yet differentiated into ego and id but which fulfils the functions of what will later become an ego—experiences anxiety *passively,* as something that sets in automatically if id impulses can find no outlet, and a damming up of a need has taken place. In that case anxiety can be regarded as a "discharge in spite of everything" of the dammed-up excitation (which is denied outlet through the skeletal musculature) along the pathway of the vegetative nervous system; or rather, it can be regarded as the way in which the ego experiences a "discharge in spite of everything" of this kind.

The so-called "harnessing" of this powerful affect by the help of the gradual formation of the ego's function of judgment is a special case of the ego's general function of acting as the representative of the external world. The development of the pleasure principle into the reality principle—that is, from the motor standpoint, the replacement of mere acts of discharge by actions, the acquisition of a certain degree of tolerance of tension, the "binding" of primitive reactive impulses by anticathexes—presupposes not only a mastery over the somatic apparatus but also the formation of the function of judgment, i.e., a capacity for forming some sort of anticipation of the future through the notion of "experimenting," which is the essence of thought in general. The expression "danger" means that the judging ego declares that a particular situation which is not yet a traumatic one might become a traumatic one. To say that the ego develops the function of a protective barrier against stimuli from the external world means no more than that it develops a capacity for judging dangers, that is, for foreseeing wherever possible any traumatic excess of excitation and so for avoiding it. Such a judgment, however, must evidently set up in the id conditions similar to those of the appearance of the traumatic situation itself, though to a lesser degree. And this too must necessarily be experienced by the ego as anxiety. Thus the *expedient* component of anxiety arising during danger (or supposed danger)—the putting into action of measures of defense—is due to the judging ego. The *inexpedient* component, which sometimes frustrates the measures of defense by paralysis, must be attributed to the fact that the ego does not produce anxiety but merely makes use of it and that it has no more expedient means at its disposal, since its judgment of "danger" creates conditions that are "analogous to trauma."

[2] *Ibid.*
[3] *Ibid.,* p. 19.

Let us proceed at once to consider the case where this analogy is carried too far. It may happen, both where there is real danger and where there is neurotic anxiety, that the "signal" is far from giving an impression of being a "small dose" but that the subject behaves in the danger or supposed danger as though it were a traumatic situation. He reacts to the situation with a major attack of anxiety, with something that overwhelms the ego violently and entirely against its will, while it maintains an attitude of passivity. Clearly the ego's intention of giving a signal has failed. With that intention in view the ego has set something going which it cannot control. The condition which causes the intention of giving a signal to fail in this way is the presence of a damming up of libido brought about by chronic inhibitions of discharge. This damming up causes the freshly received anxiety signal to act like a match in a barrel of gunpowder.[4] That an anxiety attack in an anxiety hysteric is really analogous to a trauma may be seen too from the fact that it is followed by delayed attempts to master it, corresponding exactly to those, for instance, that follow a motor accident. This has also been pointed out by Edoardo Weiss[5] in a paper upon trauma, which in other respects, however, diverges so widely from my position that I shall make no further reference to it.

It is thus only this possibility—that what is intended as a guard against a traumatic state may in certain circumstances actually produce one—that makes it necessary for the ego to make arrangements for warding off the unpleasure of anxiety. It is obvious indeed that people will seek to avoid *any* anxiety, on the ground of its being unpleasurable; but the reality principle would necessarily approve, as a serviceable institution, an anxiety signal which could be kept as small as possible and would be a protection against greater unpleasure. It is only the uncertainty as to whether the anxiety signal may not produce greater and more disagreeable results than were intended that explains the immense expenditure of anti-cathexis which, as we know, is made in order to save anxiety.

For the sake of clarification, it must be added that anxiety is not the sole answer that can be made to the increase of excitation when discharge is relatively insufficient. There may also be phenomena due to the cessation of ego functions—the organism's most primitive means of protection and one which may itself produce damming up and so still further increase the tension[6]—as well as powerful attempts of all sorts at "discharges in spite of everything" acting not only in the domain of the vegetative system but also by the help of the skeletal musculature (including that of the larynx). What these processes cannot master

[4] O. Fenichel, "Defense Against Anxiety, Particularly by Libidinization," No. 27, *First Series*.

[5] E. Weiss, "Agoraphobia and its Relation to Hysterical Attacks and to Trauma," *Int. J. Psa.*, Vol. 16, 1935.

[6] A. Kardiner, "The Bio-Analysis of the Epileptic Reaction," *Psa. Quart.*, Vol. 1, 1932.

all at once they seek to discharge or to bind subsequently by means of the no-
torious "repetitions," whether in dreams or in waking life.[7] Ferenczi[8] is certainly right in suggesting that normal dreams also perform this function. It is
well known that *unexpectedness* increases the effect of a trauma. "Anticipatory
anxiety" lays up a store of anti-cathexis ready to bind and so to diminish any
unbound quantities of excitation that may subsequently press for discharge.[9]
The essence of the ego is anticipation of the future. Consequently, unexpected,
unanticipated events are *a priori* liable to overwhelm the ego. Nevertheless I
do not agree with Ferenczi when he says [10] that anxiety corresponds to the feeling of inability to avoid the unpleasure of the trauma. What unpleasure? physical pain, perhaps? This unpleasure is surely in fact already itself anxiety. Nor
do I agree with him in regarding loss of consciousness as self-destruction by
means of the death instinct which has been preferred to patient toleration. I
should rather regard it as an act of self-protection of a regressive kind—as it
often is in other circumstances—a flight to the period before the differentiation
of the ego. It may be doubted whether *all* vegetative "discharges in spite of
everything" should be subsumed under "anxiety." Nevertheless I think we
should not be justified in entirely avoiding the term "anxiety" in referring to
traumatically determined vegetative unpleasure and in reserving it solely for
the lesser degree of anxiety intentionally brought about by the ego, while speaking of the former case as "fright." [11] This word does not picture the intensely unpleasurable sensations of a major attack of anxiety. On the other hand, it is true
that the experience of fright is essentially related to trauma: the vegetative sensations correspond to a sudden and unexpected influx of excitations.

After this long introduction I will return to my point of departure. It appears,
then, that the excessive tension which is the situation of origin of every neurosis
can be determined either by a true trauma or by damming up through a defense
against instinct. The second possibility is the more familiar analytically but the
more complicated theoretically, since in this second case it is necessary in addition to study the psychogenesis of defense against instinct. I shall therefore begin
with the first alternative.

It is easily intelligible that a shattering experience (that is, sudden and unexpected, powerful, external stimuli in all the sensory fields) cannot be mastered
immediately. I may remark here that the best opportunities for self-observation
of the effects of a trauma in small doses are afforded by experiences which are
not absolutely but relatively shattering, experiences which are not of vital con-

---

[7] S. Freud, *Beyond the Pleasure Principle*, London, Hogarth, 1948, p. 37.
[8] S. Ferenczi, "Gedanken ueber das Trauma," *Int. Z. Psa.*, Vol. 20, 1934.
[9] S. Freud, *op. cit.*
[10] S. Ferenczi, *op. cit.*
[11] T. Reik, *Der Schrecken und andere psychoanalytische Studien*, Vienna, Int. Psa. Verlag, 1929.

cern but which merely produce too much excitation in a given unit of time—such as falling down or even simply stumbling. These effects include a regression of the entire muscular activity including that of the larynx—I may recall Miss Searl's paper [12] upon screaming in children, which is certainly highly relevant in this connection—a regression varying from actions to purely senseless acts of discharge in the form of vegetative sensations and to delayed attempts at mastery by means of repetition in dreams and fantasies.

Is it possible for a sudden and unexpected increase in excitation from *within* to produce effects similar to those seen in these cases of an increase of *external* excitation? A sudden onset of *pain* is also answered by a cessation of ego func-tions (by fainting), by aimless muscular (vocal) and vegetative acts of dis-charge, and by delayed attempts at mastery; [13] but it is not so easy to say whether in this case we should speak of "external" or "internal" sources of excitation. How is it in the case of the instincts? According to Freud,[14] excitations flow into the organism from two sources: from outside through the sensations and from inside through the instincts. In the first place it must be remarked that this distinction still has a meaning even if Landmark [15] is right in warning us to be cautious in our formulation and to bear in mind that the biological modi-fication that we call instinctual tension is not an internal sensation in contra-distinction to external sensation, but only a sensitization (not perceptible as such) which determines whether succeeding sensations (either internal or ex-ternal) shall be experienced as having a quality of "incitement" or not. For the excitation, even though it always proceeds from sensations, may sometimes be determined by the nature of the object perceived but sometimes by what the object perceived stimulates us to do or to desire.

At first sight the possibility of an excitation having a quantitatively traumatic effect seems less in the case of an instinctual excitation than in that of a sensory excitation. For instinctual excitations are as a rule processes which increase by degrees, and which lead in a biological rhythm to the act of satisfaction, after which the instinctual tension disappears, to arise again gradually only after an interval of quiescence. Instinctual tension, so long as hope is present of an even-tual relaxation of tension, so long as the unpleasure of tension is in imagina-tion confronted by this hope, is in itself pleasurable and has the character of fore-pleasure. At all events this is true of the sexual instincts, and it may well be that in their case we are merely able to see more clearly what is in fact also present in the other instincts. Only under two conditions, so it seems, can in-

---

[12] M. N. Searl, "The Psychology of Screaming," *Int. J. Psa.*, Vol. 14, 1933.

[13] It is also possible, precisely on the analogy of anxiety, to speak of the pain being "harnessed" by the ego and of a "pain signal" designed to initiate measures of defense.

[14] S. Freud, "Instincts and Their Vicissitudes," *Coll. Pap.*, Vol. IV, London, Hogarth, 1948.

[15] J. Landmark, "Der Freud'sche Triebbegriff und die erogenen Zonen," *Imago*, Vol. 21, 1935.

stinctual tension lead to traumatic states and true "instinctual danger" emerge (in the sense of "danger" that I have defined above):

(1) If the external world threatens to intervene in an unpleasurable way in the process of the instinctual action. In that case the instinctual demand is not in itself a danger but is only a danger because it involves an external danger.

(2) If there is a chronic or acute inadequacy in the apparatus for producing instinctual satisfaction (whether the inadequacy is of somatic or of psychic origin), so that satisfaction is unattainable and consequently hope of satisfaction has already vanished during the excitation itself. And this is the case that deserves special study.

Human beings are born in a far more helpless condition than other mammals. Neither their perceptual apparatus nor their motor apparatus is fully formed. At the time of their birth they still possess no ego; they are not only exposed to the effects of the external world but are not even in a position to satisfy their emerging needs. Since that part of the external world which replaces their ego in the task of taking care of them cannot be always automatically at their service, traumatic situations are biologically unavoidable. It is undoubtedly these traumatic situations which make *possible* the view, which is so essential in the subsequent formation of neuroses and character, that instincts are dangers. For the judgment "danger" is always the recollection of a traumatic state that has once been experienced.

Melanie Klein [16] and other English authors were the first to attribute to this fact the essential etiological factor of the neuroses. The social factor in their etiology was thus underestimated and the neuroses were "biologized." On this view the ego, recollecting instinctual tensions in which the assistance of the external world was absent (or in which, owing to the unattainability of the instinctual aims, the assistance was bound to be absent), becomes an enemy of its instincts and seeks to repress them in order to avoid a repetition of such situations. Now it is certainly true that later experiences can only lead to neuroses if certain biological peculiarities of the mental apparatus are given. But the later actual warding off of the instincts is not explained by being traced back to the first occasion on which instinctual tensions were felt as disagreeable. The neuroses— and this was precisely the discovery made by psychoanalysis—are consequences of these later experiences. Anna Freud,[17] too, believes that it is necessary to assume the existence of a "fear of quantity of instincts" in general, which might undo the organization of the ego, a "primary hostility of the ego to instincts"; she does not, indeed, regard this as the *sole* motive for the development of a

---

[16] M. Klein, *The Psychoanalysis of Children*, London, Hogarth, 1932.
[17] A. Freud, *The Ego and the Mechanisms of Defence*, New York, Int. Univ. Press, 1946, pp. 63 and 147 ff.

defense against instinct but as one which exists in addition to "realistic anxiety" and to expectations of loss of love and of castration, which are subsequently internalized as moral anxiety. No doubt she also has in mind memory traces of the first traumatic states occurring while the apparatus for satisfaction was inadequate. I shall return to this point, but I will here remark that *after* that apparatus was developed human beings would have no real grounds for such anxiety. It would merely be that, since what is old is always retained alongside what is new in mental development, they would always, when at some later period they developed fear for other reasons, somehow or other at the same time mobilize the ancient memory traces once again.

I shall begin by bringing up still more material to remind us what a number of phenomena even in the ordinary psychoneuroses, particularly in the nature of defensive anxieties, speak in favor of the influence of memories of traumas in the strict sense. From fear of the consequences of sexual activity, the neurotic has warded off portions of his sexuality in an unlucky way, has disconnected them from his ego and has thus retained them in his unconscious in an infantile shape. The cause of this warding off, or rather of the belief in the evil results of instinctual activities which was its motive, was to begin with attributed theoretically to traumatic experiences. Subsequently, and especially in connection with the psychoneuroses, the further factor emerged of the effects of chronic sexual prohibitions on the part of the educational environment. The warding off of instinct was now extended over the whole history of childhood and the few "traumatic" experiences were merely regarded as being more marked episodes in the course of a continuous process.

Accordingly, analysis shows that the evil which it is intended to obviate by the avoidance of sexual actions and by the warding off of instinct is as a rule a threat from without. The putting into operation of instinctual prohibitions can be derived historically from commonsense experiences—a burnt child dreads the fire—but also from the situation of a child which is itself not yet capable of action. Since it stands in need of "ego-assistance" from the external world, its first general notion of a danger threatening from without is the dread of loss of love, the fear of having been or being about to be abandoned, which at this period also implies loss of ego feeling. This first general picture of anxiety is then filled out with *concrete* pictures of what it is that bad objects in the external world can do to it. The "animistic misunderstanding of the world" is of decisive importance in the formation of these fears of physical injury, which subsequently develop into the fear of castration.

To these "danger situations of the immature ego," [18] loss of love and physical injury, which threaten from without, there is then added a closely related threat

[18] M. N. Searl, "Danger Situations of the Immature Ego," *Int. J. Psa.*, Vol. 10, 1929.

from within. The ego's dread that a traumatic state which it has once experienced may return is the true content of every anxiety. An experience of the dreaded vegetative sensations can therefore lead at a very early age to a general fear of excitations in the child's own inside. So that sexual sensations, for instance, and aggressive ones as well, can only be experienced as pleasurable up to a certain degree of excitation: beyond that they become charged with anxiety. The bridge that connects fear of the external world as it is misunderstood during the child's pregenital period with fear of excitation in the inside of its own body is the mechanism of introjection, by means of which the child living in its pregenital world of thought seeks to escape from the dangers which threaten it in the external world. The experience of the dreaded sensations is then unconsciously attributed to the activity of an "introjected bad object."

I will now consider some examples of this anxiety and then examine its relation to trauma.

We know that the anxiety hysteric who avoids certain situations in a phobic manner uses that means for keeping out of the way of temptation and especially for avoiding sexual (and aggressive) excitation. But we also know from analysis that what he is afraid of are the dangers which threaten him from the external world or from his superego in the event of his performing an instinctual action. And if some anxiety hysterics flirt with their anxiety situations and even seek them out in mild degrees, and in short exhibit an ambivalent attitude to them, that may either represent an attempt at cure on the overcompensating pattern of Demosthenes or may simply show that the aggressively felt sexual situation, which is unconsciously meant by the anxiety situation, is desired by the id though at the same time repudiated by the ego from fear of punishment. So that here there is as yet no proof that instinctual excitation is feared as such, though that might be the case. There are, however, other phenomena which show it more clearly.

I will quote a case in which a pathological incapacity to experience sexual excitation beyond a certain degree without its changing round into traumatic anxiety was exhibited not in a region of the ego which had an unconscious sexual meaning but in the region of sexuality itself. I have described the case elsewhere [19] in these words: "He suffered from an acute libidinal disturbance. If he copulated with a woman, he began the copulation in a normal manner and felt normal enjoyment until the excitation reached a certain degree. Then, often before but sometimes after insertion of the penis, a sudden reversal would occur. He no longer felt pleasure but intense unpleasure of a general kind, did not know what to do, and was 'angry' with the woman because he thought she ought

---

[19] O. Fenichel, "On the Psychology of Boredom," No. 26, First Series.

instantly to take some action which would get him out of his disagreeable situation." He then further transformed the general unpleasure into a masochistic, motor restlessness or into tormenting boredom, which was found to be a tonic binding of this motor restlessness. The unpleasure had the significance of an "anxiety signal": if he were to allow the sexual excitation to proceed further, then, evidently in connection with its aggressive tinge, a "traumatic state" would emerge. By means of his restlessness and by means of his appeal for help to the object (a point to which I shall return later), he avoided this emergence. But the true content of his (ostensibly well founded) fear was not castration or loss of love but this: he could tolerate sexual excitation only up to a certain degree of intensity; from that point onward it was no longer increasing enjoyment concentrated more and more upon his genitals but a vegetative attack accompanied by anxiety and unpleasure.

In another paper [20] I have described the remarkable behavior of a frigid woman: "The patient was not entirely without excitation, but the excitation disappeared when it had reached a certain height. It was not hard to show that the patient was afraid of the increase in her own excitation. She had had a bad habit when she was a child in her gymnastics class. When she was swinging with her hands holding the rings, she used as a regular thing to let go suddenly and fall to the ground. Kindly remonstrances and punishments from the mistress were equally without effect. Now the patient was peculiarly susceptible (in other circumstances as well as in this one) to equilibrium erotism. There can thus be no doubt that while she was swinging she had particularly strong erotic sensations and corresponding fantasies. Her sudden letting-go was thus a precursor of her frigidity. When the excitation had reached a certain height, she was *obliged* to let go, however much she might want to hold on, because an increase in the sexual excitation would have involved something happening that was too bad." For our present purposes it is of less interest to learn that this something was bedwetting, or rather a fear of being punished for bedwetting. This seems, indeed, to be the typical meaning in such cases; and the fear of a person's own excitation, represented as fear of an explosion, of bursting, of falling down, etc. (especially in subjects of the female sex), seems always to be linked to the idea of losing urine or feces. (I may remark in parenthesis that in the event of excessive excitation *all* the apparatuses of discharge are set in motion, including, regressively, the anal-urethral ones. To lose control over one's ego means losing control over the sphincters as well. The fear of this is justified in so far as the "expectation of trauma" is justified: even adults wet and dirty themselves in states of anxiety and fright, or at least have an urge to do so.)

[20] O. Fenichel, "Further Light upon the Pre-oedipal Phase in Girls," No. 24, *First Series.*

For our present purposes it is more important to notice that the anxiety was experienced not as fear of punishment but as fear of excitation, as an incapacity to allow the excitation to proceed further.

These two examples show nothing out of the ordinary: this form of sexual disturbance is of course of everyday occurrence among neurotics. I therefore proceed.

Another woman patient had an obsessional impulse to pull open the doors on the subway and jump out. This again is not an uncommon symptom. It signifies in a typical fashion the avoidance and the carrying through in spite of everything of dreaded sado-masochistic fantasies.[21] And this was also so in the present case, where the unconscious sexual aim was to be beaten. (The aggressive component in the sexuality of such patients is always striking.) A more exhaustive analysis, however, showed the *form* in which the avoidance and the irruption in spite of everything were bound in the symptom; and this was exactly as with the swinging in the last case. The rapid movement on the subway train, with its vibration, produced sexual excitation in the patient, to which, to begin with, she blissfully surrendered (with unconscious fantasies). But this was so only up to a certain height of excitation. Then came the command: "Now you must get out at any price"—get out of the subway train which was causing the excitation, that is, get out of the excitation itself. If it went any further, a traumatic state would develop. (If one gets out of a moving subway train, one *falls*. The vegetative sensations of the traumatic state are sensations of the sense of equilibrium and of space. The neurotic dread of falling is a fear of the same thing. If a person jumps out or jumps down anywhere from fear of excitation, what he is warding off returns to him in the very process of warding off.)

At this point perhaps I may be allowed a brief excursion on something that is closely allied to the fear of falling, namely claustrophobia. Not long ago an extraordinarily good clinical study by Lewin [22] demonstrated the unconscious sexual wishes which are warded off by the typical content of this strange neurosis. They are sexual fantasies, which are based upon the patient's unconscious identification of himself with an embryo in the womb, and which receive their particular form as a result of infantile sexual wishes in regard to the womb and of the child's fantasies of intrauterine existence. In a review of this paper [23] I pointed out that the path that leads from the warding off of fantasies of this kind to the clinical picture of claustrophobia is especially facilitated by two physiological circumstances. In the first place, being shut up is experienced by

---

[21] S. Freud, *The Problem of Anxiety*, p. 116 footnote.
[22] B. D. Lewin, "Claustrophobia," *Psa. Quart.*, Vol. 4, 1935.
[23] O. Fenichel, Review of B. D. Lewin, "Claustrophobia," *Int. Z. Psa.*, Vol. 21, 1935.

the patient above all as an interference with movement. Such an interference, however, seems in itself and quite generally to favor the development of anxiety states, in that the external interference with movements of discharge increases the damming up of instinct; so the *idea* of an interference with movement naturally operates in the same way as an *actual* interference. Secondly, the feeling of anxiety goes along physiologically with the sensation of being "hemmed in." So that, in a reverse way, an external constriction (or the idea of one) can facilitate the reproduction of the whole syndrome of anxiety. I should now like to add to these a third factor. Being shut in is *not* felt so oppressively if the subject feels that he is able to break out. But the anxiety becomes intensified to the highest degree if the situation arises of having suddenly to leave the place and not being able to. Those who suffer from anxiety in trains, ships, or airplanes declare that the worst of it lies in the impossibility of getting out if they want to, and they get around it, for instance, on a train journey by traveling from station to station. These anxieties are constructed on the same model as the subway anxiety which I have been describing. The excitatory process is projected on to the vehicle in which the subject is traveling; and the need to escape suddenly from a place in which he is enclosed is a need to escape from his own excitation if it has reached a certain height. In this connection it may further be remarked that people with increased or repressed equilibrium erotism are particularly liable to anxieties and sensations of this kind. Owing, moreover, to the connection between these vegetative excitations, determined as they are by sensations of equilibrium, and anxiety, various forms of seasickness of organic origin are closely related to these same anxieties—whether because people with such anxieties are more inclined to seasickness or, conversely, because the experience of seasickness stirs up the memory of the anxieties and operates like a trauma that recalls primal scenes.

It is easy to demonstrate that what is feared in an excessive excitation is some kind of "collapse of the ego." One of my patients used to produce motorcar anxiety only when someone other than himself was acting as driver. "Why should I be afraid," he said, "when I can put on the brakes and stop at any moment?" Thus it is loss of voluntary control over the subject's own ego which is dreaded in vehicles that proceed independently of the passenger's wishes, in places that cannot be left at will and in sexual processes that rise to an involuntary orgasm. And there seems no difficulty now in assigning the point at which the sexual process ceases to be enjoyable for these patients and becomes unpleasurable. Reich [24] has shown in his analysis of the normal and pathological course of sexual excitation that a phase of voluntary movements is succeeded by a phase of involuntary spasms of the pelvic muscles and of concentration

[24] W. Reich, *Die Funktion des Orgasmus*, Vienna, Int. Psa. Verlag, 1927.

of the sexual process in the genitals. This latter phase, in which the sexual process can no longer be voluntarily interrupted without serious unpleasure, is the *sine qua non* of an economically satisfactory discharge in the orgasm. This "loss of the ego" at the climax of sexual excitation is normally also the climax of pleasure. Some egos—those, according to Reich, which are "orgastically impotent"—do not experience this pleasure; in their case it changes over into fear of loss of control over the ego [25] and into anxiety.

Before considering the reasons for this change-over, I should like to point out that beginnings of this fear of the subject's own excitation can be seen in many other forms of neurotic anxiety, irrespective of the fact that in their content they are also at the same time fears of castration or of loss of love. The obsessional neurotic, for instance, makes a specially great expenditure of anti-cathexis upon "isolation," is careful that ideas and the sum of emotion belonging to them shall be kept apart, and lays the emphasis of his personality (from fear of his instincts) upon the world of words and concepts which lies remote from instincts—a world into which, incidentally, the instincts that he has warded off follow him, turning an instinctual conflict, perhaps, into an obsessive doubt. In all this he is showing his fear of loss of self-control, a fear which among other things makes free association so hard for him. The endeavor to fit the whole universe into systems and to carry out everyday actions in accordance with a prescribed and formulated program always has as its aim the avoidance of what is sudden and unexpected, the prevention of any loss of control by the ego. In the case of these obsessional neurotic characters, too, the ego's dread of instinct seems to be unspecific, to radiate out from sexual prohibitions of a particular kind over sexuality in general—as is to be seen with children at the age of puberty who incline to asceticism.[26] Again, a patient of a more hysterical type filled her whole existence with restless energy which drove her into perpetual activity, into constantly starting up some new undertaking and into asking ceaselessly what she was to do now. Analysis revealed that the cause of this mania for activity on the part of her ego was a general dread of spontaneous processes overpowering her ego. Another patient, an intellectual, had to a great extent built up his life upon reaction formations against an early dread of stupidity, by seeking to prove himself a clever teacher. He displayed the reactive quality both of his success in life and of his sexual experiences by small phobic manifestations, such as a fear of swimming in deep water, a fear of passing beyond the forest belt on high mountains, and a fear of certain forms of sport, all of which had in common a fear of plunging into something greater than himself, which might wash his ego away like a flood or blow it away like a wind. It

[25] In anal erotics loss of control over the ego is equated with loss of control over the sphincters.
[26] Cf. A. Freud, *op. cit.*, p. 167.

was no accident that this patient's earliest anxiety in childhood, which came to light during analysis, was a fear of death. The phenomenon of neurotic fear of death is in itself highly complex and may be of various types; and it is easy to convince oneself, too, that Freud [27] is right in asserting that it has something to do with the relation of the ego to its superego, with the dread of losing the protection of the superego. Nevertheless, besides this it seems to have a simpler sense. Death seems to be thought of as something that is powerful and unescapable, something that overwhelms the poor little ego and makes it its plaything. The neurotic fear of death is fear of excitation washing away the control of the ego.[28] Here too belong (what are also insisted upon by Reich) the frequent anxiety pictures of bursting, of being washed away, and particularly of falling down, as well as of other physical sensations. In one case, a fear of going mad, accompanied by a fear of pains and physical sensations, also turned out to be a fear of the patient's own excitation, intensified by his mistaken belief that he was the only person who had sexual sensations. (For just as adults try to cling to the illusion that children have no sexual sensations, so many children think that such "bad" things as sexual sensations occur only in children and not in adults.) As regards hypochondria, which is related to the point we are now discussing—fear of processes occurring inside the body—I will recall what I have already said, to the effect that the experience of these dreaded sensations is often attributed unconsciously to the activity of an introjected object.

Are these phenomena, then, evidence that *before* the fear of castration and loss of love, *before* the recognition of dangers in the external world, there was present already another fear which has left these traces behind—a fear by the ego of the *quantity* of its instincts in general, a primary hostility to instinct on the part of the ego? In my opinion such a notion needs a thorough discussion, which will take us back to our problem as to the nature of trauma.

The involuntary phase of sexual excitation and the "traumatic state," however greatly they may differ—the latter being the climax of unpleasure and the former the climax of pleasure in human life—have nevertheless one thing in common, namely the fact that in both of them the ego is swept along and overwhelmed by a biological process which occurs without its having any say in the matter. If, then, we were to assume the existence of this primitive hostility to instinct on the part of the ego, the following question would suggest itself: on what does it depend whether or not the dread felt by every ego of the full quantity of its instincts is overcome sufficiently to make it possible to enjoy an orgasm? It seems more profitable to begin, rather, by doubting the primitive character of such a fear, to assume that the capacity for enjoying the loss of the

[27] S. Freud, *The Ego and the Id*, London, Hogarth, 1947.
[28] W. Reich, *op. cit.*

ego in an orgasm is normal and to investigate the findings of analysis in the case of people who suffer from a disturbance of that capacity.

One can think of two kinds of events which might be responsible for such disturbances, and which shade off into one another.

(1) They might be due to real instinctual prohibitions, or to imaginary ones arising from a projective and magical misunderstanding of the world. For the idea of danger threatening from without in the event of an instinctual activity will not merely induce the ego to take defensive measures against the instinct; these defensive measures will also result in the ego blocking the excitation's normal path of discharge. The excitation will consequently be forced physiologically along the vegetative paths, and thus the ground will be prepared for the experience of anxiety and traumatic unpleasure; and this in turn will be interpreted by the ego as the realization of the dreaded annihilation of the ego by the external world. It may be that this interpretation is the clinical basis of what Jones [29] has called "aphanisis." When once someone is in the condition of expecting castration, he interprets every experience of the powerlessness of his ego as the annihilation of his ego which he dreads; and he can no longer enjoy a pleasure in which the ego loses itself, because every time the ego begins to lose itself the situation is felt as equivalent to completed castration.

(2) They might be due to the experience of traumas in the restricted sense, which at a given moment bring about higher quantities of excitation than the endogenous instinct could have produced spontaneously: such, above all, are seductions and primal scenes. They are a continuation of the inevitable traumas of the period of suckling which have already been described and which prepared the ground for the view that "instincts are dangers." We shall return again to the possibility of "sexually traumatic neuroses" in the narrower sense; but at this point I will only remark that such experiences of primal scenes evidently increase the effect (which, as we have seen, is analogous to a trauma) of subsequent sexual prohibitions, while, vice versa, earlier sexual prohibitions are apt to lend a peculiarly traumatic character to subsequent primal scenes. The content of the sexual components involved seems not to be specific. I have already pointed out the importance of anal and equilibrium erotism, and I will only add that in men the fear of the ego being overwhelmed is certainly greater if sexual wishes of a passive-feminine kind are prominent in their unconscious, and also that in both sexes sadistic sexual components operate in the same sense.

At this point we ought to raise the question of the behavior of the "dread of instinctual quantity" in the case of the destructive instincts. May it not perhaps be that, while what has just been said holds good of sexuality, the ego's fear of its

[29] E. Jones, "The Early Development of Female Sexuality," *Papers on Psycho-Analysis*, 5th ed., Baltimore, Williams and Wilkins, 1948.

own aggressive impulses is primary? This seems improbable. In the instances in question sexual and aggressive excitation are always found to be inextricably intertwined; those concerned are always people with a pregenital orientation and an impaired genitality. Theoretically, too, what is true of sexuality must apply to aggressivity: in the case of aggressiveness, too, if it is satisfied it will not be dammed up as it is when unsatisfied; a fit of rage exhausts its fury and subsides.

We thus come back to our starting point. If the apparatus of discharge is inadequate, whether owing to the influx of excitation being too great (a trauma proper) or owing to the discharge of excitation being too small (sexual prohibitions), the result is the automatic development of severe anxiety, which may subsequently become modified into "anxiety signals" or into neurotic symptoms that are free from anxiety. The experience of traumatic states lies at the back of all judgments of danger, that is, of all realistic anxiety; traumatic major anxiety, realistic anxiety, and moral anxiety constitute genetically a developmental series.

If, however, the apparatus of discharge is adequate, and if the ego has no grounds (owing to recollections of traumas and sexual prohibitions) for actively bringing an inadequacy about by means of defensive processes, then, as it seems to me, the ego which is primarily enticed by an especially intense pleasure into allowing its organization to be temporarily overwhelmed in an orgasm, has no more reason for dreading the quantity of instinct as such than it has for dreading sleep, for instance, in which its organization is also dissolved.[30] (Fear of sleep is fear of death and, like it, goes back to fear, produced by traumas or instinctual prohibitions, of loss of the ego.)

For the sexual instincts are *periodic* processes. It is not true that the ego would be flooded by every instinct if it did not keep permanent defenses against instinct in operation. It would in fact merely be driven into a *satisfying* instinctual action. After satisfaction the demand of the instinct would vanish, and would only reappear by degrees after some lapse of time. It is only the damming up due to incapacity to carry out the satisfying action that gives to sexuality the attribute of insatiability which is so much dreaded by the educator. We can find no grounds for thinking that things are otherwise in the case of the aggressive instincts.

Anna Freud [31] has described how in puberty there is a general inclination to ward off all instincts, irrespective of their quality, and her findings can certainly not be questioned. But a thorough study of puberal life in other forms of

[30] It is only in so far as anxiety in general is a result of the traumatic situations experienced by everyone during their period of suckling, that a trace of this dread of being overwhelmed by one's own instincts survives in everyone, as a memory trace of the period in which the apparatus of discharge was inadequate.

[31] A. Freud, *op. cit.,* p. 167.

society would be essential before we could be certain that the ego would necessarily feel such a degree of dread of its instincts, would necessarily have a
primary hostility to them, if sexual education in childhood were different and
the *possibilities* of satisfaction were less severely restricted. And it seems unlikely that this would be so, in view of the fact that it is precisely surrender to
these instincts that brings the most intense pleasure to the ego in search of
pleasure. Is it the *quantity* of the instincts that the ego is afraid of? Quantity,
however, is better diminished by satisfaction than by defense. It is only owing to
a pre-existing dread of experiencing this satisfaction that the different possibilities
of a dissolution of the ego in adult life—on the one hand the *pleasurable* possibility of sexual satisfaction and of extreme fits of rage and on the other hand the
unpleasurable possibility of the traumatic anxiety attack—come to be amal-
gamated into a single possibility and that the unpleasurable one.

The intimate connection between traumatic experiences of anxiety and intense
sexual excitation is also shown by a closer consideration of the safety measures
adopted by sufferers from these disorders.

What governs self-assurance in the first instance is, as we know, the factor of
being loved. A baby feels its self-assurance diminished if it suffers loss of love.
At this level narcissistic and erotic needs still coincide completely. (Both go
back, as it were, to a primary prototype in the shape of a desire for satiation.)
Babies and people who are orally fixated have only one way of escape from all
forms of mortification or loss of strength of their ego, namely clinging to someone
bigger than themselves. A child suffering from traumatic anxiety asks to be taken
into its mother's bed, and the frightful thing about the primal scene is that its
mother does not do so but leaves the child alone with its unmasterable excitation.
Paradoxically, then, the best protection against the feeling of losing one's ego in
an unpleasurable way and of being swept away by something bigger than oneself is the feeling of being able to hide one's ego in a pleasurable way in something bigger than oneself. The question is, What determines whether this bigger
thing shall be felt as hostile or protective? My patient who suffered from boredom sought protection from his fear of sexual excitation in oral-sexual actions
by his sexual partner, whom he expected to take over his activity; if she failed to
do so he got angry and by warding off this aggressive impulse intensified his
feeling of being destroyed internally. There is thus a remarkable identity of
opposites: the sexual experience which is feared and the sexual experience which
is to serve as a protection. The fear of the act of surrender to the experience can
be overcome by a fantasy of the surrender already completed. We know this from
patients who are haunted by oral-sadistic conflicts. A fear of being devoured is
warded off by a fantasy of having been devoured (a longing to be in the womb);
a fear of devouring is warded off by a fantasy of having devoured (e.g., in

women the fear of orally robbing a penis is warded off by the fantasy of a girl being a phallus). A patient after an acute anxiety attack felt as his first phobic requirement the unfulfillable claustrophobic demand: "You must never again go indoors, you must always stay in the open air." But he described the blissful pleasure he felt when, after overcoming the anxiety, he went into a room and lay down in bed and so was able to feel at rest at last in the room and the bed—inside his mother and protected by her. It is patients suffering from fear of death who in different quantitative circumstances are capable of blissful pleasure in giving way to fatigue and in gradually losing consciousness in sleep.

If, then, we find patients who suffer from sexual disturbances of this kind constantly seeking out the conditions which cause their anxiety, namely direct or symbolic sexual excitation, we shall feel no more puzzled than when we find phobic patients flirting with their anxiety determinants. Their id drives them on, their ego drives them back. Their "repetition" is not "beyond the pleasure principle," but the consequence of the fresh somatic production of sexual desire. They are constantly *striving* toward pleasure; but their ego, under the influence of the external world (that is, of recollections of traumas and sexual prohibitions), invariably puts the same obstacle in the way, which in turn, for physiological reasons, always occasions the same unpleasurable result. Moreover, the repetition in the transference of the unpleasurable passing of the oedipus complex [32] seems to be of the same kind. The demand for repetition is not necessarily beyond the pleasure principle, but arises from the oedipus wish which has not yet been disposed of and is still striving toward pleasure. The fact that the *failure* is also repeated corresponds to an intervention on the part of the ego (attached as it is to the external world) in the nature of an anxiety signal: "Remember what happened to you the other time!" The constant pressure of sexual desire results in the endeavor to avoid a repetition, producing—a repetition.

But, it will be asked, cannot the repetition of the anxiety situation be explained also in another way, namely (on the analogy of the repetition symptoms in traumatic neuroses and in children's play) as an endeavor to gain subsequent control over excitation which had been unmasterable in the first instance, by means of a later, active repetition set in motion by the ego? Certainly. These two explanations are not in the least contradictory: they are complementary. A repetition which has as its purpose a subsequent discharge and binding must also in the last resort have as its aim the avoidance of unpleasure, and this is in fact ultimately achieved. It must be that the re-experiencing of the unpleasure of the traumatic experience is an unpleasure relatively less than the toleration of the continuously "tonic" disturbance of unmastered quantities of excitation.

A number of patients who in this fashion constantly seek out sexual excita-

[32] S. Freud, *Beyond the Pleasure Principle*, p. 18.

tions that lead to anxiety nevertheless succeed, as I have said, owing to certain quantitative relations, in attaining a relative release of tension after their great anxiety. We have here, presumably, an economic determinant for the occurrence of the paradoxical pleasure in anxiety. It is a familiar fact that in the normal sexual process the excited tension which precedes the release of tension is itself pleasurable, probably in connection with an anticipation in fantasy of the subsequent end-pleasure. If someone in whom sexual excitation always turns into anxiety nevertheless arrives eventually at a relative release of tension and if this experience impresses itself on him, he may well come at last to feel the anxiety itself as a fore-pleasure and to approve of it as the only door open to him that leads to a relative end-pleasure. This, incidentally, is by no means the only or the most frequently chosen method by which the ego can attempt a secondary warding off of this anxiety. There are numbers of individual variations in the conditions intended to exclude or reduce anxiety (e.g., perverse ones), which, so long as they are fulfilled, make it possible in spite of everything to obtain relative, though never economically sufficient, satisfaction.

I shall now return once again to the distinction between traumatic neuroses and psychoneuroses from which we started, in order to show its relative nature.

Though it may be true that in the case of the former category the influx of excitation is too great and in that of the latter category the discharge of excitation is too small, yet the fact cannot be overlooked that in practice neuroses represent combinations of both possibilities. The so-called traumatic neuroses "proper," comprising losses of ego function, anxiety, and other vegetative states, as well as epileptic reactions and acts and sensations in the nature of subsequent repetitions (which have unfortunately been little studied hitherto), are certainly never completely uninfluenced by the subject's instinctual conflicts. The discussion in *Psycho-Analysis and the War Neuroses* [33] gave examples enough of the way in which a trauma causes old infantile sexual conflicts to flare up again, whether because the trauma is unconsciously regarded as castration and consequently upsets the balance between the repressed instincts and the defensive forces, or because it operates as a temptation for unconscious sadistic instincts. On the other hand, it is possible to regard the psychoneuroses quite generally as a species of traumatic neuroses, in so far as the motive for the warding off of instinct which leads to its damming up is always in the last resort anxiety and in so far as anxiety (that is, the judgment that there is a danger) is a kind of recollection of a traumatic state that has once been experienced. But among the psychoneuroses a number of cases stand out (with symptomatologies covering every form of neurosis), which display in a peculiar sense a combination with the traumatic neuroses. There are cases in which the operative sexual de-

[33] S. Ferenczi, et al., *Psycho-Analysis and the War Neuroses*, London, Int. Psa. Press, 1921.

fenses have attained their effectiveness owing to particular infantile sexual traumas (real seductions or primal scenes). In their symptoms are to be found not only a condensation, of the sort I have described, of ideas of castration or loss of love with self-perceptions of the subject's own dreaded states of excitation, but also a competition between irruptions in spite of everything of repressed instincts and repetitions of the traumas, to which repetitions (as in the case of traumatic neuroses proper) the function must be ascribed of bringing about a gradual subsequent diminution of the excitation.

Those who suffer from neuroses of this kind, which can be described as combinations of psychoneuroses and traumatic neuroses, are worse off than traumatic neurotics proper on account of the physiological properties of sexual excitation. A person who has suffered an external trauma, let us say a motor accident, with his instincts relatively little involved, will have dreams about the accident for some time, will be unable to ride in a car, will begin to tremble at the sight of one, and so on, until the discharge of the quantities of excitation that could not be dealt with has been achieved and the dammed-up excitation "abreacted." After a certain time the whole thing passes off. What has become of the "shakers" who filled the streets of the big towns during the first years after the last war? The shaking has ceased. But if the trauma is of such a kind that it has caused the ego to make the judgment "sexual excitation, or rather the loss of ego involved in it, is dangerous," then this judgment will induce the ego to interfere every time with the normal sexual process. That process will then be diverted from the genitals into the vegetative nervous system and so once more confirm the ego's incurable mistake about the danger of sexual excitation. The fact that sexual excitation after it has calmed down is ceaselessly renewed from somatic sources results in a neurosis of this kind *never* coming to rest. It has become caught in a vicious circle. Mastery of the excitation can never be subsequently obtained, because every attempt at mastering it leads to fresh traumatic experiences. It is as though every time the person who had the motor accident makes up his mind at last to get into a car again—he had a fresh motor accident.

There are neuroses which give a stronger impression of a vain, lifelong struggle for a subsequent mastery of excitations arising from the primal scene than of a revolt against the defensive forces on the part of instincts that have been warded off out of fear of castration. In place of a case history I should like to bring forward an instance from literature.

I have in mind Céline's *Voyage au bout de la nuit,* a remarkable work and one, as it seems to me, of high artistic merit. The critics gave the most varied judgments upon this strange novel. Most frequently it was described as a piece of social criticism. It gives a moving picture of the hopelessness of the individual in the chaos of the contemporary social order and of the desperate position in which mankind find themselves in the conditions—such as war and colonial exploitation—which they themselves set in motion but which continue to operate like forces of nature. But a reader who is well informed psychologically soon gets an impression that such a view of the work only touches its surface. It cannot account even superficially for the circumstance that Nature itself is portrayed in such a fearful light nor can it explain the romantic and fantastic elements, such as the author's uncanny doubles. One has a feeling that in these pages deep unconscious impulses are struggling for expression. The strange effect of the book resembles that produced by the works of Kafka and suggests that a similar interpretation may be possible. In Kafka's case no doubt we are faced with a moving portrayal, drawn from internal sources, of schizophrenic experiences. On the same analogy, may it not be that what is revealed to us by Céline is a great depression at work and the ego lying helplessly at its mercy? But this cannot be so. It is true that the manner in which the world and our existence in it are experienced in the book shows many of the traits of a typical depression. Such, for instance, are the axiomatic manner in which only the gloomy aspects of reality are presented and the unceasing but vain attempts at becoming master of these horrors by means of self-sacrificing object relationships which perpetually fail. There are other traits, too, of what is described as "melancholia agitata," namely the restlessness which drives the hero round the world and the anxiety which intensifies a cruel reality into still more cruel delusions. But there is a complete absence of all self-reproaches, of any split between ego and superego. It was right to suppose that what is here depicted is a world of experience that approaches the psychotic; but the diagnosis of depression or melancholia was wrong. Here are the essentials. A perpetual unrest and anxiety, which allow the hero not a moment's respite, drive him on in flight from something unspeakably terrible. But he cannot escape it, since existence itself has assumed that character for him. His self is threatened with actual annihilation in the war and in the colonies; but elsewhere, too, he is in ceaseless dread of this annihilation. It seems indeed as though he only went in search of war and the tropics in order to rationalize his expectation, just as the man who is a criminal owing to his sense of guilt commits his crime out of remorse.[34] For him existence in the world has the quality of a constant threat of annihilation; and this annihilation always exhibits pregenital and sadistic (cannibalistic) attributes. Against this eternal terror there is only one protection, which he always seeks but can never attain: rest in the arms of a motherly woman who will give him "the love which is strong enough to overcome death." There are enough passages to bear out the correctness of the interpretation: a primal scene, sadistically per-

[34] S. Freud, "Character Types in Psycho-Analytic Work,' III, Coll. Pap., Vol. IV.

ceived, has changed the character of the world for the hero, so that he sways to and fro between an expectation of a repetition of the trauma and an actual repetition of it which aims at finally mastering the old excitation but is never able to master it.

It is evident that mixed neuroses of this kind must, from the standpoint of therapy, be counted among the psychoneuroses and not among the traumatic neuroses. If we contented ourselves, as in the case of the latter, with waiting for a spontaneous recovery, we should wait in vain. The responsibility for the fact that the subsequent mastery never succeeds lies with the interference of the ego, which, allowing itself to be led by an unconscious expectation of evil, sets itself to ward off the instincts. It may be possible (as in the case of the psychoneuroses) to remove the defenses by psychoanalysis, to bring about a junction of the excluded sexual portions of the ego organization with the rest of the ego and thus to change the infantile sexuality into adult, genital sexuality, capable of orgasm. If so, the experience in sexual satisfaction that it is possible for an involuntary process to be *pleasurable* will be the best guarantee of the possibility of also overcoming the quantities of excitation, unmastered since infancy, arising from an involuntary process which at that time was *unpleasurable*. Thus the removal of the pathogenic defenses, which can only be achieved by psychoanalysis, operates just as in the psychoneuroses proper. Indeed, as I have said, these do not differ in principle from the mixed conditions which I have been describing. For all defense against instinct arises from anxiety, and all (secondary) anxiety is an effort on the part of the ego to avoid traumatic experiences.

FIVE

Ego Strength and Ego Weakness*

FOLLOWING Freud, we consider the ego as an organ that gradually differentiates itself under the influence of the outside world and, forming an external layer around the core of the unconscious instinctual reservoir of the id, serves in the interchange between the organism and the outer world. On the one hand, it takes over the function of receiving stimuli (perception); on the other hand, it directs the discharge of excitations (control of motility). In the reception of perceptions as well as in the admission of impulses to motility, it works electively, and acts as an inhibiting apparatus which administers its inhibiting function with regard to the position of the organism in the outer world. To accomplish this, the ego also develops certain capacities such as the function of judgment and intelligence. It furthermore develops methods of inhibiting a direct operation of rejected impulses. This is done by means of quantities of energy held ready for this purpose —by "binding" the "primary process," which is solely guided by the striving for discharge, so that it turns into the "secondary process." All this happens through the formation of a particular organization which is governed by the tendency to fulfill its different tasks with a minimum of effort. (Principle of multiple function.)

When is an ego strong? When it fulfills these functions well and exactly. The conception of "strength of the ego" is not clear, because there can be an ego that at the same time fulfills one function very reliably and well, and another badly. An ego is strong if it can carry out its intentions even in the face of external obstacles. But an ego is also strong if it can successfully inhibit impulses that are disagreeable to it or can change their aim. Now it is possible that an ego

---

* This paper was first presented at Prague in January, 1938. Dr. Fenichel's manuscript has been translated into English, in conformity with the other papers, but no attempt has been made to give it the final form Dr. Fenichel might have given it if he had prepared it for publication.

can do this very well just *because* it is weak in the first respect; for it may very well permanently repress instinctual drives (i.e., be strong in relation to the id) because, say, it has exaggerated anxiety (i.e., is weak in relation to the outer world).

If one remembers the fact that the excitations within the organism are to begin with only striving for as prompt a discharge as possible, and that then with the formation of the ego the capacity is acquired to defer such a discharge until it seems to be expedient in relation to reality (so that in the end the most pleasure possible is after all achieved, in a roundabout way), then it is reasonable to assume that the first criterion of the strength of the ego is its ability to tolerate tension. The ego would be strong in proportion as it was able to renounce immediate satisfactions in favor of future ones and to tolerate excitations, whether arising from shattering experiences or from a damming up of the instincts— and in proportion as it was able to do this without losing its mastery over the apparatus of discharge. Toleration of tension is a quantity which cannot be measured, but it is doubtless very variable. Some people, in a situation of excitement, very soon become helpless, visibly restless, and "actual"-neurotic, using primitive defense mechanisms, while others do not. Also, the same persons behave differently at different times. Finally it seems that the ability to tolerate tension is a relative thing—as we said before about ego strength in general—since a given person at a given time may be tolerant of some tensions and intolerant of others. Thus, some neurotics who cannot stand a damming up of instinctual drives, deal with real difficulties very well.

In regard to toleration of tension we must assume in the first place a constitutional, or somatic, factor whose nature we do not know. Freud speaks of a possible "toxic impoverishment of ego-libido." But psychoanalytic observation teaches us that the ability to tolerate tension is also dependent on experience, and is greatest in conditions of a certain optimum relation between experienced satisfaction and experienced frustration. A maximum of gratifications as well as a maximum of frustrations in general reduce toleration of tension. It is true that too much gratification does not, as Jeanne Lampl-de Groot once thought, cause toxic and actual neuroses in the way in which too little does, because instinctual excitements are periodic processes which disappear after their gratification, so that too much of it cannot cause a damming up of them. The satisfied person has no instinctual tension at all for a period of time. But too much gratification is injurious through "spoiling." The ego which has not been accustomed by occasional frustrations to hold tensions in suspension later on experiences even slight frustrations which are inevitable as traumatic. Spoiling makes the ego intolerant of subsequent frustrations. But too much frustration makes for intolerance also, because its sets in operation repressions and other defense mechanisms calling for chronic anti-cathexis which cause an impoverishment of ego energy. The more energy is bound in such a defensive struggle, the less freely movable energy is at the disposal of the ego with which to hold in suspension current excitations which arise. Furthermore, the ability to tolerate is something which is only learned under the influence of the external world. It develops gradually, and is therefore less during the early developmental phases of the ego than later. Everything that tends to fixate the ego entirely or partly at early phases of development, or gives it cause to regress from an already attained higher developmental stage to an earlier one, impoverishes its ability to tolerate tension.

In relation to the outer world, that ego may be called strong which is able on the one hand to form valid judgments about reality and, on the other, to carry out its intentions even in the face of obstacles. It needs a high degree of tolerance of tension in order temporarily to put aside its own wishes and fears in judging reality, so that it may later on be able to do justice to them all the better in real life. The "mastering" of its environment is an active, alloplastic activity, which is able to make an appropriate application of past experiences to the new situation. This succeeds the better, the more accurately the ego can understand similarities and differences between past and present situations. Here we can already say what damages this capacity the most. It is all those attempts to solve infantile instinctual conflicts, which cause a single, permanent change in the ego of an anti-cathectic character, thus avoiding many later new defensive measures which would be unpleasurable and would cost a greater expenditure of energy. Wherever such ego changes occur, the subject's attitude will be rigid instead of elastic, and the present will be misunderstood in the sense of the past. No new experiences will be made; external stimuli, instead of being responded to adequately, will call out set patterns of reaction, acquired in childhood.

What are the circumstances, then, which promote a positive ego strength, in the respect mentioned? There are two opposite opinions on this point, and in spite of their contradiction each undoubtedly contains a measure of truth. The one is upheld chiefly by Bally and holds that security of existence and freedom from care during the period of ego development—a generous fostering, as it were—guarantee it, and are the best prerequisites. These prerequisites, thanks to the "biological retardation" of development in the human infant, are present to a higher degree in man than in other animals. The actual helplessness of the human infant necessitates a particularly intensive fostering by its parents, so that for a time all serious worry is kept from the growing child. He does not need to turn his energies to tasks that demand an unconditional and direct solution. Instead of that he can turn his energies to play, to the solution of tensions which he has imposed on himself. The task of tolerating tensions for some time, in order the better to solve them in the end, can be learned gradually and in a measure chosen by him at the time; for he can give himself the tensions in smaller doses than the hostile external world would do. Through this training he can learn to "master" his environment gradually and without experiencing incapacitating anxiety in traumatic situations. The opposite opinion is held by Anna Freud in her remarks about the development of intelligence. She holds that in an environment that satisfies every wish and takes away all cares, in which, therefore, a struggle with tensions caused by reality is not necessary, there is no ground for developing the ability to deal with such tensions. He who need not exert himself in order to master reality will not learn how to master it, and he will remain incapable of doing so in later life.

The truth must lie somewhere in the middle. Certainly all capacity for active alloplastic "mastery" comes from striving to satisfy one's instincts and to deal with the hindrances of the external world. If such hindrances do not occur at all, it is not necessary to develop the capacity to conquer them—a capacity which constitutes the strength of the ego in respect to the outer world; on the other hand, it is certain that too strong hindrances lead to traumatic situations and hence intense anxiety, and thus to changes in the ego which ward off anxiety but which are formed at the cost of the development of the ego. Where the child's every hope that self-exertion will lead to its goal is lost, his ego functions will be suspended and his receptive oral attitude again will come to the fore. This is because there lives on in his mind from suckling days the memory that once upon a time, in periods of need, he had all-powerful helpers.

In this connection, too, it becomes clear that not only does everything that leads to oral and narcissistic mastery of the outer world through fixation or regression weaken the ego, but that *all* the mechanisms of defense which introduce permanently rigid anti-cathectic attitudes diminish the elasticity and hence the strength of the ego and in that way cause a malformation of it. Of all of these malformations of the ego, the masochistic ones are the most fateful. In them, the subject's experience or belief that any attempt on his part to do what he wants is attended by unpleasure imposed on him by his environment, leads him not only to put forward an oral-receptive attitude to the world but also to seek out or bring into effect experiences that are injurious or restrictive to the ego. This he does prophylactically, or as the lesser evil, or at all events as a self-imposed measure, or finally only as an unavoidable prerequisite for being able to achieve his aim afterwards, at least to a certain degree.

We have long been aware that a separation of the attitude of the ego toward the environment from its attitude to the id can only be accomplished in an artificial way. Warded-off instincts which return impair everything, including the ego's strength in relation to the external world. He who suffers from a damming up of instinct does not see the external world as it is but under the influence of the instincts breaking through repression. He can deceive himself as to reality by rationalization. A strong ego must not be influenced by the id when it makes judgments about the outer world. In this respect, incidentally, one can observe during an analysis how the ego becomes stronger—how through progressive overcoming of repression it learns to assess reality more correctly. An ego which, to use Freud's simile, behaves like the clown in the circus who acts as though he were doing everything while he is really only tagging after the rest, or like the novice on horseback who pretends to dominate his steed but is in fact dominated by it—such an ego is a weak ego.

This takes us on to a consideration of ego strength in relation to the id. The ego is not by nature hostile to the instincts. Its organization serves, on the contrary, to heighten the probability of instinctual satisfaction. Only in some situations do conflicts develop between the ego organization, which represents the demands of reality, and the instincts. This is above all the case when certain external situations make an instinctual action dangerous or appear to be dangerous. However, there are also circumstances in which, apart from the external world, the arousal of instinctual excitement itself is felt as dangerous and as far as possible to be avoided. A strong ego in respect to the id would be one which is able to "master" inopportune or unwelcome instinctual impulses—that is, which is able either to postpone their activity (this being a toleration of tensions) or to hold it back altogether, or else to alter instinctual objects in the way it wants.

What are the conditions which favor the development of ego strength of this sort? Freud has repeatedly pointed out that the capacity for instinctual mastery is an economic problem, depending on the relationship between ego strength and instinctual strength. According to this, a first possibility through which ego development could be arrested would be a constitutionally heightened original strength of the instinct. (Though we know nothing about the conditions for and character of such a factor.) But since the ego which wards off the instinct works with the help of instinctual energies which have changed their direction under the influence of the external world, it could also be that ego strength, too, increases with instinctual strength. The relative strength of the instinct, however, is more important than its absolute strength. At times of excitement, instincts are more difficult to master than in the times between. Instincts which are occasionally satisfied can better be mastered than unsatisfied and hence ever-hungry instincts.

It is therefore clear what the condition is in which the ego must be weakest in the respect under consideration. It is the condition of *a damming up of instincts*, in which through a closing of the natural channels of instinctual discharge a constant high level of excitation is maintained, which the ego naturally finds hard to deal with. The greatest of the natural channels for instinctual discharge is certainly genital orgasm. Where this can be obtained at regular intervals so that the internal instinctual tension is released, or even if only the capacity for such a release exists, so that the instinct-repelling ego can be guided by the hope of a later satisfaction, the mastery of instincts is easiest of all.

An objection which could be made to this statement is that it holds good for the sexual drives but that things are different when it comes to the mastery of aggressive instincts. I do not believe that this objection is valid. If one carries pent-up anger within oneself, one breaks into aggressive excitement on a small pretext and cannot control one's self; but if one has discharged one's anger adequately in the right place, one is able to control subsequent small quantities of anger without difficulty.

This can be well demonstrated by a reflection upon emotional attacks in general. An outbreak of emotion is a transitory derangement of the ego's control of motility, during which in place of actions certain archaic discharge syndromes occur. A strong ego has learned to make use even of such syndromes. It keeps all its affects in bounds, as it does its anxiety, and employs them for its own purposes. It allows no attacks of affect during which it is unseated and does not know what it is doing. But an ego that must often experience emotional outbreaks which it cannot master is a weak ego in relation to its id impulses. And who are the persons who easily lose their self-control? They are persons with dammed-up excitations, as can be demonstrated in the simplest attack of anger as well as in a transformation of an intended signal anxiety into a severe attack of anxiety in anxiety hysteria. The ego mastery breaks down very easily when pent-up quantities of excitation are ready to use every least occasion (in the case of anxiety the mere judgment of the ego that "danger is present") to displace their energy onto it, changing the most innocent occasion into a "derivative of the repressed." Hence an inappropriate degree of affect is always the first sign to us that energy from repressed contents is being displaced to the respective occasion. Moreover, it is a question not only of the quantity but of the quality of the affects. The occurrence of obviously qualitatively inappropriate affect is also, in this sense, a symptom of a weak ego. The more excitations there are in the unconscious which we shut off from discharge, the weaker, then, is the ego, not only in the sense that it has less energy to spare for other functions, seeing that it expends its energy in maintaining the suppressive anti-cathexis (weakness toward the external world) but also in the sense that its domination is threatened by the energy of the repressed, which is always on the lookout for a breakthrough (weakness toward the id).

Once more we arrive at the same result. The strongest ego is the ego which has developed the least in the way of defensive measures of the anti-cathectic type and has undergone least alterations leading to its own impoverishment. (A remark in parenthesis: One often hears it said that the knowledge of the injury repression causes has led to psychoanalytic pedagogy setting itself the aim of bringing up children so that they need undertake no repressions. That would be an error because education which avoids renunciation and anxiety only leads to the ego's not being able to deal with hardships. But I believe that the aim of causing a minimum of repression is really correct and does not need to be reconsidered. All that experience shows is only that we took the wrong way to this right end. Spoiling which gives complete security is no protection against repression; on the contrary, it leads by by-paths precisely to repression.)

In reference to its position vis-à-vis the superego, we shall call that ego strong whose sense of guilt does not exceed a certain quantity, but which knows how to use its not too strong feelings of tension toward the superego in such a way in the regulation of its self-regarding feelings that it is largely independent of other objects in respect to its estimation of itself. There should be no open "distance" between, on the one hand, the sense of guilt and the feelings of satisfaction (arrived at through a fulfillment of ideals) which regulate its self-regard, and, on the other hand, its own reasonable judgment. In the periods between in which neither special feelings of guilt nor of self-satisfaction make themselves noticeable, there is no observable difference between the ego and the superego. An ego can deal with the claims of its superego the more satisfactorily the nearer those claims approximate to its own reasonable judgment. The more archaic in nature the superego is and the more automatic its commands and condemnations are, the more clear becomes the fact that the superego dips deeply down into the id. In short, the more the ego experiences the demands of its superego as alien to it and close to the instincts, the more difficulty will it have in dealing with them and the weaker will it be.

On what does it depend whether the superego has or maintains this archaic, ego-opposed nature? The analysis of obsessional neuroses, where the ego is particularly weak in this respect, teaches us that this character of the superego is above all the result of regression to the anal-sadistic level of organization of the libido. After such a regression the sadistic trends which the subject originally directed toward his objects are directed against himself. But even without such regression the "automatic" character of superego sanctions is understandable as a result, once more, of repressions and other defense mechanisms which necessitate a continual expenditure of energy. Just as an ego which is impoverished by anti-cathexis is not in a position to cognize reality in a differentiating manner, but responds to everything which it experiences in a schematic and automatic way, so do the commands and prohibitions and sanctions of the superego, under the same circumstances, become automatic. Here, too, then, ego strength must be inculcated by avoiding these types of defense.

What has already been said in connection with the ego's relation to the external world is especially true here. The worst weakening of the ego is once again its masochistic warping. I refer to so-called "moral masochism." If an ego cannot protect itself against the demands of an archaic sadistic superego in any way except through carrying out the threatening sanction as a prophylactic measure, and if this measure, from being the indispensable condition for pleasure, ends by also being a source of pleasure in itself—then such an ego has surrendered helplessly to its superego.

A strong ego is also strong in its organization; that is, it is an ego which does not tolerate contradictions in its own sphere and knows how to resolve really contradictory tasks in a unifying manner. Obviously what constitutes the important thing about a man's "character" or his "personality" is precisely the manner in which he reconciles with one another the demands which come from the environment, the id, and the superego. Psychoanalytic characterology, which is still in its infancy, has nevertheless already contributed much to the understanding that this factor, too, is not dependent on constitutional elements alone, but on experiential ones as well—upon the way in which the infantile instinctual conflicts were resolved in their day. We know of various pathological vicissitudes which have damaged precisely this capacity of the ego. Into the formation of every ego there have gone many identifications. It can happen that these different identifications will not blend, and as a result cause a disunited personality. This may be because the persons with whom the subject has identified himself were actually highly contradictory types, or because certain circumstances forced him to identify himself with contradictory characteristics of various objects (as, for instance, with the masculinity of a man and the femininity of a woman); or it may be that certain anti-cathected expenditures of energy of the "isolating" type forcibly hold apart the various identifications within the ego so that in respect to certain external situations or instinctual demands one identification emerges, and in respect to other such situations and demands another identification comes to light. But identification need not always be the cause which prevents the unification of the different parts of the ego. The ego has, in general, a multiple origin, and the unification of these origins may not take place, either because of isolating mechanisms or other conflict-avoiding changes of the configuration of the ego; or it may be undone through regression. In a very significant footnote in *Group Psychology and the Analysis of the Ego,* the value of which has not yet been exploited from a clinical point of view, Freud states, "In the process of a child's development into a mature adult there is a more and more extensive integration of its personality, a coordination of the separate instinctive feelings and desires which have grown up in him independently of one another. The analogous process in the domain of sexual life has long been known to us as the coordination of all the sexual instincts into a definitive genital organization. . . . Moreover, that the unification of the ego is liable to the same interferences as that of the libido is shown by numerous familiar instances, such as that of men of science who have preserved their faith in the Bible, and the like. The various possibilities of a later destruction of the ego form a noteworthy chapter in psychopathology." [1]

It is today already possible to have a glimpse of the complicated character of the factors upon which it depends whether such a pathological development of the ego occurs or not. It is once more a question of ego alterations of the anti-cathectic type which have been instituted from defensive motives and which later avoid more acute defensive struggles that demand more expenditure of energy, such as appear in injuries to the ego of this kind. The form and intensity of these changes in the ego depend on constitutional factors, on the character of the instincts against which the defense is directed, on the time when the conflict makes itself felt, and on accidents of individual history—such as external circumstances which made a particular attitude of the ego seem expedient to it or which excluded other attitudes in the subject, or finally on the behavior of the persons in his environment with whom he has identified himself.

As has already been said, what is characteristic for the "unifying" tendency of the ego is the way in which it brings its various trends into harmony with one another. Among these trends one is particularly interesting because under certain circumstances it assumes an instinct-like character, which competes with the genuine instinctual aims of the id, and can involve all the energy of the ego so greatly that nothing remains for other tasks and a very "weak" ego in fact results. I refer to the so-called "narcissistic need," the striving to maintain one's self-regard—one's "mood"—on a high level, a level which approaches as closely as possible to the feeling of omnipotence of early childhood. What weakens the ego in general here is a quantitative heightening of this need as well as a qualitative factor about it. The quantitative increase occurs in cases in which the heightening of self-regard, the striving for power and increased prestige, etc., has become the form in which one wards off a constantly threatening anxiety. The qualitative factor usually accompanies the quantitative increase and consists in this, that the regulating of the self-regard is done according to the primitive methods which the little child uses, while its erotic and narcissistic needs are not yet separated from each other. Increase of self-regard comes through the feeling of

[1] S. Freud, *Group Psychology and the Analysis of the Ego*, London, Hogarth, 1948, footnote pp. 18–19.

being loved, decrease of self-regard through the loss of love. He who still looks to receiving love and other supplies from outside for the support of his ego becomes deeply dependent on his objects, is perpetually menaced with the fear of loss of love, and seeks to overcompensate for this by attempting to be powerful in every way. It is well known that this is the behavior of so-called "oral types" (or, more correctly, of those persons who, as regards the behavior of their ego, are at a stage which predominated during the time at which their libido was at the stage of oral organization; for although this oral organization is *generally* also bound up with an oral-libidinal fixation, this is not always so). These people coincide with that class of persons who have not got away from the oral-receptive method of mastering the external world, or who have regressed to this method from an active alloplastic way of dealing with it. This enables us to understand all the better that it is precisely such people who cannot exist without support from the external world, who are completely dependent on it, and who cannot do anything on their own initiative—who have, that is, a thoroughly "weak ego."

All the sinister weakening changes in the configuration of the ego—like all the pathogenic instinctual defenses—are the result of anxiety, which causes the organism to turn away from the outer world, to withdraw into itself, and in the end to long to obtain external help through the method of "oral mastery." Certainly one must not overlook the fact that a healthy ego can actually subjugate the experience of anxiety itself, calling it up in a small degree through the judgment "there is danger here" and making it serve the purposes of reason. But the example of the grand anxiety attack in anxiety hysteria shows that such a subjugation of anxiety by the ego only succeeds when the organism is not in a state of dammed-up excitations. The avoidance of such a condition should remain the aim of educative efforts which are directed toward strengthening the ego. (But here one must freely concede that it is much easier to state this principle than to give concrete and detailed examples of how to carry it out.) Probably the same circumstance which has to a great degree made possible the differentiation and higher development of man—viz., the long period of physiological dependence of the child—has also provided the possibility that if his ego runs up against difficulties it may give up its function and activities and long for, or magically try to bring back, the time in which there was an all-powerful being in the outer world who gave him love and food and by so doing smoothed out all difficulties. But we must not forget that this physiological circumstance only makes *possible* such a regression to personalities with a weak ego. It is the socially imposed values with which the individual has later to deal, and the socially determined real misery and hopelessness of being unable to make headway against that misery with one's own means, which are to blame for the fact that these possibilities of regression are made use of on such a devastating scale. We will not hide from ourselves that the longing for an authority to relieve the ego of its tasks—a longing which weakens the ego—is increased not by social ideologies alone; there is also the fact that, since the fulfillment of this longing and the giving of real gifts is impossible, the magic thinking of man is used instead to make him receive illusory gifts, and these too have the result of inhibiting his alloplastic ego-strengthening behavior and increasing his oral-receptive behavior. In the face of such social circumstances, a system of education which aims at strengthening the ego will not have an easy time of it.

S I X

On Masturbation*

I AM not going to read a long paper here today. I hear that you are interested in the problem of masturbation, and so I want to tell you what psychoanalytical theory thinks about this matter, just to start a discussion, and what to do in the practice of pedagogy in this respect—a question which is much more difficult to answer.

Masturbation means playing with one's own genitals for the purpose of gaining pleasure. I think this definition is correct. It would be senseless to reserve the word "masturbation" only for such handling of one's own genitals as achieves orgasm. Thus little boys who quiet their bad conscience by ending their masturbation before ejaculation occurs, believe they do not masturbate at all. And it would be just as senseless to include in the conception of masturbation all the so-called masturbation equivalents, the relation of which to masturbation is only shown by psychoanalysis, and which are often performed automatically without the conscious aim of gaining pleasure.

To understand the problems involved in the phenomena of playing with one's own genitals for the purpose of gaining pleasure, I will shortly repeat the psychoanalytic basic ideas about instincts in general.

Reich, in a discussion with a Jungian analyst, once formulated the following argument: Why does a child masturbate? Adler teaches us that he does it because he wants to feel his power, or because he will carry through his purposes, or because he wants to anger the grown-ups, or something like that. But we analysts say the child masturbates because he feels an excitation there.

What is the meaning of this sentence? It reminds us that instincts are bodily

---

* This paper was first presented at Los Angeles in June, 1938. Dr. Fenichel's manuscript has been translated into English, in conformity with the other papers, but no attempt has been made to give it the final form Dr. Fenichel might have given it if he had prepared it for publication.

determined needs, resulting in a change, probably of chemical nature, in the bodily conditions. This is the so-called "source" of the instinct, which causes tension and brings into existence a psychic tendency to remove the tension. This tendency is experienced as instinctual impulses, which impel the subject to act, mostly by means of changing the way in which he makes certain perceptions of objects in the outer world as well as of sensations of his own body. The perceptions acquire a certain character of urgency ("Aufforderungscharakter"), the impulse drives to actions, which—directly or indirectly—bring about a change in the conditions of the body, so that the tension disappears once more. As a model for this discharge of tension we can, for our present purposes, use the sting of a mosquito. The mosquito puts a toxin into the skin which effects a chemical alteration of the way in which the sensory nervous apparatus works— and irritation results; there is an impulse to rub the skin, so that the influx of blood is changed. The rubbing eventually succeeds in more or less removing the uncomfortable feelings. (During the rubbing there is a strange mixture of unpleasure and pleasure—of unpleasure because the tension asks to be removed through more and more rubbing; and of pleasure because this removing of it has started and because one can look forward to further removing and one can anticipate this removing in fantasy—all just as in sexual excitement.)

The sexual instincts are much more complicated than a mosquito sting, psychic ideas complicating the physiological events, but in principle it is the same thing. The toxin which comes in the case of the mosquito from the outer world, comes here from the inner secretory glands. The difference between an irritation after a sting and the autoerotic rubbing of the skin by a child is not as great as it seems to be. And if the autoerotic activity is performed on the genitals, it is masturbation.

I am sure that you will now make the objection that masturbation is not simply an autoerotic activity. It has—as contrasted with autoerotism—two points in common with the real and complicated sexuality of the grown-ups. First, it is performed on the genitals, and secondly it is performed not only in order to remove an irritation, but with imagined objects, with which sexual acts are performed in fantasy. Let us examine this objection.

(1) The genitals.

In the beginning there is no difference between the genitals and other erotogenic organs. The genitals are just one of them, though certainly one in which the erotogenic power is particularly strong. It is not true that the child is first excited only by his mouth, next by his anus, and only after his third year of age by his genitals. The so-called organizational steps of libido do not mean anything more than that the excitement, wherever it may come from, is eventually discharged to a greater extent by the predominant zone, first by the mouth, then by the anus, and then by genital activities. Many errors in psychoanalytic literature come from misunderstandings in this respect. But the genitals in the course of development acquire a particular role among the erotogenic organs. To begin with, their irritability may be more significant than in other organs; but that is not a matter of essential difference. Of more importance is the high ability for discharge of the genitals. In autoerotic activity and also in first attempts at masturbation, there is no sharp distinction between excitation and satisfaction. When the genital apparatus is developed, this distinction becomes very sharp. The genitals are in the first respect an apparatus of discharge. Whereas in the case of a mosquito sting it has been a matter of chance whether the rubbing succeeds in achieving relaxation or not, in the case of the genitals this is guaranteed. This circumstance gives sexual excitation its particular pleasurable nature. If a sexually excited person is suddenly interrupted in his sexual activities, so that his expectation of the end-pleasure of relaxation has to be abandoned, then the pleasure he enjoys beforehand is instantly turned into an intense unpleasure. The discharge value of the end-pleasure is the specific function of the genitals. The achieving of this end-pleasure in the form of an orgasm distinguishes the autoerotic activities and the masturbation of little children on the one hand, and the masturbation at puberty and of adults on the other.

The child of from four to six stands between those two types. Though its apparatus for securing end-pleasure is not yet fully developed, a child of this age already experiences a kind of orgasm. The circumstance whether or not one achieves a specific discharge also determines the difference between successful and unsuccessful masturbation. If one speaks about the consequences of masturbation one must keep this difference in mind, because masturbation which brings about an economically sufficient orgasm has quite different consequences from an unsuccessful attempt to masturbate. Individuals popularly called "masturbatory types" are unsuccessful masturbators, who have neurotic disturbances in the apparatus of satisfaction, and who therefore masturbate again and again, trying to achieve an aim they never can achieve. They are never adequately relaxed and they constantly feel a sexual tension which, in contrast to the normal person, no masturbation can satisfy. A normal person without any suppression of his sexuality would by no means be interested in sexual matters only, as some educators assume. Normal instinctual excitements are periodic events. The hypothetically normal person, free from suppression, would achieve satisfaction through the sexual stimuli for a certain time—till new tensions arrive from bodily sources. But to return to the "masturbatory types." Being in a constant sexual tension, they do not only masturbate in response to certain sexual stimuli. Having experienced that the genitals are the best apparatus of discharge—even when the discharge they can achieve is not sufficient, but is nevertheless the best they have—they try to achieve relaxation by masturbation in every tension, even if the tension is other than genital in nature. They masturbate not only to seek sexual pleasure but also to ward off the unpleasure of tensions of every kind, but unsuccessfully. This kind of masturbation could be called pathological masturbation.

(2) The objects.

The sexual instinct has a development. In the beginning its aim of achieving bodily changes which bring about relaxation can be obtained merely by scratching. Afterward this scratching must be done in a more complicated way by another person, the sexual object. To a certain degree the adult too retains the autoerotism of the infant, but in real sexual excitement he needs an object to become satisfied with. Henceforth masturbation is not a completely satisfying method. It is a compensation. The missing object which is wanted nevertheless, is compensated for in the same way in which man can compensate for unsatisfying reality in general: by fantasy. Now you know that the ability to compensate for unsatisfying reality by fantasy must remain within certain limits. A lack of fantasy is pathological, but an abundance of fantasy at the expense of reality is pathological too. The same is true in the case of masturbation. Lack of the ability to masturbate—meaning lack of ability to resort to masturbation if under bad circumstances no sexual object is at hand—is as pathological as is a preference for masturbation to sexual intercourse. The latter occurs if anxiety or something else prevents enjoyment of a real sexual object and makes sexual enjoyment possible only if the object exists in fantasy. Thus when an adult masturbates it can be a normal phenomenon if it occurs only occasionally and in the absence of a suitable object; and it can be a pathological phenomenon, a sign of sexual suppression, if it occurs because the person prefers masturbation to sexual intercourse. That is the case when anxiety prevents real sexual experiences. This anxiety is often combined with the type of disturbance of satisfaction which we spoke about before. Masturbation is never an activity of a sensual person who gives way to pleasures that are greater than what can be achieved by a normal person. On the contrary: The individual who is hindered from enjoying normal pleasure has no better compensation than that of fantasy. Because it is a compensation and as such is not sufficient, the person must try it again and again. It is true that such an attempt is easy and quickly performed, and therefore the chronic masturbator is inclined to weaken in his tolerance of tension. If somebody has perverse sexual aims—we do not want to discuss today how perversions develop—it is certainly better for society if he is content with masturbation and does not perform his perverse desires in reality. But for him personally masturbation remains a compensation, a compromise between his instincts and his bad conscience.

So one can say that in infancy masturbation is an autoerotic and normal activity. For adults masturbation is normal only when an object cannot be obtained at the moment. How is it in childhood and in puberty? Well, in our society children are continually in the state of a grown-up whose sexual object is lacking. Children are not allowed to have sexual intercourse or to perform sexual acts equivalent to intercourse with each other. This being the case, one must say: *Masturbation at this age is normal.* It is the best discharge children can have. If tendencies to masturbate do not appear at all, one can be sure that a serious repression has already taken place. And if the educators prohibit masturbation altogether, they push the child into a state of tension, which is difficult to sustain. And more than that: They create in the child's mind the idea that sexual matters are bad and dangerous. They motivate the child to repress his instincts in the future, and in this way cause neuroses and deformations of the child's personality.

Another question would be how matters would stand in a society in which sexual activities of children were not forbidden, and sexual play of children was regarded as a natural affair. I suppose that under such circumstances children, like adults, would prefer sexual play with objects to masturbation, and would masturbate to a lesser degree than in our society. But I do not know. That has to be investigated.

Now to the question which you certainly are most interested in: Is there any danger in masturbation? To be able to examine this question in the right way, we must first consider one thing. It is clear that the continuation of masturbation or excess of masturbation, or the preference for masturbation to sexual intercourse, are less *causes* of damage than *signs* of it. Those features have the character of symptoms, and we have already spoken about their pathological character. They cannot be cured by moral approaches but only by removing the cause.

How could that be done? To advise children who show those features in their masturbation to perform sexual play with other children would be of no greater use than to advise a hysteric to get married. The inability to achieve adequate sexuality is a disturbance which is rooted too deeply to be removed by mere advice. The sexually inhibited child could take such advice only as a dangerous temptation and would respond only with more anxiety and inhibition—and more masturbation. In severe cases the basic disturbances cannot be removed without analytic help. In slighter cases, too, direct incitement could not succeed. But perhaps encouragement and persuasion which make the child feel that he will not be punished can help, because among children the motives for repression often are not yet quite internalized. The repressing forces are often nothing other than a great fear of being punished, which can be invalidated by encouragement.

Now I hope it is clear that "masturbation" is no diagnosis. It is a symptom. It is occasionally a *normal* symptom, if it appears at certain intervals and only if sexual acts with objects are not possible. It is a *pathological* symptom under other circumstances, and has to be understood as a sign that the capacity for satisfaction is disturbed. (We do not know yet in what way it is disturbed.) And really, there is no mental disorder in which the symptom of pathological masturbation does not occur. The psychic value of pathological masturbation can be manifold.

Freud nevertheless says that masturbation, whatever its kind may be, is dangerous. It is stated to be the cause of neurasthenia. What about this? Neurasthenia is a so-called actual neurosis and comes about when sexual excitement is hindered in finding its physiological outlet and is displaced from the genitals to the vegetative nervous system. That is the case if a person is afraid of the physiological discharge and therefore interferes with it. Masturbators often become masturbators from fear of the intensity of their own sexual excitement. But if they become neurasthenics too, that does not come about because they are masturbators, but because they are *unsuccessful* masturbators. This means that they fear the sensation of their own masturbation (this may be a feeling of guilt or may be a more archaic anxiety). Therefore they disturb the course of their own sexual excitement and do not let it come to its natural end. The anxiety and the unsuccessful course of masturbation produce neurasthenia, not masturbation itself.

But it is true that there are certain other dangers attendant on masturbation—dangers which are mostly less important than the dangers that are caused by prohibition of masturbation—and they become actual only in pathological forms of masturbation.

(1) The tolerance to sustain tensions is diminished if one is accustomed to flee from every tension immediately into masturbation.

(2) If reality is customarily replaced by fantasy, this circumstance causes or increases introversion; that means a general withdrawal from reality. Masturbation may furthermore fixate the disturbance of the subject's relations to his objects, of which it (the masturbation) was a consequence.

(3) If masturbation is performed with a bad conscience and anxiety which prevent its running its natural course, this circumstance has, as I have described, pathological consequences.

But we also said before that a normal person must be able to masturbate if circumstances prevent sexual object relations, that is to say, in times of a missing object and in childhood and puberty before suitable objects are available. If a person says that he has never masturbated one can be sure that a severe disturbance has taken place (assuming he was not telling a lie). And when in the course of analysis a person of this kind begins to masturbate, this can be considered progress.

The importance of normal masturbation in childhood for the development of the personality lies, I think, in the following circumstances:

Playing is a very important matter for children. The child learns to master reality by playing. What the child has experienced passively in the past or what he expects to happen in the future—that he plays actively. The tensions which have been set by passive experiences or which will be set by future events, could overwhelm him. But he himself sets this kind of tension in a smaller degree by playing, so that he can learn to master it gradually. Playing is the way to learn to master the world. By playing, a child learns to bear increasing self-imposed tension, becoming thereby slowly able to withstand reality.

But in my opinion it is to a certain degree correct to say that masturbation *is* sexual play. By masturbating the child learns to master sexual tension. One often hears the idea that the masturbating child loses self-control and becomes a victim of his bad instincts. I consider that the opposite is true: if masturbation has no pathological character (as described above) it is a means by which the child learns to control his sexual instincts. This mechanism can fail, it is true, and then the ego cannot master the ghosts it has called up. (But it is not my topic to speak now about those possible failures.) This possibility does not contradict the statement that the ego function of masturbation lies in the fact that sexual play can prepare the child for sexual reality in the same way as playing can prepare for reality in general. For this reason, disturbances to which masturbation was exposed in childhood repeat themselves later on as disturbances of adult sexuality. But it is true that after the sexual play there must follow sexual reality. If anxiety prohibits this step, the result is an inhibited person, who prefers masturbation to sexual intercourse. We know types of patients whose anxiety is so great that they prefer fantasies to reality and cannot do anything seriously, because all serious things appear to them to be dangerous. I think that the chronic masturbator is the same type as this in the field of sexuality.

Let me try to summarize the practical consequences of what I have said as I see them: There is no reason to prevent children from masturbation. I should only like to add that I would not prevent children from playing together in a sexual manner either, as far as possible—I say "as far as possible" because there is a danger of seducing a smaller child, whose sexuality is not at the same level. The best prophylaxis against the pathological type of masturbation is a supply of love and avoidance of anxiety and repression. What is of special importance is not one bit of verbal advice or another, but the whole atmosphere in which education is performed. If this atmosphere affirms sexuality, there will be no fear of occasional interdiction of masturbation of this sort: "not here" and "not now." But to what extent education in a sexuality-affirming atmosphere is possible—that depends on social and political circumstances.

SEVEN

The Drive to Amass Wealth[*]

Is THERE an instinctual drive to amass wealth? There appears to be no possible doubt about this. We meet this drive every day in widely varying degrees in different people. It can assume pathological forms, for example, in the miser, who in order to become rich foregoes the satisfaction of other more rational needs, or in the person who strives to become wealthy in order to ward off a fear of impoverishment and the like. The drive has normal forms; indeed, a person in whom it is completely lacking will in our society be considered abnormal. It manifests itself actively as acquisitiveness (with the fundamental aim of taking money away from another in order to have it oneself), as well as passively—with the essential purpose of being supported on an oral level by the strength of others, represented by money.

If we remind ourselves that Freud in "Instincts and Their Vicissitudes" [1] has rightly said: "Now what instincts and how many should be postulated? There is obviously a great opportunity here for arbitrary choice. No objection can be made to anyone's employing the concept of an instinct of play or of destruction, or that of a social instinct, when the subject demands it and the limitations of psychological analysis allow of it"; then there can be no doubt that we may call this tendency to accumulate wealth an instinct.

Doubt can, however, exist concerning the *genuineness* of this instinct. I continue the above quotation from Freud: "Nevertheless, we should not neglect to ask whether such instinctual motives, which are in one direction so highly specialized, do not admit of further analysis in respect to their sources, so that only those primal instincts which are not to be resolved further could really lay claim to the name."

[*] First published in *Psa. Quart.*, Vol. 7, 1938, pp. 69–95.
[1] S. Freud, "Instincts and Their Vicissitudes," *Coll. Pap.*, Vol. IV, London, Hogarth, 1948, p. 66.

Money is certainly not something biological and has played a rather varying rôle in different social systems. The question of the nature of social institutions, and of the method by which they can be investigated, is indeed a controversial one, particularly among authors who are concerned with the application of psychoanalysis to the social sciences. Some psychologists deny the remarkable process by which the relations of human beings to each other and to outer realities become independent entities or institutions, which then (not further derivable psychologically) act from outside as stimuli upon human beings, influencing their behavior. These psychologists will probably look upon the drive to become wealthy as a subdivision of an instinct of possession, itself biologically determined (its source would be anal eroticism); indeed they may look upon money itself as something which people endowed with this instinct have invented as a convenience, in order to satisfy the instinct with it. Sociologists, on the other hand, will be of the opinion that the craving for riches can arise only in a society in which the possibility actually exists of gaining real advantages and prestige by money and of becoming wealthy without performing work (that is, through the exploitation of the labor of others).

At the outset we have the impression that the truth must be found half-way between. Biological facts are modified by social facts (for example, the existence and function of money). This problem is to be investigated more closely in the present article.

If we remember that psychoanalysis looks upon every psychic event as the resultant of an interplay of essentially biological instinctual structures and outer stimuli acting upon them, further that the social institutions in question evidently comprise a substantial part of these outer stimuli that modify the instinctual structure of mankind, then we recognize in the problem of the drive to become wealthy a particularly good subject for the investigation of the reciprocal action between a relatively primary instinctual structure and the social influences modifying it. This reciprocal action is extremely complicated. Not only do social influences alter the instinctual structure, but the thus modified instinctual structure reacts again upon social reality through the actions of individuals. In the face of the complications prevailing here, what follows is intended only in the nature of preliminary remarks, self-evident considerations, in order to make possible an approach to the problem.

Why, indeed, does a person wish to accumulate wealth? Many quite different motives suggest themselves:

1. Because one is right in believing that the more money one possesses, the better can one satisfy one's needs. We may call this the *rational* motive. (It becomes irrational when one has illusions about the real possibilities of becoming rich.) This motive exists only when money has social validity. Its biological

basis is the total of all other human needs, not to be specified here. Only the external fact that one can purchase with money the satisfaction of needs, gives this motive the form of a drive to become rich.

2. Whoever has money can satisfy by means of it not only his own needs, but also those of others. He who has less money is dependent upon him who has more. In our society the possessor of money is honored and truly *powerful*. Now among all human needs whose satisfaction can be bought with money, particularly conspicuous are those which we call "narcissistic." The drive to become rich appears to be a subdivision of that "will to power" which first Nietzsche and later Adler so emphasized. The existence of such a striving cannot be denied. There remains the task of investigating its nature more closely. The types mentioned in the introduction, who are burdened with a drive to become wealthy because they wish to escape a pathological fear of impoverishment, can be included here as a subdivision. The analysis of fear of impoverishment shows that the loss of love and of possessions that is feared means always a loss of self-regard, a diminution of power.

3. The will to become wealthy appears as a subdivision of a desire for *possessions*. The origin of this striving has been analytically explained in detail. In the deeper layers of the mind, the idea of possessions refers to the contents of one's own body, which could be taken away. In this connection money—like all possessions—assumes the rôle of parts of the body which one could lose, or which one wishes to regain after the fantasy that they have been lost, and especially the rôle of feces, which one wishes to accumulate.

4. To these motives for the drive to wealth familiar to the psychoanalyst, there is added a fourth that is of quite a different nature, and whose relationship to the motives previously discussed represents our problem. Our system of production has become historic: it is an economy of commodities which does not produce in order to satisfy the needs of the producer directly, but in order to create products for sale, benefiting the producer only indirectly; and in such an economic system a certain commodity, *labor,* has the characteristic of producing greater value than its own market price. The possessor of money can therefore transform it into capital, which means that he can purchase both means of production and labor, and because the product belongs to him he can increase his possessions. Whoever produces on a "higher scale," whoever has at his disposal greater capital (means of production and labor), can thereby produce more systematically and therefore more cheaply, so that the producers on a "lower scale" must be driven from the field. This is the cause for the accumulation of capital, for its more and more rapid concentration in fewer and fewer hands. It forces the capitalist under penalty of his own destruction always to produce on the maximal scale. The tragedy of our system of production is that on the one

hand for the maintenance of production, an accelerating increase of it is necessary, and that on the other hand, the purchasing power of the masses is at the same time always more and more diminished thereby. It leads—and only this circumstance interests us here—to the fact that a capitalist, under penalty of his own destruction, *must strive to accumulate wealth*.

If we add to this the fact that the ideology of a society (the views concerning what is to be esteemed as good and worth striving for) is always the ideology of the ruling class, then it follows that an aim valid for the ruling class is also aspired to automatically by all other classes. That this aspiration of the masses is no mere imitation of the capitalists, but is systematically nurtured by present-day education in order to create illusions about the true class relationships ("Every soldier carries a field marshal's staff in his knapsack"), is merely alluded to here. However, the nature and mode of action of the social ideal of thrift would certainly be worth a detailed investigation.

What is the relation to one another of these four sources of the drive to accumulate wealth? The first three are of a purely psychological nature and can be investigated by the psychoanalyst with respect to their soundness, significance, mode of origin, normal and pathological outcomes. The fourth source depends psychologically upon a single general instinct of every living thing, the instinct of self-preservation, and shows us that external forces allow the self-preservation of some people—namely the capitalists—only on the condition that they accumulate wealth; accordingly what is essential in this motive would be those external forces. Accustomed as analysts to take the individual as our starting point, let us begin by investigating more closely the first three motives.

1. *The rational motive:* If a person actually were rationally disposed, there would be no drive to become wealthy, but only a reasonable ego which had gained experience in regard to its requirements, and even in their latent state, when the requirements were not acutely pressing, would provide in advance that in case of need an optimum possibility of satisfaction should exist. Here there appears to be no problem whatever. The problem springs from the fact that not all people are given the same opportunity for such rational accumulation of wealth, and that concerning this fact obscurity prevails.

Thus we come to the broad problem of propagation of the ideology of an enduring social system, the investigation of which represents the principal subject for psychoanalysis in its correct application to sociology. How does society succeed in maintaining without rebellions a state of affairs in which a majority of its members are prevented from satisfying their most primitive needs, when goods for their satisfaction are at hand in large quantities? It succeeds first by force, through the fact that in the mind of human beings a force acting contrary to their needs is produced by the influence of the environment upon the instinctual structure, namely fear of the institution of penal justice. It succeeds, however, not only by external force, but also, so to speak, through cunning, and as one of the tricks (among many others) the production of a drive to become wealthy is characteristic. For situations of deprivation are easier to bear when they are coupled with fantasies of a better future. The sight of envied, better-situated people is more easily borne when the psychological possibility of identification with them is present. Society's ideal of "thrift" serves to obscure true class relationships and to create illusions concerning the possibilities of personal social advancement.

It is clear that the action of such an ideological influence must be strongest in those classes whose hope for the future can still be sustained by a memory of the past, especially among the petty bourgeois thrown into penury by the advance of capital accumulation, who by their thrift hope to regain something lost, more than among proletarians who have never possessed anything. Thus is explained the often noted circumstance that not all people have the drive to become wealthy to the same degree, but that often just those who possess least money care least about it. This statement is, to be sure, not quite correct in the formulation just given. There are people who have very little money and nevertheless insist with extreme tenacity upon increasing this little by a minimal amount. They are those of the middle class who, in spite of the practical unreasonableness of such an accumulation of small amounts, have through social influences the illusion of a possibility of advancement. The celebrated "proletarian solidarity" which is ready to distribute what little it has, appears to us not so much possessed of a praiseworthy virtue as giving rational expression to the fact that with the proletarian class the first motive for the drive to get rich becomes untenable: an attempt to save is in fact without any prospect of achievement.

Through the existence of the right of inheritance, what is rational in the drive to acquire wealth extends even beyond the span of life. This is not the place to discuss in detail the structural alterations produced in the human mind by the social institution of inheritance, but it cannot be overlooked that the circumstance through which the death of a person brings to others the rational advantages of wealth, becomes a cause for death wishes and ambivalences of many kinds.

Why are money and money matters in our society so often considered "indelicate"? It will be said that the answer to this question belongs under point 3, since this evaluation arises evidently from the unconscious equivalence of money and feces. We are of the opinion, however, that this evaluation of money has also a rational aspect which only makes use of that unconscious equation in order to prevail. One should note what a small place in our public schools is given to instruction in finance and related fields in contrast to the enormous importance of just this field in our social system. One gains the impression that this quite general characterization of money matters as "indelicate" must fulfil a special function in the social ideology. This function must be a negative one: ignorance about financial matters and the effort to repress them as much as possible, lead to illusions about the true state of affairs in this field and about the possibilities for a rational acquiring of wealth, and thus belong to those earlier mentioned expedients for maintaining the present-day class relationships through cunning (as well as by force).

We know how much the faithful citizen repeats toward the state attitudes which as a child he had developed toward his father, the representative of the authority with which he was then faced. This naturally does not mean that the oedipus complex must have created the state in the image of the family, but that within the state an educating institution, the family, has arisen, suited to rear authority-fearing people, altered in their structure in the manner desired at the present time. The fact that in the family circle money matters (like sexual matters) are reserved for the father, who maintains his domination over wife and child through their practical economic dependence upon him, creates just that nimbus of "the mysterious" which at the present time appertains to the financial field as frequently as to the sexual. This fact is most apparent in those layers of society where the ideological influence of the family is still strong, thanks to the economic anchorage of the institution of the family—that is, among peasants and petty bourgeois more than among proletarians.

2. *The will to power:* Among the needs whose satisfaction can be bought and for whose sake a person strives to become wealthy (with or without prospect of success), a special place is taken by the will to power. What is it really? Why is this feeling of being powerful, of enjoying respect or honors, in itself a goal aspired to? As is well known, what is called ego psychology has only in relatively recent times become a subject of psychoanalytic research. We are beginning now to understand genetically the need to maintain a "high level of self-regard" which is evidently identical with the so-called "will to power." This striving owes its origin to the fact that young children all feel themselves omnipotent, and that throughout their lives a certain memory of this omnipotence remains with a longing to attain it again.

Although the work of Freud, "On Narcissism: An Introduction," [2] provided us with deep insight into this subject, the questions concerning self-regard and its regulating mechanisms remained for a long time, and wrongly, outside of the psychoanalytic sphere of interest and were relegated to the individual-psychologists, who contented themselves with confirming again and again the existence of such aspirations. The first works to make progress were those of

[2] S. Freud, "On Narcissism: An Introduction," *Coll. Pap.,* Vol. IV.

Rado,[3] which, on the basis of views acquired in the meantime, fitted the question of self-regard into the psychogenesis of the ego, and led gradually to the view that today might be formulated thus: As a motive for the actions of some individuals, the need of the ego to maintain its level of self-regard has a position of importance equal to that of the instinctual requirements of the id. (But this ego striving itself can always be shown to be a derivative of biological needs originally represented in the id, which have been altered by environmental influence and are always strengthened to overcome anxiety. The "narcissistic requirement," which plays a part in everything, including what we call love— in pathological cases a greater rôle, in normal ones a smaller—should not lead us to the point of describing love merely as a transaction that takes place between ego and superego, as if the biological force, "sexuality," played no part in its development. Such a representation, however, seems to me to be at the basis of the formulations of Bergler and Jekels concerning love.[4]) What we know with the help of Freud and Rado about the genesis and significance of self-regard, I have attempted to summarize as follows: [5]

"After the original infantile feeling of omnipotence is lost, there is a persistent desire to recover it. This desire we call 'narcissistic need,' and self-regard, the index of its quantity, is highest when this desire is fulfilled and low when fulfilment is remote. The most primitive means of satisfying this need is the sense of being loved. The small child feels a diminution of his self-regard if he loses the affection of others, and a rise of it if the contrary is the case. At this level narcissistic need and erotic need still coincide completely. This permits us to assume that both stem from a common model, a primal desire that could be stilled by an external source of supply. This primal desire is the baby's hunger, and its satisfaction the baby's satiety. . . . Later, narcissistic and erotic needs become differentiated from each other. The latter needs develop and modify in relationships with real objects (love and hate), the former come into relation with . . . the superego. Whenever there is a discrepancy between superego and ego, that is, a sense of guilt, self-regard is diminished, while each fulfilment of an ideal elevates it. As in the case of all psychic development, however, the old demonstrably persists along with the new; part of the relationship with real objects is governed by the sense of guilt."

There are indeed the most varied methods for regulating self-regard. To what extent the actions, thoughts, and attitudes produced by the ego (for example, defenses against anxieties and instincts) are in general guided by this requirement, is still in need of investigation. In so far as the drive to amass wealth

[3] S. Rado, "The Psychic Effects of Intoxicants," *Int. J. Psa.,* Vol. 7, 1926; "The Problem of Melancholia," *Int. J. Psa.,* Vol. 9, 1928.
[4] L. Jekels and E. Bergler, "Uebertragung und Liebe," *Imago,* Vol. 20, 1934.
[5] O. Fenichel, *Outline of Clinical Psychoanalysis,* New York, Norton, 1934.

appears to be a means of the ego for increasing self-regard, or for preventing a lowering of its level, this desire can be looked upon first as a derivative of that primitive form of regulation of self-regard in which the individual requires a "narcissistic supply" from the environment in the same way as the infant requires an external supply of food. Money is just such a supply. Then, to be sure, in the present-day economic system, especially with the circulation of the above-sketched illusions concerning the possibilities of getting rich, the idea of being wealthy becomes an ego-ideal. The attainment of wealth is fantasied and striven for as something bound up with an enormous increase of self-regard.

We know that such a discussion about the fact that people wish to become rich because they see therein the fulfilment of an ideal is very trite; but the consideration of this banality serves to separate for us what is relatively biological from what is sociological. The original instinctual aim is not for riches, but to enjoy power and respect, whether it be among one's fellow men or within oneself. It is a society in which power and respect are based upon the possession of money, that makes of this need for power and respect a need for riches.

3. *The will to possession:* Those who are not accustomed to psychoanalytic thinking will perhaps be astonished that we mention this desire as a separate motive. Is not the state of affairs with the will to possession exactly the same as with the instinct to become wealthy: in a social system in which possession presents the possibility of satisfying needs or of acquiring respect, is not possession aspired to just as a special case of the striving for the satisfaction of needs, or for respect? But just at this point psychoanalysts have discovered that behind these rational motives there are further irrational ones for accumulating possessions, and it is exactly the question of the relation between this specific irrational "collecting instinct" and the general "drive to become wealthy" that is under discussion.

Psychoanalytically, what is "possession"? The word itself gives the answer: Possession is that upon which one sits.† Abraham, in various works,[6] showed convincingly how literally this is felt in the unconscious. It is not only said of the miser that he sits on his money, but Abraham tells how his dog used to sit upon those objects which he regarded as his possessions. What can be the unconscious meaning of such a real or fantasied action—to sit upon certain objects? Doubtless the fear that these objects could be taken away from one. Among possessions, therefore, belong objects which are endowed with a certain ego-quality, and which one fears could be torn away from the ego. The desire

---

† In the German original: *Besitz ist das, worauf man sitzt.* Latin: *"Possidēre,"* "to possess"; from *"port,"* "toward," and *"sedēre,"* "to sit."—Trans. note.

[6] K. Abraham, "Contributions to the Theory of the Anal Character," and "A Short Study of the Development of the Libido, Viewed in the Light of Mental Disorders," *Selected Papers,* London, Hogarth, 1948.

to possess a great deal appears thus to be a direct expression of the narcissistic need to enlarge as much as possible the compass of one's own ego. What does it mean, however, "to endow objects with ego-qualities"?

"The ego is first and foremost a body-ego," says Freud in *The Ego and the Id*,[7] and he means by this that the distinction between ego and non-ego is first learned by the infant in the discovery of its body in such a way that in its world of ideas its own body begins to be set off from the rest of the environment. The idea of its own ego arises in the conception of its own body, in the so-called "body pattern." What has been termed "psychic feeling of self" is only a derivative of this "bodily ego-feeling." Now the body pattern, as is well known, is not identical with the objective body. Parts of the body that are not present, such as amputated limbs, can still belong to the body pattern; articles of clothing and the like belong to the body pattern. Articles of property are thus objects which are possessed in the same way as one's own body, and they have a portion of the quality through which one's own ego is set off from the rest of the world. *Possessions are an expanded portion of the ego.*

The psychological precursor of that upon which one sits is that which is present in one's own body. Psychogenetically, the inclination to possession is a derivative of bodily narcissism and is frequently an overcompensation for fear of loss of parts of the body. We already see by means of such considerations how intertwined in their relationships are the biological and the sociological data. As soon as we believe at all in the doctrine of evolution, no biological factor is for us constant; everything is in continual flux. The drive to amass wealth seems to be a special form of the instinct of possession, made possible by the social function of money. The possessive instinct is a special form of bodily narcissism and an expression of the fear of bodily injury, made possible because of the definite social function of possessions. The fear of bodily injury must also be investigated with respect to the social conditions of its origin, with respect to the questions when and why, that is, under what social circumstances the older generation begins to cultivate in the succeeding generation a fear of bodily injury.

The fear of bodily injuries, which forces on bodily narcissism the character of continually striving for the insurance of its integrity, we are accustomed to call "castration anxiety." This is named after the most important form of fear of bodily injury, the fear of genital injury, which appears in the fear of the consequences of sexual activity in the phallic phase of development in both sexes, but particularly in the male. Freud rightly pointed out that it would be inappropriate to give the name of castration anxiety to such precursors as the fear of suffering bodily damage through defecation or through weaning.[8] But it is just these

[7] S. Freud, *The Ego and the Id*, London, Hogarth, 1947, p. 31.
[8] S. Freud, "The Passing of the Oedipus-Complex," *Coll. Pap.*, Vol. II, London, Hogarth, 1948.

pregenital fears of bodily injury which are predominantly overcompensated in the striving for many possessions. Even though we know pathological forms of the drive to become wealthy in which money is in the unconscious unequivo-cally equated to the penis whose loss is feared, nevertheless the basis of irrational ways of behaving about money is above all the other symbolic equation dis-covered by Freud: money = feces.[9] The ability to hold back and accumulate a substance endowed with ego quality, and the fear of having to lose such a substance against its will, are acquired by the young child first of all in the train-ing to habits of cleanliness. To be sure, there is preparation for this in still earlier stages of psychic development: the infant who still considers its mother's breast a part of its own ego must experience every withdrawal of it as such a loss of ego substance. The early sadistic fantasies of wishing to tear something out of the mother's body, which evidently take place in every individual (and can have a very varied outcome), are replaced by a corresponding fear of reprisal, the idea that something can be taken out of one's own body; and this prudence concern-ing bodily integrity is reactively enhanced. It is conflicts of this kind that are later transferred to possessions.

That anal eroticism has so much greater significance in the desire to accumu-late possessions than oral or genital eroticism, may be ascribed to the fact that in the anal sphere holding back and accumulating can afford an experience of erogenous pleasure. It may be that the anal retentive pleasure is always secondary and is always mixed with a fear of experiencing the pleasure in excreting; at any rate the retentive pleasure does come to exist, at least secondarily, and analytic experience concerning anal retentive pleasure leaves no doubt but that it is the erogenous source of the desire for possession for possession's sake and the source of all irrational behavior concerning money. When Freud showed for the first time in his paper, "Character and Anal Erotism," [10] how some character traits originate in the warding off of certain impulses, he emphasized the attitude toward money as a product of development of anal eroticism.

Ferenczi has described the ontogenetic stages through which the original pleasure in dirt develops into a love of money: [11] The pleasure in retention, whether it be primary or secondary, is the model for all "saving." The child's interest turns at first from feces to the mud of the streets, then to dust, to sand, to stones, then to all sorts of made objects that can be collected, and finally to money. It is a pity that the recognition of such transformations of the collecting instinct, anal in its erogenous roots, causes even Ferenczi to see in money not something furnished by tradition and then presented to the child as an object

[9] S. Freud, "Character and Anal Erotism," *Coll. Pap.*, Vol. II.
[10] *Ibid.*
[11] S. Ferenczi, "The Origin of the Interest in Money," *Sex in Psychoanalysis*, New York, Brunner, 1950.

for such a displacement, but as something which was expressly invented for the purpose of satisfying such an instinct, regarded as purely erotogenic. In such an extrapolation to phylogenesis from ontogenetic data, he is committing the same error that we wish to discuss in greater detail later in connection with Roheim's article on sacred money in Melanesia.[12] When Ferenczi writes concerning children's interest in stones, "the capitalistic significance of stones is already very considerable," and believes that children collect stones out of pure joy of collecting, he betrays that he believes capitalism, too, originates from such a source. He says explicitly: "The not purely practical appropriateness, but the libidinal irrationality of capitalism betrays itself even on this level; the child takes decided pleasure in collecting as such." The existence of an erogenous pleasure in collecting causes Ferenczi to overlook the fact that when the capitalist strives to increase his capital, he does this on very rational grounds: he is forced to it by his competitors who produce on a larger scale. To be sure, a social system whose members are forced to accumulate because of the prevailing conditions of production or, as a reflection of this compulsion, must hold saving as an ideal for the purpose of maintaining the social system—a social system of this kind *makes use of* and strengthens erogenous drives that serve the necessity for accumulating. Of this there can be no doubt. There is considerable doubt, however, as to whether the existing economic conditions of production were created by the biological instinct in order to provide opportunity for the satisfaction of the instinct.

The varieties of irrational attitudes toward money, arising from unsolved anal-erotic conflicts, have been so aptly portrayed by Freud,[13] Jones,[14] and Abraham[15] in the classical descriptions of the anal character, that nothing can be added, except a reminder that not only the unconscious attitude toward feces but also the attitude toward introjections of every kind can be projected onto money. One thinks of kleptomaniacs, or of the women who drain men of their resources, to whom money, which they are always striving to take away, symbolizes a whole series of introjected objects that have been withheld from them; or of depressive characters who from fear of starvation regard money as potential food. There are too those men to whom money signifies their potency, who experience any loss of money as a castration, or who are inclined, when in danger, to sacrifice money in a sort of "prophylactic self-castration." There are, in addition, people who—according to their attitude of the moment toward taking, giving, or with-

[12] G. Roheim, "Heiliges Geld in Melanesien," *Int. Z. Psa.,* Vol. 9, 1923.

[13] S. Freud, "Character and Anal Erotism" and "On the Transformation of Instincts with Special Reference to Anal Erotism," *Coll. Pap.,* Vol. II.

[14] E. Jones, "Anal-Erotic Character Traits," *Papers on Psycho-Analysis,* 5th ed., Baltimore, Williams and Wilkins, 1948.

[15] K. Abraham, "Contributions to the Theory of the Anal Character," *Selected Papers.*

holding—accumulate or spend money, or alternate between accumulation and spending, quite impulsively, without regard for the reality significance of money, and often to their own detriment (sometimes unconsciously desired). In the unconscious mental life money can represent not only possessions but everything that one can take or give; therefore it can represent relations to objects in general and everything through which the bodily ego feeling and with it (as we explained above) self-regard can be increased or diminished.

In an article by Odier everything is collected that is known concerning the unconscious symbolism of money.[16] The wish to receive, or as he says, the system c. p. (captatio-possessio = seizure-possession), represents the first relationship of all to the object world. Not until much later, with the establishment of the reality principle in place of the pleasure principle, does the gradual development of the system o. (oblatio = offering) come. The realization that one must relinquish something (first the mother's breast, then feces), and the struggle between the desire to keep and the necessity for relinquishing, govern the psychological attitude toward money. "The attitude toward money is already complete before the realization of the true function of money has been awakened." However, it is not clearly expressed that an irrational desire for possession merely occupies itself with money, but does not create money. In so far as this instinctual drive is occupied with money as such, by just so much is the real function of money *damaged*.

To deduce the function of money from such a misuse of money would be like drawing from the secret sexual meaning of walking in the hysteric, shown by psychoanalysis, the deduction that we walk for the sake of sexual pleasure and not in order to get from one place to another. What is more, the function that money actually performs in reality breeds in us a reinforcement of the anal-erotically conditioned instinct of accumulation, and not the reverse—that is, a reinforcement of the instinct of accumulation has not produced the reality function of money.

Considerations of this sort are certainly important for the understanding of the development of "money-mindedness" in human beings, for here we are led further only by the recognition of the reciprocal action between basic instincts and social system, the latter modifying the former, and in turn the altered instinct structure influencing the social system. But nothing justifies the assertion that the symbolic significance of money is more important than its real significance or that its symbolic meaning is the cause of the origin of money—even though in Odier's tabulation of symbols there rightly appears not only the equation, money = feces, but also, money = *everything* which can be taken or given:

[16] C. Odier, "L'Argent et les Névroses," *Rev. Française Psychanalyse*, Vol. 2, 1928, and Vol. 3, 1929.

milk, food, mother's breast, intestinal contents, feces, penis, sperm, child, potency, love, protection, care, passivity, obstinacy, vanity, pride, egoism, indifference toward objects, autoeroticism, gift, offering, renunciation, hate, weapon, humiliation, deprivation of potency, besmirching, degradation, sexual aggression, anal penis. Indeed a tendency toward any of these can express itself with money, can express itself also in an ambition to become wealthy. The instincts represent the general tendency, while matters of *money* and the desire to become wealthy represent a specific form which the general tendency can assume only in the presence of certain definite social conditions.

The fact, correctly noted by Odier,[17] that children introduce money into instinctual conflicts of the kind we have been discussing (concerning taking and giving) before they can have any judgment of the reality significance of money, does not mean that money was invented out of instinctual drives of this sort, but that an economic system operating with money soon alters the instinctual structure of the individuals living under it in a way unsuspected before the days of psychoanalysis, by relatively increasing the anal eroticism.

It is therefore dangerous to conclude, as Odier does, that "not riches or poverty, but the persistence of unconscious infantile tendencies is decisive for the attitude toward money." For the state of affairs is not different in regard to money from what it is in regard to any other portion of reality: the persistence of unconscious infantile tendencies, that is the inclination to neurotic reactions, is decisive for the attitude toward reality. Anyone who must keep repressed material in a state of repression has to act inappropriately and is handicapped in his judgment and his sense of reality. Apart from such pathological curtailment of rationality, poverty or riches can very well be decisive in determining the attitude toward money.

Odier speaks of a "pre-pecuniary phase" in which the child acquires its attitude toward taking and giving, and of a "pecuniary phase" in which the child learns about the real function of money but in which his attitude to it is still influenced by his experiences in the pre-pecuniary phase. We can agree with him but must make two additions. In the first place, in the pre-pecuniary phase there is not yet a true desire to amass wealth but only a wish to hold on to everything, to draw everything to oneself, and psychologically it is mere chance whether

---

[17] So correct is Odier on this point, that we wish to refer to his and Ferenczi's work for a discussion of the problems of how the child learns about money and understands its use according to its conception of reality, which corresponds to the stage of development of the child's ego and libido at the time in question. Psychoanalysis is doubtless alone competent to solve these problems. To be sure, we are not concerned in the present paper with analyzing the child's behavior toward money, but with the methodological question of what analysis can contribute to the knowledge of the phylogenetic development of money.

these general aims are occupied with money or with something else. Secondly, even the pre-pecuniary phase is experienced differently according to the function of money in the particular society in which the individual is reared.

The will to power on the one hand, and the will to possession on the other, are roots of the drive to amass wealth. They cannot be laid side by side as parallels, but are most intimately intertwined. We need only remember how it happens that obstinacy develops as a character trait from the conflicts centering around anal eroticism at the time when the child is being trained in habits of cleanliness. Attaining control over the sphincters is an event of no small significance in the development of self-regard. The child who has acquired this ability, really possesses through it a bit of power, not only over its own body, but over the persons in its environment as well. Anal retentive pleasure thus contains, along with its predominantly erogenous components, a component of self-regard or feeling of power as well; the will to power and the desire to accumulate possessions are most closely geared.

4. *The sociological source:* Up to this point, the foregoing three sources of the drive to become wealthy are discussed by the psychoanalyst. Now, however, the sociologist brings our fourth argument to bear upon the origin of the drive. He believes one does not *need* all of the foregoing. From psychology he believes one *needs* only to take the existence of an instinct of self-preservation. This will suffice, together with the law that the ideology of a society is always that of the ruling class, in order to explain on external economic grounds the origin and dissemination of a drive to accumulate wealth.

To this we would first reply: What we *need* for the explanation of a phenomenon does not interest us. In psychoanalysis we have proved by scientific research that the complications discussed, the first three sources of the drive to amass wealth, *exist*. Matters actually go on in the world in a more complicated manner than might seem necessary. The multiplicity of human instinctual conflicts, the inclination of the repressed to take advantage of every opportunity for discharge, are so great that truly the "overdetermination" can hardly be overestimated; and one finds an infinite number of motives participating in a single human action. The problem is, then: What is essential, what is only accidental? With this in view, let us once more examine the first three points in order to determine how far they are comprised of the biological instinctual characteristics of mankind and how far of the social environment.

In anyone who desires to amass wealth essentially because of the first motive, the multiplicity of all his needs is active from the biological side; the need to become wealthy develops out of this multiplicity only when money has validity. The person in whom the second group of motives is stronger desires to be esteemed or to exercise power. The person in whom the third group of motives is emphasized desires to control his own affairs himself, to possess a sphere of his own, to collect something or even to distribute something and the like. Nowhere in the instinctual goal as such is money included; only the presence and the function of money in the social system furnish these unspecific instinctual drives with this specific object.

Laforgue drew from this the conclusion that this specific object, money, was placed in the world by these instincts in order that they might have something with which they could be active.[18] But they could be active in a thousand other ways without money. Anal eroticism, or the need for punishment, or any other instinctual need that is regarded as biological, is related to the drive to amass wealth, as the destructive instinct is to war—a relationship which I have investigated elsewhere.[19]

In the tendency to trace social institutions directly back to biological instincts, we see the same danger of *biologizing* which we meet, remarkably enough, in the psychoanalytic literature, especially at many points in the theory of neuroses, although in our opinion it is just psychoanalysis that has taught us to value highly enough the rôle of *actual* infantile experience.

For example, attention has been drawn to the fact that the biological helplessness of the human infant, which makes him unable to satisfy his instincts himself, frequently places him in situations where he must do without satisfaction in states of instinctual tension, that is, in "traumatic situations." Such experiences, it was thought, caused the child's ego to feel its own instincts as a danger and this feeling was then the cause of repression. Our opinion, on the contrary, is that such experiences only create the *opportunity* for repression. Whether repression later really occurs or not is decided by reality. In the same way we would say that anal eroticism produces the desire to collect something. What is collected is determined by reality. Let us consider, for example, how a child reared in present-day society becomes familiar with money in everyday life and develops his attitude towards it. Money matters must impress him as a secret; he encounters money as gift, as possession, and finally as the epitome of value. Not only does an interest in money arise from the primitive conflicts of anal eroticism, but the interest in money which is and must be instilled in the child also increases his anal eroticism and in turn arouses the conflicts which formerly raged about the latter.[20]

I would not like to dismiss ontogenetic considerations of this kind without

---

[18] R. Laforgue, *Libido, Angst und Zivilisation*, Vienna, Int. Psa. Verlag, 1932.

[19] O. Fenichel, "Ueber Psychoanalyse, Krieg und Frieden," *Int. Aerztl. Bull.*, Vol. 2, 1935.

[20] Hence it is by no means a case of the instincts being biologically determined and only their objects being socially conditioned. Instead, the instinctual structure itself, especially the relative distribution of libido between genitality and pregenitality—among the individual partial instincts in general—depends to a large extent upon social factors.

saying a few words about the only psychoanalytic attempt to approach a phylogenesis of money. The article about sacred money in Melanesia by Roheim [21] makes the same mistakes as the ontogenetic study by Ferenczi, but far more grossly and therefore more clearly.

Let us show by a single quotation how little Roheim's statements can tell us about the real origin of a money economy because they tell us nothing at all about the actual economic conditions of the peoples of whom they speak. Roheim writes about a tribe that accumulates sacred shell money: ". . . even at this early stage we have to do with an advanced form of capitalist society, . . . high interest rates, illicit tricks, plutocratic arrogance and even swindling. . . ." Since these are his criteria as to whether or not a society is capitalistic, we learn nothing further regarding the economic conditions of that people.

We are trying to study the interplay between an economic system and instinct in order to dispose finally and definitely of the wrongly formulated question: "Is this or that institution to be understood as rational or as irrational?" Roheim, however, writes: "From the very beginning there were two conflicting views of sacrifice; the soberly rationalistic view of a gift for the sake of exchange (*do ut des*) and the mystical view of oral communion." There can be no question of an "either-or" in this, however, but only of a "both-and," and the problem is simply how the mysticism of oral communion could originate from soberly rationalistic needs.

The findings of psychoanalysis regarding the participation of unconscious drives in primitive financial institutions are firmly established. But is it correct to believe that the instinctual drives *create* for themselves an external reality in order to provide a means for their satisfaction? The nature of the relationship of social institutions to the instincts is under discussion here, and this is a basic question in the group of problems concerning the place of psychology in the general understanding of social events. We shall not solve this question in the present paper, and we shall meet it often again.

Here I wish only to say this: Let us think of an invention with a practical and at the same time a sexual symbolic value, for example, a Zeppelin airship which is certainly a sexual symbol but on which people can also fly. In order to understand inventions we must not overlook the *rational necessity* which must be present before an invention can result, and which arises only in a certain social situation. The task which is imposed in reality by necessity can evidently be completed only with the help of instinctual drives. It might be conceivable that a restriction of instincts caused by material circumstances could facilitate that sort of displacement of instinctual energy. (In this connection I was deeply im-

[21] G. Roheim, *op. cit.*

pressed by a paper by Lorenz,[22] which mentions the possibility of taking literally the legends of the lame and ingenious blacksmith. Since through a bodily affliction he is handicapped in his movements and thereby in sexual enjoyment, in hunting and in fighting, he is forced to employ in other ways the instinctual energies which his comrades discharge in these ways. Invention may thus be facilitated for him.) At any rate, sexualization is a *means* for making a real task possible or at least for sweetening it. If an individual wishes to collect things, money does not result therefrom; whenever, on the other hand, a certain economic situation makes money necessary, then this necessity is realized with the help of instinctual collecting wishes.

Roheim's views concerning money and the instinctual drive to become wealthy are approximately as follows: The child wishes to *receive* milk from its mother and later any possible substitutes for milk, but must in return *give up* its excrement. That is the first exchange, the prototype of *commerce*. In itself it is certainly correct that taking and giving arise thus. We may think of the anal-erotic's frequent habit of reading on the toilet; when something is lost from below, something new must be introduced from above. The equilibrium between receiving and giving must be preserved. One's possessions, one's bodily substance must be maintained. This is now combined by Roheim with the hypothesis which Freud developed in *Totem and Taboo*[23] to the following effect: After the death of the primal father, the brothers "invested" with libido the father's corpse instead of the mother as originally desired. They devoured the father's corpse and thus identified themselves with it. Numerous funeral rites show that this corpse with which identification takes place is equivalent in the unconscious to feces. Thus in the case of many peoples the strange funeral rite prevails of defecating ceremoniously upon the grave. The explanation of these symbolic equations through tracing them back to the conditions following the murder of the primal father may be questionable because in the story itself of the death of the primal father many things are questionable that are certainly not yet sufficiently proved to justify Roheim's formulation: "It is well established that in the period following the death of the primal father . . ." What is demonstrated, however, is the unconscious connection between funeral rites and anal eroticism, and the validity of the unconscious equation, feces = dead body.

What has all that to do with money? There are tribes who deposit shell money upon the graves in exactly the same manner in which feces are deposited by the previously described peoples; there are also many legends which leave no doubt about the fact that the unconscious equation, feces = corpse, must be extended

---

[22] E. Lorenz, "Chaos und Ritus," *Imago*, Vol. 17, 1931.
[23] S. Freud, *Totem and Taboo*, New York, Norton, 1952.

to feces = corpse = sacred money = property. That this is not all very clear may be due to the fact that the pregenital thinking that is operating is in itself not clear and does not follow the laws of our logic.

At times, however, Roheim himself is to blame for the lack of clarity. For example, with reference to the association between feces and dead body, there is the following statement making death equivalent to death instinct: "There are associations between life instincts and genital eroticism on the one hand and on the other hand between the death instinct and anal eroticism." He comments further: "The ego-instincts Freud regards as narcissistically modified death instincts; and it is just in the structure of the ego (the character) that anal eroticism plays a particularly important rôle." In these few sentences there are so many distortions and misunderstandings that their more exact analysis would require much space.

We consider the statements concerning the significance of pregenital modes of thinking for the origin of money insufficient if only for the reason that any mention of the economic development is completely lacking. Money has certainly not originated because people for unconscious reasons needed a feces-corpse symbol. Instead, money was made necessary only by the development of an economic system that had reached a certain stage.[24] The same economic development has also influenced the instinctual life. A task set by reality can only be performed with the aid of a certain instinctual structure; conversely, with money once in existence, its very presence alters the instinctual structure.

Every psychological event is to be explained as the resultant of an interplay between biological structure and the influences exerted upon it by the environment. The social institutions that confront a generation act upon it as determining environmental influences. The biological structure itself has developed from the interplay of earlier structures and earlier experiences. Now, however, how have the social institutions themselves originated? Was it not, in the final analysis, through human beings who were attempting to satisfy their own needs? Yes, these individuals came into relationships with one another. But such relationships become external realities, which operate further, and the individuals who have created them can no longer escape from them. This is because these relationships continue to react through stimuli of many kinds upon human beings who thereby are themselves modified and then through their behavior again alter the environment anew.

Therefore Roheim's statement is to be absolutely rejected when he speaks of the psychoanalytic discovery of connections between money and anal eroticism

---

[24] A sociological investigation of the origin of money presupposes at the very outset a knowledge of the development of private property and its inequalities.

as "the psychoanalytically discovered origin of money" and calls the shell-money custom of primitive funerals "a historical proof of this origin."

Studies of the problems which Roheim set for himself fulfil an urgent need, but they ought to be approached with more adequate means. We ought not only to study primitive societies (their economic structure is not always easy to scrutinize) but our study should be based on as many historical examples as possible so that we may compare the drive to amass wealth in other times and societies with that of today. As far as the present is concerned, we must declare that the sociologist is right in explaining the present-day impetus to become wealthy on the grounds that the capitalist who does not accumulate wealth is practically ruined.

We shall only draw attention to the fact that the so determined impetus to become wealthy enters into complicated psychological connections and creates and utilizes modifications of instinct not only in the sphere of self-preservation. We shall also impress upon the sociologists that the study of these modifications of instinct is in no way an unessential bagatelle, but is of the greatest importance theoretically as well as practically. The statements that the production and dissemination of the ideology of a society must be understood from the actual economic conditions of this society, the "superstructure" of which is the ideology; that further they are to be understood from the fact that this "superstructure," by means of the actions of human beings, reacts back again upon the "foundation," the economic conditions modifying them—these statements are correct but general. They become more specific when we succeed in comprehending scientifically the details of the mechanisms of these transformations, and only psychoanalysis is able to help us in that.

The needs of human beings which seek satisfaction are the cause of production. The development of production and also of the principles of distribution constitute the history of mankind. It is not my task to investigate at what point and through which motives in the course of this development there arose a capitalism that had to create the general ideal of amassing wealth. I can only affirm that it cannot be the result of an "anal-erotic mutation" that has fallen from heaven. Both the invention of money and alterations in the nature of money could be possible only with the existence of a certain intensity of anal-erotic instincts and above all with the existence of a certain amount of restraint upon the anal-erotic instincts. However, the restraints in turn must likewise have their previous history and their material determinants. Thus there takes place a continual reciprocal action between external reality and the instinctual structure modified by it.[25]

---

[25] In this connection Annie Reich brought to my attention the observation that any suppression of anal-erotic instinct already presupposes a certain economic stability of possessions. If people did not

A drive to accumulate wealth exists only in certain definite social epochs. It would be a fatal error if the Marxist theory that economic reality governs the world were interpreted to mean that an instinctual drive to become wealthy governs it. On the contrary, reflection on the significant influence of economic evolution upon all the conditions of mankind shows us that such a drive at one time did not exist and at some future time will exist no longer.[26]

---

have permanent dwelling places or possessions that need to be kept clean, then no suppression of the pleasure in soiling would be necessary. Evidence for this is offered us by the different cleanliness habits of nest-perching and nest-deserting birds.

[26] Since this paper was completed at the end of 1934, the psychoanalytic investigation of ego psychology has taught us more about the ontogenesis of the ego and its peculiarities and about the drive for power and prestige, above all in its function of warding off anxiety. We have learned also that the nature and degree, not only of these anxieties but also of the relative part of the drive for power and prestige in the measures for warding off anxiety, as well as the aims (the achievement of which brings power and prestige) are socially determined. With the help of this knowledge some points in this paper could have been formulated a little differently and more precisely. The author hopes, nevertheless, that the article will be of interest as a call to reflection in the application of psychoanalysis to social questions and as a warning against "biologizing."

EIGHT

Ego Disturbances and
Their Treatment[*]

It has frequently been pointed out in recent years that the ego has taken the place originally occupied by the instincts as the chief object of psychoanalytical investigation. Freud, in his book *The Ego and the Id,* opened up the realm of ego psychology by introducing the so-called structural point of view: that is, the conception that, under the influence of the external world, an organ resembling an exterior layer covering the pith of the unconscious instinct reservoir of the id gradually becomes differentiated and acts as a mediator between the organism and the external world. In accordance with the traditions of psychoanalysis, which was from the first a genetic psychology that attempted to understand the finished structure from a developmental point of view, ego psychology has become primarily concerned with the origin and development of the ego. As a matter of history, it is by no means the case that systematic analysis was employed from the beginning to reduce to their unconscious components and historical genesis the resistances preventing the discovering of the id; to begin with, on the contrary, unsystematic analysis and every variety of suggestion had the effect of putting these resistances out of action. Only the knowledge thus gained of the instincts—the so-called "biological" part of the human personality —made the study of the rise of the opposing forces possible. With ego research, as has repeatedly been said, psychoanalysis once more approaches the nonanalytical psychologies. Adler was right in saying that problems of character, in particular those of "directive lines," "fictions," and "arrangements"—all the tricks by which the defensive ego avoids facing unpleasant realities—had long been neglected. But it was owing to this neglect that psychoanalysis was able to obtain

---

[*] First published in *Int. J. Psa.,* Vol. 19, 1938, pp. 416–438.

the means it lacked, so that today it is possible for us to make an approach to the problem which is not merely descriptive or teleological. The problem of form also admits of a genetic approach. The superficial mental variations in individual human beings as well as in different races and periods were, it is true, recognized later than the comparatively undifferentiated, more uniform instincts; they were, however, recognized in terms of their genesis and explained as the result of the influence of certain types of external stimuli on comparatively constant instinctual structures. Ego peculiarities—like everything noninstinctual in the human mind—are understood to have developed from instincts under the influence of the external world. The cellular theory, for example, does not assert that all living substance consists of cells: it is justified if it succeeds in proving that the noncellular components of living substance, peripheral nerves or intercellular substances, for example, are all produced by cellular activity. In exactly the same way, the psychoanalytical instinctual psychology will be justified if it can show that the noninstinctual mental formations are derived from the instincts under the influence of the external world. It is for this reason that Freud's short paper on "Negation" [1] appears to me to be of fundamental importance to ego psychology: in it the function of judgment, apparently far removed from anything instinctual, is proved to have arisen from the instincts.

It is essential to find a mean between two extreme points of view, both of which are obviously equally wrong. The supporters of the first are still so engrossed in the original discoveries of psychoanalysis that they are only interested in the deepest, genetically earliest, layers—the still undifferentiated basis which is similar in all men. They are not interested in comprehending the surface as the differentiated product of the instincts (which had been earlier recognized) but proceed no further than the first task—that of comprehending those instincts. They misunderstand the nature of psychoanalysis as a "depth psychology," since they think that only the depths are interesting. To explain a manifest phenomenon they mistakenly think that only its deepest and most undifferentiated instinctual basis is of importance—whereas events that occur later under the influence of experiences arising from that basis are in fact usually of greater importance. This position may be clearly exemplified by the attitude of some analysts to the phenomenon of so-called "pseudo-sexuality." Since they find the effects of concealed sexual components behind many superficial masks, they therefore believe that they are gaining access to these instinctual components whenever they meet with any form of manifest sexual activity. Sometimes, however, external sexual actions may form a superficial layer covering a strong sexual inhibition which its subject wishes to repudiate.

The supporters of the opposite extreme so concentrate attention on the dif-

[1] S. Freud, "Negation," *Coll. Pap.*, Vol. V, London, Hogarth, 1950.

ferentiated surface that they neglect the specifically analytical point of view; that is, proof of differentiation from instinctual origins. Some time ago, for example, I felt it necessary to utter a warning against the danger arising from the recognition of the so-called "libidinization of anxiety," of seeing in the libido only a neutralizing agent for anxiety and ignoring its genuine biological nature. The recently published volume upon *The Neurotic Personality of Our Time*,[2] by Karen Horney, furnishes us with an example of such neglect of the importance of ego-dystonic forces in the motivation of the human mental phenomena recognized by psychoanalysis. It speaks up courageously for ego psychology, for the complexity of the current processes in the unconscious parts of the ego, and for the necessity of a thorough investigation at precisely the points at which some analysts believe that they can pass lightly over "surfaces." Even more courageously, it stresses the importance of existing social and cultural circumstances for mental phenomena—and in particular, for the neuroses. But it empties out the baby with the bath. It discards the biological point of view along with the biologistic one. It forgets the id while concentrating on the differentiation of the ego and takes from psychoanalysis its biological basis—that of instinctual needs.

One asks oneself, when reading such works, how it is possible to forget the libido theory to such an extent when its importance has once been comprehended. One easily finds an answer: bitter necessity, rather than the systematic progress of analytical research, has turned our attention to ego processes. The neurotics who demand analytic treatment today differ from those who went to Freud thirty or forty years ago. It is clear that analytical practice and theory must be adapted to these changed forms of neurosis; thus it may happen that instead of being applied to this new field, the fundamental principles of Freudian psychology are discarded as unsuitable.

The differences between the "modern" and the classical neuroses have often been described. In the classical neuroses there was a comparatively intact personality—disturbed at certain points by inappropriate actions, impulses, or thoughts which were felt to be completely foreign to it. The personality of the modern neurotic does not appear to be uniform but is torn or deformed and, in any case, so involved in the illness that one cannot say at what point health ends and illness begins. There is a very gradual transition from neurotics to those "psychopaths" and persons with "character anomalies," who themselves feel their need for treatment less than do the people around them.

It would be a fascinating task to investigate the real cause of this change in neurotic forms. This, however, lies outside both the competence of the analyst and the scope of this paper. I merely wish to suggest where I should look for the answer to this question. The method and manner in which the ego admits,

[2] K. Horney, *The Neurotic Personality of Our Time*, New York, Norton, 1937.

repels, or modifies instinctual claims depend to a large extent on the way in which it has been taught to regard them by the surrounding world. During the last decades morality, this educational attitude to the instincts, has changed very much in our European and American cultures. Classical hysteria works chiefly with the defensive mechanism of genuine repression, which, however, presupposes a simple prohibition of talk concerning the objectionable instincts, chiefly sexual, which upbringing has consistently represented as bad. The inconsistency of present-day education, itself undecided as to which instinctual claims to allow and which to suppress, results in initial license and subsequent sudden, unexpected, and therefore more cruel deprivation. This inconsistency in education corresponds to the inconsistency of the neurotic personality. The change in the neuroses, it seems to me, reflects the change in morality. In order to understand this, however, one would have to investigate the sociological changes which have taken place in our culture in the last decades. In any case, the present-day neurotic characters appear to us to possess egos restricted by defensive measures: they lose energy through their continual anti-cathexis, and lose differentiation through renunciation, because, owing to their inability to respond to external stimuli by any but set reactions, they are lacking in vivacity and elasticity. Freud [3] has said that "it is always possible for the ego to avoid a rupture in any of its relations by deforming itself, submitting to forfeit something of its unity, or in the long run even to being gashed and rent. Thus the illogicalities, eccentricities and follies of mankind would fall into a category similar to their sexual perversions, for by accepting them they spare themselves repressions." Since the maintenance of these eccentricities must surely correspond to the reaction type and demand an expenditure of energy, it would perhaps be more correct to say that their formation corresponds to a single definite act of repression, so that the necessity for subsequent separate repressions, which would require more energy, and separate anxiety situations is avoided. In this way, the ego-restricting attitudes, which act as chronic anchorages of instinctual defense, are not experienced as ego-dystonic symptoms but are worked into the ego. Their constant operation prevents the instinct from becoming manifest so that we see no living conflict between instinct and defense but something rigid which does not necessarily appear to the patient himself as questionable. The question for us lies in the relative constancy of the defensive attitude assumed by the ego when faced by different demands both from the external world and from instinctual contents.

It might be asked whether we are justified in considering that all these ego alterations are built according to the plan of obsessional neurotic reaction formations, that is, as displays of anti-cathexis, hindering the expression of contrary

[3] S. Freud, "Neurosis and Psychosis," *Coll. Pap.*, Vol. II, London, Hogarth, 1948.

instinctual attitudes, which, nevertheless, can still break through in various ways. Some pathological attitudes give the impression of attempting to satisfy instincts directly rather than to suppress them.

It would, of course, be incorrect to consider that the word "character" is synonymous with the expression "defensive attitudes rooted in the character." The organization of instinctual energies, the way in which the ego behaves in relation to instinctual actions, how it combines its various tasks in order to find a satisfactory solution—all these, too, go to make up character. Psychoanalytic characterology will probably have to make a fundamental distinction between those character traits in which, possibly after alteration of aim and object under the influence of the ego, the original instinctual energy is discharged freely and those of the defensive type—in which psychoanalysis, as an "unmasking" psychology, has proved that the original instinctual attitude, which is contrary to the manifest attitude, still exists in the unconscious. The second type of attitude is betrayed either by its cramped nature, by the occasional breaking through of that which has been repressed, or merely by the amount of energy consumed, resulting in inhibition due to general economic impoverishment. Since we wish to discuss ego disturbances, we shall confine our attention to this second type of attitude.

We must also remember that just as there is a pseudo-sexuality which appears to be a sexual attitude, but in which there is in reality a sexual defense, so there are ego attitudes which appear to be instinctual but which serve chiefly a defensive function. We must therefore learn to use the expression "defense" and "instinct," and "ego" and "id" in the relative sense in which they are intended.

To explain what I mean, I should like to remind you of an idea advanced by Alexander.[4] He considered that there were two types of neurosis. The first type was produced by a fundamental conflict between an instinct and a defensive impulse on the part of the ego—for example, an oedipus wish and a fear of being castrated for it; the second type was produced by a conflict between two instincts —for example, between an oedipus wish and a passive, feminine desire for castration. I am of the opinion, however, that the nature of the id is such that no contradictions are possible in it: instincts with contradictory contents can be satisfied one after the other—sometimes even by common derivatives (representation by the opposite). There is, of course, the second type of neurosis; but the instinctual conflict at the bottom of it is always a structural conflict as well, in that one of the opposing instincts is always nearer to the ego—sustained by an ego defense or strengthened for purposes of ego defense, so that although it is an instinct, it acts as an instinctual defense relatively to the more deeply repressed instincts. We have only to imagine the dynamics of the mind clearly enough.

[4] F. Alexander, "The Relation of Structural and Instinctual Conflicts," *Psa. Quart.*, Vol. 2, 1933.

It is not a case of one instinct fighting against a defensive impulse; there are always variations—a lively fight and a reciprocal penetration. A defense rarely brings a fight to a decisive standstill, since the rejected impulses nearly always break through the defense and there follows further repression of the defense, which itself includes instinctual components. There are reaction formations against reaction formations. In addition to the three-layer arrangement—instinct, defense, instinct breaking through again—there is the arrangement—instinct, defense, repression of the defense. A man, for example, who has become passively feminine from castration anxiety may overcompensate this defense by particularly accentuated masculine behavior.

The technical rule, "Defense interpretation precedes id interpretation," does not always mean dealing with one topic while ignoring another; it often means that certain qualities or connections of a topic are dealt with before certain others. I would remind you that the analysis of so-called "impulsive characters" showed that in them there is not a genuine lack of instinctual suppression—that they do not, like animals, give free expression to their instinctual impulses with unbroken narcissism. It showed, on the contrary, that—in so far as there has not been a complete breakdown of certain defenses—their structure is like that of the perversions, where the necessary condition for maintaining the defense against one instinct is the expression of another.

We can therefore describe all the ego disturbances which interest us as, fundamentally, "defensive attitudes." In considering the defensive attitudes of an individual, we can divide them into those which are occasional and those which are habitual. We can further divide the habitual group, since there are some individuals who adopt a certain defensive attitude only in certain situations, while others remain in a comparatively constant defensive attitude, suggesting that the instinctual temptation which must be repressed is continually present. There are people who are impudent, polite, indifferent, or ready to prove others at fault, in all situations and to all or nearly all people. Such attitudes may be described as "character defenses" in the narrower sense in contrast to other types of defense.

Can the appearance of such character attitudes in relation to the analyst be described as "transference"? If one defines transference as the repetition toward the analyst of attitudes previously found in other situations, or if one defines transference as misunderstanding the present in the sense of the past, the answer is "Yes." These, however, are not specific reactions to the analyst which change as the situation changes; these attitudes are neither specific for the analysis nor for any past situation, but are rigid, general, and unspecific. They cannot therefore be compared with the "transference situation" in that more exact sense which means that the patient reacts in an agile and specific manner to the analyst just as in the past he reacted, or wished to react, to a definite person. What factors determine whether a patient produces lively transference resistances or rigid character resistances? Is the determining factor the question whether the defense was formed at an earlier period, at a time when the ego, still only capable of relationships with part-objects, was indifferent to the people around it? Or is it that real object relationships were present only in the first group, while, in the second, people in the external world were used only as a means to relieve an endopsychic conflict? It is certainly more valuable to assume that the difference depends on whether an instinctual conflict has developed from its original position and spread over the subject's whole life, or whether it has remained localized in one place. It depends, in other words, on whether the ego shuts out the anxiety and the symptom after their first appearance by continued repression—a repression which is then broken through in the transference situation—or whether the ego builds them into itself and so changes its own nature. I wish here to make a slight digression. Alexander [5] has asserted that the "neurotic character" (defined by him as one in whom the unsettled conflicts of childhood continually urge him on to perform purposeless actions in the present day) is more easily influenced by psychoanalysis than a patient with a symptom neurosis. The reason for this, he says, is that in the latter the subject has regressed from the alloplastic to the autoplastic, so that after a successful analysis he must pluck up courage in order to make the next step, which is to take action in real life; whereas this necessity does not arise with the neurotic character, who is continually acting out his conflicts in real life. I should like to contradict this thesis emphatically. The pseudo-alloplastic attitude of the neurotic character cannot be changed into a healthy alloplastic one except by first being turned, for a time, into a neurotic autoplastic attitude, which can then be treated like an ordinary symptom neurosis. Internal conflicts which involve hardened pseudo-object–relationships must first of all be changed back into internal conflicts and must be dealt with as such before normal object relationships can take their place. We may thus state a technical rule: in order to be able to treat character resistances, one must first of all change them into transference resistances.

We have now reached the technical problem about which I really wish to speak, namely, the treatment of ego disturbances. Once one has grasped the nature of these ego disturbances, the therapeutic task is easy to describe theoretically. It is only necessary to keep the principle of the psychoanalytic method in mind. That method demonstrates the derivatives of repressed material as such and so leads to the toleration of less and less distorted derivatives and gradually confronts the ego with its repressed contents; in thus removing the isolation of those contents from the whole personality and allowing the repressed instincts

[5] F. Alexander, "The Neurotic Character," *Int. J. Psa.*, Vol. 11, 1930.

to catch up with the development which the ego as a whole has passed through in the meantime, it changes infantile into adult sexuality, and so makes an ordered sexual life possible, with consequent development of sublimations and condemnatory judgments on the part of the ego.

In applying this principle to the chronic defensive ego attitudes, we see first of all that we can only reach the repressed instincts by gradually undermining the opposing defenses, which can always be demonstrated earlier than the repressed impulses themselves. When analysis wishes to make unconscious material accessible to the ego and to connect up with the ego apparently involuntary happenings, this connection seems incredible to the patient as regards his symptoms. Attempts of this sort in relation to the symptoms are therefore contra-indicated as being what might be described as "too deep" interpretations. The secretly active component in apparently passive experience can only be demonstrated by showing at the most superficial point that the patient hinders his impulses and their outlet and how he does so. There is one difficulty about this. The unconscious instinct which presses forward to consciousness and motor discharge is our ally, the defending ego is our enemy. This is true, but we are in the position of a general who is separated from his allies by the enemy's front. In order to combine our strength with that of the rejected instinct, we must first of all reach it. For this we need to enlist a further ally, the reasonable ego, which is accessible to us. This requires to be separated from the defending element. To continue the comparison, we must first of all undermine the enemy's front with propaganda and win over a large part of his force.

When, therefore, a patient with ego disturbances actively demonstrates them in the same way in which (let us say) an obsessional neurotic draws attention to his obsessive symptoms, the further procedure of the analyst seems fairly straightforward. Difficulties may arise, however, when the patient does not recognize in himself what the analyst perceives—i.e., a rigid attitude in which the chief part of the energies which the analysis aims at setting free is tonically bound—or when the nature of such an attitude is such as to interfere with the process of analysis. The analytic procedure relies on the co-operation of the reasonable ego, to which it demonstrates unnoticed instinctual derivatives. Freud,[6] therefore, has said that "a fairly reliable character" is one of the preliminary conditions for successful analysis. And yet we are now discussing the possibility of treating an "unreliable character" by analysis. Freud, in his recent paper,[7] has emphasized the fact that the ego disturbances which result from some infantile instinctual conflicts form one of the chief hindrances to the therapeutic efficacy of analysis. Analysis has often been forced by necessity to occupy itself with the problem of

[6] S. Freud, "On Psychotherapy," Coll. Pap., Vol. I, London, Hogarth, 1948.
[7] S. Freud, "Analysis Terminable and Interminable," Coll. Pap., Vol. V.

character analysis, a problem which also arises from the simple reflection that, from the dynamic point of view, in analysis our aim is to remove resistances, not to strengthen unconscious instincts. The recent book by Anna Freud [8] which has been quoted by Freud, also shows the principle on which we base our work: we split the ego, as it were, and demonstrate its attitude to the observing reasonable element which is still present. We let the observing element feel that this attitude is tendentious and self-made; we disclose its purpose and finally reduce it to the historical situation in which it was formed, just as we do with symptoms, which are more in the nature of distorted id expressions.

"This must not be taken to imply that they [the ego difficulties] make analysis impossible. On the contrary, they constitute half of our analytic task." Freud is here referring to the confrontation of ego analysis and id analysis by Anna Freud. She is of the opinion that in order not to be one-sided both are necessary; the task is to make the id accessible by means of ego analysis. Before the defensive front has been broken down, it would be useless to point out an unconscious instinctual claim. But this half of the work is very difficult. First of all, it is necessary to bring about the division of the ego previously mentioned. The defending part of the ego, which is interested in maintaining the resistance, is our enemy, and the reasonable element, the ego which could help us, is, to begin with, powerless against this defending element. It belongs to the nature of resistance that it will not let itself be discovered without resistance. The possibility of mastering this difficulty depends upon quantitative factors. In addition, a part is played in the ego attitude by constitutional factors over which we have no influence. "The psychological peculiarities of families, races and nations, even in their attitude towards analysis, admit of no other explanation." We also think it possible that an exact historical analysis of the defenses would teach us that members of the same families, races, and nations are often exposed to similar external influences in childhood; even if this factor is taken into consideration, however, a constitutional remainder is left. Those factors described by Freud in *The Problem of Anxiety* as "resistance of the id" must also be considered. An obsessional neurotic patient once compared the attempt at curing a neurotic with the help of his reasonable insight, precisely when that insight has been disturbed by his illness, with trying to dry a man, who has fallen into the water holding a towel, with the towel that has been made useless by the very set of circumstances which it is hoped to remedy. What one must do is to find the "dry places" in the towel—that is, to work with the healthy remainder of the personality, which increases in size as analytic work progresses; in cases where this healthy remainder appears to be lacking, it must be produced by a preparatory pedagogical period.

[8] A. Freud, *The Ego and the Mechanisms of Defence*, New York, Int. Univ. Press, 1946.

This, then, is the situation with which we are concerned. To begin with, there was a conflict, urgent and alive. The subject withdrew from this struggle by means of a permanent ego alteration. The forces which at one time opposed each other are now wasted in the useless and hardened defensive attitudes of the ego: the conflict has become latent. It is only by dividing the reasonable observing ego from the automatic, defensive, experiencing element, that we are able to set free the bound energy, and thus to reactivate the old conflict, in much the same way as we do with every transference interpretation.

Does it therefore follow, according to our view, that every obsessional character must experience acute anxiety during the course of an analysis? I do not think he need necessarily experience these anxiety attacks in their full force; though this is true only because they can be avoided by correct doses of analysis. I am, however, of the opinion that he is theoretically liable to experience such attacks as had been previously avoided by means of his obsessional character. The substitution of mobility at points which have become hardened must not be produced by shock; analytic results must of their nature be produced gradually. Obsessional neurotics may experience anxiety attacks during the course of an analysis, and one need not fear them. I am, however, skeptical about analysts who are too fond of such upheavals. When a patient is too phlegmatic at the beginning of an analysis, one does not know immediately whether this is due to a real lack of affect, or to the suppression of a particularly strong affect—just as in the case of a dream fragment that is devoid of affect, where it is not clear at first whether the lack of affect is due to the unimportance of the fragment or whether the expression of affect has been prevented by anti-cathexis. Two locomotives of the same strength under full steam and pulling in opposite directions do not move any more than two unfired locomotives. But just as the consumption of coal would show which was the actual state of affairs, so in the case of the patient does the consumption of energy. The phlegmatic attitude as a form of defense is either very fatiguing or is revealed by rigidity in all or particular parts of the muscular system. A patient can inform us that the action of his bowels is in order in a manner that shows that his anal-erotic conflicts are unsettled just as clearly as if he informs us that he suffers from continuous constipation or diarrhea. In such cases, the associations, too, emerge so characteristically "in order" that it is clear that one must first reduce them to disorder before bringing them back into real order. It is comparatively easy to see what must be done; the correct analytical task is to thaw the frozen energies of the phlegmatic attitude. It is, however, much more difficult to fulfill this task—to find the place where the system is most insecure, where the neurotic defense is weak, the points and times, in other words, where the fight between instinct and defense has remained most alive. What has to be done is to rectify displacements, undo isolations, and lead back affect traces to where they belong.

I am therefore of the opinion that the general technical rule that "The patient determines the subject of the session" requires a reservation. One cannot, of course, force on a patient what does not interest him. You will remember, for example, how the attempt of Little Hans's [9] father to interpret the oedipus complex necessarily failed because, at the time, anal-erotic material was uppermost. It is by no means always by what he talks about, however, that the patient "determines the theme," but often by not talking, or by the way in which he talks, or by what he does. In this connection attempts at more systematic analysis are frequently misunderstood. We cannot give the analyst directions that will be applicable to every case. It seems, however, that some things which are not mentioned by the patient spontaneously are shown involuntarily, and that it is then the task of the analyst to speak about them. This is not a particular kind of "activity" on the part of the analyst, it is dynamic interpretation. One must always work at the point at which the affect is really located at the moment; moreover, since the patient may not know where this is, one must seek first of all to find it.

Our opinion—that ego disturbances are only amenable to analytic treatment in so far as latent conflicts are changed into current ones—appears to contradict Freud's statement in "Analysis Terminable and Interminable" that precisely this is impossible. We must, however, ask ourselves whether by the mobilization of latent conflicts Freud means the same as we do. His arguments as to the incompleteness of what analysis can achieve, since something of that which has been overcome must always remain even when a higher stage in mental development has been reached, are extraordinarily clear and compelling. It seems to me, however, that precisely this statement of Freud's indicates the task of an economically correct guidance of analysis, namely, of attacking at the exact points at which the decisive conflicts are present at that moment in a latent form. To our surprise, however, Freud writes that one would have to "turn a possible future conflict into a present one," but that this is not possible: for, he says, "tempting as it may be to our therapeutic ambition to propose such tasks for itself, experience bids us refuse them out of hand."

In order to transform a latent instinctual conflict into a present one, he goes on, "clearly there are only two things we can do; either we can bring about situations in which the conflict becomes actual or we can content ourselves with discussing it in analysis." The first is not possible because "we have so far rightly left to

9 S. Freud, "Analysis of a Phobia in a Five-Year-Old Boy," *Coll. Pap.*, Vol. III, London, Hogarth, 1948.

fate" the task of bringing fresh suffering into life. The second is useless since mere discussion will not help any more than reading Freud's works will cure a neurosis. It is easy to reject these two alternatives; but it is not so clear that these are the only two possibilities. There is a third one. It is a question of mobilizing latent conflicts, not of creating conflicts which are not there. Latent conflicts are never entirely latent. The analyst is accustomed to divining the presence of great conflicts lying behind the smallest sign. It is his task to show so clearly to the patient the "reality" of these conflicts, to make these signs so objective, that his ego can recognize them as rationalizations, irruptions, and derivatives of the latent conflict behind them. It seems to me that if we wish to settle the latent conflict, to make the decisive part of he hardened instinctual energy capable of discharge, and so to restore mental health, we must indeed first "turn a possible future conflict into a present one." This means that we must in fact provoke situations in which the conflict becomes actual—but neither by playing the part of fate in the real life of the patient, nor by joining in the transference through systematic, artificial behavior of our own, but by psycho-analysing those points at which the latent conflicts show themselves and by demonstrating their derivatives and making objective the attitude toward them taken by the observing ego.

What is the aim of this mobilization? It is the reduction of the ego attitudes to those historical situations in which they were originally formed. The special quality of those attitudes depends on a number of factors: partly on the hereditary constitution of the ego, partly on the nature of the instincts against which the defense is chiefly directed, partly on the age at which the child experienced this instinctual conflict. In most cases, however, the analysis succeeds in showing that the special attitude was forced on the individual by the external world, either because it was the most suitable attitude in a given situation or because of some past identification.

A special problem in the investigation of this historical situation is the so-called "defense transference." This is no doubt caused by two things. The first is the general human tendency to order one's actions according to experience, to retain whenever possible something which has once proved to be expedient, to encounter a danger in the same way that has previously proved useful against a similar danger, even when in the meantime changes have taken place which make what was previously suitable manifestly unsuitable. The problem remains why a previous "danger situation" is experienced as such even when it has ceased to be one. The answer is a dialectic one: precisely because of the defense achieved at that time, the whole conflict was separated from the reasonable ego; the capacity to judge this type of danger has consequently not developed in the meantime with the rest of the personality.

In the second place, the individual wishes to "transfer his instincts." He always strives after the same satisfaction, but his ego always responds to these strivings by producing memories which once aroused anxiety. When, in the process of psychoanalysis, the highly unpleasurable "passing of the oedipus complex" is repeated in the transference, it is only in a relative sense that this repetition appears to be "beyond the pleasure principle," since the individual still strives for the pleasure of instinctual satisfaction: it is the external world which forces the ego to experience pain instead of the desired pleasure, in order to avoid even worse pain.

If it be possible to reduce "ego fixation" and "ego regression," like "instinctual fixation" and "instinctual regression," to a definite historical psychogenic situation, then one must be clear as to the exact meaning of these words. Ego fixations and ego regressions may involve the *whole* ego—constitution and experience functioning, as usual, as a complemental series—in which case we are faced with an "infantile type"; or *part* of the ego may be involved, which, again, can have various implications.

Single ego functions may retain certain features of the primitive phases for an unduly long time, or may assume them again. In this sense we can describe the "eidetic type" as perception fixations. Or the way of thinking may have retained a more magical character than is normal. This happens, for instance, with every obsessional neurotic, in whom a very early and strong intellectual development contrasts sharply with the beliefs in omnipotence and the law of talion which characterize the unconscious parts of the ego. The manner of treating objects may also show primitive features: there may be fixation at the preliminary stages of love, at the aims of oral incorporation, or at the regulation of self-feeling of little children. Finally (and, despite its fundamental importance, attention has only been turned to this during the last few years) the ego fixations may be restricted to certain kinds of defense—about which we have already spoken—which the ego habitually uses whenever it objects to an instinct.

It is, perhaps, also important to mention that the words "ego" and "id" (here as elsewhere) must not be taken too rigidly. On closer examination of even an ordinary instinctual fixation, one usually finds that this is due not only to a particular satisfaction or frustration of the instinct in question, but that the fixation serves, at the same time, as a defense or a reassurance, in that the satisfaction of an instinct is particularly suitable for the purpose of denying or repudiating the anxiety produced by another instinct. "Instinct fixations" thus have a structure similar to that of the perversions. On this matter, I must therefore admit that Mrs. Riviere † was right when she maintained that this was true of jealousy,

---

† Mrs. Riviere contributed a paper on "Jealousy as Mechanism of Defence" to the *Int. J. Psa.*, Vol. 13, 1932. It was discussed at some length by Fenichel in his "A Contribution to the Psychology of

whereas I was of the opinion that an oral-sadistic fixation could only be explained by the mere experience of having been "spoiled" in that sphere. (She reproached me for not taking the unconscious fantasies of the patient seriously enough because I put *"etwa"* before a formulation which remained vague. My answer to this is that the fantasies of the pregenital period *are* vague and can never be exactly reproduced in words.)

I should now like to attempt to show the historical genesis of defensive attitudes by a few examples. Lack of time forces me to choose examples in which the attitudes in question are anchored in the character and of a very conspicuous nature, so that the historical circumstances which necessitated these attitudes may appear macroscopically understandable. As I cannot give three complete case histories, I must limit myself to relating their chief features. I am convinced that these cases do not offer any very special features but that similar features can be found in every analysis. It is precisely because of this that they appear to me such characteristic examples of what occurs in the treatment of ego disturbances.

The first patient I am going to describe could be called "a Don Juan of achievement." A successful and, in his own line, prominent man, he was in fact always dissatisfied with himself, always striving after higher achievements, with external success, but no sense of inward satisfaction. In a like manner, he was always trying to increase his quite adequate income and was unable to overcome his anxiety that it might be insufficient. He behaved in the same way in his love life: although women ran after him and he had one success after another, he always felt inwardly dissatisfied—which is understandable, since these relationships were completely lacking in tenderness and had none of the characteristics of a real object relationship. It is clear that the man was so dominated by an overwhelming narcissistic necessity that the libidinal aims of his instincts were completely overshadowed. The man was married to a woman considerably older than himself, who, in some ways, behaved toward him as a mother does to her child; she acted, that is, in many ways as a guardian to him, so that he, the big, successful man, was more like a little child at home. He found this dependence very oppressive, it is true, and was in the habit of revenging himself on his wife by attacks of rage, by continual unfaithfulness, and by complete lack of consideration. Thus each of them made life a torture to the other. The first defensive function of his persistently unsatisfied wish to be a great man must therefore have been to deceive himself with regard to the fact that he was a little child in so many ways—one of which was his complete lack of consideration for the person who mothered

Jealousy" (No. 31, *First Series*), to which Mrs. Riviere replied in a postscript to the German translation of her original paper: "Eifersucht als Abwehrmechanismus," *Int. Z. Psa.,* Vol. 22, 1936.—Trans. note.

him. This impression is strengthened by the knowledge that his wife was continually goading his ambition, just as his mother was in his childhood. The realization that there was something behind his continued dissatisfaction, which persisted despite all his external successes, and the truth of which he did not wish to admit, was gained in transference analysis. As in every other province, he was very ambitious in analysis and wanted to impress both me and himself by his quick success. At the outset, after he had read Freud, he was forthcoming with theories about his childhood; he grasped comparatively quickly, however, that this was not what mattered to me, and then began to observe himself and his behavior, and to behave like a "favorite pupil," continually stressing, however, the fact that the analysis progressed too slowly and that he was not satisfied with himself. On one occasion, at the last session before the holidays, he came late, because, just as he was starting for his analysis, he had a sudden attack of diarrhea, and this for the first time shook him very much. The bowels putting in their say made him experience the reality of the analysis in an entirely new way. He realized that his continual haste only served the purpose of drowning something else in him. The analysis explained this richly overdetermined diarrhea in the first place as an anxiety equivalent; it then brought this at first incomprehensible anxiety into relation with his anxiety of insufficient success, insufficient sexual objects, and insufficient earning. It was then discovered that the character formation of the patient had been complete in childhood. He had always been go-ahead, cheeky, outwardly successful; he had always been the first, even in being naughty, but had, nevertheless, always been dissatisfied with himself. In this behavior he had obeyed his mother, who had always been very ambitious for her son and had always urged him on to further deeds. When it appeared that, at bottom, his mother had despised his father, who was a tradesman, and had always said to the boy, "You must do better than your father," etc., it became clear that his behavior expressed a particular form of the return of the oedipus complex out of repression; it was not yet intelligible, however, why it had taken this form—why it had this essentially narcissistic note. Various things soon became more obvious, however: his father had illegally sold certain goods, the sale of which was only permitted by special concession; the policeman, therefore, was a dreaded figure in the patient's childhood. In the eyes of the boy, this considerably reduced the power of the father; he determined not to be frightened when he was big, but to make policemen afraid of him. (He remained faithful to this intention: as a motorist, he loved to get policemen to intervene unjustifiably, and then afterward prove them to be in the wrong.) The circumstances at his home, moreover, were such that at times he had to stand behind the counter and serve when he was six years old. The customers liked the little boy, and chose to buy from him; he felt this to be a triumph over his father, whom he already regarded as weak. There were, also, two later experiences, which particularly accentuated both the continuous need to show his superiority in some such way and the impossibility of satisfying that need.

At the age of fourteen, in the first place, he was seduced by a maid, with whom he had regular sexual intercourse from that time on. This episode had been changed in memory, to make it appear that it was he who had, at this age, seduced the grown-up girl. It needed analysis to convince him that it had happened the other way round, and that the whole of his later attitude to women was an attempt to alter this to him painful memory in accordance with his wishes. This attempt, by the way, failed in a typical manner: he intended that the large number of women whom he persuaded to have intercourse with him should convince him of his active masculinity, which he unconsciously doubted; more detailed analysis, however, showed that he arranged it so that he seduced the women into showing their willingness and that it was only when he saw this that he was not able to resist them. At seventeen, in the second place, he had an abscess on the lung for which he was operated on several times and which kept him in bed for months and convalescent for years—so that he had to be passively nursed like a little child.

He gradually became afraid of the transference in analysis, afraid that he might become "enslaved" to the analyst. His transference attitude was intended from the beginning to repudiate this anxiety. He attempted, even then, to disparage the analyst and to find "policemen" who were superior to him. The expected then proved to be true: the six-year-old salesman could not feel completely superior to his grown-up father in the role of tradesman. His father, who used to beat him a great deal, had been greatly feared by him in earlier years. His relation to him had completely overshadowed his relation with his mother, and, in consequence, his being needed by his father for business purposes had an additional libidinal value. The passive narcissistic attitude was suggested to him in his early childhood by particular circumstances including, among others, illness, strict prohibition against masturbation which put an end to his early phallic attempts, and the strictness of his father who beat him. It was, however, owing to the same set of circumstances that he feared this attitude. In this conflict, his mother's ambition, the disadvantageous comparison of his dreaded father with the policemen, and his own success as a salesman showed him a way out: by a continuous outward fight against his passive-narcissistic attitude, he was able to retain it at other points. The seduction by the maid and his illness after puberty then fixated these latter defensive attitudes in his character.

In a paper upon pseudologia,[10] I have reported the case of another patient.

[10] O. Fenichel, "The Economic Function of Pseudologia Phantastica," No. 9 in this volume.

Her lies obeyed the formula, "If I can make them believe what is not true, then perhaps what I remember as true is only a lie," and so contradicted her sadistically understood memories of the primal scene. The attacks of anxiety which brought her into analysis arose at precisely the point at which this system of repudiation had broken down. Originally she had deceived not only others but also herself, in that she pretended that what she wished to refute, in order not to be afraid, was a "lie" or a "game." She sometimes, for instance, decided, in order not to have to go to school, to simulate an illness by rubbing the thermometer until it reached 100° and then going to bed. It happened on one occasion that when she took the thermometer out it showed 101°. She had the impulse to simulate illness when she really felt ill; she did not wish to become aware of this fact and sought to dispel it by means of "truth-lies." The analysis then showed how deeply rooted was her fear of illness: she had used the warnings of an over-anxious mother, who was herself continually thinking of prophylaxis against tuberculosis, in order to displace her anxiety in relation to the primal scene onto an anxiety in relation to illness. In my paper I did not have an opportunity of describing the terrible extent to which this patient was "introverted" as a whole—that is, had withdrawn herself from reality and lived only in her fantasies. Her latent anxiety was only bearable on condition that she regarded reality itself as a kind of game. In the course of analysis she discovered that she was continually in a state of tension, always waiting for a curtain to fall so that the play would be over and she could begin with real life—an idea which of course she could not define. We know that there are two kinds of thinking, one in words, which is a preparation for reality, and an archaic visual kind, the imaginative preconscious thinking, which takes the place of reality when it is unpleasant. Some people appear to have completely given up the first kind out of fear of reality, and to have developed the second kind very highly. One might ask why wish-fulfilling, pain-denying fantasies are not used much more generally. In an adult person this would surely mean an almost psychotic condition, and my patient could be called almost psychotic in more than one respect. That does not explain why almost psychotic defensive types are not much more common. It is certain that, wherever possible, the ego acquires "excrescences, oddities and peculiarities," hard to get rid of once the period of primitive denial is finally past.[11] This is one more reason why we must try to understand the determining condition for the retention of denial in this case, since we are now dealing with this kind of ego disturbance.

The peculiar character of my patient's parents was a sufficient explanation of the conditions which made this way out possible. The patient was an only

[11] A. Freud, op. cit.

child, and was loved and spoiled by her parents to an unusual extent. Her mother's exaggerated fear of illness had pleasant as well as unpleasant consequences for the child: the fact that all her cares were taken from her, her well-being always cared for in every way, and all her wishes fulfilled was certainly pleasant; but the fact that she was given an enema every day, and that early disturbances of eating led to a great fuss being made about her meals (she was not allowed to eat this and that, and had to eat other things which she did not like) was highly unpleasant. She was relieved of the need for any sense of reality. "I did not know when I ought to go to the lavatory," said the patient, "because Mother always sent me out at the right time," and analysis showed that she was right. She learned at home and did not go to school until she was about ten; at that age she could not eat alone or put on her coat unassisted. It was no wonder that the other children thought she was an idiot. Since her aloofness from everything practical had proved compatible with good intellectual development, she revenged herself by becoming "clever," by making up stories and boasting that she was "intellectual." The whole attitude of her character served the purpose of avoiding being separated from her games and fantasies and coming up against reality, which would then show that she was an idiot. Two important conditions which helped to develop her character can be added: one was the existence of an old cook who told creepy stories, and to whom the patient fled from the terror of her parents' bedroom. I have related more about her in the paper which I have already mentioned. Her attitude made possible the defense: "It is all a tissue of lies and not true." The second condition was that her father, who appeared to be completely enslaved to her mother, spoiled the child just as much as she did. He was himself a very imaginative person, and she used to have long conversations with him, which consisted of daydreams; these lasted up till puberty, and provided the satisfaction of her oedipus wishes.

When a person substitutes fantasy for reality to a large extent, then reality must be particularly repulsive and fantasy particularly attractive. The first condition was produced by a series of traumas, among which repeated primal scenes and the daily enema played the chief role; nor did the fact that the child was artificially isolated and surrounded with precautionary measures, that she had to be alone with her parents every day, that later she met with dislike and was laughed at as an idiot, make reality particularly attractive. What seems to me, however, to be more important in this case is what made fantasies particularly attractive; this was certainly not so much the presence of a cook who told her stories and of a bragging father, as the situation which made complete introversion possible, and as the fact that the abnormal environment of the growing child prevented any confrontation with reality, just as is usually the case with a baby. The attempt to substitute fantasy for reality fails with the normal child because the child who attempts this is sooner or later brought face to face with reality. This encounter was prevented here by an external world which took over from the child the fulfillment of functions which otherwise the ego would have been forced to develop. The result of this was that the patient's ego remained undeveloped.

The third case is one in which the introversion was not nearly so highly developed; I will merely mention it for the sake of a comparison with the second one. This third patient was characterized by the haste with which she always undertook every more or less indifferent enterprise. She was physically, as well as mentally, continually in a state of tension, always occupied with tomorrow, never living in the present. This continual activity of the ego remained on the surface to an amazing extent. Her associations spread in every direction without ever getting any deeper. Her interests and occupations also bore the stamp of a superficiality which did not correspond to her intelligence and talents. She avoided everything which had a "serious" character. In describing her experiences she expressed a peculiar sense of inferiority: "Nothing that happens to me can be serious or real." The activity, restlessness, and continual worry about what would happen tomorrow served the purpose of forestalling any serious experience which might happen, by means of her own, superficial, ego-determined, i.e. play-like, activity. This patient was passionately in love with a man. She could not leave him, although serious conflicts were aroused in her as a consequence. In all her anxiety and trouble, and, in particular, at the beginning of a depression, she escaped—in the same way as a drug addict escapes by means of his drug—with the help of real or imagined experiences with this man. It soon became clear that it was not real love that drove her to him, but that he satisfied narcissistic necessities whose fulfillment repelled anxiety or depression. However, it was not clear in what way he did this. Only gradually did we realize that the chief quality of this man—and in this he was the diametrical opposite of the patient's husband—was that he was humorous, apparently frivolous and witty, and never called things by their right names. What the patient really wanted from him was the reassurance: "I need not be afraid of sexuality, it's only fun." In a first analysis the patient had, from the very beginning, developed the resistance of not speaking, and no progress was made. Only later did we understand that this had happened because the analysis was "serious" and that its aim was to call things by their right names, which the patient wished to avoid at all costs. The analysis with me, on the contrary, appeared to make very rapid progress. It took us a long time to understand that this progress was only apparent and was the result of a particular resistance. I had, by chance, laughed at some remarks which the patient had made during her first sessions. This enabled her to work "in isolation." What she had with me was a "fun-analysis" (in the same way that she enjoyed "fun-sexuality") without the analysis really attacking her anxieties about her real instinctual life. When a child experiences something that shakes it deeply, or when it is afraid of some occurrence, it plays this occurrence afterwards. It forestalls in its fantasy what is expected, or repeats the past occurrence, so changing its own passive role into an active one, in order to practice mastering the dreaded tensions with the reduced quantities which it measures out for itself. Our patient had apparently begun this process but never ended it. Her anxiety was too great for her to make the step from playing to reality. Just as the former patient continually said to herself, out of fear of reality: "It is only a fantasy story and not true," so this one said: "It is only a game and not serious." The analysis showed that the "serious" sexuality had acquired its frightening character as the result of a sadistic component aroused by the birth of a younger brother at the end of the patient's fourth year. This had evoked unconscious anxiety that, if she gave in to her real impulses, she would tear the penis from men and the child from women. It is interesting to note that the escape into "playing" which was suggested to her by various circumstances in the external world was due, among other things, to a particular incident in the nursing of this younger brother. An elder sister had suggested to the patient that she should push over the perambulator and so get rid of the intruder. From that time on the patient was very much frightened of touching her little brother, particularly after she had once noticed how her mother and the nurse had laughed over the little boy as he was micturating. Her mother had persuaded her out of this aversion to touching him by saying: "Take him in your arms; I'm standing here; you're only playing at being his mother; you're not really his mother."

NINE

The Economics of Pseudologia Phantastica*

A PATIENT recounted in his analysis the following recollection. When he was about four years old he had lain with his parents in their bed. Owing to an accidental exposure he had seen his father's penis, and was frightened by its size. Amazed, he had asked himself whether his mother too had such a large penis. He had waited for a suitable opportunity to lift her nightgown inconspicuously, and underneath, to his great satisfaction, he saw an equally large penis. The patient, of course, realized the absurdity of this memory. Nevertheless it stood before his eyes so vividly that he felt he could swear to its correctness. The contradiction in his story, that first the size of his father's penis frightened him, and then the size of his mother's reassured him, helped in the analysis. It became probable that the true state of affairs had been just the reverse. During an accidental exposure the boy must have caught sight of his mother's genital, been frightened by it, wondered whether his father looked like that too, lifted his nightshirt, and seen with relief his large penis.

This screen memory—a common example of tendentious falsifications of memory—had thus exchanged father and mother, for what purpose it is easy to see. The exchange denies the unpleasant, indeed probably traumatic, sight of the woman's lack of penis. This seems to be a special case of the "pre-stage of defense," quite recently described by Anna Freud,[1] which consists in a denial of disagreeable external stimuli. Indeed it is a special case which is reminiscent of an already familiar one, namely, the perverse behavior of fetishists by which they seek to deny the woman's lack of penis. Freud, as we know, has shown

---

* First published in *Int. Z. Psa. & Imago,* Vol. 24, 1939, pp. 21–32.
[1] A. Freud, *The Ego and the Mechanisms of Defence,* New York, Int. Univ. Press, 1946.

that the denial of realities regarded by patients as a threat, were they to engage in instinctual activity, is not limited to psychoses.[2] It is probable that perverts in general are people whose sexual pleasure is threatened by a danger expected from without, and whose symptom is an attempt to deny this danger by over-emphasizing a trait of infantile sexuality, so that sexual pleasure becomes once again possible for them, in so far as during the sexual act the danger is denied by means of the perverse measure.[3]

In a screen memory such as the one described above, we may observe the same mechanism under simpler conditions. If there is a general endeavor to deny unpleasant facts, this endeavor must be all the more marked when the unpleasant fact is one which makes one's own drive appear as a danger. In phenomena such as the tendentious forgetting of external experiences which represent drives, no rigorous distinction between "denial" directed outward and "repression" directed inward seems possible. It is just as possible to "repress" or to falsify perceptions of all senses and of deep sensibility which represent proscribed instinctual impulses, as it is to repress representations of instinctual aims.

Such a tendency to deny is opposed by the maturing perceptual apparatuses of the ego. The tendency to experience and the tendency to deny engage in a struggle with each other, and the results of this struggle vary greatly. As is known, the solution which is typical of childhood is that reality is denied in an affectively successful way in fantasy and play, while simultaneously an ego that is adequate to reality is aware of the imaginary or make-believe character of this denial. I have described another symptom which is characteristic for the same duality in the so-called "craving for screen experiences." [4] In this, forgetting an unpleasant experience is made easier if the subject's recollection which reminds him of it is offered an experience which is associatively similar to it but altered precisely in respect of its offensive element. The feeling which children so frequently have, often about quite innocent experiences, "I must remember this all my life"—the so-called "command to remember"—is in reality always an economic aid of this sort to repression, and means: "By remembering this, I can forget the other." In our case there was no need for a second experience, displaced from the sexual field. The sight of the father's genital, following almost at once upon that of the mother's, sufficed for such a "screen experience"; it could be duplicated in remembrance. Here something untrue is represented as true, to make it possible to represent something true as untrue. Of course we

[2] S. Freud, "Fetishism," *Coll. Pap.*, Vol. V, London, Hogarth, 1950.

[3] O. Fenichel, *Perversionen, Psychosen, Charakterstoerungen*, Vienna, Int. Psa. Verlag, 1931.

[4] O. Fenichel, "The Economic Function of Screen Memories," and "The Inner Injunction to Make a Mental Note," Nos. 11 and 16, *First Series*.

cannot call such an "untruth" a "lie," since the patient did not intend to deceive others with it and believed in it himself.

Before passing on to similar functions of lying, I would like to mention yet another result of the same conflict between faithfulness of memory and the tendency to repress which seems to have great importance in psychopathology; namely, the obsessional doubting, so common in children, of their own perceptions, because "what should not be, cannot be" (Chr. Morgenstern). The frequent compulsive doubting of news of death, which occasionally leads to a paradoxical "Thank God!" of relief when the news has been confirmed, is explained on a deeper level by anxiety concerning the omnipotence of one's own thoughts, which would like to deny the news of death, lest one's bad wishes be responsible for it. On a higher level, however, it is explained contrariwise: had one, by a slip of the ear, heard news of a death which actually had not been conveyed, it would become obvious that one entertained such thoughts; therefore, the confirmation of the news is a relief, since it frees one from the suspicion of having imagined it without grounds. Children develop quite similar compulsive doubts toward sexual or other perceptions in regard to their parents, about which the official view is that they do not happen—as, for instance, quarrels between them. When a child, upon asking what happened between his parents during the night, is told that nothing happened, that he had merely been dreaming, and now begins to doubt whether his own memory or this reply is true, then it is perhaps easy to discover in his belief "Yes, I was only dreaming" an element of mockery against his parents. But apart from this, what happens here is also like what happens in doubts attending news of death. Once the child has developed feelings of guilt about instinctual events, he will, on deeper levels, refuse to perceive any instinctual events at all, because he wants to deny that part of the world; but on higher levels he will be afraid to have "only dreamed" these events because then they would be entirely his own fault, whereas their being real would free him from guilt. I had the opportunity of analyzing a case in which such doubts concerning sexual scenes which the patient had witnessed led to the fear of being insane—that is, of having seen and heard things which had not happened.

Such compulsive doubts may persist unresolved. As a rule they are resolved, in keeping with experience, on the side of reality. We know that if the capacity to "deny" is retained to a greater degree, it is a dangerous mechanism which can easily lead to psychosis. Only in tendentious forgetting of external events, in "screen memories," and in perversions, does "denial" seem to be victorious.

Thus the formula of screen ideas is: "Not *that* is true, but *this*." The same formula holds for many fantasies and games which serve to master and (completely or partially) deny overpowering impressions, though in these cases there exists at the same time a reality-adequate ego, which knows the deceitful nature of the "this." In a subsequent repetition of the events which have made such impressions it is precisely their offensive points which are altered.

There is a class of fantasy and play which seeks to achieve the same goal—the denial of powerful impressions or their mastery by alteration of their specific offensive parts—by somewhat different means. Their formula is: "Just as this is only fantasy or play, so that was not true either."

Freud has already elucidated the meaning of "absurd" games and fantasies of children in "Little Hans." [5] They serve to ridicule the incredible assertions of others: "If you lie to me, I'll lie to you!" There are, however, games and fantasies of this kind which are not so much directed against the external world as calculated to pour scorn in a similar fashion on the subject's own memory. His own incredible perceptions are made even more incredible by absurd exaggeration, in order to facilitate their denial. In this way the child's games in later years may deny his memory of sexual games of earlier years by repeating them absurdly in self-irony—this time without conscious sexual coloring. The aid rendered to repression by such "screen games" is especially great when the denial is common, i.e., when the same siblings who in their day had the sexual experiences together later on play the games they scoff at. We shall come back to the subject of "common daydreams" as a form of denial. [6]

It is now time to remember that fantasy and play serve not only to deny unpleasant realities, but primarily also to replace these by better ones. Fantasy is a "refuge" in which otherwise proscribed wishes may be lived out, as long as the fantasying person knows that it is "only fantasy." Introverted people who live only in fantasy are people who are afraid of real instinctual activity. We know too that they do seek contact again with real objects in a secondary way, in that they attempt to seduce them into taking part in their fantasies, instead of—as healthy people would—taking part in their sexual activities. The socially most significant example of a return from fantasy to social life is to be found in art, in which the fantasying person influences objects affectively through the products of his fantasy. The "common daydreams" which are preparatory to art also serve people who are inhibited in reality to get together with equally inhibited people to form a substitute for sexuality. Naturally such a sexual substitute—like a neurotic symptom—finds room both for what is repressed and what represses. It can, as we saw in the example of "screen games," serve

[5] S. Freud, "Analysis of a Phobia in a Five-Year-Old Boy," *Coll. Pap.*, Vol. III, London, Hogarth, 1948.
[6] H. Sachs, "The Community of Daydreams," *The Creative Unconscious*, Cambridge, Mass., Sci-Art, 1942.

either a (limited) instinctual gratification or common denial of unpleasant facts.

Here, at last, we should like to bring in the function of pseudology as well. It is obvious that representing certain fantasies as real occurrences is something between a screen memory which the subject considers real, and an ordinary fantasy which he distinguishes strictly from reality. Likewise, it needs no psychoanalysis to see that stories of imaginary sexual experiences told by a sexually inhibited woman are a compromise between her wish to seduce sexually, and the inhibition opposing this. We wish rather to stress the negative side of the phenomenon—namely, the fact that the lies serve as a denial and how they do so. The formula is: "If it is possible to make someone believe that untrue things are true, then it is also possible that true things, the memory of which threatens me, are untrue."

Helene Deutsch has demonstrated that the contents of the pseudologies are screen memories for true things.[7] She believed that such demonstration justifies the theory that pseudology is a distorted break-through of repressed memories. We agree with her findings completely, but we think that they must be complemented to the effect that it is not *merely* a break-through; the fact that the break-through occurs in this distorted form—i.e., in the form of fantasies represented to others as real, though the subject knows that they are not—indicates that pseudology is an economic measure for the further *maintenance* of the repression.[8] The screen fantasy and the screened memory belong together. The fact that the patient knows that the former is untrue is designed to aid him to regard the latter as untrue also.

Lack of time prohibits the inclusion here of a case history of pseudology. I will limit myself to marshaling a few data from an analysis which illustrates the point very well.

The complaints which brought the patient in question, a woman, into analysis were exceedingly frequent, compulsively performed masturbation, and a fear of burglars, murderers, etc., which, under certain circumstances, rose to the pitch of major anxiety attacks. The neurosis had become manifest on the occasion of a dramatic incident: the patient had unexpectedly become the witness of an attack of rage of an insane person. The analysis of her fantasies and dreams showed that the burglars and murderers represented in the first place this insane person who might do her harm. When we found out that the fantasies which accompanied her continual and tormenting masturbation were thoroughly sado-masochistic and that they were always about a villain or a madman or a murder gang attacking an innocent person, then it became clear that the two symptoms,

[7] H. Deutsch, "Ueber die pathologische Luege (Pseudologia phantastica)," *Int. Z. Psa.*, Vol. 8, 1922.
[8] Cf. H. Sachs, "Zur Genese der Perversionen," *Int. Z. Psa.*, Vol. 9, 1923.

masturbation and anxiety, belonged together. It was apparent that her experience with the insane person had mobilized a repressed part of her infantile sexuality, but, also at the same time, her defense against it. The masturbation fantasies had obviously been pleasurable only as long as the patient was convinced of their imaginary character. Her experience with the madman brought their realization within the realm of possibility, and to this she responded with her great anxiety, and also—in a manner not as yet understood—with a change in the character of the masturbation so that it became compulsive. What the patient liked most to paint in imagination was what she most feared in reality.

It turned out that the fact that masturbation was the patient's essential sexual activity was not the only respect in which she had replaced real experience by imagination. Like a dreamy child, she had put the accent of her entire personality on fantasy. Daydreaming, attempts at writing which had a daydream character, and a few little "romantic" experiences, which seemed to be no more than secondary attempts at a realization of daydreams—all these stood in contrast to her real life, which was relatively uneventful, dependent, and turned away from the world. An intense anxiety, of which the episode with the insane man had again reminded her, must early in her life have prohibited every real instinctual action whatever, and have displaced instinctual excitation into the realm of fantasy. It soon became clear that here fantasy was not only a substitute for sex, but also an explicit denial of reality; for the patient related that she often concocted fantasies with the idea that it was unlikely that what one thought of would actually come to pass in exactly the way one imagined it, so that by fantasying she defended herself from a dreaded reality. The content of the fantasies proved throughout to be replicas or derivatives of her sado-masochistic masturbation fantasies.

The patient's pseudology—in which she was in no way inferior to her national hero, Peer Gynt—was clearly an attempt to find her way back to reality, after having withdrawn from sexual reality into fantasy. It was a special way in which the patient sought contact with her environment. As usual, the lies consisted of sexual and self-glorifying boasts. At first the patient would not believe that her lies had to do with her masturbation fantasies. One day, however, she related how in puberty she had made up her first big lie: she told a loved teacher that the class had conspired to attack her and that several girls planned to attack her collectively and beat her up. The connection between the (sexually meant) ideas of attack and the lies was unquestionable. The many variations in which she partly thought out these attacks and partly related them as real events in her tall stories gave the impression that she was attempting to achieve a "deferred mastery" of the trauma of an attack.

The patient had several entirely fantastic screen memories. The improbability of the events which she remembered definitely as actual happenings, surpassed even that about the mother's penis, described above. Once, for instance, she had seen a ghost floating into a room through the air, without touching the ground, and doing all sorts of things there, etc. These screen memories thus seemed always to be intended to prove to her against her better sense: "This absurd nonsense is actually true." It was not difficult to get at the origin of these images. The patient remembered as her own experiences stories which, it is true, she had not experienced, but which had been told to her. In her childhood there had been an old cook in the house with whom she had liked to sit, and who had told her many fairy-stories and fantastic tales of horror, and especially stories about mad people. What had to be interpreted analytically, therefore, was the patient's obvious attempt to tell herself: "What the cook tells me is true." Her tendency, exhibited in her lies, to tell others untrue stories as true, seems to stand in contradiction to the other, more understandable, line of emphasizing the *untruth* of all such tales of murder and horror. The developmental history of the patient's entire neurosis and the further course of the analysis also showed this line of thought: "Sexual enjoyment is possible only as long as I know that the horrible things which I have to think during it do not really happen but are just imagined." The absurdity of the screen memories was so excessive that it could already be surmised that this line was the more fundamental one, i.e., underlying the question concerning the truth or untruth of the horror tales, there must have been the above-mentioned struggle between the tendency to repress and a recollection of something she had perceived.

I should like to add here that it was the character of the parents which made possible and, indeed, actually forced on this only child such an extensive introversion. The father loved his daughter very much, and expressed this affection in long "talks" with her, which resulted in the sexualization for her of talking and producing ideas; thus he perpetuated the tradition the cook had begun, and made possible the resistance which characterized the entire analysis, namely, the patient's hidden sexual pleasure in analytic talk about sexual matters, whose reality she persistently sought to deny. The mother brought the child up in complete dependence, shielding her and caring for her, and making it possible for her to ignore reality to an inconceivable degree, and yet making herself burdensome to the child by her continual excessive care of her. The patient remembered that early in her life she had already begun to withdraw to the cook from the embraces of her mother, which were unpleasant to her. Her love for the cook clearly had an edge against the mother; it meant: "I don't want to be in the living room, I want to go into the kitchen." And this—as the analysis showed—meant in the depth of her mind: "I want to hear horrible stories, but

I don't want to witness the horrible things which happen in my parents' bedroom." The patient fled from the primal scenes, which she conceived sadomasochistically, to the reassuring old cook, in whose fantastic tales she found a "return of what has been defended against in the defense"—but a return which had become bearable through the conviction: "This woman's tales, which I like to hear so much, are only imaginary; there is no such thing in reality."

Of course, this defense against the memory of the primal scenes which the patient had witnessed was unsuccessful. Both the drive, which sought real satisfaction, and memory, which obeyed the reality principle, made her feel: "Something of what the cook tells me is true all the same." But this aroused anxiety; therefore, she picked out the most fantastic and absurd of the cook's stories and clung to them. In the fantastic screen memories we recognize, therefore, on the one hand the defensive strivings of the ego: "Just as the crazy stories the cook tells are not true, so it is not true that my parents go mad at night and attack each other"; on the other hand, we observe in them the failure of the defense— the reminder that incredible things really did happen in the bedroom.

Thus the patient imitated the cook in her lies: "If I can make others believe that things which I know to be untrue are true, then it is also possible that my memory is deceived and what I remember as true is untrue." To assert something untrue meant to deny something true. (Of course this interpretation does not exclude other, simpler ones. The patient's lies were also courting-substitutes of a person who had regressed from sexual activity to fantasy, as well as revenge for not having been told the truth about sexual matters.) The aforementioned compulsive doubting of one's own perception, which is so characteristic for children who develop lying on this basis, was present here too. When she first heard about "the thing in itself," in puberty, she developed feelings of depersonalization, in which she thought that perhaps the whole of life was untrue and just a dream. Moreover, just as she lied to adults, so did she feel herself to be lied to in a fanciful way; she had to wonder, for instance, whether it were true that there was an England or an English language.

Let us remember the patient's saying that she lied and daydreamed so that the lies should not come true in reality. In the analysis we gained the conviction that this reflected her state of mind while listening to the cook's tales: "What she thinks up here cannot be true, *because* it has been thought up," and that she took up with the cook and later on with masturbation not only in order to partake in sexuality in an aim-inhibited manner, but also in order to deny the actuality of these things by imagining them. This explained the compulsive character which her masturbation assumed after the episode with the insane man had confirmed the actuality of those sado-masochistic horrors. The denial magic of the fantasy "I think something so that it won't happen" seems not to be at all rare. Another woman patient once told me: "As a child I always used to think up everything bad, so that it wouldn't happen." There is no doubt that this belief arises from the positive omnipotence of the thought "by thinking this I could make it happen," through negation of it; but this is of no interest to us here. In relation to the object the lie was thus doubly determined. It meant not only, "As I was taken in, so do I now take in others," but also, "As I now take in others, so it may be that I was only taken in when I saw what I was afraid was true." The object plays the role of a witness, which the repressing ego wants to summon against perception or a memory, as the case may be.[9]

It can now be seen in what direction I propose to complement Helene Deutsch's findings, which I have been able to confirm. Pseudology is an attempt at seduction made by a person to whom sex is permitted only in imagination, and it takes the form of a break-through in distorted form of infantile-sexual experiences. But the economic significance of this break-through lies in the special form of the distortion, which—as in perversions and screen memories—serves to maintain the repression and to deny the truth of the reality contained in the lie.

Finally, I would like to discuss a phenomenon which, despite the frequency of its occurrence, has received little attention so far, and which may be considered to be the compulsive counterpart of hysterical pseudology. Many obsessional neurotics find it compatible with their characteristic conscientiousness and meticulousness, and even with compulsive fanaticism for truth, to falsify facts crudely on some points, both in analysis and life in general. Of course, in accordance with the obsessional neurotic "displacement onto details," the points in question are mostly objectively unimportant nuances or trivialities. A patient of this sort, for instance, would, in reading a text aloud, make slight

---

[9] A few confirmatory details from this case history: The fear which the patient had of the "actuality" of her instinctual experiences finally led her, among other things, to regard everything as being not real, but only play-acting, and to wonder—after the fashion of a depersonalization—that anyone should really eat, go to the toilet, etc.; because people just talk about things to do with the instincts, but actually there are no such things. In the course of the analysis she discovered that she felt in a constant state of tension, waiting for a curtain to fall so that she could at last stop "acting."

The flight into "it is all nothing but a story" she had learned from the cook; the flight into "it is all nothing but play-acting" was made possible for her later by the following experience: As a child she had a bear phobia, and once she was taken to a play in which a man appeared disguised as a bear. She shrieked and cried. But then the man raised his mask and showed that he was a man and that the bear was but a stage disguise.

How extensively the patient used this "it is only lies" as a means of denial is shown by the fact that she occasionally decided to simulate illness so as not to have to go to school. She would rub the thermometer until it showed 100° F. and would only then insert it. Occasionally it happened that it showed 102° F. when she took it out. She was *really* sick but did not want to perceive this and tried to deny it by means of "lying a sickness." The analysis then showed how deep was her fear of sickness; for she had used the cautionings of her overanxious mother who was continually concerned with the prevention of tuberculosis, to transform her anxiety about the primal scene into anxiety about sickness.

changes in it wherever the language permitted, or would leave out a small detail of the story, or add to it from his fantasy. These minor obsessional falsifications of reality are sometimes the center of compulsive self-reproaches, but more often they are free of guilt. (One can occasionally succeed, too, in showing that guilt feelings appearing in quite another place have been displaced there from such falsifications.) If now we analyze these falsifications, we notice in the first place what is unspecific about them. The small alterations of truth represent intended greater alterations, which serve the purpose of pressing the world into a certain system. Facts must not be what they are, but what the compulsive system requires. Moreover, the lie is intended to force the system not only on the facts, but on the subject's fellow men: "You shall see things not with your own eyes, but only as I present them to you." This violence done to others by the obsessional neurotic who puts forward *his* "reality" can serve to give him all sorts of neurotic instinctual gratifications (such as exhibitionism or anal stubbornness). But these do not interest us here. Further analysis of the *specific* nature of the falsifications yields specific causes too. Freud once compared the statements of unanalyzed persons about their childhood to the formation of legends, in which historical facts are also arranged and recast according to the wishes of the people concerned.[10] In the obsessional neurotic falsifications I have in mind, we can see such legend formation in *statu nascendi.* Just as the systems of obsessional neurotics serve in general to assure them that they need not fear that their instinctual life will spring something unexpected on them, since with the aid of their systems and programs they can foresee all and protect themselves against surprises, so is this lying an attempt to put into effect the universal validity of systems and programs against the internal perception of proscribed instinctual impulses as well. We know that obsessional neurotics' attempt to have a general conspectus of the whole world is designed to enable them not to see a certain part of it; their tendency to remember everything, to assert about everything that they already knew it, serves the purpose of allowing them to forget something in particular; and their complete sincerity is meant to let them be insincere in some special respect. We also understand that such a single piece of insincerity—in accordance with the process of "after-expulsion" [11]—necessitates further insincerities, which are then displaced to trivialities. I am reminded here of the obsessional who, in his systematic striving to have only natural frontiers between countries, considered the Pyrenean peninsula as a single country and Portugal as nonexistent. One day, having been told by a foreigner that he was a Portuguese, he described what passed in him in the following words:

[10] S. Freud, "The Interpretation of Dreams," *The Basic Writings,* New York, Random House (Modern Library), 1938.

[11] S. Freud, "Repression," *Coll. Pap.,* Vol. IV, London, Hogarth, 1948.

"I thought to myself, 'as he says he is Portuguese, he's probably Spanish.'"[12]

The minor obsessional neurotic falsifications of truth differ from such processes in regard to the social factor. It is not, or not only, in the subject's own eyes that they are meant to distort the truth which contradicts their system, but principally in the eyes of the object. Of course, desire for power, stubbornness, exhibitionism —in short, narcissistic and anal-sadistic instinctual impulses—are strongly involved here. But the main thing is that the subject can, by empathizing with his object—who knows reality only through his (the subject's) mediation—convince himself that the world is as his system says it is. (In the same way, too, he makes the object join him in other obsessions, such as, say, that of remembering everything.) Whereas "negative lies," which suppress something that has happened, confirm a desired denial directly, being only displaced from something important to something unimportant, "positive lies," which add an imaginary detail to a piece of reality, confirm it indirectly, in that they, for their part, adduce the possibility of convincing someone that something untrue is true, as a proof of the possibility that something which has been experienced could be untrue as well. The person who is lied to serves once again as a witness whose testimony is thrown into the scales of the subject's internal struggle between his tendency to repress on the one hand, and, on the other, his recollection or his instinctual perception.

A special case of "isolation"[13] is not infrequently involved in this. We often find that obsessional neurotics, and children too, attempt to keep two spheres of life—for instance, analysis and home life, or school and home life—strictly isolated from each other. The parents, let us say, are not to see the teacher, but to know him only through the child's stories; likewise the teacher is not to know the parents personally, but only through the child's eyes. This often results in falsifications that are characteristic for the instinctual conflicts of the child. The anxiousness with which the isolation is maintained now corresponds to the anxiety lest these little falsifications might be discovered.

Obsessional fanaticism for truth, like screen experiences attended by a "command to remember," is connected with a compulsive remembering whose intensity betrays its character of a reaction formation, and this is in keeping with the fact that both have the same origin.

We are used to finding that when viewed topographically psychic phenomena prove to be determined by several strata of the mind superimposed on one another, and that when viewed dynamically they turn out to be maintained by conflicting instinctual forces. This also holds good for the type of pathological lie which we have been investigating. Quite other types, too, may exist, but

[12] O. Fenichel, *Hysterien und Zwangsneurosen*, Vienna, Int. Psa. Verlag, 1931, p. 145.
[13] S. Freud, *The Problem of Anxiety*, New York, Psa. Quart. Press and Norton, 1936.

hysterical pseudology and obsessional falsification seem to belong to this type. On its most superficial level it was seen that the lie served to hide the truth; Helene Deutsch then showed that it also betrayed it; and we have recognized that it is in the manner of this betrayal that the denial of the truth first takes root.

TEN

Trophy and Triumph[*]

A Clinical Study

I

IN "EGO psychology," as it is called, psychoanalysis investigates matters which have for long been studied by other psychologies as well. But it does this in a different way from them, prepared as it is by its previous exploration of the instincts (or drives). It approaches the subject from a *genetic* standpoint, in that it represents ego phenomena as originating from the interplay of instincts and environmental influences. Thus, one no longer exposes oneself to the suspicion of being an adherent of "individual psychology" if one wishes to investigate problems concerning the *will to power* which—in our society even more than in others—is a powerful motive of human action. It is only a question of *how* one conducts this investigation.

The problems of self-regard and its fluctuations—of which depression and mania are pathological caricatures—are best approached, I think, by taking Rado's conception as our point of departure.[1] In his view, the infant in its narcissism feels omnipotent. Later on it learns that its power is quite limited. The longing to attain once again this lost sense of omnipotence persists throughout life, manifesting itself as a "narcissistic need." A high degree of self-regard means coming close to the lost feeling of omnipotence, a low self-regard means remoteness from it. The desired closeness is at first attained by the ego from external sources, so long as "narcissistic" and "erotic" wants are insufficiently differentiated; later on, by fulfilling ideals. Similarly, low self-regard arises first from the feeling of being unloved or rejected, later on from feelings of guilt. The

---

[*] First published in *Int. Z. Psa. & Imago*, Vol. 24, 1939, pp. 258–280.

[1] S. Rado, "The Problem of Melancholia," *Int. J. Psa.*, Vol. 9, 1928; "The Psychoanalysis of Pharmacothymia (Drug Addiction). I. The Clinical Picture," *Psa. Quart.*, Vol. 2, 1933.

explanation of this is that the child retains a strong belief in omnipotence after the loss of his own omnipotence, by regarding as omnipotent the persons who so seriously limited his omnipotence—indeed, as far as he is concerned, they are almost omnipotent in reality. To get something from them means to be again united with them, to *participate in their power;* to be rejected by them means to be even more exposed to helplessness. As we know, it is this narcissistic dependence upon external supplies in the form of being loved that makes children in the first instance *educable.* Education attaches conditions to these indispensable supplies: the child receives these only by abstaining from instinctual actions which its upbringers regard as undesirable. Such promises of protection or power to the helpless, conditional upon the observance of certain moral regulations, are encountered later on again, at various points in social life. This, too, is the formula of religion. The Almighty promises protection, help, and a certain participation in power to the helpless human being, provided he fulfills certain ethical requirements.

When one asserts that those who obediently fulfill the commandments of God thereby somehow partake in the glory of God, one must be prepared for the objection that a Prometheus, who defies God—that is, who denies or even actually conquers his helplessness and dependence on Him—must feel more omnipotent than the pious man; and that is so, provided that the conquest or the denial are successful. The defiant man chooses the more direct path, whereas the pious one is forced to make a *detour* because he considers any attempt at defiance hopeless. But both have the same goal, viz., to become once again as powerful as they once were and as someone *outside of their own ego* in the external world now is. The discoveries of psychoanalysis concerning the instinctual foundations from which, under the influence of the external world, the differences of the so-called superficies of the mind develop, enable us here once more—in contrast to individual psychology—to take a *genetic* view. A particularly excessive need for power usually turns out to be an attempt to compensate for an anxiety; and it is precisely this means of defense against anxiety which is fostered by our culture. A first attempt to achieve such an aim of power consists naturally in the individual's putting himself in the place of him who is powerful in the external world, in eliminating him (actually or in fantasy), or in robbing him of his power. If this cannot be achieved, another means is adopted. The individual allows the powerful being to remain, but in some way partakes of his power— re-introjects the power he has projected. One important way of once more sharing in the lost omnipotence seems not to be the fantasy of devouring the powerful one, but of somehow dissolving in him, being devoured *by* him.[2] All those later

[2] G. H. Graber, *Zeugung, Geburt und Tod. Werden und Vergehen im Mythus und in der Vorstellung des Kindes,* Zurich, Rascher, 1934.

narcissistic feelings of well-being in which one's own insignificance feels sheltered within a something infinitely great which nevertheless has an ego quality, are of this sort. Such are: patriotism ("my nation is infinitely greater than I, and yet is I"); religious ecstasy (God is infinitely greater than the self, yet the believer is one with Him); hypnosis (the hypnotizer is infinitely greater than the subject, and yet he now fulfills functions which are otherwise those of the subject); and the relation to authority in general (the authoritarian leader is infinitely greater than any single individual of his nation—and yet he himself is a single individual of the nation).

The methods employed for acquiring the power of the mighty one—by seizure or theft of it or by participation in it, and the fantasy substitutes for these— are indeed fundamental subject matters for psychological research. Consideration of them is justified even if its results add nothing new to Freud's exposition in *Totem and Taboo* and in *Group Psychology and the Analysis of the Ego,* but merely relate various actual phenomena to what he has said in those works.

Since sexual aims also are derived from the original instinctual aims of incorporation, and indeed, female sexuality in particular reaches its culmination in an actual temporary incorporation, the striving of man for the "incorporation" of power is in many ways linked with sexual aims, and particularly with feminine ones. This circumstance, however, will not be specially considered in what follows.

II

In my paper, "The Symbolic Equation: Girl = Phallus," [3] I cited the case of a young man whose castration complex was constructed more in accordance with the feminine type; that is, it did not take the form of a fear that something might happen to his penis, but rather of the fantasy that something had already happened to it, and he had to conceal this. (This fantasy, nevertheless, was only used to cover a normal castration anxiety in a deeper layer of his mind.) The patient also had a strong exhibitionistic tendency. This came into conflict with his feeling, which corresponded to the fantasy just mentioned, that he had to conceal his inferior penis. He rescued himself from this conflict by acting the knockabout comedian. I was able to show that he was adopting the line, here, of "Though my penis is small, it is nevertheless powerful." I mentioned that the figure of the *clown,* which is certainly of a phallic nature, has nevertheless definite pregenital attributes, and I believed I could explain this simultaneity of genitality and pregenitality by supposing that a regressively debased phallic exhibitionistic impulse was at work: "Though I am small, and you laugh at me, I am omnipotent, in spite of my size. If my penis is small, very well then, the whole of myself

[3] O. Fenichel, "The Symbolic Equation: Girl = Phallus," No. 1 in this volume.

is a penis and that you will have to respect!" One feels oneself to be small and powerless and the adult, the father, as big and omnipotent. One cannot, as one would actually like to, put oneself in the place of the omnipotent father, but one can—though at the price of a regressive debasement—in some way feel oneself to be him, to be a part of him, his only important part, his penis which represents his power. How this fantasy—representing, as the case may be, revenge upon the father or reconciliation with him—was still further complicated by the fantasy of being a girl, was a special issue which I was investigating in the paper referred to, and it does not interest us here.

The same phenomenon presents itself in the case of women with the "girl = penis" fantasy. They feel themselves cheated of something (of an "instrument of power") which another person has. They want to steal it; and this impulse runs up against anxiety or feelings of guilt. If they manage in fantasy to *be* this object ("to have already stolen it," as it were), then they *participate* in its possession. The achieved identification is an equivalent of the seizure by force.

Narcissistic injuries are made up for by supplies from without. If these supplies are not forthcoming, the narcissistically injured person will seek to obtain them by force. If his fear, or love, or both, of the more powerful being inhibit the use of force, then an identification with the retained object—an identification which has yet to be more closely studied—may become the equivalent of forcible seizure, since it implies a participation in the might of the more powerful being. The fantasies of being a penis indicate that identificatory tendencies which are associated with destruction of the object can be replaced by partial identifications which preserve the object as a whole. In the same way, it was already a substitution when the idea of seizing the insignium of power, the idea of castration, took the place of the original idea of murdering the powerful being whose place one would like to take. In magical thinking "power" is conceived of absolutely *concretely:* one can kill the powerful one, or rob him of his power-substance, or, finally, partake of that substance through partial identification, and even through mere contact. This last is a compromise between the craving for power on the one hand and, on the other, fear of the powerful being and passive love for him.

III

Now we pass to a quite different clinical theme. I shall review briefly a paper by Nunberg.[4]

The kind of love according to which one loves the person who is what one would like to be oneself is particularly frequent in homosexual forms of love, which, in general, tend more frequently to follow the narcissistic pattern of object choice. Now there is a type of passive homosexual who loves ideal men—

[4] H. Nunberg, "Homosexuality, Magic and Aggression," *Int. J. Psa.,* Vol. 19, 1938.

men that are like what he himself wants to be—in whose analysis, however, it soon turns out that this love is in fact extremely ambivalent and built upon hate. These are men whose castration complex is of the feminine pattern mentioned above. They feel castrated and unmasculine, and they are drawn to strong men in order *to become masculine themselves through contact with them*. This is contagious magic.

Nunberg's patient wanted to seize possession of his partner or rather of his penis in the sex act, or to be given a present by him. The secret aim of his love was the *castration* of the partner. It is noteworthy that he always thought of his aggression in *oral* terms. It became clear that his homosexuality was, so to say, an intermediate act on the way toward the gratification of the normal oedipus complex. His own penis is too feeble for the conquest of the mother, and so he submits sexually to the father, who is strong enough for this, in order to emasculate him and thus obtain the strength to carry out the heterosexual task. This intention, to be sure, failed because every attempt in this direction took the form of primitive pregenital sadistic impulses. Therese Benedek has described a similar case.[5]

I should like to venture the assertion that rudiments of such an attitude, and fantasies belonging to this sphere, are very frequent in men. I can recall a number of cases in which externally feminine-masochistic behavior served to conceal sadistic fantasies of seizing the penis in the homosexual act.

A patient who consciously despised and almost hated his mother—and who related only after a prolonged period of analysis that until puberty and occasionally even later he had slept in her bed—was always extremely courteous and submissive, and always had "superiors" after whom he modeled his thoughts and actions. The analysis showed that what he wanted to get from these models was the strength he lacked to desire his mother. We learned eventually how under castration threats from an older sister he had regressed to pregenital stages and how he began to associate with older boys. He developed the fantasy that he would learn from them how to treat women, in order one day to take revenge upon this sister by using the means which he would have stolen from his older friends. This revenge had, through regression, assumed an oral form. This "being a little boy with the big boys," this identification with them in fantasy, while actually submitting to them (otherwise they would not have taken him along with them), became the point of departure for widely ramifying homosexual fantasies, the basic aim of which was the oral-sadistically conceived castration of his sexual partner.

Nunberg mentions in his paper the three hitherto known psychogeneses of

[5] T. Benedek, "Some Factors Determining Fixation at the Deutero-Phallic Phase," *Int. J. Psa.*, Vol. 15, 1934.

homosexuality: (1) identification with the mother, and the choice of a young man representing the subject's own ego as object; (2) identification with the mother, and the choice of the father as object; and (3) overcoming feelings of envy, jealousy, and hatred against the older brother (or the father) by means of an overcompensating identificatory love. He points out also how frequent are combinations between these three types, as well as between these and the fourth type which he describes. I would add that the third and fourth types are particularly closely related. There is scarcely a case of "altruism," as described by Anna Freud,[6] which does not at one point or another betray the original hate and envy. Freud has shown that a (never altogether successful) way to master an undischargeable hatred for a rival is to feel that one belongs to him, and participates in his power.[7] It might be added that identificatory love of this sort demands a particular kind of behavior on the part of the object such as makes the identification possible. Corresponding daydreams also always depend on the object, the demand upon whom is: "Behave so that I can identify myself with you." If the object does not meet this demand there is a strong tendency to revert from the budding love to the original hostility. Thus it is understandable that these fantasies which I list here should shade into each other: "I will surrender myself to a great man, so that while doing so I may take away from him his insignium of power, which I want for my own use"; "I will surrender myself to a man whom I originally hated, so that I can feel like him and participate in his masculinity"; and "I will do something to him to compel him to let me participate, if he does not do so of his own accord."

Again we see, then, the same thing: there is an originally aggressive form of seizing from the possessor of power his power, in order to possess it oneself; and there is a milder form, made peaceful by identification, of partaking in the power-substance, which is a compromise between the hunger for power on the one hand, and the fear of the mighty one and passive love for him on the other.

I recall the case of a man who had a kind of monopoly of his profession in his home town and who, when a professional colleague moved into town, immediately made friends with and indeed subordinated himself to him. It was only after prolonged analysis that it became clear to the patient how much he had hated his colleague and what, upon the news of his coming, he had wanted to do to him. Moreover, he realized that his submission not only served as a defense against his own aggressive tendencies, but on a deeper level was meant as a trick to insinuate himself into the other's favor in order to steal any superior knowledge he might have, and thus later on the more securely to castrate him.

---

[6] A. Freud, *The Ego and the Mechanisms of Defence*, New York, Int. Univ. Press, 1946.

[7] S. Freud, "Certain Neurotic Mechanisms in Jealousy, Paranoia and Homosexuality," *Coll. Pap.*, Vol. II, London, Hogarth, 1948.

To be an "apprentice" makes it possible to adopt a passive attitude toward the "master," to receive his protection and enjoy the advantages of being small, while, anticipating the future in fantasy, one aims at taking away his mastery, at becoming greater than he was. Is this not also the usual ambivalence of the small son who loves his great father?

IV

I will now shift again to two quite different clinical themes. The first of these concerns the exaggerated "animal friendships" of children which have been made intelligible by Anna Freud.[8] They are preceded by a fear of animals or at least the beginnings of such a fear.[9] The warding off of the anxiety then ensues through identification with the aggressor. The result is that the ego enjoys the advantage not only of converting passive experiencing into active doing, but also of belonging to the brotherhood of the powerful animals. The strength of the animal which would have pursued him is now at his disposal to pursue others with. This method of warding off anxiety is often not entirely successful and only works if certain conditions are fulfilled. There exists the danger that the might which is at present allied to oneself may, through regression, once more turn against one. The subject's apparent love for animals often bears traces of a considerateness for them which is still shot through with anxiety, indeed of a certain subordination to their power; in return, however, he has become one with them and participates in their strength. I once wrote [10] about a youngster who was extremely fond of the animals in the zoo, and who when he was pecked by his beloved jackdaw felt nothing but pride in the strength of this jackdaw which "belonged to" him, and considered his wound only as a proof of his bond with it. (How remote from his consciousness was that stratum of the mind which contained his passive-feminine desire to be castrated!) Here we have precisely the same process as the one by which the final mild identificatory love of the feared older brother comes about. In the same category belongs perhaps an attitude which is important in the psychology of examinations: "I am not only not afraid of the examiner, I am even on friendly terms with him." This not only means that one purchases the examiner's good will by submission; it also signifies a participation in his power, and it often even implies a readiness to become aggressive against him in the event of his being unwilling to recognize this. A nice study by Stengel [11] demonstrates the irrational character of modern examinations and their origin in initiation rites. To be sure, Stengel saw in this

---

[8] A. Freud, op. cit.

[9] This does not contradict the possibility that a child may in a primary sense choose an animal for love object.

[10] O. Fenichel, "Defense Against Anxiety, Particularly by Libidinization," No. 27, First Series.

[11] E. Stengel, "Pruefungsangst und Pruefungsneurose," Z. psa. Paedag., Vol. 10, 1936.

primarily the expression of the "eternal struggle between generations," instead of the eternal struggle between those who have power in society and those who have not—or rather, those who aspire to power and to whom *under certain conditions* some participation in it is granted. The irrational meaning of all examinations is that those in power grant the candidates a real participation only if they at the same time make the latter believe that they must in return renounce all more radical attempts to seize power.[12] "Pull" consists in a candidate participating in power before he is thus officially admitted to the ranks of those who may do so.

Perhaps it is not at first sight clear why I choose as my subject for discussion the psychology of the collector. Our knowledge of this is founded on Freud's paper "Character and Anal Erotism," [13] and it has been further developed by others, recently by Winterstein in his study "Der Sammler." [14] We know that the objects of the collector's hobby are fecal symbols. Collecting is a sublimation of anal-retentive desires, and the collector's pleasure in it is a continuation of his infantile-narcissistic pleasure in his own feces. But we must proceed from there to ask: In what individuals will it be particularly strongly developed? Firstly, in people with a constitutionally heightened anal erotism; but this does not interest us here. Secondly, however, in those who because of their experiences have either persisted in their infantile retention narcissism or have reverted to it later on. Perhaps it will be a help to us if we interpolate between the term "object of collection" and "feces" the term "possession." What is possession? That on which one sits.† In the final analysis, the prototype for it was certainly what one had inside the body.[15] Possessions are things which are now in the external world, but were once in the subject's own body (that is why possessions are symbols of feces). Thus they are the external world, and nevertheless they have ego quality. Obviously the possession is always in danger of losing this ego quality. The over-emphasis of the desire to retain—an overemphasis which is certainly erotogenic as well—means, "I will not let myself be robbed of anything," and the more one is afraid of being robbed of anything the stronger it is. The collector convinces himself by his collecting activity that "I still have it," but also (for what constitutes the narcissism of the obstinate child who will not part with his stool?) that "I still can." Great

---

[12] This is probably also the real meaning of initiation rites, in which social and sexual rights are granted to the young men, but in which it is impressed on them through painful ordeals and symbolic castration that these are granted only on certain conditions by which they must abide.

[13] S. Freud, "Character and Anal Erotism," *Coll. Pap.*, Vol. II.

[14] A. Winterstein, "Der Sammler," *Imago*, Vol. 7, 1921.

† The German word for "possession" is *"Besitz,"* and the word for "to sit" is *"sitzen"*; *"Besitzen"* ("to possess") means something like "to be-sit."—Trans. note.

[15] Cf. K. Abraham, "A Short Study of the Development of the Libido," *Selected Papers*, London, Hogarth, 1948.

possession is also *great power*. If one cannot do something that the more power-ful person can, one wants to appropriate his possession which makes him powerful. We know from the psychoanalysis of kleptomania that its object is often the penis (therefore it is more frequent in women than in men), but only if the penis envy was dealt with in a certain pregenitally determined way. For to the kleptomaniac, the stolen goods are basically always the external supplies that are necessary for his self-regard.[16] If in addition there is a par-ticularly anal-erotic constitution and an inclination to compensate the feeling of lack of manifold possessions—then there arises the tendency to collect. It is well known that passionate collectors easily overcome their moral scruples. Objects of collection are often recognizable as symbols of the collector's having or being able to do what others do not possess or cannot do. The relation be-tween the collector and his objects ought some day to be studied to see how frequently it reflects the feeling "I have acquired something by force or fraud that originally belonged to someone more powerful, but which is now a talisman for me, or which connects me magically with the previous possessor."

We should like to point out, lastly, that—in accord with the *oral* origin of the regulation of self-regard by external supplies—the penis or fecal symbol, that was obtained by robbing, stealing, or trickery, or by voluntary admittance to par-ticipation, is in the final analysis always thought of in all these forms as having been acquired orally by swallowing.

V

What prompted me to collate these clinical phenomena was a non-clinical problem. A small group of analysts of which I was one were inquiring into the use of analytic knowledge for the understanding of historical events and we came, among other things, upon the following problem: In all wars, whether external or internal, there have been and are *cruelties* that are far in excess of tactical necessities and of the amounts of hatred actually mobilized in the single individual. Only psychology can explain these. Glover considered this to be proof that deep-rooted instinctual motives are the true causes of wars, while what is ordinarily regarded as their cause are mere "rationalizations" of these destructive drives.[17] One can disagree with Glover's view without denying the existence of biologically founded pleasure in cruelty. One of the problems is that at most diverse periods the cruelties of war assume very similar and quite definite forms, in particular cruelties inflicted in order to dishonor the adversary. Perhaps psychoanalysis may enable us to see in this some more specific psy-

16 Cf. chapter on "Impulshandlungen," in O. Fenichel, *Perversionen, Psychosen, Charakterstoerun-gen*, Vienna, Int. Psa. Verlag, 1931.
17 E. Glover, *War, Sadism and Pacifism*, London, Allen and Unwin, 1933.

chological factors. These involve always either a chopping off of limbs or cannibalistic acts, or symbolic allusions to them. For instance, to quote Engels: "Many prisoners were executed in the cruelest manner; the rest were sent home with noses and ears cut off." [18] "The peasants were attacked and dispersed by Zapolya; Dosa himself was taken prisoner, roasted on a red-hot throne, and eaten alive by his own men, whose lives were spared solely on this condition." These atrocities were committed not by the rebels but by the representatives of law and order; and one often has the impression that in the history of the world such things have been done more often and more extensively by the defenders of the legal state than by the insurgents. For this an explanation is not far to seek: representatives of the prevailing traditional order act with a *good conscience,* and are thus on the whole better able to "idealize" [19] cruel instinctual actions, whereas their opponents are inhibited by feelings of guilt. (Since, however, they also have ideals, they too can become cruel enough; and another circumstance contributes to this, namely, the explosion of long pent-up quantities of aggression—"Fear not the free man; but tremble at the slave who breaks his chains." ‡)

In the cutting off of nose and ears they but imitate the criminal procedure of their time, or, more accurately, they anticipate it—for the regular penal code too inflicted such cruelties. We may also ask whence such forms of punishment originate. It can be established that roasting alive and eating a human being is not a prescribed punishment in any judiciary system (or if such occurs among certain primitive peoples, it certainly did not any more in sixteenth-century Germany). What was the purpose of this cruel command? To scorn and humiliate a beaten foe. And what determined the form of this scorn and humiliation? We often find that what was once one's own longed-for instinctual aim, but later succumbed to repression, is imposed on others in mockery and scorn. If the civilized man of today insults somebody with the famous quotation from Goethe's *Goetz von Berlichingen,* he wants to pour scorn on him with it, although, or *because,* it refers to what had precisely been his instinctual aim at a stage of his libidinal organization which he has since surmounted. The same holds for cannibalism: the vanquished must do for his humiliation what the victor had originally done for his gratification. It might be possible to conceive of lopping off of hands as an expression of a kind of inborn "castration drive." But seeing that it is done particularly to thieves and is thus a talion punishment, one should be cautious about such an assumption. There can be no doubt that such measures have a complicated magic meaning which is only no longer

[18] F. Engels, *The Peasant War in Germany,* New York, International Publishers, 1926.
[19] Cf. S. Rado, "An Anxious Mother," *Int. J. Psa.,* Vol. 9, 1928.
‡ From Schiller's poem "Die Worte des Glaubens."—Trans. note.

clear in their derivative forms: the wish is to cut off and eat the insignium of power—the body of the powerful one, his penis, his head—in order by this means to take his place, to become one with him. Primitive peoples eat the conquered enemy whose strength and valor they admire. All the other strange cruelties are derivatives of this.

It seems that this is the prototype from which the clinical phenomena discussed above derive. The wish is to acquire and devour the penis of the powerful one, to bring and keep many such penises within one's own power in order to be powerful oneself. As we know, this attempt is usually unsuccessful, and it leads to the phenomena of fear of revenge by the introjects (the social counterpart of the problem of depression).

The basic theme of all the phenomena discussed is, as has been said, that the subject's self-regard is heightened by his reuniting himself orally with the person to whom he has yielded up his own omnipotence. The omnipotent object must again acquire ego quality. The wish is to possess something of the object whereby, so long as that something is possessed, one is, in a magical way, the object, and thus once more omnipotent. That is what the collected object does; it is the sign that one possesses something of the power of the other person— in the final analysis, that one has robbed him of it. If one collects mementos of journeys what one has done is to conquer Nature which makes traveling fatiguing.[20] When in the folk tale the devil is cheated of his spoil, when Esau is defrauded of Isaac's blessing—as though the quantity of blessing were constant, and if Jacob got it, Esau lost it—then the concrete character of the magical concept of power comes to expression: the task is to steal a bit of power, and then one has it. One must only guard it well lest it be stolen from one in turn. Besides, the stolen bit of power is rather like ı stolen dog, which out of fidelity to its former owner may turn against the new one.

VI

The concrete concept of power is the trophy—and concerning this we already have a considerable analytic literature. I may assume that we are all familiar with Marie Bonaparte's excellent paper on the subject.[21] She points out that the trophy is a product of magic thinking, which rests on the notion that power (she calls it "honor") is a constant quantity, that "honor lost by one is always gained by another." Where head trophies preponderate, phallic ones are correspondingly scarce, and *vice versa*. The ambivalence toward those from whom trophies are taken is important. They are held in honor, since part of them is made part of one's self. (There is here undoubtedly a fluid transition from naked

[20] Mementos in general signal a victory over the one-way direction of time.
[21] M. Bonaparte, "Ueber die Symbolik der Kopftrophaeen," *Imago*, Vol. 14, 1928.

robbery to acts of piety: to preserve mementos from the legacy of a dear departed is to have appropriated a trophy from him who died before oneself and so to have compelled him to protect and not attack one.)

In the hunt the totem animals are treated as is the enemy in war; and the probable reason why the stag is the noblest game is because of his antlers, which are particularly suited for trophies. (The powerful man, who has no such phallic head decoration, creates for himself an artificial trophy as a substitute—for instance, a kingly crown.) As far as the betrayed husband is concerned, I do not share Marie Bonaparte's view that his being horned only depicts castration, through "representation by its opposite"; it is precisely its meaning as a symbolic substitute for his erect penis, which he cannot use with his wife, who is occupied elsewhere, that makes him—as I have shown in my paper on "The Long Nose" [22] —the target of ridicule. An important point, it seems to me, is the recognition that trophies are themselves substitutes, just as "possession" stands for "what has been incorporated." First there is the wish to kill and devour; then only comes the wish to possess the corpse, its parts, and their substitutes. And it is only after that that the wish arises not to kill, but only to steal and thereby to participate—and, last of all, the wish to receive from its previous possessor, under the observance of certain conditions, a trophy authorizing participation in his power which is voluntarily yielded by him. From this point there is a bridge to phenomena of fetishism and of normal love play. The lover, too, collects objects which have had some contact with his love object in order—literally or figuratively—to incorporate them. The lists of Don Juan's conquests which Leporello carried about for him were also a collection of trophies. Here "ocular" introjection certainly plays a large role; [23] and in this connection we have to stress the importance of respiratory introjection also,[24] since many customs, compulsive rituals, and fantasies aim at inhaling the spirit, or soul, or the like, of a beloved, or powerful, or deceased person.

VII

There are two groups of problems with which the trophy must be brought into relation: the primitive regulation of self-regard, and totemism. We have already spoken of both. As we know, the first of these also occurs in the cycle of ideas concerning the subject's own omnipotence—its loss to another person—the wish to regain it—introjection of the other person. The person who is caught up in this cycle is always primarily confronted—as the psychology of depression

---

[22] O. Fenichel, "The Long Nose," No. 17, *First Series*.
[23] O. Fenichel, "The Scoptophilic Instinct and Identification," No. 33, *First Series*.
[24] O. Fenichel, "Respiratory Introjection," No. 23, *First Series*.

shows—with this problem: shall the external supplies, which are indispensable to life and are cruelly denied by the external world, be got by him through oral-sadistic actions, or shall he obtain the favor of his objects through submission and thus induce them to make a voluntary delivery? Prayers are probably first of all signs of humility and submission, offered in the hope of purchasing the favor of God; nevertheless whole societies and some modern neurotics also think that by means of prayer they can, by force or fraud, *compel* God to grant them his favor, willy-nilly. Psychoanalytic clinical experience has made us familiar with the manifold forms of extortion of love, in which external devotion only gives opportunity for the expression of deeper-lying sadism. And not only do the subjects of a king seek forcibly to extort his favor by feigned obedience; King Friedrich Wilhelm himself was guilty of this contradiction toward his subjects when he cried to them as he beat them with his stick, "You shall not fear me! You shall love me!" This alternation between violent oral sadism and a humble devotion which conceals it belongs also to the sphere of our inquiry. We have a continuous series ranging from murder followed by cannibalism to "mild" homosexuality, from head-hunting to the peaceful memento-amulet received as a present.

Freud's theory of totemism is familiar to all.[25] Considerations like the ones put forth here show again the full depth of that theory. It may be that Freud's hypothesis of the murder of the primal father disregards many questions—for instance, that of a primary period of matriarchy or that of the role of external (i.e., economic) reality in cultural development—and this is certainly not the place to enter upon an evaluation or critique of Freud's far-reaching theory; but in one respect it makes clear at one stroke the relationships of the phenomena under discussion: all the totem rites serve to restrain the members of the totemistic society from rebellious acts of murder against social authority (as I should prefer to say instead of "the primal father"), from "repeating the primal deed," partly by prohibiting situations of temptation (incest taboo), but partly also by offering illusory substitutes. The totem is the primal ancestor, and as such he is not only something unattainably more powerful than the single individual, but is also flesh of his flesh—something with which the individual is indissolubly united, in which he partakes, so that he need not seize it by force. (The totem feasts, about which we have yet to speak, seem, it is true, to show that this safety device is insufficient; a social institution must afford a substitute for rebellion which channels off the rebellious impulses of the society in a harmless way, or directs them so that they serve, on the contrary, to strengthen the existing society.) The illusion of a purely magical participation in power can reconcile one, to a certain extent, to actual helplessness.

[25] S. Freud, *Totem and Taboo*, New York, Norton, 1952.

VIII

And now let us consider social reality from this point of view. This varies greatly, it is true, according to different times and places; but there have so far always been the opposed interests of those who could get gratifications, and those to whom these were denied, of the powerful and the powerless, and these are nowadays represented by social classes. Ever and again the question arises how societies can maintain themselves when the majority of their members are deprived of all possibilities of gratification, although the goods necessary for their satisfaction are available. How can the enormous quantity of pent-up hate which must accumulate under such conditions be prevented from erupting? This, as we know, is done first of all by external force; secondly, however, by a psychic "restructuring" of the members of society whose instinctual and ego formation is bent by education in a direction desirable to the society. Part of this "restructuring" is made intelligible, it seems to us, by what has been said here. Those who are in fact helpless are offered illusory participations in power (such participations being very different in different societies).[26] All danger of revolt would of course really be avoided if, in a "democracy," an *actual* participation in power could be offered to everybody; but this is not possible, because fire and water can make no compromise with each other. Instead, magical participation is offered, the operation of which can be explained only by psychoanalysis. Actual social trophies are, for example, orders and decorations which of course are conferred by the superiors and are not wrested from them by force. The *mana* of authority is personified in all badges of distinction. He who has received them can count himself as participating in that authority, regardless of how he fares in other things, and he who has not received them can hope to do so. "Every man carries his marshal's baton in his knapsack" was always an illusion of this kind, and some class societies manage to maintain in the members of the op-pressed class, despite all the evidence to the contrary, the illusory hope that they individually can rise into the ruling class and partake in power. Where the absolute boundaries of the caste system obtain, this illusory participation is conceived differently, being still more magical and less realistic. Even the "better world to come" after death is nothing else than this. Still more clear was this participation by magical sharing in the power of the mighty when nobility was conferred by a tap of the sword; the power substance was conveyed to those thus distinguished through contagious magic. The mighty of today merely extend the hand—and therewith afford us an insight into the psychological

---

[26] After completing this paper I became acquainted with the studies of A. Kardiner, "The Role of Economic Security in the Adaptation of the Individual," *The Family*, Vol. 17, 1936, and "Security, Cultural Restraints, Intersocial Dependencies, and Hostilities," *The Family*, Vol. 18, 1937.

meaning of our greeting by handshake. The erotogenic factor certainly also plays a part here. But what is more important is that one man's physical substance is allowed to flow into the other person magically by contact, so that he and they become of one blood, thereby excluding enmity.

The soldier's uniform is "the king's coat"—and whoever wears it partakes in the king. Fromm considered the meaning of the uniform to be primarily that it distinguishes sharply the uniformed person from the non-uniformed one and the officer from the rank and file.[27] This may also play its part, since in general it is characteristic of "illusory social participations" that, seeing that they serve to eradicate the striving for *real* participation, they often at the same time inculcate the fact that any other participation than that proffered is forbidden. (It is characteristic of God and of all authority that they—like the omnipotent adult in relation to the helpless child—are at once unattainable for the self and yet have ego-quality. But it seems to me even more important that the uniform creates *uniformity*—makes all alike. *Flags* are trophies *par excellence*. Those of the enemy are to be conquered; one's own are something unattainably exalted, outside one's own ego, yet having ego quality.[28] The relation of this to Freud's formulation of the group-uniting character of the collective superego [29] will be discussed later.)

Fromm goes so far as to say that when the superordinated power seems much too unattainable, the individual will, upon appropriate inducements from above, renounce not only his personal superego but—as in hypnosis—parts of his ego as well.[30] Fromm is correct in this. He writes: "If another person proves so powerful and so dangerous that fighting him is hopeless and submission seems the best defense, or so benevolent and protective that the individual's own activity seems superfluous—in other words, if there arises a situation in which the exercise of ego-functions becomes impossible or superfluous, then the ego disappears for as long as the functions in connection with whose exercise it arose cannot or may not be exercised by it." Those functions thus "participate" in the alien ego of the more powerful person. Where this occurs, masochistic characters develop. If it is true that the "bodily-part" fantasy—i.e., "only together with the other person am I a whole"—is the psychological formula of bondage, then the masochism of the bondsman is precisely of this kind. It is built on hidden

[27] E. Fromm, "Authority and Family, social-psychological section," *Studien ueber Autoritaet und Familie*, Paris, Alcan, 1936. (*Schr. Instit. Sozialforsch.*, Vol. 5.)

[28] A. Kielholz has called my attention to the fact that at the battle at Sempach the mayor of Zoingen swallowed the pennant of the Swiss so that it should not fall into the hands of the enemy, and that he was celebrated on this account as a national hero. He has pointed out to me also the connection between the word "trophy" and the verb τρέφομαι ["I am nourished"].

[29] S. Freud, *Group Psychology and the Analysis of the Ego*, London, Hogarth, 1948.

[30] E. Fromm, *op. cit.*

sadism; for the masochist there is peaceful "participation" where once there was a sadistic wish to rob. According to Freud the overcoming of hate through identificatory love always plays a part in the "social feelings." In our society this is certainly so. Fromm says that the mechanism which underlies such participation should not be termed identification, and that on the contrary there can never be any identification with the powerful one because he is alien in essence from the subject's ego; it has to be admitted that this identification must be different from other "identifications in the ego," but would not Fromm consider that the mechanism which brings the superego into being was an "identification"? The unbridgeable distance between the introject and the rest of the ego is characteristic for the superego too, and, indeed, becomes the cause of the forming of a "grade" in the ego and thereby of the establishment of a specific superego.[31] It is true enough that in these "participations in power," as in the development of the superego, the fantasy of dissolving into the great person, of *losing individuality,* of being devoured,[32] is also an executive mechanism, in addition to introjections. But these two mechanisms underlying identifications seem to merge in practice to such an extent that it is scarcely possible to separate them. Perhaps their differentiation will some day become important for the problem of empathy.

And now let us ask ourselves, What is "triumph"?

IX

To this end we must consider two of Freud's basic concepts of psychoanalytic theory.

The first is the concept of the superego.[33] The superego is a structurally distinguished part of the ego which has arisen through the introjection of persons belonging to the external world. It is more or less set over against the rest of the ego, which it observes, on which it makes demands, but to which it also extends protection and approval. It is an intrapsychic and desexualized continuation of an external sexual object relation. In introducing this concept, Freud wrote, among other things: "Clearly the repression of the oedipus complex was no easy task. . . . The strength to do this was, so to speak, borrowed from the father. . . . The superego retains the character of the father. . . ."—though it derives its sternness, not alone from the father's real sternness, but also from the child's original aggressiveness. What seems to me important in our present inquiry is the concept here of "borrowing." If we put this together with the fact

---

[31] S. Freud, *The Ego and the Id*, London, Hogarth, 1947.
[32] G. H. Graber, *op. cit.*
[33] S. Freud, *The Ego and the Id*.

that the introjected former objects of the oedipus complex cannot merge with the ego because their powerfulness makes them incongruous with the rest of the ego, so that the superego, though it has ego quality, towers high above the ego, then it becomes obvious that we are in the very middle of our problem. With the help of the superego the ego "participates" in the more powerful father's might, and the acquisition of the superego is the equivalent of the acquisition of a trophy. Here too participation, in the final analysis, is accomplished through oral incorporation. The acquisition of the superego is a special case of the reacquisition of lost omnipotence by reintrojection, and the course it follows is already laid down by the very *first* object relation, the one to the mother's breast and milk. The first experience is: "I feel unpleasure—I swallow what is offered to me from outside—the lost pleasure returns." And in accordance with this we have the later sequence: "I am helpless—I swallow the power which is in the external world—the lost pleasure returns." It is in keeping with the supposition that all trophies are somehow personified "superegos" that they all have one thing in common with the superego: they both protect and threaten their possessor. As long as one keeps a trophy in one's house, one has the power-ful being in the house, and compels it to protect one. But, just as behind the peaceful "participation" there always lurks the original intention of robbing, so is this protection always conditional too, and the hidden deeper layer, the "revenge of the introject," threatens to break through. The deer, whose antlers hang in the room, may again change into a threatening enemy. "Noblesse oblige"; the possessor of the trophy owes certain considerations to the memory of the original bearer of it.

The second concept I wish to bring up here is Freud's formula for the forma-tion of "groups." [34] As we know, it is to the effect that a number of persons set the same man or the same idea in the place of their superego, and identify them-selves with one another on the basis of what they thus have in common. It is thus assumed that the superego, an internal agency, can be projected back into an object in the outer world—a thing which is amply confirmed by psychoanalytic clinical experience. Following such projection there are, therefore, once again people who both appear unattainably lofty and yet possess ego quality—or, rather, "superego quality," as we should say here.

Now according to Fromm [35] this is the essence of all authority. He writes: "External power is transformed through the superego, in that it is changed from an external into an internal power." But this, it is true, is then "always again projected onto the prevailing authority in the society; in other words, the

34 S. Freud, *Group Psychology and the Analysis of the Ego.*
35 E. Fromm, *op. cit.*

individual invests the actual authorities with characteristics of his own superego. As regards this sort of projection of the superego onto the authorities, the latter are largely exempted from rational criticism."

Clearly human beings have only two ways of facing a power which restricts them: revolt; or else a (more or less illusory) participation, which makes it possible for them to bear their suppression—a submission (with more or less masochistic sexualization) in which their hostility, their "latent revolt," persists somewhere, but is combated by the fantasy that it has been already accomplished, and that they are already one with authority.

Freud, as we have already quoted, says that "social feelings" are primarily of latent homosexual character (he speaks here of our own society), and he explains it thus: The mechanism at work in the development of social feelings is the same as the one implicated in the genesis of the aforementioned "mild identificatory love." Where there was once envy and hate toward the other, there is now the feeling of "mea res agitur." It is understandable that the aggressions against the person with whom one has thus identified oneself then become restricted. According to Freud, in view of man's destructive tendencies, only these limitations of aggression make society possible at all.[36] And this is true; for it is by means of identifications that we learn to love and to be considerate of others and for that reason to tolerate tensions, and when necessary renounce immediate discharges. But it is also obvious that in this way inhibitions of aggression are formed which are no more and no less than inhibitions of a vital function of the ego, paralyzing aggressive energies with which one could defend one's interests against the interests of those more powerful than oneself. For the latter interests, although diametrically opposed to one's own, now become, with the help of "participation," experienced *as* one's own.

So far we have spoken of the primitive regulation of self-regard by external supplies. The less primitive later regulations, however, occur in normal people by means of a "fulfillment of ideals." If the difference between ego and superego is great, the subject's self-regard is low; in turn, every convergence of ego and superego, every feeling that the ideal is after all not totally and forever inaccessible, every assurance that the "unattainably high" does have "ego quality," augments his self-regard. Every removal of feelings of guilt brings him closer to his original feeling of omnipotence; every fulfillment of an ideal is, one might say, equivalent to the "acquisition of a trophy," in that it brings back to him a part of the omnipotence which he has relinquished to the external world. If such a removal of the sense of guilt is especially rapid and extensive, his narcissistic gratification attains an exaggerated, hilarious character, and the suddenly

[36] S. Freud, *Civilization and Its Discontents,* London, Hogarth, 1946.

released energy, hitherto tied up in feelings of guilt, is discharged in laughter and in a general agility of the ego.

The same process takes place, though much more convulsively, in *mania*. Here, the sudden disappearance of a hitherto valid superego demand comes about not by means of the "fulfillment of an ideal," but by the use of the defense mechanism of "denial" against persisting superego demands.[37] If, as Freud put it, mania gives the impression of a successful rebellion of the ego against the superego,[38] then the satisfaction felt after a "fulfillment of an ideal" gives the impression of being a reward by the superego, of a participation in it. Mania and self-satisfaction from the "fulfillment of an ideal" are, in this sense, basically the same phenomenon as the defiance of Prometheus on the one hand, and, on the other, the believer's devotion to God.

We know that Freud has compared mania with the universal human institution of feasts.[39] Feasts are periodically recurring events in which social rules which are otherwise valid are suspended. According to Freud's well-known interpretation, the totem feast is a symbolic repetition of the forbidden primal deed, and the festive mood corresponds to the sudden liberation of the energy usually tied up in necessary inhibitions. The social meaning of this institution is thus clear: The existing order prefers a symbolic rebellion to a real one. The people must be given *"circenses"* as well as *"panem"*—must have an opportunity to discharge their rebellious and sadistic tendencies in an innocuous place.

When the deed is repeated, the uprising executed, the mighty deprived of power, then the inhibitions disappear—and previously tied-up energies are liberated in the form of manic actions and feelings. *Triumph is the disappearance of fear and inhibition as a result of the acquisition of the trophy; it is the joining of the hitherto powerless with power.* (It is also due to the disappearance of fear, to conquer which the will to power was especially intensified.) As intoxication can be followed by a hangover, so can triumph be followed by an intensified fear of the trophy's continuing independent existence.

X

And now I would like to return again to clinical experience, particularly to that concerning laughing fits, which, as far as I know, have not as yet been studied psychoanalytically. We are familiar, however, with the compulsive laughter on receipt of news of death which is so common in obsessional neurotics. The typical, familiar interpretation of this is, as we know, as follows: The

[37] H. Deutsch, "Zur Psychologie der manisch-depressiven Zustaende, insbesondere der chronischen Hypomanie," *Int. Z. Psa.,* Vol. 19, 1933.
[38] S. Freud, *Group Psychology and the Analysis of the Ego.*
[39] S. Freud, *ibid.*

neurotic, who unconsciously hated the dead person, or is reminded by his death that another individual whom he hates might likewise die, experiences the news of his death as a gratification of his unconscious wishes; he attempts to suppress his satisfaction which nevertheless breaks through in the form of laughter. It is not difficult to state the economic reason why this compulsive laughter should occur in sudden bursts; upon the news that the enemy is dead, the anxieties and considerations relating to him become *suddenly* superfluous— and it is their energies which are discharged in the laughter. The strangeness, the compulsory element of the laughter, is explained by the fact that the ego is not in agreement with it.

I had the opportunity recently to analyze in a female patient a direct shift from a severely depressive mood to a laughing fit. During the analysis the patient developed a passing but extraordinary intensification of her feelings of inferiority. External events and transference fantasies seemed to her to prove that she was useless, "internally destroyed," etc. Feeling insignificant, empty and worthless, she began (using the defense mechanism of projection) to cast aspersions on analysis and the analyst: they were useless, and did not help her. The analyst just sat there without doing anything. He was an old, impotent man. He might not even be listening to her, might not even be there, might have died during the hour. Perhaps there was a trap door under the analyst's chair through which he would vanish while the patient was suffering on the sofa, and would return only at the end of the hour. Of course, he said something, occasionally. Perhaps he came up through the trap door every time again for this purpose—but that would have to happen very quickly sometimes—down, up, down, up—and at this point the laughing fit broke loose.

The first obvious thing is that the patient in her imagination makes the analyst into an old, impotent man, that is, she has castrated him; the second, that the rhythmic appearance and disappearance which she consciously fantasied as a symbol of feebleness represents the rhythm of the sexual act and that the patient is thus in her imagination clearly watching an active phallus.

Anna Freud has shown that laughter frequently appears as a substitute for sexual excitement. We find this confirmed, but must add that in this case it is a sexual excitement of a special kind. It seems contradictory that the analyst is conceived of on the one hand as a castrated man, and on the other as a "penis." But this paradox is explained: the penis which the patient watches is a cut-off penis. In the case of another patient too, a very compassionate and easily "touched" person, the "poor child" with whom she sympathized so much was both the penisless creature and the penis. "Little Hans, all alone, went into the world so wide" § is the phallic figure as an object of compassion, because it is

§ "Haenschen klein ging allein in die weite Welt hinein."—Trans. note.

connected with the idea of a performed castration. In our present case, however, the castration called out not pity but *triumph:* the analyst vanishes into the ground, that is, into the grave, and he is forced to copulate with the patient— and thus to give her what she needs to lift her depression. The initial situation is that she is the "have-not," the analyst is the "have." She fantasies a robbery and the inverse situation: she is the "have" and the analyst the "have-not." In her sadistic-sexual excitement, which was forced into the form of laughter by repression, she has taken possession of the analyst's penis, has acquired it as trophy, so that what is left is an impotent old man who might well vanish entirely; and she savors the *triumph* of her union with this trophy by playing with it, by making it dance before her, copulate with her, and satisfy her, at her whim.

Since this case, I have analyzed a male patient's tic, which was a suppressed laughter, and which also proved to be his triumph about a fantasy of having carried out a castration.

Why does the suddenly released excitement which cannot be recognized as sexual, take precisely the form of laughter? Freud explains laughter as a sudden release of hitherto dammed-up energy.[40] These conditions are present in our case. An inhibition, an anxiety, has turned out to be unnecessary. Now, in the presence of something dangerous we hold our breath. The somatic equivalent of the "anxiety signal" is a tonic tensing of the diaphragm. But if the mighty one can be killed or rendered powerless, or if he changes so that one can participate in his power and thus need fear him no longer, then the spasm of the diaphragm is relaxed, in such a manner that the tonic spasm first changes into a clonic one which then executes the discharge; the triumph is introduced by a triumphant laughter.

XI

I prefaced this study by saying that I could say no more than had already been stated in *Totem and Taboo* and *Group Psychology and the Analysis of the Ego.* But I hope that we have seen what has been stated there in new connections and particularly in relation to clinical facts of a different kind. Yet, to my mind, the significance of the topic here discussed lies not in its clinical but rather in its socio-psychological aspect. The needs of men cannot for long be left unsatisfied and suppressed without calling out in them a tendency to revolt. The suppressed see that the others are powerful and want to strike them down so as to attain the power for themselves. If they succeed, they feel themselves to be in the place of the others, they have the *trophy*—originally, through cannibalism, inside their body, later, through "castration," as a possession—and they experience its

[40] S. Freud, "Wit and Its Relation to the Unconscious," *The Basic Writings.*

acquisition as triumph. The attempt frequently fails, owing to ambivalence, anxiety, passive love, and consequent remorse after the deed; the trophy retains its independent existence in the form of the supergo and threatens the ego just as it is itself also continuously threatened by the ego. The conflict becomes permanent in the form of a rhythmic alternation between depressive and manic moods —between distance from the superego and approximation to it—between dissatisfaction and satisfaction with the self. These feelings are frequently used by society to change the structural configuration of its members.

It is in the interest of the mighty to make voluntary concessions to the helpless whose aggression is to be forestalled; for trophies voluntarily surrendered, they can demand and obtain compensation in the form of respect and submission. Since, however, *magical* participations may have the same aggression-preventing effect as real ones, such magical participation in power of all kinds can induce the helpless to remain voluntarily in their state of helplessness. The illusion that the authority which has robbed a man of his activity and brought him into a masochistic-receptive position, loves him and gives him the supplies which maintain and raise his self-regard is obviously one of the means by which class societies maintain themselves.

ELEVEN

The Counter-Phobic Attitude *

ERNEST JONES pointed out in his study on "The Phallic Phase" [1] that not all the manifestations characteristic of that phase of libidinal development are directly parallel to the effects of the erotogenic sensations which emanate from the penis or from the clitoris and which finally establish the primacy of those organs. He showed that in part these manifestations are, on the contrary, determined by the very fact that the subject has to deal with fears which arose when he yielded to those sensations. Accordingly, Jones distinguishes a "proto-phallic" phase, in which the primacy of the phallus entirely dominates the picture, from a "deutero-phallic" phase, in which the task of dealing with these fears complicates the picture. In fact, considering the abundance of actual manifestations, it is not easy to recognize which are determined primarily and biologically, and which arise only when fear has to be dealt with. Sometimes it has seemed as if writers who have attempted to investigate the interrelationships psychologically have underestimated the primary biological component. I have already expressly pointed out the danger of such an underestimation.[2] I have since learned, however, to what an extent efforts toward defense against fear, and even the pleasure derived from successful efforts, actually complicate the picture of primary erotogenic pleasure.

In the present paper I should like to devote my attention to a definite type of these fear-defenses, which is usually referred to under the inexact name of "overcompensation against fear," but which could much more precisely be called the "counter-phobic attitude." Its manifestation is by no means confined to the phallic phase.

---

* First published in *Int. J. Psa.* Vol. 20, 1939, pp. 263–274.
[1] E. Jones, "The Phallic Phase," *Papers on Psycho-Analysis*, 5th ed., Baltimore, Williams and Wilkins, 1948.
[2] O. Fenichel, "Defense against Anxiety, Particularly by Libidinization," No. 27, *First Series*.

The phobic attitude consists of avoiding certain situations or certain parts of situations, such as objects, perceptions, feelings, or sensations, because they would be connected with anxiety. This anxiety is the symptom of an existing instinctual conflict. The situation feared usually represents a temptation toward an instinct whose activity is unconsciously regarded as dangerous. At times the situation feared corresponds merely to a supposed confirmation of an unconscious expectation of punishment. Or the situation may represent temptation and threat of punishment simultaneously. We know that this anxiety is initiated in a judgment on the part of the ego "Danger ahead!"—a judgment whose purpose it is to introduce defensive attitudes.[3] What is of most importance to us at the moment, however, is that this purpose should have failed and an attack of anxiety have occurred. The signal given by the ego, "A traumatic situation may arise," has in itself produced a traumatic situation, probably owing to an already existent damming up of instincts. In the "phobic attitudes" the ego has learned to avoid the repetition of such very painful traumatic situations.

This all seems perfectly clear. But it becomes less so when we observe that such anxiety situations are not avoided but are sought after, at least under certain conditions. It often happens that a person shows a preference for the very situations of which he is apparently afraid. And even more frequently he will later on develop a preference for the situations which he formerly feared.

The first explanation of this lies in the nature of the phobic anxieties already mentioned. It is not the total personality that fears the phobic situation. That situation represents an unconscious instinctual impulse. Originally, there was an active striving for it. Only the veto of the external world or the superego produced the anxiety. The original striving may reappear.

We must now investigate under what conditions this reappearance may take place. It presupposes that the opposing anxiety has been overcome, so that we have here to deal with the problem of defenses against anxiety. On the other hand, in the very cases in which situations once feared are especially sought after, the anxiety seems not to be completely overcome. Otherwise the situation would have lost its whole importance. The libido which had been displaced from a certain instinctual situation onto its phobic substitute would have flowed back to its original instinctual aims. But the preference displays the character of an overcompensation and shows that unconsciously the anxiety is still alive. We must ask what this means, and under what conditions the paradoxical state of affairs becomes possible, in which a still present anxiety is warded off more effectively by *seeking* situations in which it usually appears than by *avoiding* them.

With this in mind let us consider the normal ways of overcoming anxiety—

[3] S. Freud, *The Problem of Anxiety*, New York, Psa. Quart. Press and Norton, 1936.

that is, of bringing about, not a mere external "defense" behind which the latent anxiety still operates, but a real conquest, such as occurs thousands of times in the course of normal development.

A child, as we know, at first wishes to discharge as quickly as possible the excitations which flow in upon him from without as well as from within. He is incapable of controlling his motility himself. As the environment cannot always immediately take steps to satisfy him, the child frequently reaches a dammed-up condition. This state, or rather, an undesired vegetative discharge caused by it, is then experienced as the prototype of anxiety. As the child slowly learns to control his motility, purposeful acts gradually take the place of mere discharge reactions, which means that he can prolong the time between stimulus and reaction, and achieve a certain tolerance of tensions, a binding of the immediate reactive impulses by means of anti-cathexes. What is prerequisite for a purposeful act is not only the control of the physical apparatus, but also the establishment of the function of judgment, that is, of the capacity for anticipating the future in the imagination, the capacity for "trying out," which is characteristic of the functions of the ego in general. With the establishment of this function of anticipating the future in the imagination and of planning later actions accordingly, the idea of "danger" is justified. The judging ego declares that a situation which is not yet traumatic might become so. This judgment obviously sets up in the id the same conditions as the traumatic situation itself, but in a lesser degree. This, too, the ego must experience as anxiety.[4]

Freud has shown us that in small children a phenomenon can be observed which we also find in traumatic neurotics. If the organism is flooded with quantities of excitation it attempts to get rid of it by later repetitions of the situation which induced the excessive excitation. This takes place not only in the play of little children, but, as Grotjahn has recently pointed out, in their dreams as well.[5] Between the original flood of excitation and these repetitions there is one fundamental difference. In the original experience the organism itself was passive—it was flooded with stimuli from without or from within the body. In the case of the repetitions, the organism is active and can, at least to a certain degree, determine the admissible measure of excitation. At first, the passive experiences which roused anxiety are reproduced actively by the child in his play in order to achieve a belated mastery. Later on, the activity of the ego becomes even greater: the child in his play not only dramatizes the exciting experiences of the past, he also anticipates what he expects to happen in the future. It is precisely this anticipation which the function of judgment determines, and

[4] For this and what follows cf. S. Freud, *ibid.*, and *Beyond the Pleasure Principle*, London, Hogarth, 1948; and O. Fenichel, "Early Stages of Ego Development," No. 3 in this volume.

[5] M. Grotjahn, "Dream Observations in a Two-Year-Five-Months-Old Baby," *Psa. Quart.*, Vol. 7, 1938.

eventually directs to purposeful "action" and also to the suppression of action in case of "danger."

When the organism discovers that it is now able to overcome without fear a situation which would formerly have overwhelmed it with anxiety, it experiences a certain kind of pleasure. This pleasure has the character of "I need not feel anxiety any more." It makes the child's play evolve from immediate discharge to mastery of the external world by means of repeated exercise. Probably what German psychologists have called "functional pleasure" is nothing other than this pleasure—that is, pleasure in the fact that the exercise of the function is now possible without anxiety.[6] This pleasure is the basic component of the counter-phobic attitude.

What does this functional pleasure mean economically? If it were merely that the ego, engaging in activity without fear, has become able to avoid a damming up which would previously have appeared in a similar situation, that would explain the non-appearance of a specific unpleasure, but not the positive appearance of pleasure.

But a certain expenditure of energy is associated with the anxiety or the fearful expectation felt by a person uncertain whether he will be able to master the excitation connected with the experience. It is the sudden cessation of this expenditure of energy which is experienced by the successful ego as a sort of "triumph" and enjoyed as functional pleasure. Usually the pleasure originating from this source will be condensed with an erotogenic pleasure, which again has become possible owing to the overcoming of the anxiety.

If, however, functional pleasure is based upon the fact that an ever-ready anxiety proves to be superfluous, then the anxiety must disappear as soon as the ego is absolutely sure of itself and no longer holds an anxious expectation in readiness. And this proves correct in innumerable cases. In general, adults do not enjoy any special functional pleasure when they engage in long-familiar and automatic activities, which made them very proud when first accomplished in their childhood. If an adult has this special kind of pleasure, it can be for only two possible reasons, or rather for a combination of these reasons. Either his pleasure is actually of a different kind and merely disguises itself as functional pleasure, or the person in question is by no means really convinced of his ability and, before he engages in any such activity, actually passes through a sort of anxious tension of expectation, though he may not consciously recognize it as such.

Let us consider the first possibility. We have said that the functional pleasure

[6] This idea was put forward by E. Kris, "Ego Development and the Comic," *Psychoanalytic Explorations in Art*, New York, Int. Univ. Press, 1952.

of children is usually condensed with erotogenic forms of pleasure. Fixations to this combination may occur, in the sense that certain erotogenic forms of pleasure later retain the external form of functional pleasure or assume it again. It is not merely that in certain circumstances a pleasure experienced during an apparent sexual act may prove to be functional pleasure. The reverse is also true. Among the sexual component instincts, exhibitionism is particularly suited to such a use. Actually, the exhibitionist, though interested in objects, remains narcissistic to a remarkable degree. We see that for perverse exhibitionists as well as for other people engaged in actual or fantasied performances before an audience, the person of the object is relatively unimportant and that he is merely used as a sort of "witness" in endopsychic conflicts. The idea of the subject that the object is excited is intended to help the former to get away from his castration fear. Similarly a functional pleasure may also be condensed with other instinctual pleasures.

The second possibility is of more importance. If the primary anxiety has not been entirely overcome, and the inhibition is still effective in the unconscious, then the adult who must in every instance conquer his anxiety anew is like a child succeeding for the first time.

And in this respect the "counter-phobic attitude" may really be regarded as a never-ending attempt at the belated conquest of an unmastered infantile anxiety. It is easy to say what determines whether or not the infantile anxiety will be overcome. It cannot, as we know, be overcome if the activity against which it is directed has a hidden sexual significance. The defensive processes undertaken have cut off the defending anxieties, as well as what is being warded off, from any contact with the rest of the personality. More difficult is the decisive question, the consideration of which we shall postpone for the moment, of what determines the fact that even in the case of failure certain derivative anxieties may be overcome in the counter-phobic attitudes—a conquest which is experienced pleasurably even though the primary anxiety remains alive.

If both conditions are effective simultaneously, the instinctual pleasure felt in conquering an acute anxiety (which is still alive in the unconscious) is never identical with the pleasure which the unblocked primary instinct could give. This difference is of paramount practical importance.

The best example of this is the pride in potency of some obsessional neurotics. Under certain conditions that allay his fear, such a patient is able to carry out the sexual act and enjoys a narcissistic functional pleasure in it. Naturally, he also feels a certain sexual pleasure, but not the complete relaxation of a full orgasm. Here one might refer to the wide field of pseudo-sexuality in general, where acts of an apparent sexual character serve the purpose of satisfying narcissistic needs and in this way of defense against anxiety. The sexual pleasure is then interfered with, since other needs have become intermingled with it.[7]

Only in especially favorable circumstances is it possible for counter-phobic attitudes to result eventually in the dissipation of the original anxiety.[8] But unquestionably that is what the counter-phobic individual really strives for. He seeks out what was once feared in the same way as a traumatic neurotic dreams of his trauma, or as a child experiences pleasurably in play what he is afraid of in reality. What pleasure, for example, does a child feel when an adult tosses him in the air and catches him? Undoubtedly on the one hand erotogenic equilibrium (and skin) pleasure, and on the other hand the overcoming of a fear of falling. If he is certain that he will not be dropped, he can take pleasure in having thought that he might have been dropped—he may shudder a little, but realizes that his fear was unnecessary. To make this pleasure possible, certain conditions must be fulfilled. The child must have confidence in the adult who is playing with him, the height must not be too great, etc. Here obviously a real learning through exercise may occur. When repeated experience has shown that the fear is groundless, the conditions under which enjoyment is possible become wider and wider, and finally the fear disappears entirely. The counter-phobic individual remembers this process and tries to repeat it. We know why his attempt usually fails.

When, however, we see that many people with counter-phobic attitudes nevertheless consciously feel a good deal of pleasure in spite of this failure and can avoid becoming aware of the anxiety still operative in them, we must admit that they are relatively well off. And we can thus turn now to our principal question: What makes such a relatively fortunate outcome possible?

(1) We already know what the first condition is: the transformation of passivity into activity.[9] The child fears that undue quantities of excitation may break in upon him unexpectedly from the outside. He creates actively in play a tension within himself in a degree and at a moment which are bearable for him. Gradually he learns to increase the degree of tension. (It would be interesting to enquire how far masturbation in children is sexual *play* in this sense, that is, to what extent the ego learns through self-established sexual tension how to deal with sexual excitation.) We frequently see that in adults, too, the search for situations which were formerly feared becomes pleasurable precisely because they are actively sought. If, however, the same situation arises at an unexpected

---

[7] It would be entirely wrong to state that these other needs are the "unconscious meaning" of the sexual act.

[8] Just as it is only in especially favorable circumstances that a phobia results in the dissipation of the anxiety. Cf. S. Freud, "Repression," *Coll. Pap.*, Vol. IV, London, Hogarth, 1948.

[9] This condition was mentioned by Freud in *Beyond the Pleasure Principle* and was discussed by him later on several occasions, and finally at considerable length in "Female Sexuality," *Coll. Pap.*, Vol. V, London, Hogarth, 1950.

time and without activity on the part of the subject, the old fear reappears. A phenomenon which has already been studied in detail in analytical literature belongs to this category: the so-called "identification with the aggressor." [10]

(2) The overcoming of anxiety is not always so "progressive." Children overcome their anxiety not only by playing actively at what has threatened them, but also by letting a loved person, whom they trust, do to them what they fear to do themselves. Or they try to convince themselves that such a person's omnipotence will protect them in their activity. To this type belongs a very common counter-phobic precondition: that pleasure may be enjoyed so long as one believes in some magical fashion in the protection of an outsider. There are hundreds of varieties of this mechanism which requires one to secure a protective or permissive promise, actual or magical, before engaging in an activity which would otherwise be feared. It is of importance to notice that a passive-receptive condition of this kind may frequently be later bound up with a transformation of passivity into activity: the counter-phobic individual can engage pleasurably in the activity which he originally feared, if during the procedure he demonstrates to an object with which he is unconsciously identified that he is protecting or pardoning it.

(3) If the originally infantile sexual excitation was feared because of its sadistic component, then the mechanism which we have just described is simultaneously operative in still another way. The promise of protection which the subject seeks to enjoy, or, in the case of identification, to give, is well calculated to contradict the unconscious belief in the violent nature of the intended act: "If the object concerned *itself* allows me to do this, then this act cannot injure it." So, too, in many other cases, certain accompanying circumstances are necessary, which seem to contradict one or another of the factors which originally aroused anxiety. There is a similar position in the perversions, where sexual pleasure is made possible in the face of a severe fear of castration by overemphasizing a component instinct whose activity apparently contradicts the possibility of castration.

Thus I once found in an analysis that an interest in literature was based upon a phobia of picture books. The scoptophilia, associated with the functional pleasure "I am no longer afraid of books," had become possible owing to the narcissistic striving "to know all books." In this way the subject was protected from surprises which involved a sudden danger of castration. I had an opportunity of observing a similar mechanism at work in a marked interest in railways, which went back to a forgotten infantile fear of railways. Here also the primal scene that had been displaced onto the excitements of traveling by rail was

---

[10] A. Freud, *The Ego and the Mechanisms of Defence,* Chapter IX, New York, Int. Univ. Press, 1946.

experienced above all as the "overwhelming unknown." Through the heightened interest and the knowledge of railway traveling acquired as a result of it, this fear was eliminated, and the previously feared sexual enjoyment of the rhythm of the railway again became possible. Moreover, this was also connected with the mechanism "active instead of passive." For between the passive experience of the feared railway journeys and the later predilection for railways a long period of actively "playing at railways" took place. During the analysis its unconscious significance was recognized in the fact that the rhythm of the railway game was actively performed in contrast to the rhythm of the feared sexual excitation.

Here we may interpose that much of what, in libidinal development, we are accustomed to call "fixations" not only goes back to special experiences of satisfaction or frustration, but is built in a fashion analogous to the perversions. The attitudes to which the subject has become fixated often simultaneously contradict an opposing anxiety. Now it is true that he is not fixated to the attitudes which were at one time feared, but to those which contradict that anxiety. But there are also cases which are analogous to many compulsive symptoms—in which the patient feels compelled to repeat the same action a certain number of times. In analysis it comes to light that, whereas the conscious compulsive command runs, "You must carry out exactly the same action once again," the unconscious significance is that the repetition is to differ in one fundamental point from the first execution: it is to be executed with a different mental attitude (e.g., without disturbing instinctual thoughts, or, accentuating the superego instead of the instinct). Similarly there are fixations which consist of doing exactly what had been originally feared, and so contradicting the anxiety.

(4) And with this we come to the cases in which we may speak of a true "libidinization of fear," which occurs with people who have gone through a certain masochistic development.

A mechanism destined for instinctual defense may also be secondarily libidinized outside the realm of fear. It may happen owing to the return of the repressed or by the use of a defensive attitude for attaining a pleasurable secondary gain. Fear, like any other excitation, may be a source of sexual excitation. But this is true—just as in the case of pain—only so long as the unpleasure remains within certain limits, for example, in feeling sympathy for the hero of a tragedy. This is—just as in the case of masochism—a procedure of secondary adjustment.[11]

(5) All of these mechanisms are usually connected with another factor. Search for the anxiety situation has the character of a "flight to reality." This means that

[11] O. Fenichel, "Defense against Anxiety, Particularly by Libidinization," No. 27, *First Series*.

the reality of the situation with which imaginary expectations of punishment were connected is sought, presumably to convince the subject that this connection was purely imaginary and that actually only the situation itself occurs.

The experience that imaginary ideas connected with a certain situation actually do not prove true, is precisely the basis of most counter-phobic attitudes. The situation must be sought again and again, because although, owing to this experience, reassurance is obtained that on this occasion the imaginary expectations are not realized, it is not a final proof that they never will be realized.

Recently, in connection with research into the theme of the "misapprehended oracle," [12] I investigated certain phenomena of depersonalization, which were felt pleasurably during the experience that something perceived was "really true." Their significance is: "That real occurrence over there is true, but what I had imagined must happen when this occurrence comes to pass, and what my fear was directed toward, is not true." As the fear still exists in the unconscious, the persons in question often try to keep alive the recollection that on this one occasion nothing did happen. This is one of the motives for collecting "trophies" as a proof of having taken a risk.

In counter-phobias, just as in anti-cathexis of the reaction-formation type in general, leakages occur. Behind such attempts at repression or denial of anxiety, the over-tense nature of the attitude, general fatigue, symptomatic acts, or dreams may betray the fact that the anxiety is still operative. Sometimes a leakage of this kind may be avoided at the last minute by setting in motion an emergency mechanism of defense. We may see, for example, combinations of counter-phobic and phobic attitudes: to a certain degree and in favorable circumstances counter-phobia, at a higher degree and in other circumstances phobia. The very thing which is preferred if the conditions are fulfilled is avoided if the conditions are altered. An emergency mechanism of this sort does not always succeed. When the conditions or the degree are changed, one often sees a sudden reversal of pleasure into anxiety. Kris has described this phenomenon in certain forms of unsuccessful humor, and has mentioned the "double-edged character" of comic phenomena, the ease with which they pass from pleasurable success to unpleasurable failure.[13] The same thing holds true for our phenomenon. In the midst of the "triumph" which the counter-phobic individual can enjoy because of his saving in emotional expenditure, unpleasure may break out if something occurs which seems to confirm the old anxiety.

An example of a failure of this kind may be seen in cases in which the fear of entering a fight is overcompensated by a counter-phobic tendency to struggle and to compete with everyone on every occasion. For such people the meaning

12 O. Fenichel, "The Misapprehended Oracle," No. 16 in this volume.
13 E. Kris, "The Psychology of Caricature," op. cit.

of "I am not afraid, for I can already do that" is "I can do it better than anyone else"; which means unconsciously a wish to castrate the others. In certain qualitative or quantitative circumstances this pleasure may suddenly fail and, in place of the intended castration, an unwanted and terrifying identification with the victim appears.

The anti-cathexis is much more apparent in the counter-phobias than in the phobias. Whereas in phobias it arranges for the avoidance of the situation in question, here it operates in the form of a special interest, which in the search for these situations tries to convince the subject that no anxiety is necessary.

The mechanisms which I have described have been observed in character analyses. Reflection teaches us, however, that no deep-seated character analysis is necessary for the observation of this phenomenon, but that similar things can be seen in everyday life as well. The most outstanding example is probably the entire field of sport, which may in general be designated as a counter-phobic phenomenon. No doubt there are erotic and aggressive gratifications in sport, just as they are present in all the other functional pleasures of adults. Certainly not everyone who engages in sport is suffering from an unconscious insoluble fear of castration; nor does it follow that the particular sport for which he shows a later preference must once have been feared. But it will generally hold true that the essential joy in sport is that one actively brings about in play certain tensions which were formerly feared, so that one may enjoy the fact that now one can overcome them without fearing them. I should like to go further and suggest that the people for whom sport or at least certain kinds of sport (as for example mountaineering) are not a mere occasional relaxation but a matter of significance in their lives, are true counter-phobic subjects. It would be interesting to investigate the careers of famous athletes with reference to occasional sudden attacks of anxiety while they were taking part in sport.[14]

Another easily accessible class of objects that belong here are certain works of art, in which the artist, in a constant endeavor to shake off anxiety, seeks and describes what he fears, in order to achieve a belated mastery. And, of course, there are similar phenomena in the realm of science. Here again some investigators keep trying to get close to an object onto which they have projected their anxiety, so that they may feel they have it under control and do not need to fear it. And finally one may assert generally that all abilities in which people take special pride fall within the same category.

And now a few words in regard to analytic practice. Counter-phobic attitudes which are frozen into character attitudes are often residues of once powerful instinctual conflicts. They must be resolved in analysis. This is accomplished by

[14] H. Deutsch came to the same conclusion years ago in her paper "A Contribution to the Psychology of Sport," *Int. J. Psa.,* Vol. 7, 1926.

the same means that are used in thawing out rigid attitudes in general. The attitudes have first to be revealed to the patient and then made to appear problematic, the complex nature of the pleasure attached to them must be detailed, and their tendentious character shown by a demonstration of the resistances which oppose their resolution. The principle that analysis must break down a neurotic condition of stability in order later to erect a truly stable equilibrium holds true equally for counter-phobic attitudes. In the course of the analytic treatment anxiety must be experienced again, not only where compulsion or lack of feeling is present, but also where there is a tense one-sided pride in certain activities or attitudes. There is no reason to expect that special abilities attained as a result of counter-phobic overcompensations will be lost owing to the analysis of the underlying anxiety conflict. These abilities will merely lose their cramped character and will gain in sureness. An analysis conducted in an economically correct manner will carry out the necessary process as painlessly as possible for the patient.

TWELVE

Two Dream Analyses*

I

It infrequently happens in a psychoanalytic case that the interpretation of a dream is continued until a complete understanding of all its elements is obtained, or that a dream analysis succeeds in throwing light on the total personality structure of the patient. I shall give one example of each type, though neither dream is extraordinary.

I shall go directly to the point and report the dream of a woman patient: *I am buying two pounds of fish. It occurs to me that I might buy fish for Mrs. X. too, which would make eight pounds. It then occurs to me that perhaps Mrs. X.'s cook might already have done her marketing. I then would have too much fish and would appear to be extravagant.*

Most of the elements of the manifest dream text came from an experience of the previous day. The patient had really bought two pounds of fish. When she arrived home she learned that her cook had already bought some other food, so that the fish was superfluous. The fear of appearing extravagant also had another root in happenings of the previous day. It was just before Christmas and the patient had spent much money for presents. She was afraid that her husband would reproach her for being extravagant. She was in general afraid that her husband was dissatisfied with her.

At this point in her associations, the patient interrupts herself: Somehow, she states, she did not tell the dream correctly. She was not sure whether in the dream she bought two pounds of fish—as she did in reality—or *whether it was four pounds.* She did not know why she had not mentioned this doubt and the words "or four." The figure two, she says, is the more probable one, because she actually bought two pounds. (My suspicion was, however, that the contrary

* First published in *Bull. Menninger Clinic*, Vol. 3, 1939, pp. 129–138.

174

was correct: the figure two is determined by the day remainder; the figure four, which she did not mention first, must have a certain significance in the unconscious.)

With the idea "fish," she associates that in her childhood her family used to have fish very seldom and then only haddock. Only as a married woman did she learn that there are other kinds of edible fish than haddock. Her mother prepared the same food over and over again; she was a poor shopper, and in no respect whatever a good housewife. Since we already knew from the analysis that the patient was very ambitious as a housewife, we could understand that the purchase of fish in the dream represented a competition with her mother. In this way it becomes possible to formulate provisionally the first dream thought as follows: *"I would like to do better than my mother, so that my husband will become more satisfied with me."*

At the time of the dream we already knew that all her intense feminine ambitions were centered in a pedagogic ambition. She was very proud of the way she was bringing up her two little daughters, very sensitive about minor difficulties in their behavior, and eager to hear that she knew how to rear children better than all other women. She also used to compare the education of her children with her own upbringing. I therefore called her attention to the possibility that the wish to do things better than her mother might also here concern the pedagogic field. Thereupon, the patient recalls another day remainder which led to Mrs. X., who appeared in the dream text. The day before, the patient had been skating with her children and on this occasion could not help observing that Mrs. X.'s youngest daughter was a much better skater than her daughters. At first she was so hurt that she felt a deep hatred toward this child, so intense a hatred that she was horrified, and then laughed at herself. She continues that she has bought Christmas presents for Mrs. X.'s children as well as for other friends' children. Among the presents were several dolls. She remembers how she, as a child, used to play with dolls. At that time she was distressed that her sister's dolls always seemed to her to be nicer and cleaner than her own. Sometimes she even smashed one of her sister's dolls in rage. And recently, too, it had happened that she accidentally broke a doll.

Now it was clear that the patient in her pedagogic ambition behaved toward Mrs. X.'s children in the same way that she had behaved as a child toward her sister's dolls.

The question "Who educates children better, Mrs. X. or I?" had to be translated on the one hand into: "Who educates children better, my mother or I?" and on the other hand into: "Who keeps the dolls cleaner, my sister or I?"

She was very ambitious in the matter of cleanliness and was never satisfied with herself in that respect. This was the outcome of a deep anal-erotic fixation, brought about by the measures taken by her mother, who herself was obviously very anal-erotic. Behind the competition with her sister for cleanliness was hidden the competition for her mother's love. The mother's exaggerated anal behavior went so far that she even used to inspect the daughters' stools until they were quite big children. The wish to show clean dolls was based on the more infantile wish to produce a more impressive stool. That was not the sole factor which showed us that her ambition to educate children was based on an ambition to give birth to children. Now we are able to modify the dream thought formulated above approximately as follows: *"I would like to surpass my mother in giving birth to children so that my husband will become more satisfied with me."* The fear of being reproached by her husband for extravagance was a repetition of her fear of making her mother angry by her uncleanliness.

What is the meaning of "I might buy fish for Mrs. X. too"? To this the patient says that Mrs. X. has to buy large quantities of food every day. Yesterday, the patient compared the consumption of her family with that of Mrs. X.'s. She figured how many people had to be taken care of in each family. She and her husband have two children and a maid, that makes five people; Mrs. X. has four children and not less than three maids, that makes nine persons.

With this the patient revealed the meaning of the dream element "two or four," which at first was repressed. Two and four refer to children. She has two children, Mrs. X. has four. The patient's mother, too, had two children, namely the patient and her sister. And so we understand: The originally repressed dream element "or four" contains the key to the most important dream thought, that is: *"I would like to have more children than my mother (for instance, four children like Mrs. X.) to demonstrate that I do better than my mother, so that my husband will become better satisfied with me."*

The patient replied to this interpretation: "Have I already told you that a child died in our house this week?"

She had not mentioned this fact before. But the doll she had broken, proved that when she learned about the death of that child, she must have thought: "This is what should happen to the children of all women who have more than two children."

Hence her fear of seeming extravagant to her husband becomes understandable as representing the opposite: She was afraid her husband would find her too miserly in bearing children. He could, for instance, compare himself with Mr. X. and find her inefficient. (This interpretation does not exclude the anal-erotic interpretation of the fear of extravagance which we indicated above. The circumstance that the wish to give birth to children is displaced precisely into the element of the number of children is anal too.)

Now only one detail of the dream text still remains unexplained: the number eight. (Eight pounds of fish would have had to be bought if she had had to take care of Mrs. X., too.) The patient answered this question in an unexpected way: "I figured out, you know, that the X. family are nine persons. If one of them dies, there will be eight." There is no doubt who was to die: Mrs. X.'s youngest daughter as a punishment for her good skating. That explains why the patient was so terrified at herself when she realized to what extent she hated this child. In her anger that this child was superior to her children, she probably thought of the sad event which had happened in her house a short time previously.

The main dream thought, the revelation of which advanced the whole course of the analysis, was as follows: *"I should have four children instead of two, and at X.'s there should be eight persons instead of nine."*

Of this thought only the numbers came undistorted into the manifest dream text.

The dream was very much overdetermined. It was my intention especially to demonstrate content and distortion of one latent trend of thoughts. Two other trends of dream thoughts I will mention briefly: First, the patient's sister has no children. The patient has surpassed her in bearing children, and therefore feels very guilty toward her. She feels as if she were the murderess of her sister's unborn children—just as she actually broke her dolls. To compensate for this, she developed the fantasy that she should give herself to her sister's husband in order to bear a child which she then would present to her sister, a fantasy which is an excellent example of "the return of the repressed out of repression." This fantasy was the basis of the dream idea that she had to take care of Mrs. X., too. Secondly, the fish which she bought was, as might be expected, a penis symbol. This was also the point of departure for several latent thoughts and wishes which we did not mention.

II

A male patient dreams:

"A professor is holding a lecture outside the room. The room is filled with water; it is a lake. It is just low tide. Big fish become visible as well as two hares making love to each other."

In this case it is necessary for me to give some data about the patient before telling his associations to the dream.

The patient is a man in his forties, who came to analysis on account of certain character troubles. Although he is married, he is an active homosexual. But this fact does not trouble him much. It is in another respect that he desires a change in his personality. He rightly feels that he lacks the capacity for full emotional expression. The structure of his personality makes an impression similar to those obsessional characters who have learned to defend themselves against strong emotions of every kind. It was relatively easy to understand that, among the emotions that he unconsciously feared, guilt feelings—as a consequence of aggressive tendencies—were predominant. He felt at his best if he could prove that an injustice had been done to him. Unconsciously, he had developed certain tricks to induce others to act unjustly and unfairly toward him. This gave him a feeling of superiority corresponding to a relative decrease of his unconscious guilt feelings. He also understood how to make use of his emotional coldness as a kind of self-justification. He felt superior if in the company of an excited person he himself remained calm and remote. He behaved in the same way during his active homosexual adventures. And further, he liked to make presents to others in an unexpected way, whereas he became stubborn and negative if anything was demanded or expected of him.

At the time of the dream, the analytical situation was as follows: After his blocking of emotions as a mechanism of defense had been broken up, we had started to analyze his homosexuality. In his dreams dangerous women who roused feelings of fear in him began to appear. It was possible to connect this with a screen memory which had long since been known to us: As a small child he and a little girl had been photographed in the nude. The children had had a quarrel, during which the girl had scratched him, and he had cried. An uncle of his had scolded his mother for letting the children be together in the nude, but his mother had laughed and said that they were still small. From two details we saw that this memory represented the fears which had determined his turning to homosexuality: His dreams of "dangerous women" always contained allusions to nails and scratching; the patient had later developed a kind of hand fetishism: he classified the hands of persons of both sexes into "male" and "female" ones and preferred the male ones. His fear of women had, besides its manual importance, a significant oral note. The women in the dream were "vampire" in character, and tried to suck him or to take something away from him.

However, it was interesting that the appearance of those fears was limited to his dreams. In his daily life the old mechanism of defense against his emotions continued. I called his attention to this difference and told him that the emotions he experienced in his dreams were real and that the analytical task would be to find some indication of the same emotions in his everyday life. Thereupon he admitted that for several days he had had a slight diarrhea. I assured him that this was the sign of anxiety we had been looking for. I added that the dreams showed that this anxiety must be rooted in a certain passive attitude toward women. He replied that he thought he was perhaps afraid not only of women, but of any passive attitude generally; perhaps, he said, he emphasized an active homosexuality in order not to become aware of the passive homosexual longings. We had some material which seemed to confirm this idea: I have already mentioned that he liked to spend money and to make presents when he could surprise people, whereas he refused to make a gift whenever he felt that he was expected to give. He liked to walk through the town, acting like Harun al Raschid: he would bestow a large sum upon a beggar and play Santa Claus to street urchins. In this behavior the activity without doubt served the purpose of covering passivity. Originally, he would have liked to receive gifts in the same way that he now gave them. If he now showed obstinacy when gifts were demanded of him, it was in revenge for his unsatisfied longing to get presents. So for the time being we could not decide whether women or men were primarily feared. But certainly this much could be stated: The patient had a great longing to have someone hold his hands, to be soothed and to be presented with gifts, but this longing was blocked by an anxiety that the person to whom he gave himself might injure him, that the hands to which he clung might unexpectedly begin to scratch him.

Another fact should also be mentioned. It had become clear to us that in the transference the "interpretations" which the analyst gave him also had the significance of gifts. He was very much hurt if the analyst did not speak enough to him, but felt himself appreciated if he got "words" from his analyst.

It was in this analytical situation that the dream occurred.

When asked for associations, the patient began to talk about a matter which seemed to have no connection with the dream. He usually did not bother very much about his money. Often, he was greatly surprised how much he had spent when he got his monthly bank statement. But this time the opposite had happened. The day before he had received the statement and had discovered that the balance was much higher than he had anticipated. This pleased him greatly. I remarked that perhaps he felt like the children who got gifts from him—he had presented himself with a gift. He did not respond to this interpretation, but instead began to associate to the details of the dream text: The night before the dream he had attended a concert. A concerto called "Past Happiness" was performed. As the patient did not know the language of the country very well, he at first misunderstood the title. In this language the word "past" is similar to the word "hare," and he was at first astonished about "hare-happiness." Later he recognized the mistake.

It was now clear what the "hare-happiness" of the dream meant. It simply was a "past happiness." The dream exhibited an aquarium, a spectacle, in which his past happiness was demonstrated to him. But besides the hares that make love to each other, there are the big fish. What about them? To this the patient made no reply. Apparently, the question was put too soon. Instead, he talked about the professor. A few days before I had said that I analyzed only a few neurotics; that the majority of my cases were physicians undergoing analysis for training purposes. This remark of mine made the patient very happy. He said that I seldom made remarks about myself and that he knew how to appreciate it. In other words, he took my remark as a present. Of course, the patient added, the professor represents the analyst. He is "outside the room." In a certain sense the analyst likewise is outside the room, because the patient cannot see him. Thus we see he dreams that the analysis shows him his past happiness, and that this demonstration has the value of a gift for him.

He further recognizes the professor in the dream as a certain person in his environment. This acquaintance is a paranoid person who up to now did not need hospitalization. During the last few days the patient has thought a lot about this person, consciously because he feared that the man in his delusion of persecution might hurt him; unconsciously, because he felt tempted by the homosexuality of this paranoid man. Now we can provisionally formulate a dream thought: *The analyst, who gives him a present, might do him some harm. He does not do so but shows him his past happiness.*

The patient had been told that his lack of emotion was a defense mechanism; hence the "past happiness" refers to the time when he was still able to enjoy his feelings. His thought was probably something like this: Perhaps there is something to psychoanalysis and I will regain my emotions (as one gets a gift); but still I am afraid of that gift.

When the patient heard that, he replied: "Now I remember another part of the dream which I had forgotten":

"There was a bottle full of small fish, which one can drink."

He immediately knew the day remainder of that part of the dream: The bottle is one filled with sweets that he saw yesterday in the window of a candy shop. Following a sudden impulse he bought this bottle to present it to his wife. But his wife, unfortunately, is not permitted to eat sweets because of stomach trouble. He had taken it for granted that she would be allowed to eat these small sweets at least. At this point I must add that his wife had been pregnant some time previously, but had had a miscarriage. It was problematic whether she should have another child because of her stomach trouble. The fact that he bought her something which she was forbidden to eat was not only an indication of his ambivalence toward her, but also expressed his wish that she become pregnant in spite of the contraindications. There was also no doubt that since she was forbidden to eat sweets he would eat them. The sudden impulse to buy them must have represented a sudden desire to eat them. Thus we see that in the matter of pregnancy he identified himself with his wife. The patient had always been suspicious of medicines. Medicines may be helpful, but then again they may be poisonous. To give sweets to his wife may be a sort of substitute for the lost child (by giving her another child), but may also do her some harm. He had always been dubious as to whether medical advice is helpful or harmful. He had at one time suffered from rheumatism, about which he had consulted many physicians. The prescriptions given by them had had no effect. On a trip to the Orient a native woman had given him a medicine for his rheumatism. He was very dubious whether he should try the "magic drink" of this "gypsy" or not. He had always been interested in Oriental people and other exotics, who seemed to him wise and dangerous at the same time. He must admit that he has similar feelings toward the Jews. However, he tried the medicine and it worked promptly. The pains disappeared. And then he again remembered how happy he was to learn there was more money in his bank account than he had expected. Incidentally, the day before he had also given money to some beggars.

We now can interpret: He fears to get "interpretations" or "health" from the analyst, because those gifts may hurt him. But he nevertheless hopes that the analysis will work in the same way as the Oriental medicine and succeed in bringing his lost happiness back to him. This dangerous bringing back of his past happiness is connected with the thoughts about pregnancy. There is no doubt that the thought of the Oriental woman represents the analyst, who is a Jew. But it is significant that the patient replaces the analyst with a woman. In reality he has not received a gift but has given one away, namely to his wife, unconsciously to make her pregnant. When this was brought to his attention, he interpreted the little fish which were in the bottle: they represented spermatozoa. That spermatozoa were thought of as a "gift" was clear in other connections as well: his *ejaculatio retardata* was due to his unreadiness to give when it was expected. He associated to this the love drink of Isolde, and further thought of the relation of balsam to poison, and of good drinks to bad drinks. He had a longing to receive and also an anxiety about it.

Two elements of the dream text still remain unexplained. Why is this spectacle an aquarium and the room filled with water? And why besides the hares in the spectacle are there big fish there? The first element may be interpreted symbolically: water represents pregnancy. As for the second the patient gives an unexpected explanation: he now recognizes those fish. They were the salamander fish of New Zealand, pictures of which he had seen in a magazine a few days before. The article stated that explorers in New Zealand had reported that these fish have both gills and lungs, and that they are able to live on land as well as in water. The explorers had not been taken seriously—everybody had thought the story a lie. It was later proven that these fish really exist. Similarly he had been dubious about the analysis. Now he began to feel his forgotten emotions again, which brought him joy and anxiety at the same time.

The ambivalently expected "past happiness" which the analyst was to give back to him as a "gift," had on the one hand the meaning of a passive homosexuality (spermatozoa, pregnancy), but on the other hand in place of the analyst he put an exotic woman of the magic vampire type.

As the principal dream thought we can formulate:

"Though I am afraid of what may happen if I really give myself to free associations and emotions, I hope that it will bring me sexual satisfaction and happiness, which I have known only in times long past."

The difficulty of his giving way to his emotions is due to the circumstance that he understands this formulation sexually. The active homosexual behavior of the patient, as well as his ambivalent attitude toward making gifts, served the purpose of repressing his passive attitude, which he both longed for and was afraid of. The question whether the first objects of this ambivalent passivity were men or women cannot, even after this dream, be answered clearly. The unconscious attitude toward his male analyst was doubtless a passive homosexual one. Nevertheless, the fact that in the dream a gypsy woman is substituted for the analyst seems of greater importance. The deep anxiety which was represented in the screen memory of the nude girl who scratched him, may be expressed as follows: "If I seek security, protection, and passive satisfaction from my mother, I may be terribly disappointed and hurt."

THIRTEEN

The Study of Defense Mechanisms and Its Importance for Psychoanalytic Technique*

WE ALL know psychoanalysts whose papers abound in unclear theoretical expressions, whose juggling of the concepts "id," "ego," and "superego" provokes dizziness, and who give the impression that they employ psychoanalytic theories to avoid recognizing psychic realities. This obvious misuse of psychoanalysis has been criticized often enough. But there is also the opposite extreme. There is a distaste for theoretical conclusions, which goes so far as to interpret all interest in psychology as resistance. We hear that (in this country) analysts refer to themselves as "clinicians" in contrast to the theoretical speculator Freud, and attempt to substitute for metapsychology exact descriptions of facts which then thin out, in reality, into flat generalities. We hear how someone else argues that the facts which Freud discovered should be recognized, but not the way in which he interpreted those facts. Libido theory, oedipus complex, the theory of the instincts, the significance of childhood experiences, the concepts of narcissism and transference, the theory of anxiety, the structural conceptions, the recognition of the importance of feelings of guilt—all these are regarded as theoretical superstructure. Still others are of the opinion that "theory" and "speculation" are equivalent, and demand that anyone who wishes to investigate clinical reality should refrain from theorizing. In a discussion on psychoanalytic instruction one teacher said that teachers of psychoanalysis should limit themselves to teaching

* This paper was first presented at Ojai in March, 1940. Dr. Fenichel's manuscript has been translated into English, in conformity with the other papers, but no attempt has been made to give it the final form Dr. Fenichel might have given it if he had prepared it for publication.

that which they really understand, and not touch upon theory; whereupon I indulged in the interruption that perhaps some teachers of psychoanalysis also understand theory. To be brief, the principle is frequently not understood that psychoanalysis is a natural scientific psychology, which may be applied—among other things—to the cure of neuroses; on the contrary, it is degraded to a subdivision of psychotherapy.

Such undervaluation seems to me to be a greater danger (in this country) at the present time than the very much feared misuse of theory. This is due to a fundamental misunderstanding of the role of theory in every science. It is a means *of achieving better methods of practice.* Those of my colleagues who boast of their clinical point of view are destined to be disappointed in their all-too-impatient expectations as to practical results. In renouncing theory, they also renounce the science itself—and thereby the dependability of everything they do. This is the reason why I entertain no fear that if Freudian analysis is to continue to exist at all, Freud's scientific method will likewise endure. Whoever, like Freud, takes heed of the dangers of overweening ambition in the therapy will have the better therapeutic results. He does not have to argue; he can demonstrate his results. Therefore, I do not wish to speak today—as was incorrectly announced—about "Practical Ways to Handle Ego Defense," but rather about "The Study of Defense Mechanisms and Its Importance for Psychoanalytic Technique."

Every science begins with practical problems which it first tries to solve by the method of "trial and error," borrowing its first general assumptions elsewhere. Then it proceeds to compare its results more systematically and thus arrives at general principles which are corrected in accordance with new data. The erection of ever more precise hypotheses follows, and finally there comes the formulation of theory, which in turn presents new problems, the solution of which leads to modification of the theory. The road leads from practice to theory, and from theory to better practice.

This interdependence of theory and practice is much more evident in psychoanalysis than in other sciences, inasmuch as the research methods of psychoanalysis and its therapeutic applications largely coincide. Psychoanalytic theory was not formulated at a desk, but, as the historians of our science know, was evolved through slow, painstaking, practical work. Though the theory may still have loopholes, it is nevertheless so far advanced today that it is possible deductively to arrive at conclusions as to what the psychoanalytic therapist should do and what he should refrain from doing. In the introduction to my *Problems of Psychoanalytic Technique,*† I stated why a theory of psychoanalytic technique is necessary and what it can accomplish, but also what its limitations are.

† O. Fenichel, *Problems of Psychoanalytic Technique,* Albany, Psa. Quart. Press, 1939.

To comprehend a psychological phenomenon in accordance with psychoanalytic theory means to investigate it in terms of the three points of view of topography, dynamics, and economics. It would not be quite correct to maintain that these three approaches were discovered and evaluated in the above-mentioned sequence. None the less, the topographical approach can be described as the most general, and it was also the first to make its appearance in a theory of analytic technique. The task of practical analysis, it was maintained, was to make the unconscious conscious. That was a topographical formulation. The practice that corresponded to it was the effort of the analyst to get at the unconscious of the patient through his utterances and to communicate it to him. Sometimes such an explanation had therapeutic success; and sometimes it did not. When the therapeutic effect did not follow, it was said that the patient's resistance was too great, and this really meant that it was the fault of the patient and not that of the analyst. Obviously the interpretation had in some way not touched off a corresponding thought in the unconscious of the patient. Freud wrote that such a patient had the same thought content in two different "copies," or imprints, in different divisions of his mental apparatus: once in the unconscious and once in the perceptual apparatus. This was a purely topographical description. What Freud really meant was that certain dynamic forces prevented the confluence of these two imprints. But in general theoretical formulation and in practical application the dynamic point of view found acceptance only very gradually. The theoretical formulation found expression in the recognition that repression is not so much characterized by the fact that a certain ideational content does not become conscious, but by the fact that a specific impulse, which is merely represented by that ideational content, is cut off from consciousness and thereby from the possibility of discharge; but that it nevertheless remains effective as a tension of energy in the organism, striving for discharge. The practical application found expression in the formula that bringing the unconscious to consciousness had to be effected by eliminating the resistances. (Parenthetically, let it be said that this formula of therapeutic psychoanalysis that resistances are to be eliminated has been misinterpreted to the effect that the psychoanalyst is to do nothing but to point out resistances and their senselessness to the patient. But the mention of preconscious, not unconscious, content, if undertaken at the right place, is an excellent and important means for the elimination of resistances.) Finally, a correct consideration of the economic point of view made its appearance relatively late in practice, which teaches us how, when, and where we are to eliminate resistances.

In the beginning of psychoanalysis, it was not by systematic analysis that resistances were, for the first time, reduced to their unconscious components or traced to their historical genesis, but rather by unsystematic analysis and suggestion. The knowledge gained in this way concerned the repressed instincts and not the repressing ego. In 1916, even after the psychology of the unconscious processes had been formulated in detail, Freud could still write: "We can say nothing more precise on this point, for we know as yet too little of the nature and mode of operation of the system Cs." [1] It is only in appearance paradoxical that the unconscious was studied before the conscious, the instincts before the defensive forces, the id before the ego. It was essential to proceed in this order so that psychoanalysis could hereafter view the so-called "surface," the modes of behavior and attitudes, the differences between individuals—in short, the ego—in a different way from that of the pre-analytic psychologies—that is to say, genetically. The characteristics of the ego, like everything non-instinctual in the human mind, it is now clear, have developed from instincts under the influence of the outside world. The psychology of the ego, especially the study of the defensive mechanisms, has its strength in its dynamic-genetic method of observation. The fact that many neurotic attitudes are not to be understood as eruptions of instincts, but as components of unified defense systems against anxiety or against instincts, should never lead us into misconstruing all the properties of the human mind as intended arrangements. Ego psychology does not nullify Freud's fundamental discovery that within the human mind ego-alien forces are at work; on the contrary, it explains the unfolding of the personality in terms of these ego-alien forces, which under certain conditions may in turn disturb the personality which has evolved from them.

However, it was not only the systematic progress of analytical research which turned our attention to the processes of the ego. Rather, it was bitter necessity. The neurotics who today demand treatment from the analyst are different from those who went to Freud thirty or forty years ago. In the classical neuroses there was a comparatively intact personality, and at certain points actions, impulses, or thoughts broke through, which did not fit in with the whole. Today the personality which is the bearer of the symptoms does not appear at all uniform. It is rent or deformed, and in any case it is itself involved in the illness. It would be a fascinating task to investigate the real cause of this change in the forms of the neuroses. It certainly is connected with changes in morality. The classical hysteria worked chiefly with the defensive mechanism of repression; this, however, presupposes that education designates the objectionable instincts consistently as "bad." Present-day education is inconsistent. It does not know which instinctual claims to allow and which to suppress, and it often first seduces and then frustrates suddenly and unexpectedly and therefore all the more cruelly; to this inconsistency of education there corresponds an inconsistency of the neurotic

---

[1] S. Freud, "Metapsychological Supplement to the Theory of Dreams," *Coll. Pap.*, Vol. IV, London, Hogarth, 1948, p. 149.

personality. The neurotics of today appear to us to be egos restricted by defensive measures which through their permanent anti-cathexis lose energy, and through renunciation lose in differentiation, because they respond to exterior stimuli with set reactions and so diminish in vivacity and elasticity. Freud formulates it thus: It is often possible for the ego to avoid a rupture in any of its relations by deforming itself, by forfeiting something of its unity; thus the irrationalities, eccentricities, and follies of man would be similar to sexual perversions, for by accepting them man spares himself repressions. As the maintenance of these eccentricities certainly follows the anti-cathectic pattern and demands an expenditure of energy, it would perhaps be more correct to say that their formation corresponds to a single definite repression, by means of which later separate repressions, which would take more energy and separate anxiety situations, are avoided. In this way the ego-restricting attitudes which act as chronic anchorage of the instinctual defense are worked into the ego. Their constant operation prevents the instinct from becoming manifest, so that instead of a living conflict between an instinct and a defense we see something rigid which to the patient himself does not appear problematic, or at least not always. But there *is* a problem. This is the relative constancy of the defensive attitudes under varying demands of the outside world or the instincts.

Attitudes of this anti-cathectic type betray themselves through their overstrained nature or through an occasional breaking through of what has been repressed, or simply by the amount of energy needed, which can have as a result "inhibition due to general economic impoverishment."

When we consider defensive attitudes of this kind, we can divide them into occasional and habitual ones. The habitual ones can be divided further. There are people who only adopt a certain defensive attitude in certain situations, and others who remain in the defensive attitude comparatively constantly, as if the instinctual temptation were continually present.

Not all defensive attitudes are recognizable as such at first glance. Some of them may give the impression of instinctual impulses. We must learn to take the expressions "defense" and "instinct" as relatively as they are meant.

In order to explain what I mean I should like to remind you of an idea advanced by Alexander. He was of the opinion that there were two kinds of neuroses. First, those at the bottom of which there is a conflict between an instinct and a defensive impulse, as for instance between an oedipus wish and a fear of being castrated; secondly, those at the bottom of which there is a conflict between two instincts, for example between an oedipus wish and a readiness for passive feminine castration. But it belongs to the nature of the id that there are no contradictions. Instincts with contradictory contents can be satisfied one after the other or even in common derivatives. Of course, the second type of neurosis does exist, but the instinctual conflicts at the bottom of it are always a structural conflict as well. One of the opposing instincts is always nearer to the ego, is held by an ego defense, or is strengthened for the purpose of an ego defense. It is therefore, although an instinct, one of a relatively *defensive* kind, in comparison with the deeper repressed instincts. What we have is not one instinct struggling against a defensive impulse, but always a variety, always a lively struggle, a reciprocal penetration. A defense rarely brings the struggle to a definitive standstill. Nearly always the rejected impulses break through the defense, and there is further repression of the instinct-laden defense as well. There are reaction formations against reaction formations. We see not only the three-layer arrangement of instinct–defense–instinct breaking through again, but also instinct–defense–repression of the defense. For instance, a man who has become passively feminine through castration anxiety might overcompensate this attitude with a particularly accentuated masculine behavior.

The technical rule, "Interpretation of the defense goes before interpretation of the id," does not always mean that one content shall be dealt with and another not, but often means that certain qualities or relations of a content are dealt with before certain others.

Now we have finally arrived at questions of technique. We will not and cannot summarize all results of the "study of defense"; we want to find out the consequences which those results have for our technique, especially for the economic correctness of our interpretations.

If a patient develops his usual defensive attitudes toward the analyst, these have this in common with the phenomenon of "transference"—that they are a repetition of attitudes which he has previously formed in other situations. The present is misunderstood in the sense of the past. But these attitudes are not specific reactions to the analyst, which change in changing situations. They are rigid, general, unspecific, and therefore cannot be compared with the "transference situation" in the narrower sense, in which the patient reacts in an active and specific manner to the analyst—the manner in which in the past he reacted to, or wanted to react to, a definite person. What determines whether a patient produces more lively "transference resistances" or more rigid "character resistances" cannot be discussed here.

Alexander stated once [2] that the "neurotic character" is more easily influenced by psychoanalysis than a symptom neurosis. This is because the symptom neuroses have regressed from the alloplastic to the autoplastic level, and therefore, after they have been successfully analyzed, have to pluck up courage to make the next step in real life. This necessity does not appear with the neurotic character, who is continually acting. This I would like to contradict emphatically.

[2] F. Alexander, "The Neurotic Character," *Int. J. Psa.*, Vol. 11, 1930.

The pseudo-alloplasticism of the neurotic character cannot be changed into healthy alloplasticism except by first being transitorily turned into a neurotic autoplasticism and treated like an ordinary symptom neurosis. Internal conflicts which have hardened into pseudo-objectual relationships must first of all be changed back into internal conflicts and be dealt with as such, before normal object relationships can take their place. The technical rule runs accordingly: *In order to be treated, character resistances have to be changed into transference resistances.* The therapeutic task is theoretically easy to characterize once one has grasped the nature of these disturbances of the ego. We must just keep in mind how psychoanalysis works in principle. It demonstrates derivatives as such, and then leads to tolerance toward constantly less distorted derivatives, and so gradually confronts the ego with the repressed contents. In this way it removes the isolation of the latter from the whole personality, and lets the repressed instincts catch up with the development which the ego as a whole has passed through in the meantime. Infantile sexuality is changed into adult sexuality through intervention of the ego, which makes possible an ordered sexual life and sublimations.

When we wish to apply this to the chronic defensive attitudes of the ego, we see first of all that we can only get to the repressed instincts by gradually undermining the defenses opposing them, which can always be demonstrated earlier than the repressed impulses themselves. When analysis wants to make unconscious material accessible to the ego and once again relate to the ego what apparently happens involuntarily, this certainly cannot be done with symptoms or deep instincts in the beginning. At first the secretly active behavior of the patient in what is passively experienced by him can only be shown in the fact that he inhibits his impulses and their outlet and how he does so. It is true that the unconscious instinct which presses forward to consciousness and discharge is our ally, the defending ego our enemy. But we are in the position of a general whose troops are divided from his allies by the enemy's front. In order to combine our strength with that of the rejected instinct we must first break through to it, and for this we need first of all another ally accessible to us, the reasonable ego, which must be separated from the defending element. To continue the comparison, we must first of all undermine the enemy's front with propaganda and win over a large part of his force.

Therefore, when a patient with ego disturbances actively demonstrates this, the further procedure of the analyst does not seem very problematic. The difficulties begin where the patient is unaware of that which the analyst perceives as a rigid attitude in which the chief part of the instinctual conflicts is tonically bound, or where this attitude contradicts the process of analysis itself.

A short time ago, Freud emphasized in his paper "Analysis Terminable and

Interminable" that the ego disturbances which are the result of infantile instinctual conflicts form one of the chief hindrances to the therapeutic effectiveness of analysis. It is relatively easy to formulate theoretically what ought to be done. We have to divide the ego, as it were, and to demonstrate its attitude to the observing part of it. We let the patient feel this attitude to be tendentious and self-made; we disclose its purpose, and finally take it back to the historical situation in which it was first formed, just as we do with the symptoms, which tend more to be distorted expressions of the id. It is much more difficult to do this in practice. But this difficulty, Freud says, must not be taken to imply that it makes analysis impossible. On the contrary, it constitutes half of our analytic task. With this remark Freud is referring to the concepts of ego analysis and id analysis suggested by Anna Freud, who is of the opinion that both must be done to avoid one-sidedness. I do not find that the formulation that the analyst has to carry on his work from a position equidistant from ego, id, and superego is quite clear. The task is to make the id or the superego accessible by means of analysis of the ego. We are concerned with the following situation. At one time there was a conflict which was pressing and alive, and the subject withdrew from this fight by means of a permanent alteration of his ego. The forces which at one time opposed each other are now wasted in the useless and hardened defensive attitudes of his ego; the conflict has become latent. We must, if we want to set free the energy bound up there, remobilize the old conflict through a division of the sensible observing ego from its automatic, defending, experiencing element. The technical rule, "The patient determines the subject of the session" needs, therefore, a limiting commentary. It is by no means always by what he talks about that the patient "determines the theme," but often by not talking, or by the way in which he talks, or by what he does. Some things are not mentioned by the patient spontaneously, although they are shown involuntarily, and it is the task of the analyst to speak of these things. This is no particular kind of "activity" on the part of the analyst, but it is dynamic interpretation. For the analyst must always work where the affect is really located at the time. And we must add that the patient does not know where this is, and the analyst must look for the points where the affect is located.

I think that now the principal importance of the study of defensive attitudes for technique is clear: Only the approach through what is known as ego analysis gives us the possibility of an economically correct analysis. It is especially important to approach instinctual attitudes which represent defensive purposes from the viewpoint of defense first. Remember, for instance, the so-called "pseudo-sexuality" where apparently sexual acts serve a narcissistic purpose, or the "reversed transference interpretation" where you say to the patient, "Your feelings are not at this moment aroused about your father but about me."

Our opinion, that latent conflicts have to be changed into current ones, appears to contradict Freud's statement in "Analysis Terminable and Interminable," that this is just what is impossible. But we must ask ourselves whether Freud understood the same thing by "mobilization of latent conflicts" as we do. His arguments as to the incompleteness of what analysis can achieve (since that part of what was overcome in the mental development always remains beside or behind the higher stage that is reached) are extraordinarily clear and compelling. But it seems to me that precisely this statement of Freud's indicates the task of the economically correct guidance of analysis, which is to attack at just those points where the decisive conflicts are, at that moment, latently represented. To our surprise, however, Freud writes that "one would have to change the possible future conflict into a current one," but that this is not possible. "Tempting as it may be to our therapeutic ambition to propose such tasks for itself, experience bids us refuse them out of hand." Then, in order to make a latent instinctual conflict current, "clearly there are only two things we can do, either we can bring about situations in which the conflict becomes actual, or we can content ourselves with discussing it in analysis," and pointing out that it may possibly arise. The first is not possible because the task of bringing fresh suffering into life "we have so far rightly left to fate." The second way does not work because merely discussing does not help any more than reading Freud's works will cure a neurosis. The refutation of these two methods is obvious. Not, however, the assertion that these are the only possibilities. There is a third one. It is not a case of creating conflicts which are completely missing but of mobilizing latent ones. Latent conflicts are never quite latent. The analyst is accustomed to guessing the big conflicts lying behind the smallest signs. It is his task to show the patient the reality of these conflicts so clearly—that is, to "objectivate" his ego to these signs to such an extent—that the rationalizations, ruptures, and derivatives of the latent big conflict concealed behind them can be seen by the ego. It seems to me that we must then really actualize the latent conflict if we want to settle this, and to make the decisive part of the hardened instinctual energy capable of discharge, and so restore health; and this means that we must in truth provoke situations in which the conflict becomes actual— but neither by playing the part of Fate in the real life of the patient, nor by joining in the transference through a systematic artificial behavior on our part, but by analyzing those points in which the latent conflicts show themselves, through naming their derivatives and "objectivating" the observing ego toward them.

What is the aim of this mobilization? It is the historical reduction of the ego attitudes to those situations in which they were originally formed. Their special quality is dependent on a series of circumstances—partly on the hereditary constitution of the ego, partly on the nature of the instincts against which the defense is chiefly directed, and partly on the age at which the child experienced this instinctual conflict. In most cases, however, the analysis succeeds in showing the special attitude as having been forced on the person by the outside world either as the most suitable in a given situation, or owing to an identification.

A special problem in the investigation of this historical situation is what we have already mentioned, the so-called "defense transference" (Anna Freud). This is no doubt caused by two things. The first is the general human tendency to order one's actions according to experience, to retain where possible what has once proved expedient, to encounter a danger in the same way as that which proved useful against a similar danger, even when changes have taken place in the meantime which make what was previously suitable unsuitable. The problem remains why something which was formerly a "danger situation" is experienced later as such, even when this is no longer the case. The answer is a dialectic one: Precisely because of the defense which was at that time accomplished, the whole conflict was removed from the reasonable ego, and the evaluation of this particular kind of danger has not taken part in the development which the rest of the personality has gone through since. The second cause is that the person wishes to "transfer his instincts." That means that he always strives for satisfactions; but the ego always responds to these strivings with memories which at one time produced anxiety. When the highly unpleasurable "decline of the oedipus complex" is repeated in the transference during the analytic treatment, this is only *relatively* "beyond the pleasure principle." The person strives for the pleasure of instinctual satisfaction; it is the outside world which forces the ego to experience unpleasure in place of the pleasure it wanted, largely in order to avoid worse unpleasure.

I am sure you have already heard more than enough about theory here. You may find more about it in my papers, "Ego Disturbances and Their Treatment" ‡ and "Problems of Psychoanalytic Technique." I will now give a clinical example of the historical reduction of ego attitudes. It must be a case in which the relations are macroscopically understandable; though they appear very simple, they are the product of long and troublesome analysis of the ego attitudes.

A patient with specific character difficulties evinced first and foremost the following contradiction. On the one hand he had clear-cut feelings of inferiority, which manifested themselves in constant ambitious strivings (the impossibility of really satisfying his ambition, together with certain disturbances of potency, was the reason for his coming to analysis); on the other hand he was in reality completely inert, led a retired life, had never had genuine object relationships, and felt contented when he was undisturbed by the outside world. His ambitious

‡ No. 8 in this volume.

fantasies were of a very childish character and centered around the idea that he wanted to show himself the stronger person. The imagined competition was extremely primitive. It was comparatively easy to see that victory was of less importance to him than the recognition and affection which would be his because of his victory. The common goal of his ambition and his laziness was to live in narcissistic self-sufficiency with supplies flowing in from the outside. Although he was quite successful in his career, and had developed adequate pseudo-contacts as substitutes for object relationships, so as to avoid the external appearance of being pathological, his inner life was astonishingly poor. He regarded his professional work as a necessary evil that was to be got over with as quickly as possible; he had no particular outside interest, at least none on the level of his intellectual abilities; he tended to become depressed if he felt that he was not immediately loved by everyone. His relationships with women were so superficial that no long analysis was necessary to sense the latent homosexuality behind them; but his relationships with men were also narcissistic in nature and fundamentally consisted only of childish competitive fantasies. The better one knew him, the more one saw to what an extent he was dominated by a primitive narcissistic need: he expected that as soon as he felt a need the object world should gratify it, without his showing the slightest inclination to do anything for others—indeed, without his being able to feel that other people had needs. He lived completely in that narcissistic preliminary phase of love which Alice Balint has recently so well described: the mother is to satisfy the child's needs, then she can go away again.

As in all character cases, it was some time before both the infantile elements of this narcissistic fixation of the patient's became clear. One of these elements was his mother's attitude. She had been a very active person who used to make incessant demands on both her boys in many ways, especially as regards their training in cleanliness. The patient recalled that he had felt "bothered" by his mother and her demands all through his childhood and kept striving to evade them. But the second element was of greater importance. During his entire childhood there had been an old nurse in the home who had functioned in every respect as a "counter-mother." Through her the patient was enabled to realize his narcissistic fantasies of spite aimed at his mother. For he was absolutely certain of the love of this nurse; he could do anything he pleased as far as she was concerned, and he got everything he needed from her without ever having to recognize that she, too, was a person with feelings.

Now, is this pampering of the primitive narcissism of a child sufficient to explain a character fixation that permits the avoidance of every vital activity, not only of love relationships, but of intellectual activities as well? Certainly not. Karen Horney might attempt to impose such a conception on psychoanalysis.

But it is not in accord with Freudian thought. There is absolutely no doubt that in this case the avoidance of vital activities was equivalent to a general phobic attitude, so that the patient tried to avoid the full intensity of life just as an agoraphobic avoids going out in the street. That he carried out this evasion by clinging to a primitive narcissistic attitude toward the outside world was sufficiently explained by the existence of the nurse; but this did not explain what the dangers were that caused him to withdraw to this nurse. The dreadful demands of the mother had to be understood and supplemented.

The never-ending competitive fight to which the patient abandoned himself in his fantasies, but which he avoided in reality, as well as a corresponding attitude in the transference situation, kept reminding us of the fact that he had a brother three years older than himself and that the few childhood memories which gradually appeared always showed him as the younger one in the company of his brother and his friends. His "fighting boy's" point of view must have corresponded to the wish at some time to be stronger than the older boys around him, and the hopelessness of this wish obviously made him recoil from these boys to the nurse. Even at this point one could correctly presume that his attitude of oral demand toward the nurse was based upon a "return of the repressed from the repression"—that in his relations with the older boys he had developed a passive-receptive homosexuality; that he had overcompensated for the wish to be stronger than they; and that then, because this ambition was unrealizable, he had again regressed to receptivity. When this was explained to the patient—at the right moment and, of course, not in these words—he responded with a surprising recollection. At about ten years of age and afterward, he had surpassed his brother in physical strength. There were frequent fistfights between the boys, and the patient was always the victor. This circumstance resulted in his trying to repress his recollection of having been the weaker at earlier periods, by means of developing the ideal of the "fighting boys" and adhering to it throughout his life. But the unconscious passive-receptive yearning for the period when he was the weaker, was the reason why the "victor" ideal remained theoretical, and why in reality he lived only in the "world of the nurse."

The patient's statement about his withdrawn attitude certainly confirmed our insight into the situation. When he could not surpass others he always felt the impulse either to insult or to attack them, and he was afraid that sometime he might give in to this impulse in a compromising way. Actually he avoided, above all, any active-sadistic step, which would have served the purpose of denying a certain pleasure in being the weaker. But then again this kind of denial would not have been possible if in the depths of his mind there were not some more fundamental sadism, and this betrayed itself in his continual fantasies about fighting, as well as in the oral avidity with which he demanded immediate satisfaction of all his needs.

This sadism evinced itself likewise in the patient's only hobby, which alone seemed to him to make life worthwhile—namely, hunting. The analysis of this hobby brought us first and foremost the realization that his joy in shooting the hunted animals was as little a direct expression of instinct as was his fantasy of suddenly beating to death those rivals whom he so feared that he avoided attending social gatherings. By steadily treating his pathological peculiarities of character it was possible gradually to bring the patient to a point where he relived the fear which was still within him, but which he had not felt since his childhood (except for several interesting circumscribed fears—for example, the clear-cut syphilis phobia from which he suffered). Various fears made their appearance at first in dreams, then in daytime symptoms as well—fears which increasingly assumed the form that certain demands were being made of him which were dreadful, and from which he tried to escape through stubbornness. (He sometimes used to lock himself into his office and go to sleep, meanwhile experiencing great pleasure in the thought that others believed he was working, and that no one could reach or disturb him.) He observed that it was fear again that always caused him to break off his love affairs as well as his friendships with men, when a certain intensity of feeling was reached. And finally to his surprise he noticed that the sole source of pleasure for him, the hunt, likewise had fear as a basis.

The hunt offered the patient opportunity to satisfy certain fetishistic traits: he loved high boots and rough clothing. To be sure, he did not know the sexual character of this preference, inasmuch as the fetishistic character of boots and clothing was limited to masculine attributes and he was, for example, uninterested in women's shoes. In speaking of the odor of leather in new boots, which was associated with the odor of rubber, we came upon an indistinct memory of rubber sheets that had been used on his bed in the nursery. Here for the first time the topic of enuresis was touched, and the impression arose that the "masculine" boots and clothing were intended to deny some sort of passive-childish ideal, just as the idea of conquering his brother covered the recollection of a time when he had been the pet of bigger boys.

The story of his passion for hunting brought out for the first time his relationship to his father. The latter had not been a hunter, but a fisherman. While he was standing in or near the water to fish, the youngsters were allowed to shoot small birds with popguns. During such outings the little fellow always felt very "manly," a feeling which he relived in his present joy in the hunt. But anxiety dreams relating to water which occurred with ever greater frequency brought us finally to the realization that this joy likewise had a hidden meaning: "But I am a hunter and not a fisherman." His father's fishing must have aroused anxiety in him; he had overcome this anxiety in a sort of counterphobic pride that he was allowed to go off with his father on a masculine jaunt; but nevertheless he could enjoy this counter-phobic pleasure only in the hunt, whereas it now grew increasingly clear that a hitherto unconscious anxiety was connected with fishing and all activities associated with water. Several peculiarities in his behavior while hunting showed that he always strove to connect his hunting activity in some way with "water," but that this connection must never be too close. Although as a child he had been afraid of swimming, he now tried to force himself to swim, but it gave him no pleasure whatsoever. Dreams and fantasies brought out that the water he was afraid of represented dirty water, which was revealed by the analysis of his inordinately intense anal and urethral eroticism, against the demands of which his entire pathological character had in truth been erected as a defense mechanism.

I do not intend to speak much more about these deeper levels. It will suffice to indicate two things:

The first of these refers to the father, who had impressed the youngster as exceptionally "masculine," whose chief interest was certain athletic activities, and who himself seems never entirely to have overcome the "fighting boy's point of view." Moreover, he laid great stress on the matter of clothes. The homosexual ties of the patient were directed toward the father. The latter often used to go out with the boy, especially to take him along to parties, and to show off with him. These were the situations in which the patient on the one hand experienced manly pride, and on the other hand, fear that as a little boy he was not equal to his manly task—and for this reason preferred to stick to his nurse and to his primitive narcissism. The idea of always being handicapped in social gatherings because he could not yet compete with the more adult men, as well as the other idea of avoiding such gatherings because he might injure the others in a sudden sadistic outburst, went back to his ambivalence toward his father, who had used him in an exhibitionistic way.

The second thing is that during the early years of childhood the patient shared a bed with his brother. What he fantasied hazily as enticing and dangerous in connection with his father, he actually experienced with his brother. These homosexual excitations, which he sought to counter by regressing to a primitive oral narcissism, had found their expression in constant bedwetting. He was shamed by his "exacting" mother for this bedwetting; and he resolved, as a revenge for her belittling him, henceforth to live only for his own gratification and to have consideration for no one else. This determination finally was shattered and led to secondary conflicts. Of all this the patient had been, of course, completely unaware.

I should like to add that the pregenital fixation, which found expression on the one hand in bedwetting and on the other in oral regression, went back to early stomach and intestinal disturbances.

This crude and schematic résumé suffices to show how the characterological peculiarities of this patient were determined by a combination of circumstances in his childhood environment: the nurse who pampered him, the exacting mother, the older brother, the fact that this older brother later was physically weaker, the exhibitionistic, boastful character of the father; only when all these circumstances are taken together can the development of this patient become clear to us. These etiological factors would never have come to light if we had not made the systematic treatment of his peculiarities of character the central point of his analysis.

FOURTEEN

Psychoanalysis of Character[*]

As is well known, psychoanalysis started as a therapy of neuroses; therefore, the neurotic symptom was its first main subject. In a neurotic symptom something happens which the subject experiences as strange and unexplainable—either involuntary movements, or other changes of bodily functions and various sensations, as in a hysterical symptom; or an overwhelming and unjustified emotion or mood, as in attacks of anxiety or depression; or queer impulses or thoughts, as in compulsions and obsessions. It is always something which seems to break in from without upon the personality and which disturbs the continuity of the personality and appears like an invasion from something outside the usual habits of the subject, coming as a vivid proof of the limits of the conscious will. It cannot be controlled by means of the usual controlling apparatus of the mind.

Before psychoanalysis undertook to study the essence of "personality," it had to investigate the disturbances of personality and the disruptions of its continuity. It was the study of the insufficiencies of conscious control and those habitual patterns of behavior which we call "character," which enabled us later to attack the problems of character itself. The result of those preliminary studies showed that the impression that the neurotic symptoms represent an invasion from another country was correct. Their ego-alien nature can be explained by the fact that they break in from a region of the mind which the subject had previously purposefully alienated from it—viz., the unconscious. Neurotic symptoms are the outcome of forces which are always at work but which are usually prohibited from expressing themselves. The essence of the psychology of the

[*] This paper was first presented at Santa Barbara in April, 1941. Dr. Fenichel's manuscript has been translated into English, in conformity with the other papers, but no attempt has been made to give it the final form Dr. Fenichel might have given it if he had prepared it for publication.

neuroses is the explanation of how this normal prohibition became insufficient. For repressed instinctual forces which are striving for discharge are to a certain extent present in everybody. The first proof of this fact was given by the interpretation of dreams. Dreams, like symptoms, are disguised expressions of the repressed, and that is the reason why they appear to the coherent and reasonable ego to be strange, as neurotic (or even more, psychotic) symptoms do. Normal persons may dream, too. And so we see that the unconscious is operative in normal people also. We can understand that it is the state of sleep itself which, with the suspension of consciousness, weakens the suppressing forces of the higher levels of personality, and so enables the deeper parts of the mind to make their appearance. In the case of neuroses, however, the insufficiency of the prohibiting forces proceeds from other causes than the state of sleep. It is a consequence of a too far-reaching suppression of instinctual satisfactions. That is not of much interest for us today. What matters is the fact that the human mind seems to consist of two principal parts: the so-called "continuous personality," the activities of which seem at least to be of a suppressing nature; and unconscious instinctual forces which usually are suppressed, but which make their appearance in neurotic symptoms and dreams, and also—we hasten to add—in other sudden acts, emotional feelings, or attitudes which are experienced as strange and which have always an impulsive and instinctual character, opposed to intellect and reason. The situation is really very analogous to brain physiology, where it was also ascertained that the activity of the higher centers, the cortex, partly consists in suppression of activities of deeper and more archaic centers, and that the latter find expression whenever the higher suppressing forces become insufficient. Sometimes it looked, therefore, as if the two parts of the human mind might have to be represented by two different psychologies. It has been thought that psychoanalysis, as a "depth psychology," has to study the unconscious and the instincts, but that other, non-analytic psychologies, would have to study the "surface," the personality which suppresses the instincts and which governs the mind of the normal person during the day—the "character."

But such a viewpoint is wrong. It is the genetic point of view which shows us that the relationship of the deep instincts and the unconscious, which are studied by psychoanalysis, and the ego and the so-called character, is more complicated. We certainly do not assume that there are no other phenomena in the human mind than instinctual phenomena, but we do assume that the non-instinctual phenomena can be explained as derivatives of instinctual ones, which took shape under the influence of the outer world. Just as the cellular theory is not contradicted by the existence of bones and nerves, and bones and nerves may be studied by means of the same principles as the cells, as long as it is possible to demonstrate that the bones and nerves are derivatives of cells—so, in the same way, does psychoanalysis, which first studied the unconscious and the instincts, remain competent for the whole human mind as long as it succeeds in demonstrating that the conscious and non-instinctual phenomena are derivatives of unconscious and instinctual ones.

What the "ego" undertakes with the deep unconscious forces is certainly not only their suppression. It is their organization and guidance as well. And so it becomes understandable that an apparatus whose function is suppression, guidance, and organization cannot be understood before the material which is suppressed, organized, and guided is thoroughly known. First comes the psychology of what is comprehended, then the psychology of comprehension. In the so-called "ego psychology," psychoanalysis approaches the same subject as other psychologies, but it approaches it in a different way, namely genetically. I have already anticipated that it can be shown that the whole "daytime personality" which we call the ego is to be regarded basically as being a result of conflicts between primitive instincts and inhibiting outer forces.

By taking symptoms and dreams as its first objects, psychoanalysis has succeeded in studying the nature and genesis of the unconscious instincts which find their distorted expression in them. It is not my task today to talk about this part of psychoanalytic research. I remind you only of the fact that the immense field of infantile sexuality was not known before Freud.

There are three reasons why psychoanalysis could not fail to be extended to ego psychology. To begin with, there were theoretical reasons: The repressing forces are also an object for psychological study and the preliminary study of the repressed forces enabled psychoanalysis to make the next step. In addition, there were two other, practical, reasons, the importance of which has to be estimated still higher. In the first place, when the psychoanalyst tried to get at the hidden meaning of the neurotic symptoms he met the suppressing—or, as I might say in this connection, the repressing—force of the ego in the form of what we know as "resistances." To overcome these resistances became his main practical task. How was it to be done? Everything was tried in this respect, and Freud has said in his *Introductory Lectures* that every means of suggestion is justified for the purpose of overcoming resistances. But if, for example, a patient did not obey the basic rule which tells him to say everything which occurs to him, a scientific mind was tempted not only to influence this unreasonable behavior by means of suggestion, but to get to understand this ego, which had hitherto figured as a reasonable ego, but which in such cases seemed not to be reasonable at all. Consciously, the man was trying to do everything to co-operate; but unconsciously a "suppressing" part of his ego was antagonistic. Here was a conflict at work inside the ego; other material, associations or dreams or sleeping states of the patient, had to be used to analyze this conflict, to make the patient aware *that* he had the resistance, *why* he had the resistance, and why he had it in that form. The principle is that this is always done by the discovery that the patient, even if he does not feel any fear today, was once afraid (or ashamed or disgusted or full of bad conscience) about certain instinctual experience, and that this fear is unconsciously still working in him, so that he develops resistances against utterances which might be connected with the instincts in question. Thus it was the necessity for analyzing the resistance which in practice started psychoanalytic ego psychology. Moreover, in this way two other things were discovered: first, that certain attitudes of the patient's which always recurred when similar instinctual dangers were mobilized served the purpose of resistances, and second that not only was that purpose fulfilled by them in the psychoanalytic treatment, but that the same behavior patterns were also used by the patient in his ordinary life, either to prevent his expressions of certain instincts or to prevent his becoming aware of them. This discovery opened the way to the first "psychoanalysis of character"—that is, to the analysis of the purpose and the historical genesis of certain characterological attitudes as repressions. In the second place, it is an interesting fact that the neuroses themselves, which the analyst had to deal with, have changed. We began today with the statement that in the classical neurosis a continuous personality was suddenly disturbed at certain points by inappropriate actions, impulses, or thoughts. In modern neuroses that is no longer the case. Here the personality does not appear to be uniform, but open, torn, or deformed, and in any case so involved in the illness that one cannot say at what point the "personality" ends and the "symptom" begins. There is a very gradual transition from neurotics to those "psychopaths" and persons with "characterological anomalies," who themselves feel their need for treatment less than do the people around them. I know that you here are especially interested in so-called "criminals," a term which I do not like as a description for psychological facts, because "criminality" is a juridical and not a psychological term. But certainly "criminals" are among such "characterologically deformed" people.

It would be a fascinating task to investigate the cause of the changes in form of neurosis. I merely wish to suggest where I should look for the answer to this question. The method and manner in which the ego admits, repels, or modifies instinctual claims depend to a large extent on the way in which it has been taught to regard them by the surrounding world. During the last decades morality, this educational attitude toward the instincts, has changed very much in our European and American cultures. Classical hysteria works chiefly with the defensive mechanism of genuine repression, which, however, presupposes a simple prohibition of talk concerning the objectionable instincts, chiefly sexual, which upbringing has consistently represented as bad. The inconsistency of present-day education, itself undecided as to which instinctual claims to allow and which to suppress, results in initial license and subsequent sudden, unexpected, and therefore more cruel, deprivation. The inconsistency of the neurotic personality corresponds to this inconsistency in education. The change in the neuroses, it seems to me, reflects the change in morality. In order to understand this, however, one would have to investigate the social changes which have taken place in our culture in the last decades. In any case, the present-day neurotic characters appear to us to possess egos that are restricted by defensive measures, and psychoanalysis has had to adapt itself to this new object—and that might be the decisive reason for the interest in "psychoanalysis of character" and the recent progress which psychoanalytic characterology has made.

Now to the next question: what have "character anomalies" and "neurotic symptoms" in common, and in what respect do they differ from each other? A neurotic symptom is, in general, as you know, a distorted expression of a repressed instinct. But sometimes it is more an expression of the repressing forces—of what safeguards an executed repression. Think, for example, of neurotic impotence or frigidity; this may perhaps occasionally express some masochistic or sadistic instincts too, but it is certainly to a much greater extent, and in all cases, a method of insuring that the subject shall not give in to sexuality, which he unconsciously holds to be dangerous. Or think of the compulsive symptom which reassures the patient against unconscious death wishes. The degree in which repressed instinct and repressing forces participate in the structure of the symptom may vary; but in principle we can say that every symptom is an expression of a conflict between an instinct and counter-forces (anxiety, feelings of guilt, shame, or disgust). The same is true for dreams—cannot the same formula be applied to attitudes or patterns of behavior?

There are some attitudes in which the possibilities for instinctual satisfaction are so obvious to the observer that it does not need psychoanalysis to discover it. Consider, for instance, the amount of sadism which can be satisfied provided the subject thinks that he does it for a higher aim. There are many more attitudes still in which the purpose to repress some instincts, or to defend the subject against an instinctual danger, is obvious. Take, for example, all attitudes of the type of "reaction formation"—that is, overstrained and rigid attitudes that hinder the expression of contrary instinctual attitudes—which nevertheless may sometimes break through in various ways. Thus it seems that in principle these attitudes which a person's ego develops toward his objects as well as his own instincts are also compromises between the instincts and the anxiety which opposes them, just as symptom and dream are. The problems which, after this discovery, are now of more interest, are:

1. What are the differences between dreams and symptoms on the one hand and ego attitudes on the other, and why are those attitudes of an "ego" nature, while dreams and symptoms are alien to the ego?

2. Are all attitudes and behavior patterns such results of instinctual conflicts, or are only a certain type of them of this sort, so that besides them there may exist attitudes which are psychologically of an entirely different character?

We can divide the "attitudes" of an individual into those which are occasional and those which are habitual. The habitual ones may be summarized as "character." Character traits may once more be subdivided in those which appear only in certain situations and those which are comparatively constantly present, suggesting that the instinctual temptation which must be repressed is continually present too. There are people who are impudent, polite, indifferent, ready to prove others at fault, etc., in all situations and to all people. Such attitudes may be called "character defenses" in the narrower sense, in contrast to other types of defense.

It would, of course, be incorrect to consider the word "character" as synonymous with the expression "defensive character attitude." The way in which a person behaves in relation to instinctual actions, how he combines his various tasks in order to find a satisfactory solution—all that too goes to make up "character." In all probability psychoanalytic characterology will have to make a fundamental distinction between character traits in which—most likely after an alliance between them and the object—the original instinctual energy is discharged, and those traits in which psychoanalysis as an "unmasking" psychology can prove that the original instinctual attitude which is contrary to the manifest attitude still exists in the unconscious. We can call the first the "sublimatory" type of character trait, and the second the "reactive formation" type. This second type is betrayed, as already mentioned, either by its forced and rigid nature, or by the occasional breaking through of that which has been repressed.

It can easily be understood why the reactive type is much better understood than the sublimatory type. It is the reactive type which forms characterological anomalies and resistances whose investigation was required of psychoanalysis for practical reasons. They show themselves as frozen residues of former vivid instinctual conflicts. Freud once wrote that "it is always possible for the ego to avoid a rupture in any of its relations by deforming itself, submitting to forfeit something of its unity, or in the long run even to being gashed and rent. Thus the illogicalities, eccentricities and follies of mankind would fall into a category similar to their sexual perversions, for by accepting them they spare themselves repressions." Since the maintenance of these eccentricities must surely correspond to the reactive type and demand an expenditure of energy, it would perhaps be more correct to say that their formation corresponds to a single definite act of repression, so that the necessity for subsequent separate repressions, which would require more energy, and for separate anxiety situations, is avoided. In this way, the ego-restricting attitudes, which act as chronic anchorages of instinctual defense, are not experienced as ego-alien but are worked into the ego. Their constant operation prevents the instinct from becoming manifest, so that we see no living conflict between instinct and defense but something rigid which does not necessarily appear to the patient himself as questionable. The problem for us lies in the relative constancy of the defensive attitude assumed by the ego when faced by different demands both from the external world and from instinctual contents.

This relative constancy could also be understood for certain kinds of attitudes of the reactive type. The special quality of those attitudes seems to depend on a number of factors. It depends partly on the hereditary constitution of the ego, partly on the nature of the instincts against which the defense is directed. (As an example of this, I may quote the classical triad of the anal character: sense of order, parsimony, and obstinacy.) It depends partly, too, on the age at which the child experienced the instinctual conflict in question. At a certain age certain defensive mechanisms and attitudes are more in the foreground than others. In most cases, however, the analysis succeeds in showing that the special attitude was forced on the individual by the external world: either it was the most suitable attitude in a given situation, or all other possible attitudes were blocked in a given situation, or this attitude was promoted by similar modes of behavior in the child's personal environment with which the child identified itself; or else the attitude was exactly the opposite of these modes, which the child was trying *not* to assimilate. In this way the ego which develops a character of a defensive type becomes more and more rigid and unelastic, reproducing the same pattern of behavior instead of reacting individually to individual stimuli. Such an ego becomes increasingly poor and loses more and more possibilities of behavior—till analysis succeeds in reawakening the old conflicts and enabling the individual to reach a better solution.

Certainly you will not expect to find that if the analysis succeeds in remobilizing the old conflicts, the once-repressed infantile instincts will come into the open immediately. The child was once afraid of those instinctual impulses, and as a rule its anxiety was actually manifest in the form of an infantile anxiety neurosis. It took time to develop the character attitude of the defensive type with which the individual, as we have seen, escaped from subsequent repressions and anxieties. Thus we can say that in the defensive attitudes anxiety has been *bound*—and we find the proof for this in the fact that in remobilizing the old conflicts the first thing we usually see is that the patient develops more or less severe attacks of anxiety. The analysis of this anxiety which follows, however, brings the instinct in question to the surface. A layer of anxiety has been laid down between the original instinct and the ensuing defensive attitude.

This view that such character attitudes serve the purpose of binding anxiety is not contradicted by what Mrs. Deri has recently said when she stressed the fact that probably of all the attitudes which an individual has developed, those are selected to build up the character—i.e., to become chronic—which are suited to provide satisfactions as well, though it may be in a distorted form. This apparent contradiction can be overcome if two circumstances are borne in mind. First, the defensive attitudes which we are discussing are only one half of the characterological attitudes. There are also the attitudes of the sublimatory type. These have been as yet less inquired into. It may be that the reactive type represents more anxiety, the sublimatory type more satisfaction. The other circumstance which we have to consider is that "satisfaction" does not necessarily only mean "satisfaction of genuine instinctual desires." There exists also a "satisfaction" in the sense of "security"; and the defensive character attitudes certainly are selected because they seem to give to the individual a maximum of security, namely, an avoidance of anxiety situations.

It must be admitted that this whole discussion of character traits as results of conflicts between instincts and the judgment that giving in to the instinct might be a danger, presupposes the existence of a psychic function of judgment or of a psychic instance which is able to experience fear. The question of how the function of judgment develops and how there is gradually established in the infant an apparatus which serves the purpose of communication between the individual and his surroundings, certainly goes beyond the subject of "character analysis." But it was undoubtedly the progress of character analysis which made it possible to see more clearly into that field as well, so that it can be said that the basic functions also of the ego—perception and action—can in principle be explained by the inner actions of outer influences and primitive biological needs. Mention must be made, however, of another complication in the structure of the so-called ego—a complication which occurs much later in life, say from the second to the seventh year of age. I refer to what is known as the "superego." The new elements which are brought into the picture by this agency are of special practical and theoretical importance for character analysis.

I am presuming that you are acquainted with the Freudian conception of the superego as the psychic agency which turns fear into a feeling of guilt. We have said that the first reason why the organism, which is interested in the satisfaction of its instincts, sometimes paradoxically turns against its instincts and tries to defend itself against them—the first reason is fear, based on the judgment that the instincts are dangerous. Some of the feared dangers are real and natural—as when the child gives in to the instinctual demand to grasp at the beautiful fire and burns itself. Some are real and artificial—as when the educating adults punish the child for certain instinctual acts, or threaten to withdraw their affection from the child when it behaves in certain ways (and the child needs this affection urgently), or promise premiums of higher supplies of affection if the child suppresses certain instincts. Others of the feared dangers are imaginary, in so far as the child judges its surroundings according to its own instincts, misunderstands the world in an animistic sense, and therefore expects more dreadful punishments than ever occur in reality. However this may be, in all cases giving in to the instincts becomes connected for the child with the idea of danger. It is a danger which threatens from without, and the executors of it are, to the child's mind, its parents. The child is afraid that its parents may either punish it bodily (the so-called "castration anxiety"), or by a withdrawal of their affection. But later on there comes a time when the child begins to act as a "good child" even when the parents, who might punish it, are not present or will certainly not become aware of its behavior. Then fear has been turned into a feeling of guilt. The parents who might punish it are now, so to say, inside the child itself; they are always present and are to be differentiated from the real parents. Those "inner parents," who watch the child, who give commands and prohibitions, but also prizes and protection—they are the superego, and their "incorporation" is a result of a long instinctual development which we cannot discuss today.

Now I think you already understand why I am talking about this point at considerable length. It has much to do with "character analysis," in so far as the functions of the conscience are a very important component of the character of personality. Very characteristic for a personality are (a) what he considers good and what bad; (b) whether he takes the commands of his conscience seriously or not; (c) whether he obeys his conscience or tries to rebel against it, etc. On what does that depend? It depends, as all psychic structure does, on constitution and experience, and it is the experience part which we can investigate psychoanalytically. The structure of the superego, its strength, and the way in which the ego behaves toward its "id" depend in the first place on the actual behavior of the parents (for the superego, being the incorporation of the parents, is strict when the parents are strict). They depend in the second place on the instinctual structure of the child; and this in its turn depends on the child's mental constitution and all its previous experiences. The child who unconsciously hates his parents fears retaliation—his superego might act toward his ego in the same way as once his ego wished to act toward his parents. But for the most part the superego depends directly on the models which the child had before him in his environment and on the nature of his object relationship, the incorporations of which are represented in his superego. You know from the analysis of so-called criminals that in all probability the most severe deficiencies of the superego are to be observed in persons who in their childhood had no opportunity to develop lasting object relationships because they changed from one more or less loveless foster home to another. But it is not only the *content* of what is to be considered good and bad—what the father first teaches and the superego later demands—that is transmitted from one generation to the other through the superego structure; it is also the *idea* of good and evil itself and the way in which this idea is thought of in our society—it is the authority which asks obedience and promises protection if obedience is given—which are created through this change from fear into feelings of guilt.

We have spoken of the neurotic conflicts as conflicts between instincts on the one side and anxiety or guilt feelings on the other. In our structural terminology we should say that they are conflicts between the id on the one side and its ego, or an alliance between the ego and the superego, on the other. But sometimes there are also conflicts between the ego and the superego. Not all egos accept the demands of the superego without contradiction, and rebellions which were once attempted (or not attempted) against the parents may be continued against the superego. The extreme case of disunion between ego and superego is given in melancholia, where the whole weight of the personality is laid on an extreme pathological feeling of guilt which destroys the remainder of the per- sonality. But you know that when the subject has a certain degree of such a feel- ing of guilt he may try to prove that it is not justified or to repress and to deny it. Many character anomalies turn out to be attempts of the ego to defend itself against a sense of guilt. There are personalities in whom the need to contradict the superego is so overwhelming that it overshadows all object relationships. They need "supplies of affection" from everybody in the same way as they needed them as little children, using the feeling of being loved as an argument against in- feriority and feelings of guilt (and anxieties) into which they fall back when they feel that those supplies are denied. This continual passive asking to be loved —and in a very primitive way, asking to be loved by everybody, without evolving any real relationship to real objects, this being a regression into the ways in which the little child used to center regulation of its conflicts round its self-regard—this asking for love may either be a defense of the ego against the strong superego ("when I am loved, I cannot be as bad as that, after all"), or it may be a de- ficiency in the development of the superego, in the sense that the individual still is more governed by outer anxiety than by guilt feelings. Such a deficiency of supplies of affection blocks all real object relationships; and it also forms the basis for manifold secondary conflicts. The most characteristic of these is the conflict between the tendency to get by force the supplies which are denied and the tendency to repress every aggression, because the aggressed person might refuse all supplies.

I have repeatedly used the term "real object relationship," but we have not yet discussed what that means.

Love and hatred have a long history of development, and in every phase of this development disturbances may occur which are then reflected in the subject's character. The considerateness for the object which characterizes love is not present from the beginning. The infant's "love" consists only in taking and not in giving; he acknowledges the objects in so far as he needs them for his satisfaction, and when this satisfaction is attained they may disappear. The subject's first experiences in this respect, the way in which he got or did not get his satisfactions as a very small child, may be decisive for his later attitudes toward his objects. His general optimism or pessimism, his relationship to "getting," his capacity or incapacity for being patient, the dependence of his self-regard upon outer supplies, or its independence of them—all this may be determined by his earliest infantile experiences with objects. Later, in the so-called anal period, he is more obliged to take the objects and their demands into consideration. The training in cleanliness is the first occasion on which he has to give up primitive erotogenic pleasure for another person's sake, or rather, for the sake of getting the affection which he needs from his mother. Psychoanalytic characterology has especially studied the different ways in which those conflicts influence the later attitudes of the ego. Certainly here are the first social conflicts, whose specific nature has a formative force. But it would be an error to assume that it may be more or less a matter of chance that those social conflicts cover the anal phase. What we have learned is that it is precisely the anal instincts which, under the influence of these so-called social conflicts, change their aim or object, thus becoming incorporated into the ego. The "anal character traits" have developed, instead of anal-erotic instincts. It is not a "modern alchemy" that instincts may be turned into ego attitudes, as a critical author stated a short time ago. It is a clinical fact which can be observed again and again; and it is proved by the experience that an analysis of the conflicts which resulted in the development of defensive ego attitudes turns them back, after the interposition of overwhelming anxieties, into the original instincts once more.

The same is true for the relation between so-called "orality" and dependence. Their connection is not an accident but an essential one. Man is a mammal, and the human infant is born still more helpless than other mammals and requires feeding and care on the part of adults so that he shall not die. This undoubtedly provides a biological instinctual basis for the fact that every human being has a remote recollection that there were once powerful or, as it must seem to him, omnipotent beings on whose help, comfort, and protection he could depend in time of need. Later the ego learns to become independent and active and to use active means to master the world by itself. But the possibility of a "passive oral attitude" remains as a relic of infancy. Often enough the adult person gets into situations in which he is as helpless once again as he was as a child. Sometimes the forces of nature are responsible, more often social forces which have been created by people. Then he longs for just such omnipotent protection and comfort as was at his disposal as a child. He regresses, as we are used to saying and as we can prove by observing his instinctual behavior, to orality. There are many social institutions which make use of this biologically predetermined longing. To be sure, none of them promises the longed-for help without expecting some return. The conditions that they make vary greatly in different cultures. But all of them combine the promise of comfort and help with ethical conditions. The formula "if you obey me, I will protect you" is the one which all gods have in common with all earthly authorities. It is true that there are great differences between the idea of an almighty god or of a modern employer on the one side and the mother who feeds her child on the other: nevertheless it is the similarity between them, it is the instinctual bond between child and mother, which explains to us the psychological effectiveness of authority. It has been said that a man's character is formed by the social institutions in which he lives. The psychoanalytical instinct psychology does not contradict this statement in the least. On the contrary, it is psychoanalysis which makes it possible to understand how the social institutions work in detail in forming the characters of the individuals who live under their rule. The instincts are interposed between the institutions and the changes of the personalities. It is clear that the individual's character, which is the result of infantile instinctual conflicts, must depend upon the content and intensity of prohibitions and encouragements which the different instincts get in different social institutions. Actually, we see that various cultures produce various character formations.

But we must return from sociology to psychoanalytic practice. What are the basic consequences of what we have been discussing for psychoanalytic practice? It is clear that all mere talking about unconscious instincts or about reconstructions of the historical past of the patient cannot change anything, as long as the energies of those old conflicts, to liberate which is the aim of psychoanalysis, are bound in certain more or less pathological character attitudes. Where there are rigid attitudes instead of living conflicts, the latter must be remobilized. For that purpose it is necessary first to make the patient aware of the peculiarity of his behavior when he is not aware of it spontaneously. When the patient is aware of what he does, he has to become aware of the fact that he is forced to do so, that he cannot do otherwise; then he will understand that it is an anxiety which makes other behavior impossible, and that he needs the behavior in question for purposes of defense. He will learn to understand historically why these defenses were obliged to assume the form they have, and eventually what it is he is afraid of. If the mobilization succeeds he will experience anxiety; and later on, instead of the rigid and frozen attitude, there will appear once again the instinctual impulses in question, the old full emotions. I have shown elsewhere in detail that and how this procedure can be described by the formulas: we change character neuroses into symptom neuroses, and we change character resistances into living transference resistances, in order to handle them afterward as ordinary symptom neuroses and transference resistances are handled. The aim of this mobilization is the reduction of the ego attitudes to those historical situations in which they were originally formed. A special problem is the investigation of this historical situation and the so-called "defense transference"—the fact that the patient seems to "transfer" to his relation to the analyst not only his past instinctual demands but also the past situations in which he developed one particular form of defense. But the explanation of this fact is not very difficult. The character defenses in general have been developed precisely for the purpose of being applied again and again in every similar situation. The patients behave as if they were careful to make continuous application of a method which had previously proved useful against the danger, just as though they never could know when a similar danger might not reappear. What the patient is really striving for unconsciously is certainly the pleasure of instinctual satisfaction. But his past experiences (real or imaginary) force the ego to produce in every situation of temptation memories which once aroused anxiety, and against those memories the same defensive patterns have to be developed over again.

The next question is whether there are any analyses at all which are not "character analyses." And perhaps in a very strict sense there are no such analyses. A certain part of the energies which are bound in useless defensive conflicts and have to be put at the disposal of the individual once again, is always bound in certain defensive attitudes. But undoubtedly there is a difference of degree between real "character analyses" and "symptom analyses."

I should now like to attempt to illustrate by a few examples the historical genesis of character defenses and their treatment. But this is not an easy task. To demonstrate what is really meant, long case histories would be needed, for which the time is lacking. I must limit myself to relating the chief features of two cases which certainly do not offer any very special characteristics. Similar features can be found in every analysis. And since the cases are rare in which the historical circumstances that necessitated certain attitudes are easily and microscopically understandable, you will excuse me if I use examples which I have once published in a similar connection. I hope that you have not read the paper in question.

The first patient I am going to describe could be called "a Don Juan of achievement." A successful and, in his own line, prominent man, he was in fact always dissatisfied with himself, always striving after higher achievements, with external success, but no sense of inward satisfaction. In a like manner, he was always trying to increase his quite adequate income and was unable to overcome his fear that it might be insufficient. He behaved in the same way in his love life: although women ran after him and he had one success after another, he always felt inwardly dissatisfied—which is understandable, since those relationships were completely lacking in tenderness and had none of the characteristics of a real object relationship. It is clear that the man was so dominated by an overwhelming narcissistic necessity that the libidinal aims of his instincts were completely overshadowed. The man was married to a woman considerably older than himself, who, in some ways, behaved toward him as a mother does to her child; she acted, that is, in many ways as a guardian to him, so that at home he, the big, successful man, was more like a little child. He found this dependence very oppressive, it is true, and was in the habit of revenging himself on his wife by attacks of rage, and by continual unfaithfulness, and by complete lack of consideration. Thus each of them made life a torment to the other. The first defensive function of his persistently unsatisfied wish to be a great man must therefore have been to deceive himself with regard to the fact that he was a little child in so many ways—one of which was his complete lack of consideration for the person who mothered him. This impression is strengthened by the knowledge that his wife was continually goading his ambition, just as his mother was in his childhood. The realization that there was something behind his continued dissatisfaction, which persisted despite all his external successes, and the truth of which he did not wish to admit, was gained in transference analysis. As in every other province, he was very ambitious in analysis and wanted to impress both me and himself by his quick success. At the outset, after he had read Freud, he was forthcoming with theories about his childhood; he grasped comparatively quickly, however, that this was not what mattered to me, and then began to observe himself and his behavior, and to behave like a "favorite pupil," continually stressing, however, the fact that the analysis progressed too slowly and that he was not satisfied with himself. On one occasion, at the last session before the holidays, he came late, because, just as he was starting for his analysis, he had a sudden attack of diarrhea, and this for the first time shook him very much. The bowels putting in their say made him experience the reality of the analysis in an entirely new way. He realized that his continual haste only served the purpose of drowning something else in him. The analysis explained this richly overdetermined diarrhea in the first place as an anxiety equivalent; it then brought this at first incomprehensible anxiety into relation with his fear of insufficient success, insufficient sexual objects, and insufficient earning. It was then discovered that the character formation of the patient had been complete in childhood. He had always been go-ahead, cheeky, outwardly successful; he had always been the first, even in being naughty, but had, nevertheless, always been dissatisfied with himself. In this behavior he had obeyed his mother, who had always been very ambitious for her son and had always urged him on to further deeds. When it appeared that, at bottom, his mother had despised his father, who was a tradesman, and had always said to the boy, "You must be better than your father," etc., it became clear that his behavior expressed a particular form of the return of the oedipus complex from repression; it was not yet intelligible, however, why it had taken this form— why it had this essentially narcissistic note. Various things soon became more obvious, however: his father had illegally sold certain goods, the sale of which was only permitted by special concession; the policeman, therefore, was a dreaded figure in the patient's childhood. In the eyes of the boy, this considerably reduced the power of the father; he determined not to be frightened when he was big, but to make policemen afraid of him. (He remained faithful to this intention: as a motorist he loved to get policemen to intervene unjustifiably, and then afterward prove them to be in the wrong.) The circumstances in his home, moreover, were such that at times he had to stand behind the counter and serve when he was six years old. The customers liked the little boy and chose to buy from him; he felt this to be a triumph over his father, whom he already regarded as weak.

There were also two later experiences which particularly accentuated both the patient's continuous need to show his superiority in some such way and the impossibility of satisfying that need. The first experience was that when he was fourteen he was seduced by a maid, with whom he had regular sexual intercourse from that time on. This episode had been changed in memory to make it appear that it was he who had, at this age, seduced the grown-up girl. It needed analysis to convince him that it had happened the other way round, and that the whole of his later attitude to women was an attempt to alter this to him painful memory, in accordance with his wishes. This attempt, by the way, failed in a typical manner: he intended that the large number of women whom he persuaded to have intercourse with him should convince him of his active masculinity, which he unconsciously doubted; more detailed analysis, however, showed that he arranged things so that he seduced the women into showing their willingness, and that it was only when he saw this that he was not able to resist them. The second experience was that at seventeen he had an abscess on the lung for which he was operated on several times and which kept him in bed for months and con-valescent for years—so that he had to be passively nursed like a little child.

The patient gradually became afraid of the transference in analysis, afraid that he might become "enslaved" to the analyst. His transference attitude was in-tended from the beginning to repudiate this anxiety. He attempted, even then, to disparage the analyst and to find "policemen" who were superior to him. What he expected with fear then turned out to have been true: the six-year-old sales-man could not feel completely superior to his grown-up father in the role of tradesman. His father, who used to beat him a great deal, had been greatly feared by him in earlier years. His relation to him had completely overshadowed his relation with his mother, and, in consequence, his being needed by his father for business purposes had an additional libidinal value. The passive narcissistic attitude was suggested to him in his early childhood by particular circumstances including, among others, illness, strict prohibition against masturbation, which put an end to his early phallic attempts, and the strictness of his father who beat him. It was, however, owing to the same set of circumstances that he feared this attitude. In this conflict, his mother's ambition, the disadvantageous comparison of his dreaded father with the policemen, and with his own successes as a salesman showed him a way out: by a continuous outward fight against his passive-narcissistic attitude, he was able to retain it at other points. The seduction by the maid and his illness after puberty then fixated these latter defensive attitudes in his character.

Another patient, a woman, was characterized by the haste with which she always undertook every more or less indifferent enterprise. She was physically, as well as mentally, always in a state of tension, always occupied with tomorrow, never living in the present. This continual activity of the ego remained on the surface to an amazing extent. Her associations spread in every direction without ever getting any deeper. Her interests and occupations also bore the stamp of a superficiality which did not correspond to her intelligence and talents. She avoided everything which had a "serious" character. In describing her experi-ences she expressed a peculiar sense of inferiority: "Nothing that happens to me can be serious or real." The activity, restlessness, and continual worry about what would happen tomorrow served the purpose of forestalling any serious ex-perience which might happen, by means of her own, superficial, ego-determined, i.e., play-like activity. This patient was passionately in love with a man. She could not leave him, although serious conflicts were aroused in her as a conse-quence. In all her anxiety and trouble, and, in particular, at the beginning of a depression, she escaped—in the same way as a drug addict escapes by means of his drug—with the help of real or imagined experiences with this man. It soon became clear that it was not real love that drove her to him, but that he satisfied narcissistic necessities whose fulfillment repelled anxiety or depression. However, it was not clear in what way he did this. Only gradually did we realize that the chief quality of this man—and in this he was the diametrical opposite of the patient's husband—was apparently that he was humorous, frivolous, and witty, and never called things by their right names. What the patient really wanted from him was the reassurance: "I need not be afraid of sexuality, it's only fun." In a first analysis the patient had from the very beginning developed the resistance of not speaking, and no progress was made. Only later did we understand that this had happened because the analysis was "serious" and that its aim was to call things by their right names, which the patient wished to avoid at all costs. The analysis with me, on the contrary, appeared to make very rapid progress. It took us a long time to understand that this progress was only apparent and was the result of a particular resistance. I had, by chance, laughed at some remarks which the patient had made during her first sessions. This enabled her to work "in isolation." What she had with me was a "fun-analysis" (in the same way that she enjoyed "fun-sexuality") without the analysis really attacking her anxieties about her real instinctual life. When a child experiences something that shakes it deeply, or when it is afraid of some occurrence, it "plays" this occurrence afterwards. It forestalls in its fantasy what is expected, or repeats the past occurrence, so changing its own passive role into an active one, in order to practice mastering the dreaded tensions with the reduced quantities which it measures out for itself. Our patient had apparently begun this process but never ended it. Her anxiety was too great for her to make the step from playing to reality. Just as another patient continually said to herself, out of fear of reality: "It is only an imaginary story and not true," so this one said: "It is only a game and not serious." The analysis showed that the "serious" sexuality had acquired its frightening character as the result of a sadistic component aroused by the birth of a younger brother at the end of the patient's fourth year. This had evoked unconscious anxiety that, if she gave in to her real impulses, she would tear the penis from men and the child from women. It is interesting to note that the escape into "playing" which was suggested to her by various circumstances in the external world was due, among other things, to a particular incident in the nursing of this younger brother. An elder sister had suggested to the patient that she should push over the perambulator and so get rid of the intruder. From that time on the patient was very much frightened of touching her little brother, particularly after she had once noticed how her mother and the nurse had laughed over the little boy as he was micturating. Her mother had persuaded her out of this aversion to touching him by saying: "Take him in your arms; I'm standing here; you're only playing at being his mother; you're not really his mother."

FIFTEEN

The Ego and the Affects*

I

AFFECTS and emotions are but rarely discussed in psychoanalytic literature.

In the *Studies in Hysteria* [1] the affects still were—in the conception of "strangulated affects"—the kernel of the theory. Later the interest decreased considerably, and it is only lately that several psychoanalytic writers have again taken up the subject.

If we wish to investigate the problem of how the ego, i.e., the organized part of the personality which physiologically controls the relations to the outer world, adjusts itself to the affects, we must first determine what we mean by "affects." Psychoanalysis does not usually have a simple time with the conceptions taken over from psychology, because these are descriptive, whereas psychoanalysis strives for dynamic-economic definitions. But these can only be the end, not the starting point, for a psychoanalytic investigation. Hence we cannot set forth from ultimately defined conceptions, but only from described phenomena, and we must come to an agreement as to which phenomena we mean. Most of the textbooks make no fundamental differentiation between "affect" and "emotion." It is my impression that the word "emotion" means rather the feeling sensations themselves, "affect" more the outcome of those sensations, the discharge phenomena, as they, for example, come to light in an emotional spell. In German we use the word *"Affekt"* for both; the sensations which accompany certain specific tensions are likewise called *"Affekts,"* e.g., "grief," though no discharge phenomena or movements occur, or at least are not in the foreground of the picture. Glover therefore suggested subdividing the affects into "tension affects" and "discharge affects." [2] However, we shall start with the discharge phenomena. Phenomena

---

* First published in *Psa. Rev.*, Vol. 28, 1941, pp. 47–60.
[1] J. Breuer and S. Freud, *Studies in Hysteria*, New York, Nerv. Ment. Dis. Pub. Co., 1937.
[2] E. Glover, *Psycho-Analysis*, London, Bale, 1939, and "The Psycho-Analysis of Affects," *Int. J. Psa.*, Vol. 20, 1939.

like a spell of rage, a sudden anxiety, sexual excitement, overwhelming disgust, or shame, or a general unspecific excitation will be our first objects.

What is the common denominator of all these different phenomena? In all of them we find: (a) movements and other physiological discharges, especially changes in the mimic-muscular and glandular functions; (b) emotional feelings. Both the physical and the psychic phenomena are specific—and in particular the correlation of both phenomena is specific. What determines the syndrome of physical and psychic phenomena? Certainly not the conscious will. It is characteristic of the phenomena in question that they occur more or less without the consent of the conscious will, that the normal function of the ego is partially eliminated. Persons who undergo emotional spells have "lost control." Apparently something of a more archaic nature is substituted for the normal ego. These spells seem to be a kind of regressive phenomena, and there is no doubt that children and infantile personalities are more "emotionally labile," adult persons with a so-called strong ego more "stable."

Under what circumstances do such spells occur? There may be two situations: (1) A spell may be a response to extraordinary stimuli, the quantity or quality of which makes the temporary insufficiency of the normal control apparatus of the ego understandable. In this case the emotional spells seem to be a kind of "emergency control"—substituting for the normal ego control in case of emergency—to use a term proposed by Rado.[3] (2) Or a spell may be the response to ordinary stimuli when certain conditions obtain in the organism. What are those conditions? The simplest example of an emotional spell without adequate stimulus is displaced rage. A slight precipitating factor evokes a fit of anger, if there was a readiness for it in the organism, rooted in a previous experience which afforded this tendency no means of expression. In general we can say that the organism tends to "emotional regressions," if it is in a state of "tension." This is why unduly intense emotional reactions generally show that this reaction is a "derivative" of something which has been suppressed previously. To summarize: Emotional spells occur when the normal ego control has become relatively insufficient (a) by too much influx of excitement ("emergency control") or (b) by a previous blocking of the efflux.

Such a definition must perplex us. Is it not also valid for quite another type of phenomena, namely, for neurotic symptoms? The neurotic symptoms, too, are discharge phenomena which occur without the consent of the ego; and if we analyze their precipitating factors we likewise find that either an increased influx of excitation has taken place (traumatic neuroses) or that the defense mechanisms of the ego have previously blocked certain discharges and have thus

---

[3] S. Rado, "Developments in the Psychoanalytic Conception and Treatment of the Neuroses," *Psa. Quart.*, Vol. 8, 1939.

brought the organism into a state of tension (psychoneuroses). Yes, it seems to be true that the causation of emotional spells and of neurotic symptoms is essentially the same: a relative insufficiency of the ego control, either by increased influx or by blocking of the discharge. We may state that emotional spells and neurotic symptoms are indeed dynamically very similar to each other. Both are partial substitutes—of a more archaic nature—for healthy ego motility. The difference lies in the nature of what is substituted: in the case of neurosis the substitute is subjectively determined, in the history of the individual; in the case of affect the substitute is objectively determined, the syndrome is more or less the same in different individuals—just how we do not know. The similarity is more striking in the conversion symptom, especially in the hysterical fit, which could be called a "subjective affect" by the same token that an emotional fit could be called an "objective neurosis." This similarity is likewise the reason why Freud, having discovered the historical determination of the hysterical fit, also tried to find a historical determination of the syndrome of anxiety. The similarity seems less striking in the case of compulsion neurosis. But we know that the compulsion symptom is less primitive than the conversion symptom. It is not simply a breaking through of the repressed out of the repression, but more a compromise with the repressing forces; it corresponds probably more to the "tension affects" like grief. If we may compare the conversion symptom to an outburst of rage or to the intractability of sexual excitement, then probably the compulsion symptom is paralleled by the more gradual work of mourning. The so-called tension affects in all probability likewise represent a secondary elaboration of the original tendency toward stormy discharge. We shall return to this question later.

Whatever significance is attached to the conception "weakness" or "strength" of the ego, there is no doubt that an ego which shows insufficient control over a rather small quantity of excitement can be called weaker than one which has mastery over larger quantities. Unquestionably children and "neurotic personalities," i.e., persons with many repressions, and therefore greater tensions, in general have more frequent emotional spells than normal adults. It is obvious that the normal adult does not lack emotions. But he does not have overwhelming emotional spells. Apparently the ego's increasing strength enables it somehow to get the upper hand of the affects at the moment when they arise. The ego is no longer overwhelmed by something alien to it, but it senses when this alien something begins to develop and simultaneously upon this recognition it re-establishes its mastery, binding the affects, using them for its purposes—"taming" them, as it were. To be sure, even the most adult ego can do this only to a certain degree. Too much excitement is emotionally upsetting for everyone. Thus we see that the first stage, in which the ego is weak and the affects dominant, is followed by a second in which the ego is strong and has learned to use the affects for its purposes. But a third state is always possible in which once more an elemental affect may overwhelm the organism.

This triple stratification has been studied with special reference to anxiety. We have (1) traumatic anxiety, i.e., the specific sensation displeasure, which is experienced when the organism is overwhelmed by excitement; (2) fear of danger—the ego, which has learned to anticipate the future, expresses the judgment that the imminent situation might turn into a traumatic one. The judgment itself has the effect of a trauma and produces anxiety. But it is an anxiety of slight degree, which is purposefully used by the ego as a "signal" to initiate defense measures. (3) In the hysterical attack of anxiety, this tendency of the ego to "tame" anxiety fails, and the judgment which is intended to avert the traumatic state actually induces it. (This can happen if the organism, as a result of previous repressions, is in such a dammed-up state that the "slight anxiety" added by the "danger judgment" acts like a lighted match in a powder barrel.) We can, however, observe this triple stratification with respect to other affects, too. If, for instance, we ask ourselves what "disgust" really is, we answer as follows: (1) An archaic physiological defense syndrome that is automatically produced as soon as something repulsive reaches the digestive tract. (2) The strengthened ego learns to use this reflex for its purpose and turns it into a defense against sexuality. (3) There are neurotic "attacks of disgust" in which the ego, thanks to previous blockings, is completely overwhelmed by the affect which it wanted to use for defense purposes. We may assume that there is an analogous situation with respect to pain. First pain is the way in which stimulation of certain nerve-endings is experienced, automatically as it were. This experience is then used by the ego to initiate defense measures ("pain signal"). And finally it may happen that this effort entirely fails, because the pain is so strong that every defense function is paralyzed.

II

We have seen that affects first of all make their appearance as a force alien to the ego in situations where the normal mastery of excitations by the reasonable ego fails; that then the strengthened ego learns to anticipate the affects, to apportion them, and to use them purposefully. In so doing, it behaves toward the affects just as it does toward overwhelming outside impressions. Toward all surprising and strong impressions which the ego experiences without its consent, whether they originate from within or without, the ego has but three possible ways of responding: (1) The impression may be *traumatic,* i.e., it may, because of its quantity, wholly or partially block the healthy functions of the ego for the time being; in this case the ego, seeking to re-establish its equilibrium, makes various attempts at belated control, as may best be observed in the traumatic neurosis. (2) The ego is no longer overwhelmed. It opposes the impression with counter-cathexes. The impression may be so painful that the ego seeks to flee from it, as it were, a procedure which presupposes that the ego is in a position to take active measures against the impression: it attempts to *ward off* the impression. (3) The ego is strong enough to absorb into and to *use* within its structure that which befalls it. Which of these three reactions will actually be employed by the ego, depends upon the relative strength of the ego and of the impression.

We can observe these three forms of reaction in relation to external experiences (shell-shock, denial or distortion of unpleasant perceptions, and reasonable learning from experience), as well as, for instance, in relation to sudden neurotic symptoms (repetition dreams after an attack of anxiety, denial or rationalization of neurotic symptoms, and last, their employment for secondary gains) as well as in relation to affects.

An unduly strong outburst of affect, or an unforeseen one, or finally one whose quality is still unknown may assuredly have a real traumatic effect. Originally, *every* outburst of affect was indeed, as we have seen, *per definitionem,* a trauma, i.e., an occurrence which overwhelmed the ego and made the usual ways of behaving inadequate. That such "affect traumas" can also provoke a sort of "traumatic neurosis" can be observed most clearly in children. They are prone to repeat an initially overwhelming affect situation actively again and again in play and dream. In real traumatic neurosis, too, we sometimes observe that the overwhelming factor, which is subsequently to be brought under control, consists not only of exciting sense impressions, but of affects aroused by these sense impressions, e.g., the person's own aggression. Later the ego learns to defend itself against affects and to master them.

III

Let us begin with defense. The conception "defense" was originally introduced by Freud in the sense of "defense against affects." In the *Studies in Hysteria* he and Breuer had recognized that hysterical symptoms should be regarded as a discharge of affects in changed form, which at one time had been obstructed in their natural expression, and had become dammed up in the organism and "strangulated." Since then we have gained a deeper understanding of the neurotic conflict, and view it less as a conflict between a tendency toward affect and a resistance toward its expression, more as one between an instinct striving for discharge and an anxiety or guilt feeling opposing this instinctual activity. But it is obvious that this more recent formulation supplements and clarifies, but does not nullify the older one. The opposing anxiety or stirring of conscience, as well as the dreaded "punishing" intervention of the environment, would transform the instinctual enjoyment into an unpleasant experience, into an unpleasant affect, and the avoidance of this displeasure is the real motive, not only of the pathogenic, but of every instinct defense. Frequently it is very clear that defense against instincts is undertaken by the repressing ego, not only because of the danger of "loss of love" or "castration," but also because the person's state of instinct excitation itself—for reasons that the history of the individual can explain—is regarded as dangerous. That which is sometimes described in the literature as "fear of the strength of the instincts" really ought to be called "fear that intense affects may appear and overwhelm rational behavior." In another place we have shown why it seems improbable to us that every ego basically should be guided physiologically by such a fear, providing that its apparatus for gratification and mastery are functioning normally.[4] (Such an assumption is valid only in so far as "danger" is always anticipated "trauma"; in the last analysis every fear is actually a fear of a traumatic state.) But in so saying, naturally the phenomenon itself is not denied, only the assumption that it is normal and needs no further analysis. The analysis of such cases gives us, on the contrary, innumerable examples as to how a person comes to undertake defenses against his excitation, respectively his affects.

Inasmuch as many neurotic symptoms, e.g., compulsions, may be comprehended as secondary bindings of anxiety, the psychology of neuroses often uses the terms "instinct defense," "affect defense," and "anxiety defense" interchangeably, and indeed we often speak simply of "defense." But there are situations where we have to distinguish between these various types of defense. Probably such a differentiation will become more significant if we do not limit ourselves to the investigation of neurotic symptoms but study character and ways of behavior. We shall then see, for example, that a defense may be intended less for a situation regarded as dangerous than for an experiencing of the anxiety affect itself. Affect defense is implicitly contained in all neurotic manifestations.

Defense attitudes toward affects which from the beginning are unpleasant, are at least as primitive as defense attitudes toward unpleasant perceptions. Closer investigation shows us that we cannot differentiate so exactly between defense attitudes directed toward without and within, between "denial" and "repression," for instance, as we should theoretically like to do. For the very perceptions which seem unpleasant to us are those which mobilize unpleasant affects in us.

If we now inquire into the mechanisms of affect defense, we shall certainly not be able to give any new information. The general and primitive character of affect defense makes it a matter of course that *every* known mechanism is also employed against affects. We cannot describe new mechanisms, but can only examine the ways in which the already known mechanisms are directed specially against

[4] O. Fenichel, "The Concept of Trauma in Contemporary Psychoanalytical Theory," No. 4 in this volume.

affects, particularly against affects which themselves have already been applied in defense against still other, more primitive affects, such as sexual excitement.

The most primitive defense is complete *blocking* (restraining) of the affect. But how is such a thing possible? Did we not *define* the outburst of affect as an insufficiency on the part of the ego which normally regulates discharge? And now we are to assume that this ego is nevertheless in a position to hinder the development of affect? Yes, it seems that the ego, after having been overwhelmed by affects, can regain its strength to such an extent that in similar recurring situations it can have adequate counter-cathexes on hand to ward off a new, full development of the affect. Assuredly it is not possible to "repress" affects in the same sense as ideas. According to the definition which we gave for "affects," an "unconscious affect" would be a *contradictio in adjecto*. But there is a similarity between the affects and the data on "depth sensibility." (The psychic component of the affects is nothing other than a complex of such data.) And as for "unconscious sensations," Freud investigated their content in *The Ego and the Id*. We can speak of "unconscious affects" in no other sense than of "unconscious sensations." In both instances there are certain states of tension in the organism which, were they not hindered in their development and discharge by counter-cathexes, would result in affects, respectively sensations. There are unconscious "dispositions toward affects," unconscious "longings for affects," strivings toward the development of affects, which are held in check by opposing forces which hinder the development of affects. Such "unconscious dispositions toward affects" are naturally not theoretical constructions, but may be observed clinically just as unconscious material in general may be clinically observed: they develop "derivatives," they betray themselves in dreams, symptoms, and other substitute formations, they betray themselves through the rigidity of the opposing behavior, or finally they betray themselves merely in a general weariness, which is occasioned by the consumption of energy in the unconscious struggle over the affect.

Complete blocking of affect discharge, which betrays itself in rigidity and weariness, has as a natural consequence a heightened readiness for the development of derivatives. We said at the beginning that people in a state of dammed-up affects are ready, even on slight provocation, to produce violent outbursts of affect. Disproportion between precipitating factor and affect reaction is therefore an index of the presence of repressions. Thus we can say that a general affect *lability* is the first consequence of affect defense through blocking of discharge. (The person, particularly if it is someone whose development has been in the direction of a so-called compulsive character, can then learn to defend himself in turn against this affect lability by strengthened counter-cathexes. If affect lability is the first result of affect defense, general affect *rigidity* is the second.)

The "derivatives," which break through the attempt at blocking, may represent stronger or weaker signs of the distorting influence of the defensive forces. The simplest derivatives are the *delayed* outbursts of affects, with which we have become acquainted in the typical example of the belated attack of fury on slight provocation. The displacement in the temporal connection which results in the affect reaction simply appearing *later,* whereby the motivating connection becomes unrecognizable, is the most frequent special case of the so-called affect displacement. As is well known, dream distortion makes frequent use of such affect displacement. It can scarcely be coincidence that this defense is more frequently instituted against the affects of *irritation* and *grief.* Irritation can obviously be endured without discharge for a short period, but only for a short period; then it must be aired, no matter against whom. And in the affect *grief* this postponement itself seems to be an essential component: the conception, "work of mourning," says nothing other than: an affect which, in its full strength, would overwhelm the ego (the quantity of cathexes released through the loss of the object) is gradually "worked through." Hence it is comprehensible that the general mechanism of affect postponement has been studied in the case of grief especially. The classic example is Freud's Wolf-Man, who upon the death of his sister showed no reaction, but burst into tears at Pushkin's grave.[5] Helene Deutsch has since devoted a paper to this question.[6] What we today call "grief" is, taken as a whole, obviously a "postponed" and apportioned neutralization of a wild and frequently self-destructive outburst of affect. Such an outburst is all the stronger, the more ambivalent the attitude toward the lost object had been, and is one which we meet in the uninhibited self-destructive or self-abasing mourning reactions of primitives, and which is associated with the fear of revenge by the dead person. Our "work of mourning," extending over a period of time, is a successful defense against this primitive affect which threatens the ego. (Hence, according to Glover, "mourning" is a "tension affect"; but originally it was, like all affects, a "discharge affect.")

Affect postponement is, however, by no means limited to irritation and grief. Pfister investigated the reactions of the ego to acute mortal danger, and repeatedly found absence of fear during the period of acute danger—but a subsequent appearance of enormous fear when, objectively, the danger was past.[7] Such postponement of fear reaction may have a life-saving effect, because it makes possible purposeful action which otherwise might be paralyzed by fear. Similarly the fear symptoms of the typical traumatic neurosis are in part such "delayed fear."

[5] S. Freud, "From the History of an Infantile Neurosis," *Coll. Pap.,* Vol. III, London, Hogarth, 1948.

[6] H. Deutsch, "Absence of Grief," *Psa. Quart.,* Vol. 6, 1937.

[7] O. Pfister, "Schockdenken und Schockphantasien bei hoechster Todesgefahr," *Int. Z. Psa.,* Vol. 16, 1930.

A "delayed fright" sounds like a contradiction, because we only call a sudden and immediate reaction "fright." And yet there is such a thing. Anyone who has seen Walt Disney's *Pinocchio* will have noticed that repeatedly in the picture frightful experiences are calmly accepted by the person in question—only a moment later to be "caught up" by the fright. During this one moment the ego has been able to prepare itself a little, to protect itself from being completely overwhelmed.

I once had the opportunity to analyze a case of delayed *disgust:* A patient had, in the course of his analysis, resumed an infantile habit of anal masturbation. He explained in his analysis that in so doing he had soiled his fingers; it was striking that he showed no disgust reaction, although his entire character would have led one to expect such a reaction. A few days later he responded to a relatively slight provocation with a disproportionately strong outburst of disgust.

There is no doubt that *all* affects can be postponed in such a way. Certainly there is delayed *shame*.

We have already said that postponement is just one special case of affect displacement known to us from the interpretation of dreams. The next special case is displacement in respect *to the object;* the affect, which was suppressed in relation to a certain object, bursts forth against another object. It is clear that this type of displacement can be combined with "postponement." We think again of the example of displaced irritation, and of the Wolf-Man at Pushkin's grave. The displacement of the feared object is known to us from animal phobias.[8] Important clinically is the displaced feeling of guilt, which finds expression because of some other provocation, but is not felt at the place where it genetically belongs.[9]

The defense activity of the ego has gone further, if not only time and object, but also the quality of the affect itself has been changed. The Wolf-Man experienced his excitation at the wrong place, but the excitation had not changed its nature of mourning. The defense is more successful if the subject can deceive himself as to the character of his own excitation, not merely as to its significance. This is possible in various ways.

The first possibility is the following: The typical discharge-innervations occur wholly or partially, but their psychic significance remains unconscious. This is the way in which the so-called "affect equivalents" originate. "Anxiety equivalents" were described by Freud in his earliest work on anxiety neurosis.[10] The "mourning equivalents" were collated by Landauer.[11] It cannot be doubted that

---

[8] S. Freud, "Analysis of a Phobia in a Five-Year-Old Boy," *Coll. Pap.,* Vol. III.

[9] S. Freud, "Notes upon a Case of Obsessional Neurosis," *Coll. Pap.,* Vol. III.

[10] S. Freud, "The Justification for Detaching from Neurasthenia a Particular Syndrome: The Anxiety-Neurosis," *Coll. Pap.,* Vol. I, London, Hogarth, 1948.

[11] K. Landauer, "Aequivalente der Trauer," *Int. Z. Psa.,* Vol. 11, 1925.

all other affects can likewise be replaced in such a way by "equivalents" of somatic sensations. It is characteristic of certain compulsive characters that when analysis has deflected their affect blocking, they begin to complain about certain bodily changes of sensations, without sensing their psychic significance. Before they rediscover their affects fully, they find, first of all, the route to affect equivalents. In place of feelings of guilt, intestinal sensations frequently appear, and oral and stomach sensations in place of disgust. Schreber's somatic "basic language" [12] consists in the affects reduced to body sensations.

The denial of the true significance of the affects may be anchored in a convulsive adherence to the opposite emotional attitude. We can speak of "reaction formations" against affects. We see perhaps how impudence is developed as a defense against a feeling of guilt, courage as a defense against fear, etc. What happens in the case of shame and disgust? We are so accustomed to these affects being used as sexual defenses that we are prone to regard strikingly shameless behavior, or ostentatious recourse to the disgusting, rather as an eruption of infantile sexual instincts than as a reaction formation against affects. But such an "eruption of instincts" is not always necessarily simply constructed. In other connections, too, we very well know that "eruption of instincts" and "defense against instincts" are relative conceptions, that an eruption of instincts at one point may serve as a defense at another point. Editha Sterba's analysis of a "shameless" girl at least showed beyond doubt that in this case there was not a definite lack of shame, but a complicated reaction formation against a preceding period strongly characterized by intense shame.[13] Reaction formations against affects betray themselves, like all reaction formations, in their convulsive nature and in occasional eruptions of the original attitude in dream, symptom, or symptomatic behavior. We have also to mention those "reaction formations against anxiety" which I recently collated under the name "The Counter-Phobic Attitude." [14]

Further self-deceptions as to the significance of one's own affects are finally made possible by complicated phobic and counter-phobic attitudes toward those situations which originally induced the affect in question.

Finally it is also conceivable that through certain defense mechanisms of the ego, the quality of the affect experience is really specifically changed. Freud's old conception that under certain conditions "sexual excitement" is transformed directly into "anxiety" seems to us by no means as yet refuted.

Up until now we have said that the derivatives of averted affects can make their appearance at the wrong time, can be directed toward the wrong object,

[12] S. Freud, "Psycho-Analytic Notes upon an Autobiographical Account of a Case of Paranoia," *Coll. Pap.,* Vol. III.

[13] E. Sterba, "Nacktheit und Scham," *Z. psa. Paed.,* Vol. 3, 1928.

[14] O. Fenichel, "The Counter-Phobic Attitude," No. 11 in this volume.

or can show the wrong quality. They can also be *isolated* from their entire psychic connection by a particular expenditure of counter-cathexis—and the analysis of affect disturbances consists, as we know, in large part of re-establishing connections which have been lost through resistance. Affects may be *projected,* i.e., perceived in someone else, to escape perceiving them in oneself. The idea of "introjection" of one's own affect seems to make no sense (it may be that the expression "to swallow one's emotion" is to be taken seriously), but there certainly is an affect defense through introjection of the object for whom the affect was intended, e.g., the feared object. Under the heading "isolation" there should be included the situation that certain affect excitations are admitted only under certain guarantees, but not under others; for example, only so long as a real and serious character is not ascribed to them.

There is a continuous line from the compulsive characters who have completely isolated the affect excitations from the content to which they belong to the persons who *are really blocked as to affect,* who more or less feel no affect whatever. To them, as is known, there attaches a special significance from the therapeutic point of view: an analysis, which discusses the content of their infantile instinctual conflicts, remains fruitless unless an analysis of affect defenses has made the patient accessible to experience of affect.

Like all defenses, affect defenses may *fail.* People who deny their affects may under some conditions be completely overwhelmed by the return of their affects. Hence we frequently see a "double-edged character" in affect defenses: [15] absense of affect can reverse into an attack of affect, a reaction-formation affect can reverse to its original opposite. We said that "affect lability" is in general a sign of defensive struggle against affects.

From the life-saving "displacement" of an anxiety or of grief to the affect-paralyzed hebephrenic, there is a continuous line.

IV

It seems simple to distinguish between "defense" and "synthetic infiltrations into the structure of the ego" theoretically. Let us consider the instincts, for example. We speak of "defense" when the opposing forces of the ego prevent the complete discharge of the original instinctual energy; of "sublimation," when object and goal are changed without interfering with the discharge. (The "nevertheless discharge" of averted instincts in symptoms and other derivatives is in principle never sufficient.) A similar differentiation must be established for affects: The "averted" affect readinesses" require a constant expenditure of energy. The healthy ego, however, experiences affects, knows them, discharges them

---

[15] E. Kris, "Ego Development and the Comic," *Psychoanalytic Explorations in Art,* New York, Int. Univ. Press, 1952.

and uses them for its own purposes. In practice this differentiation is not always so simple as in theory. With most manifestations which we discussed in the previous chapter, there can be no doubt about their "defense" nature. With some, however, such doubt is entirely possible. For instance, how about the "work of mourning"? For the healthy person, it serves not so much for the suppression of released energies which constitute a threat to the ego, but rather for the attainment of the capacity to apply those energies elsewhere. "Belated mastery" of affect quantities does not always mean preventing expression of "affect readinesses" which tend to rebel against such "binding"; there may be a real mastery, an infiltration of these energies into the realm of the ego.

Such a "synthetic employment of affects" certainly is present when the strengthened ego is no longer content to master outbursts of affect belatedly, but proceeds to anticipate them, to create them, and make use of them, when necessary. The "taming" of initially automatic id reactions for ego purposes through anticipation and active apportionment is the method of the ego in general.

Two particularly impressive examples of such active use of affects have already been mentioned: the one consists in the use of the initially automatic protective affects, disgust and shame, for the purpose of sexual defense. The other is given in the conception "affect signal" which, as was shown in the first section, is by no means limited to "anxiety signal." The reader is reminded of shame-, disgust-, and pain-signals. Instead of being overwhelmed by demonic affect forces, there is autonomous, active, free play of the victorious ego with its multiplicity of affects. Of course, there is no such thing as the "normal person" having no affects. But he is the master of his affects, whereas the weak ego is mastered by its affects. Whereas complete outbursts of affects do interfere with coming to terms with reality, the function of reality testing, "affect signals" are absolutely a means for reality testing.

It is almost superfluous to mention that there are also various "secondary gains" from affects. These may be narcissistic in nature, e.g., a sort of pride in one's own affectivity, or object-libidinal. They may be used for many rationalizations, may bring gains in object relationships. Finally they may also take over various functions in conflicts between ego and superego, e.g., incite others to unconsciously longed-for attitudes, which are needed for release from feelings of guilt.

V

It should be repeated again that practically there are combinations of defense and synthetic application. Averted affects, too, find certain possibilities for discharge in their derivatives, and not all "additions" of affect to the ego express themselves in discharge manifestations; some are shown in tension attitudes.

As the entire ego, in the last analysis, is an apparatus for detaining direct discharges, the transitions are fluid, and everyone constantly has certain unconscious "affect readinesses" within himself. We shall call them "pathological" only if, from the unconscious, they disturb conscious intentions. Such "affect readinesses" can be decisive for the interest and the vivacity of conscious actions. It would be better not to call this "sublimation of affects," but rather "sublimation of instincts whose energy, had they not been sublimated, would have appeared in the form of affects."

❋ ❋ ❋ ❋ ❋ ❋ ❋ ❋ ❋ ❋ ❋ ❋ ❋ ❋ ❋ ❋ ❋

SIXTEEN

The Misapprehended Oracle*

I shall use Freud's significant paper "A Disturbance of Memory on the Acropolis"[1] as a point of departure for further study. In the year 1904 during an unexpected trip, Freud was standing in front of the Acropolis and suddenly had the feeling, "So all this really exists just the way we learned about it in school." Analysis showed that this astonishment about reality had been displaced from another situation and actually meant, "So it is really true that I was allowed to come to Athens." He had been doubtful of this, not about the reality of the Acropolis. He compares his own emotional setting with that of "those wrecked by success."[2] He was afraid of something like the envy of the gods when his wishes to travel were fulfilled; and his feeling of guilt made him believe that it would not be right for him to experience the gratification of such a wish. The feeling that it was all "real" was to soothe the anxiety which made its appearance when his desire was fulfilled. The origin of this anxiety, i.e., feeling of guilt, was a consideration of filial duty. He thought he was not allowed to be more successful than his father.

Let us bear in mind the anxiety situation which, according to Freud, underlies such situations of doubts about reality: A wish which is inhibited by a sense of guilt is suddenly gratified, and a conflict results between the inclination to enjoy this gratification and the opposing feeling of guilt. And let us now examine other examples of similar experiences.

One of them concerns the screen memory of a patient who, as an adolescent boy, saw a girl wearing short socks which showed her legs. He thought in

---

* First published in *American Imago*, Vol. 3, 1942, pp. 14–24.

[1] S. Freud, "A Disturbance of Memory on the Acropolis," *Coll. Pap.*, Vol. V, London, Hogarth, 1950.

[2] S. Freud, "Some Character-Types Met With in Psycho-analytic Work," *Coll. Pap.*, Vol. IV, London, Hogarth, 1948.

astonishment, "I must always remember that girls also have legs." [3] The second case concerns a woman patient who suffered from pseudologia phantastica. She often thought she had fabricated something which actually turned out to be true; then she would become very frightened and suffer from uncomfortable feelings of estrangement.

The first case is not difficult to understand. The command to remember directs the boy's attention to the existence of girls' legs and serves to cover up something else, namely that these girls have no penises. Here, too, the doubt has been displaced. The command to remember, which certainly is an equivalent to the experience "so it is really true," is utilized in this case to substantiate the idea: "Something else which is true, is not true"; it is used in the service of repression.

The second case is somewhat more complicated. The patient was apparently frightened by a magical experience of her own omnipotence of thought: What she believed she was making up, turned out to be true. But analysis showed that her attempt to "make up" was an attempt to deny an unpleasant reality—and what appeared like "omnipotence of thought" was actually a failure of such an attempt.

For example: Owing to specific childhood situations, the patient was very much afraid of being sick. As a child she sometimes wanted to avoid going to school and told her mother that she felt ill. She rubbed the thermometer which was given her until the mercury indicated a fever of, let us say, 100° and then introduced it. It happened that the thermometer registered 101° when it was taken out. Here the "estrangement" represents a failure of repression. It sets in when the patient is forced to acknowledge something which she had tried to deny. [4]

These two cases have one thing in common: They contain the element "so it is really true that." But in the first case the stressing of reality facilitates the repression (the stressed reality being of a reassuring nature), whereas in the second case the repressed reality comes back and repression fails. In the first case a substitute for that which should remain repressed is perceived as "real," which insures the desired repression; in the second case the unwanted reality makes its appearance in opposition to the tendency to repress. Both cases feel a kind of astonishing estrangement. But the ego of the first case—feeling reassured—is relieved; that of the second is terrified. If it is permitted to compare

[3] O. Fenichel, "Defense against Anxiety, Particularly by Libidinization," No. 27, *First Series*.

[4] In this connection it is interesting that this tendency to "make believe" (which sometimes failed and thus aroused the "estrangement" in question) was this patient's main mechanism of defense. I described elsewhere ("The Economics of Pseudologia Phantastica," No. 9 in this volume) that her pseudologia was formed according to the formula: If it is possible to deceive others, it may also be possible that my memory is deceiving me, that what I have experienced, but would prefer not having experienced, may be mere fantasy. She was frightened when it proved to be real, nevertheless.

the Acropolis case with these two cases, Freud's experience is nearer to the former case. His disturbance is of a pleasant nature, and reality is experienced as a reassurance against superfluous anxieties. In so far as there was a feeling of guilt in the case of the Acropolis, opposing the desired gratification, there has also been a tendency to feel that standing in front of the Acropolis might be not true; and this tendency now dropped out.

So we have a conflict between either the perception or the expectation of a terrifying reality on the one hand, and the tendency to repress on the other. What actually happens serves in the cases of the Acropolis and the girl's legs to devaluate the fear which made the perception or the expectation terrifying; in the case of the fever reality confirms the danger of impending punishment.[5]

We said that the mechanism of denial, which might fail, is utilized not only against outer realities, but also against inner guilt feelings and such outer realities as seem to confirm the validity of guilt feelings. We know people whose whole personality is determined by a denial of guilt according to the formula "Not I am guilty, the other fellow is guilty." Now we would like to interrupt our trend of thought and first consider a particular manifestation of this mechanism where the situation may be formulated as follows: "Not I am guilty, but fate or God is guilty."

If such a defense could be successful, the individual would be free from guilt. But we all know cases where this mechanism fails or is insufficient. So the accusations against God, fate, or parents must be tenaciously repeated since with-

---

[5] Many persons try to repress their guilt feeling by denying reality, either by denying any danger of punishment, which is done by denying the truth of ominous facts, or by denying the full reality of the punishable instincts. In those cases fantasy not only serves as a substitute for an unpleasant reality, but as a denial of a (magically perceived) reality. To the patient who denied her fever by simulating it, thinking was a charm used against the coming true of what had been thought. The patient said to herself, it was very improbable that anything might happen just the way she had thought about it beforehand. Eventually she did not believe in any reality. During analysis she found out that she was under chronic tension, constantly waiting for a curtain to fall so that at last the play might end and real life begin. With a kind of depersonalization she sometimes felt amazed that people eat or go to the bathroom—as if she had been of the opinion that instinctual things are only thought of but never actually done. She used to daydream horror stories about lunatics; and her first great anxiety spell occurred when she suddenly witnessed a temper tantrum of a psychotic.

The well-known phenomenon of "dream within a dream" may serve a similar purpose. It attempts to deny the reality of instinctual pleasure in order to render possible the enjoyment, which is "only dreamt of," in spite of a fear of punishment. And in the same way as we have described a failure of such an attempt in the fever-fright of our patient—a failure of the consolation "it is only a dream" may also occur. A patient remembered that at puberty he often experienced in dreams tempting situations which he did not dare to make use of, doubting whether this was dream or actuality. He tried to escape from this dilemma by making the following mental note in daytime: "Whenever I feel a doubt whether this is reality or a dream—I may be sure that it is a dream; when actually awake, I do not feel such doubts." It was to no avail; he doubted again in the next sexual dream.

A novel and play of Andreyev, *The Thought*, described such a failure of an attempted denial by "making up." A strange and doubtless schizoid man suddenly gets the idea of simulating madness and of killing his friend for that purpose. In the insane asylum after the deed he begins to doubt whether all this was merely a game.

out such pertinacity the unconscious but still active expectation of punishment would instantly reappear. In the *Schicksalsdrama,* where tragedy is the outcome of predestined fate, all the artistic effort is directed toward showing that man cannot escape his doom. It was first demonstrated by analysis that in such cases the tragedy ensued not because of the inexorable course of fate, but because of the undeniable consequences of the hero's guilt.

And therewith we come to the function of the oracle. In ancient times it was customary to consult the gods when confronted with a weighty decision in order to shift the responsibility. If the words of the oracle were obeyed, somebody else could be held responsible for what happened, and a sense of guilt or perhaps a fear of impending punishment became unnecessary.

Now what takes place, when, as in the Oedipus myth, the oracle foretells the future, and the drama is based on the fact that the individual tries to escape from the prophecy but is eventually unable to do so? We can formulate the situation of Oedipus in the following fashion: "Something which is bound to happen must not happen—but finally it happens anyhow." And now we come back to the problems previously discussed. We said about the fever patient: "Something which has taken place should not have taken place, but it happened anyhow." We have added that this formula as related to the past is also significant for the future in so far as the past was only to be denied in order to deny the future punishment resulting from it. Oedipus tries to escape the oracle in the same way as the visitor at the Acropolis fights the envy of the gods, the lover of the girl's legs the possibility of castration, the simulating girl the existence of real fevers. The modern cases' denial is directed against the guilty act, or against the culpability, or against the possibility of punishment. The ancient hero denies the responsibility for the act and so his punishability—for everything was predetermined by fate. The prophecies of the oracle are in fact a retrospective projection of the guilt-oppressed ego.

The oracle was consulted not only to obtain advice about an external situation, but especially when a decision had to be made about an inner conflict: whether what the individual had in mind was permissible or whether a punishment was to be expected. In such a case the oracle was asked for permission, that is for a divine decision, which might act as a counterweight against the twinges of conscience.

We can still detect this oracular function in the analysis of the modern oracle seeker, the superstitious compulsion neurotic. For instance, one patient remembered that he habitually performed a ritual in order to decide whether or not he should give way to the temptation of masturbation; that is, whether masturbation might be permitted just once more. If luck were with him, he gave way to the drive in the hope that he might displace the guilt upon the gods. If luck were against him, he invented an excuse in order to repeat the oracular process until he obtained the desired permission. I hardly need to add that the displacement of guilt upon the gods was unsuccessful, that he did not escape his pangs of conscience, that he felt it to be absurd that the same gods who had forbidden masturbation should permit it on this occasion. An oracle of this kind seeks to accomplish the impossible. The parents who forbid certain activities should be made to permit and even to encourage them.

The well-known ambiguous meaning of oracular predictions must by its very nature have a social significance: The priests reject the responsibility which has been foisted upon them and express themselves in words of double meaning so that they are protected against all future eventualities. But such double meanings may meet the demands of the ambivalent oracle-seeker halfway, who wants permission to gratify his instinctual needs and expects an unavoidable refusal. He tries to interpret a prognostication of double meaning as a permission, but remains unable to rid himself of the feeling that he should have interpreted it as a prohibition and as a warning of punishment. Kris called to my attention the connection between interpretation of the ambiguous prophecies and the solution of riddles. The individual who rejects all knowledge of guilt and represses the significance of his act misunderstands the task. And the wise man who can solve every riddle is not the most intelligent, but he who can recognize the hidden truth because he is emotionally free and unhindered by repressions.

The motive of the *misapprehended oracle* must have something to do with such a conflict. This motive means that an oracular pronouncement is apprehended as a pacifier until a moment comes when the uncanny thought comes up: "This utterance of the oracle, in which I believed, is true, but in an entirely different sense from that which I had supposed. It brings me misfortune—and only now when I can no longer escape it, I understand and do not know how I could have misconstrued it before." This sensation is probably related to the uneasiness which the patient with the temperature of 101° experienced and corresponds to the feeling, "It is as though I had been blind, since I now see clearly the fatal truth when it is too late to escape." Let us take the story of Macbeth as an example of this frequently recurring theme. Macbeth thinks he is secure because the witches predicted security. But Birnam Wood does come to Dunsinane, and no woman did give birth to Macduff.

Many things are condensed herein: The weird quality of irrevocable fate, the uncanniness of sudden clear vision, the consequent inevitable knowledge of what is to come, and a feeling of guilt: I ought to have known before what I know now.

We have already mentioned the analysis of "Ananke." "Ananke" who cannot be escaped is identical with the furies. What cannot be escaped from are the consequences of one's own guilt. And it is, as we have already said, only a defense against the guilt feeling, that this guilt is made to seem predestined. What actually is predestined is talion law: Who has committed the deed cannot escape punishment. Macbeth's first crime is the murder of the father, which draws the other murders after it. He murders and believes that he can get rid of the responsibility by calling upon the soothsaying of the witches. The prophecy, which apparently exculpates him, must actually mean: "Do not believe that you can escape conscience. Punishment is inevitable."

How does it mean that? And what purpose is served by the motive of the misunderstanding?

The prophecy about the wandering wood and the man who has not been born of a woman sounds like a paradox. Dream interpretation and the analysis of compulsion neurosis have taught us that a paradox means derision. Then who is deriding whom? The witches Macbeth? Macbeth thinks that the witches tell him one thing when they are really telling him something else. They cradle him in apparent security, but really foretell disaster. Perhaps there is something of derision in the idea that someone who has committed such a monstrous deed could believe that he might be able to escape punishment. But the fact that Macbeth allowed himself to be soothed by the witches points to the conclusion that the derision is directed against himself by Macbeth's own conscience. He tries to think: "It is as unlikely that I will be punished as that a wood could move or an unborn man injure me." Such a cynical rejection of the conscience naturally arises from a repression of guilt and even precipitates a repetition of the act. The misunderstanding itself is guilt: "I understand the prophecy foretelling my misfortune as though it were announcing my salvation"; and this means, "I may go on acting without listening to my conscience."

Let us consider now the sensations arising at the moment of sudden clarification. A patient emphasizes the déjà-vu-like character of certain feelings in repetitive dreams in which something he has always known suddenly takes on a different and disastrous meaning. In such dreams he is feeling: "Now I understand what once happened. Now it repeats itself and that is why I know that I can no longer escape disaster. I know and could say exactly what will happen at any moment. What is going to happen now had to happen because that is how it happened before."

In this particular type of déjà-vu sensation the individual not only feels that everything that is going to happen has already happened in exactly the same fashion, but also feels that he knows exactly what is going to happen in the next moment, since it is the repetition of a past experience. Isakower recently compared sensations of this sort with retrograde amnesia: "Just as the tendency to repress can retrogressively involve extensive areas, the tendency to reactivate a latent attitude has the tendency to extend itself in the form of sensations of the return of a previously experienced past. The relationship may be expressed as follows: The amnesia takes the place of the (unpleasant traumatic) experience and tends to extend beyond it retrogressively. The déjà-vu attitude takes the place of an experience which urgently seeks reactivation and tends to extend beyond it into the future (anterograde). The similarity is a formal one: In either case the process has the tendency not only to prevent the true content from coming into the foreground, but also to extend itself in a certain direction over all similar and connected experiences." [6] We are now able to add the explanation as to what earlier experience seeks reactivation, and in what way this is done. We are dealing with the repressed memory of a guilt-laden act which now threatens to return as a punishment turned against the ego. It is experienced that it necessarily has to return in such a form from which there is no reprieve. The fact that the individual repressed the deed and hoped to escape from its consequences means a magnification or repetition of the guilty act in the same way as remorselessness in criminology is regarded as an aggravating circumstance. When in this déjà-vu phenomenon the experiencing of reality is stressed so much, this is due to the fact that the tendency to repress has tried to cast doubt upon this reality or its true meaning.

The misapprehension of the oracle corresponds to a guilt which revenges itself with sudden revelation. Now, how can it be that the overpowering sense of guilt for murder or incest can be displaced upon a misunderstanding of the meaning of veiled words? Freud designates as "spiteful defiant obedience" that frequent phenomenon which manifests itself through apparent obedience which conforms with the exact wording of the command rather than with its true intention.[7] Such a literal pseudo-obedience is often also used to make a forbidden instinctual satisfaction possible in spite of a definite prohibition. We could imagine a stubborn child who has been told not to touch himself "down below," and who might lift his behind up, and masturbate. The child is trying to create a situation in which it is possible to declare that the order has been obeyed and that the father is unjust if he metes out punishment. Such a maneuver cannot be entirely successful because the child who has misinterpreted the prohibition knows that he has actually disobeyed. The sense of guilt which tends to inhibit the instinctual gratification is held in check by the misunderstanding which creates a sense of obedience and conformity. *It is this mechanism of defense which is the essence of the misunderstanding of the oracular utterances.* In this way the misunderstanding itself becomes a double of the deed: The person has been

[6] O. Isakower, "A Contribution to the Patho-Psychology of Phenomena Associated with Falling Asleep," *Int. J. Psa.,* Vol. 19, 1938.

[7] S. Freud, "Notes Upon a Case of Obsessional Neurosis," *Coll. Pap.,* Vol. III, London, Hogarth, 1948.

in doubt not only about the reality of incest, primal scene, or absence of a penis, but about the reality of his own guilt or the fatherly prohibition. The recognition that the prohibition really is effective brings again into consciousness the expectation of the punishment which the individual had unsuccessfully tried to escape.[8]

We are dealing with the return of the repressed, but in this case the repressed is a superego demand which was denied, but returns, nevertheless.

The fright at a 101° fever is absolutely comparable to Macbeth's fright. The stress which is laid on the reality of the Acropolis or of girl's legs, however, is a defense against this fright: I do not need to feel guilty; the reality is mere reality, no revenging furies. There reality confirms, here it contradicts magic expectations.

According to Freud, the nature of the uncanny depends upon the fact that something once believed, then disbelieved, is eventually proved to be true.[9] The law of talion is so closely interwoven with the world of magical thought which our ego pretends to have conquered, that any sudden warning that magical power might be potent is apt to remobilize a latent expectation of punishment.

When a man signs a pact with the devil and hopes to fool him, and then nevertheless is caught by the devil, his position is similar to that of Macbeth. The invitation of Don Juan to the dead commander is also a cynical duplicate of his intention to murder him, and the unnatural way in which the latter accepts the invitation opens his eyes about something which he should have known before and from which there is no longer any escape.

That the misunderstanding represents a rebellion against the prohibiting power—a rebellion which fails—is shown very clearly in stories in which a misunderstanding is purposefully simulated to negate the plans of fate. In a Grimm fairy tale, death gave a physician the special power to foretell whether or not his patients would die: If he appeared to the doctor at the foot of the sickbed, the patient would live, but if he appeared at the head, the patient would die. As Death appears at the bedside of the princess whom the physician loves, the doctor quickly has the bed turned around so that Death will stand at the foot and the patient live. But the doctor is soon punished for this misdeed.

The misapprehended oracle, where a threat of punishment is taken to mean the security of the narcissistic integrity and where this misunderstanding leads to a horrible and uncanny awakening, is a tragedy not without comedy correlates. In those parallels there is a misunderstanding of something which is harmless or secures narcissistic integrity as though it were a threat, thereby

---

[8] And recognition that the prohibition actually is *not* effective brings about the comfortable type of estrangement which Freud felt on the Acropolis.

[9] S. Freud, "The Uncanny," *Coll. Pap.*, Vol. IV, London, Hogarth, 1948.

betraying the guilty conscience. These comic elements are comparable to the liberating experiencing of the realness of reality which is shown in analysis as a release from the anxiety expected in connection with fantasies related to certain subjects; but the difference is that the subject now does not enjoy this liberation but is ridiculed for his need of such a liberation. The frequent jokes which introduce an anxiety situation, which then turns out to be neither mysterious nor frightening but a well-known truth, where we discharge the energy of the saved anxiety by laughing, show this character. The Jew, who is dressed as a lion in the circus and suddenly sees himself face to face with another lion, and who becomes frightened and begins to say his prayers (whereupon the other lion continues the prayer), demonstrates a misunderstanding which is the opposite of that of Macbeth. When the seven men from Schwaben think the hare is a dragon, then this grotesque mistake shows a guilty conscience derived from the desire to murder the father. Finally the fools and rogues, who usurp the seat of kings or judges who are expected to render serious and weighty decisions, and who find a solution for anxieties, serious difficulties, or troublesome situations by means of a silly misunderstanding, symbolize the attempt to reassure the effectiveness of the misunderstanding and to eliminate the anxiety of a rude awakening.

Other jokes illustrate the function of the misunderstood oracle—not in the way that a guilty man overhears the prophecy of his punishment, but that a conceited braggart misunderstands a prediction deflating him as one that praises him—and we laugh at his expense. There are many anecdotes about rabbis who, asked for an opinion about a book written by one of their disciples, make a remark which sounds like an expression of praise but which actually divulges their criticism: "Your book might give the crown back its former glory." In Jewish this means "to explain clearly and precisely an incomprehensible part of the Talmud." But the rabbi elucidates, "It is well known that paper is made out of dirt; but you took paper and turned it back into dirt."

SEVENTEEN

The Psychopathology of Coughing*

TODAY everybody agrees that the question whether a given phenomenon is somatic or psychogenic in origin is incorrectly put. There is no either-or. The task is to study the interrelationship of somatic and psychic forces. The journal *Psychosomatic Medicine* has made this study its principal task. In studying the special case of coughing, I hope to avoid a backsliding into the very question which I have refused, and try to show—as briefly as possible—what types of interrelationship psychoanalysis sees in this special case.

Nervous coughing is seldom the primary indication for a psychoanalysis. It is, however, a rather common symptom, which can frequently be studied in the course of analyses undertaken for other indications. Then, the following six possibilities may be observed:

1. A severe organic cough is, as a rule, a rather annoying or even painful symptom. The patient has to adapt himself to it—and this adaptation may become difficult or even fail entirely under certain psychological circumstances. Psychic reaction to coughing is overshadowed in acute, feverish states like pneumonia by the other, more acute symptoms of the disease; but in chronic states, like tuberculosis or chronic bronchitis, emotional reactions to coughing may be very plain. These reactions may vary considerably, but one factor is always present: that annoying, or painful, coughing absorbs attention; and that the coughing person is more concerned with himself, becomes more introverted and less ready to react to other persons. He either becomes entirely uninterested in others or else shows his interest merely by demanding care or help. Freud compared the interest we have in other persons with pseudopodia which an ameba extends and which it may withdraw again in case of pain. Sick people withdraw their pseudopodia. The degree of their withdrawal depends on the previous

---

* First published in *Psychosom. Med.*, Vol. 5, 1943, pp. 181–184.

history of the personality. The tolerance of a given person toward tension and pain depends upon unknown constitutional factors as well as upon early experiences. An intolerant person with a chronic cough becomes irritable, restless, angry, ready to accuse others; or he may develop, by overcompensation of these tendencies, just the opposite characteristics. All this is typical for the psychology of sick people, and is not specific for coughing.[1]

2. It is more specific if some patients develop the habit of coughing in a cramped, "exaggerated" way. This may be the expression of an unconscious interest in coughing or at least in being sick in general. In this article we are interested in a specific unconscious interest in coughing only. Some persons continue to cough even after the organic cause has ceased to exist. If a symptom which was organically determined continues to exist after the organic cause has ceased to be effective, we talk about a hysterical superstructure over an organic disease. In such cases, coughing unconsciously serves the purposes of the patient and is in some way advantageous to him. This does not necessarily mean that the patient "escapes into sickness" or enjoys being taken care of (although it might mean that). The terms "purpose" and "advantageous" are used here in a much more general sense. The advantage might consist only in a gain in the economy of his psychic energy. The psychic apparatus has a general tendency to get rid of tensions; external stimuli are (sooner or later) answered by reactions which discharge the excitation and re-establish the psychic equilibrium. In the case of "repressions," certain discharges of this kind are blocked. The persons with repressions are in an unconscious conflict between a tendency to discharge the inner tension and a repressing force which tends to stop this discharge. The more intensive the repression, the higher will be the inner pressure and the inclination to find other permissible discharges which might serve as substitutes for what has been repressed. *Coughing might be such a substitutive vent for relieving an inner pressure caused by repressions.* This is a kind of conditioning; coughing has now become connected with other stimuli whose presence provokes it. Many "psychoanalytic mechanisms" can be described by "conditioned-reflex" terminology. But the fact remains that only certain persons develop such "conditioning," whereas others with the same experiences do not. Psychoanalytic description throws light upon this difference.

Thus, coughing may serve for relieving an inner pressure. But "inner pressure" does not necessarily mean an unconscious need for punishment, aimed at the relief of an unconscious guilt feeling. Coughing is a reflex means of discharging mucus. In certain neurotics, it may serve as a means of discharging something else, of discharging a kind of "mental mucus." Coughing is the response of the organism to an irritating physical stimulus in the air passages.

---

[1] S. Freud, "On Narcissism: An Introduction," *Coll. Pap.,* Vol. IV, London, Hogarth, 1948.

In neurotics, it may be the response to some other inner stimulus of which the patient tries to rid himself as if it were mucus. Fantasies of disturbing foreign bodies in the interior of the organism are abundant in everybody's unconscious, fantasies of having incorporated some magical substance which has to be expelled again. The old belief of demons who enter the organism and have to be exorcised illuminates best this type of fantasy. We talk in psychoanalysis about "introjection" and "reprojection of what has been introjected." Mostly the introjection is unconsciously thought of as an act of eating, and many a nervous vomiting has to be intrepreted as an attempt at reprojection. But it is not only the digestive tract which is used for fantasies of this type. Breathing often has a magic function also, and the beliefs of primitive nations are full of material of this kind. Primitive men as well as children are aware of the fact that by breathing they are taking in some substance from the outer world, and returning a substance to it, but the substance is invisible and therefore suitable for bearing magic ideas. Inhaling the same air as another person might mean union with him, while exhaling might mean separation.[2] The ideational "hysterical superstructure" of coughing as a rule represents an unconscious attempt to cough up some harmful or dishonestly acquired magical substance.

3. In certain persons whose respiratory tract—by constitution or by some early psychic experiences—has acquired a particular sensibility towards psychic stimuli, psychological tendencies of this kind may produce a cough, even without any preceding organic disease of the respiratory organs. This is the case in hysterics who have the disposition to express their psychic conflicts and fantasies by changes in their somatic functions. This is called "conversion." Freud, in one of his earliest cases, had the opportunity to psychoanalyze a classical example of hysterical cough (combined with aphonia) as a conversion symptom.[3] His patient, Dora, produced coughing spells, the analysis of which showed the following factors involved: (a) Dora imitated the sickness of an acquaintance, Mrs. K., who happened to be the wife of the man with whom Dora was unconsciously in love; (b) the cough expressed the rejection of the fantasy of being raped by Mr. K., which rape (out of certain facts and fantasies in Dora's earlier life) was imagined as a fellatio.

The imitation of Mrs. K. makes it advisable to add a few words about so-called "hysterical identification." Hysteria, as is well known, is ready and able to imitate all diseases—something which used to puzzle physicians of the pre-Freudian era. A hysterical cough is likely to occur when a hysterically disposed person lives in the neighborhood of a patient with a chronic cough and has some unconscious reason for identifying himself with the cougher. In the case of Dora

[2] O. Fenichel, "Respiratory Introjection," No. 23, *First Series*.
[3] S. Freud, "Analysis of a Case of Hysteria," *Coll. Pap.*, Vol. III, London, Hogarth, 1948.

such a motive for identification was obvious: she envied Mrs. K. for her sexual relations with Mr. K. and would have liked to be in her place. It is the result of Dora's guilt feelings for her rivalry that in putting herself in Mrs. K.'s position she has to select a disease as the point of identification.

But not in all cases is such an intimate relationship between a coughing hysteric and the organically coughing person whom he imitates to be found. There are also "hysterical identifications" with persons who personally have played no important part in the life of the hysteric, if there is the "same etiological claim" present. Freud uses the example of a girls' school, where a sick girl may react with a fainting spell to a love letter, and then all the other girls may get spells too. The unconscious meaning is: "We should like to get love letters, too." [4]

In Dora's case the unconscious fantasy of fellatio was at the basis of the cough. That is quite typical, but other fantasies concerning in some way the respiratory tract may have a similar effect. In speaking of the "respiratory tract" in this connection, not the anatomical definition is meant but the popular conception in which the mouth also is included.

Hysterical conversion may also develop in persons who are not living with other persons suffering from tuberculosis, chronic bronchitis, or other diseases in which coughing is a chronic symptom. Everyone has had colds at some time in his childhood connected with coughing which he might revive in a later hysteria whenever an old conflict of childhood is mobilized which has been acute at the time of the original coughing experience. A temporary coincidence of coughing with a traumatic experience of conflict situation in the past is in such cases the basis of psychogenic coughing. Such a conflict which has originated at the time of a childhood cold will cause later nervous coughing only if its underlying idea is to get rid of some "respiratory introject." This introject may represent different things on different mental levels. I know about a case of a pregnant woman whose nervous coughing represented an unconscious desire to get rid of her child.

4. There is a type of psychogenic cough which is not a conversion symptom, but is more related to the group of "tics." It is common observation that public speakers who feel embarrassed and nervous are in the habit of clearing their throat or even coughing before they begin to speak. Certain neurotics do the same thing in an exaggerated way. They may cough whenever they begin to talk, using coughing for procrastination. Talking, sometimes, might be not only inhibited to a greater or lesser degree, but made entirely impossible. It is obvious that the "normally" nervous speaker by clearing his throat tries to gain time for preparing his words. A person who actually inhibits his talking in such

4 S. Freud, *Group Psychology and the Analysis of the Ego*, London, Hogarth, 1948.

a way must have some unconscious motive *not* to talk. He may have a specific conflict whether or not to say a certain thing; or what is more probable, the function of "speaking" as such has a certain unconscious meaning. He may, for example, use speaking for the gratification of an exhibitionistic trend, and therefore feel afraid or guilty. This exhibitionistic trend may not be restricted to speaking alone but may perhaps be the whole idea of appearing in public and being the center of attention. In such cases nervous coughing might be an equivalent or a part of the stage-fright syndrome.

Some people do not cough when they are supposed to talk, but when they are supposed to listen. Their unconscious intention then is not to disturb their own, but the speaker's talk. This and various other types of hostility, directed either against certain persons in particular or speakers in general, play the same part in such cases as embarrassment does in the case of inhibited exhibitionism.

If this throat-clearing or coughing becomes automatic to such a degree that it is no longer a concomitant sign but an equivalent of embarrassment or hostility, it assumes the quality of a tic.[5] Instead of feeling embarrassed or hostile, the patient has a spell of coughing without knowing why. He is not even aware of any emotional upset at all. The whole innervation of the reflex has lost the connection with the emotion in which it originated, and has become an automatic physical equivalent of an emotion which is no longer felt. Such a cough may eventually become an unspecific expression of a general uneasiness toward the environment.

5. The most frequent form of nervous cough is one whose genesis is a little more complicated. A continuous habitual and forced clearing of the throat, over weeks and months, has a drying effect upon the throat and may lead eventually to a pharyngitis. In such cases the coughing is organic but the conditions which brought it about are psychogenic. The habit of sleeping with open mouth also dries the throat and may cause a pharyngitis and coughing. This habit sometimes has organic causes; at times it might be the expression of certain unconscious wishes which become mobilized during sleep. This type of etiology in which a psychogenic condition in time leads to organic symptoms has been described by Freud as different from "conversion," [6] and has been studied in great detail by different authors, especially Alexander.[7] An unusual attitude which is rooted in unconscious instinctual conflicts causes a certain behavior; this be-

---

[5] S. Ferenczi, "Psycho-Analytical Observations on Tic," *Further Contributions to the Theory and Technique of Psycho-Analysis,* London, Hogarth, 1950.

[6] S. Freud, "Psychogenic Visual Disturbance According to Psycho-Analytical Conceptions," *Coll. Pap.,* Vol. II, London, Hogarth, 1948.

[7] F. Alexander, *The Medical Value of Psychoanalysis,* New York, Norton, 1932, and "Psychological Aspects of Medicine," *Psychosom. Med.,* Vol. 1, 1939; F. Deutsch, "Biologie und Psychologie der Krankheitsgenese," *Int. Z. Psa.,* Vol. 8, 1922; L. Saul, "A Note on the Psychogenesis of Organic Symptoms," *Psa. Quart.,* Vol. 4, 1935.

havior in turn causes somatic changes in the tissues. The chronic psychogenic condition causes inflammations which secondarily cause coughing. We call such somatic results of psychogenic attitudes "organ-neurotic symptoms," and Saul has written a very interesting paper in which he summarizes the possible psychogenic and neurotic causes of common colds.[8] We have in mind cases in which the colds themselves are not psychogenic, but in which persons behave in such a way as to catch cold, without having intended this result of their behavior.

6. In practice, probably most cases of nervous coughing represent a combination of these five types. Such combinations may occur in mixtures of every conceivable degree.

Concerning therapy, the administration of drugs, such as sedatives or expectorants, depends upon the preponderance of the different etiological factors. The choice of psychotherapeutic methods, on the other hand, depends exclusively upon the character of the whole case, and not on the type of coughing. Such simple psychotherapeutic measures as the use of will power and relaxation may occasionally work, but in general not much can be expected from them. If will power were sufficient to control the cough, why didn't the patient apply his own will power previous to the doctor's suggestion? The patient who accepts the doctor's suggestion and applies it successfully is not using his own will power, but rather that of the authoritative doctor, which he has incorporated and borrowed from him: he is obeying the doctor's order as a hypnotized person obeys the orders of the hypnotist. As to relaxation—whether or not it helps—most patients because of their unsolved unconscious conflict are *unable* to relax; and first some other type of psychotherapy must be applied to make relaxation *possible*.

Psychoanalysis, in the case of conversion symptoms or tics, is aimed at uncovering the unconscious meaning of the symptom, and undoing pathogenic repressions. In the analysis of organ neurotics, the symptoms themselves will not be discussed very much, but the underlying emotional attitude revealed. The patient should understand the unconscious background of his behavior, and with the change of this behavior the symptoms will disappear.

We have attempted to explain the *dynamic relations* which form the basis of the different types of nervous coughing. The special details involved in each case of nervous coughing can be understood only in the light of case histories.

[8] L. Saul, "Psychogenic Factors in the Etiology of the Common Cold and Related Symptoms," *Int. J. Psa.*, Vol. 19, 1938.

EIGHTEEN

Brief Psychotherapy *

BRIEF psychotherapy is the child of bitter practical necessity. This eternal necessity is now—due to social conditions—rapidly increasing. Exactly twenty-five
years ago, Freud prophesied: "Some time or other, the conscience of the community will awaken and admonish it that the poor man has just as much right
to help for his mind as he now has to the surgeon's means for saving life." [1] His
prediction has come true, and this is fortunate, even if it is impossible for the
neurotic misery of our time to be overcome or even successfully combated by
therapeutic means alone. For science, however, it is not entirely fortunate.
Freud also prophesied: "It is very probable   . ." that we shall be compelled "to
alloy the pure gold of analysis . . . with the copper" of other therapeutic
measures.[2] Actually, many of us today are using such modifications, which is
quite right as long as we are clearly aware of the fact that we are doing it. But
unfortunately we see that the use of copper frequently makes people despise
gold. We come across fake pretenses that the physical characteristics of copper
are the same as, or even better than, those of gold; after all, psychoanalysis is
merely one type of psychotherapy, and it takes years. Other psychotherapists
achieve success in weeks. Thus . . .

No, it is not a question of psychoanalysis *versus* brief psychotherapy. Psychotherapy has always existed. It has been practiced by physicians as well as by
friends; for as long as there have been human worries there has also been help
for them by talking them over with friends.

---

* This paper was first presented at Los Angeles in October, 1944. Dr. Fenichel's manuscript has
been translated into English, in conformity with the other papers, but no attempt has been made to
give it the final form Dr. Fenichel might have given it if he had prepared it for publication.

[1] S. Freud, "Turnings in the Ways of Psycho-Analytic Therapy," *Coll. Pap.*, Vol. II, London, Ho·
garth, 1948, p. 401.

[2] *Ibid.*, p. 402.

Such psychotherapy, however, was intuitive and unsystematic. A scientific understanding of what actually takes place in "interpersonal relationships" did not come into being prior to psychoanalysis. And though there are many psychotherapeutic methods, and psychoanalysis is only one among them, there is but one psychology of neuroses. Only psychoanalytic theory can explain, too, what happens in non-analytic psychotherapy. The understanding derived from this theory can evolve a systematic and scientific basis for non-analytic therapy. But such understanding will also show its limitations. The use of psychoanalytic psychology for purposes of non-analytic psychotherapy is a new application of psychoanalytic science—and as such comparable, for instance, to an analytic psychology of propaganda. This application is new, not yet very much developed, limited because of the depth of the anchorage of neuroses, and, owing to its relative lack of organization, *more difficult* than a psychoanalysis *lege artis*. One sometimes hears that this or that young doctor, who still lacks assurance in the application of psychoanalysis, is practicing "non-analytic psychotherapy only" in the meantime. This is frank quackery. Non-analytic psychotherapy is more, not less, difficult than psychoanalysis. Only he who has studied psychoanalysis thoroughly and has acquired analytic understanding is capable of conducting good non-analytic psychotherapy. Everyone else does what all physicians have done for centuries; this, however, in emergency situations, may mean quite a lot.

We do not intend to investigate what actually takes place when so-called non-analytic psychotherapies are successful, for we have not the time to do this here. Instead, we prefer to ask what can be done to attain a probable maximum of success.

For this purpose, let us first consider how psychoanalytic theory looks at neuroses:

All neurotic phenomena are based on insufficiencies of the normal apparatus of control. They can be understood as involuntary emergency discharges which supplant the normal ones. The insufficiency can be brought about in two ways. One way is an increase in the influx of stimuli, by which too much excitation enters the psychic apparatus in a given unit of time and cannot be mastered. Such experiences are called *traumatic*. Another way is that a previous blocking of, or decrease in, discharge has resulted in a damming up of tensions within the organism, so that normal excitations now operate relatively like traumatic ones. These two ways are not mutually exclusive. A trauma may initiate an ensuing blocking of discharge; and a primary blocking, by creating a state of being dammed up, may cause subsequent stimuli to have a traumatic effect when they would not be traumatic for the average person.

The nearer a given neurosis is to the traumatic end of this complementary series, the greater is the probability that external efforts to support the subject's spontaneous attempts at regaining mental equilibrium may be successful; but the more success depends on an annulment of "previous blockings," that is, of methods of defense and of the belief in the necessity of defenses, the smaller is the probability of easy psychotherapeutic cure.

In traumatic neuroses we observe two apparently contradictory kinds of spontaneous attempts at recovery—which, in a certain percentage of cases, are successful even without any treatment. First, attempts to get "distance" and rest, to collect energy, as it were, for the task of belated mastery: a stopping of, or decrease in, ego functions, an undoing of differentiations, a withdrawal in order to make a fresh start for the reconstruction of the collapsed equilibrium. Second, attempts at belated discharges, restlessness, motor phenomena of all kinds, emotional spells, repetitive dreams, and repetitive symptoms during the waking state. The first set could be called the "quieting-down method," the second the "stormy" method—both aimed at the same end of achieving belated mastery.

Psychotherapy can and should imitate *both* methods. On the one hand, the therapist may give the patient rest, reassurances, satisfaction of his wishes for passivity and dependency and "take it easy" suggestions. On the other hand, he may give catharsis, opportunity for stormy discharges and for repeated re-experiences of the trauma, and a verbalization and clarification of the conflicts involved. The second method, when applicable, is a more direct help; the first one becomes necessary where the ego is too frightened, where a working through of the traumatic event is still unbearable and would still be too much of a repetition of the traumatic character of the experience. Clearly the therapeutic task in traumatic neuroses consists in finding out which blend of the two methods is necessary in a given case. To find the relatively correct amount of catharsis and reassurance is the main task of therapy. It is theoretically of comparatively minor importance by which methods cartharsis as well as reassurance is achieved.

Only a minority of mental difficulties are of a "traumatic" nature. However, there are precipitating factors for psychoneuroses or for non-neurotic states of acute upheaval which can be compared with traumas. A person may have evolved from old infantile conflicts into a state of relative equilibrium between repressed and repressing forces. An external alteration may mean a disturbance of this equilibrium, and thus make a hitherto attained adjustment more difficult. And even a normal person who suffers a loss of love or a failure, or a change in his standard of living, or a shift from a civilian to a military situation, must make an adaptation to the new conditions. In carrying out a "work of learning" or "work of adjustment," he must acknowledge the new and less comfortable reality, and fight tendencies toward regression, toward misinterpretation of reality, toward longing for passivity and dependency, toward wish-fulfilling fantasies. If, however, in a person with latent defensive conflicts, the new situation implies temptation for a repressed impulse, or an increase in an anxiety (or guilt feeling) which opposes a repressed impulse, the infantile conflicts are remobilized and the external change may become the precipitating factor of a neurosis.

The more such a precipitating factor resembles a trauma, the more sudden and the more frightening it is, the greater is the possibility that the same help given to normal persons in such situations may suppress the neurosis *in statu nascendi* and re-establish the relative equilibrium that existed prior to the change. In acute difficulties of life, counseling may be helpful. It works by the same means as therapy in traumatic neuroses: on the one hand, we may verbalize and clarify the task set by reality and help to suppress the tendencies toward irrational reaction by bringing them to the conscious level; on the other hand, this help may be mixed with relative allowances for rest and for small regressions and compensatory wish-fulfilments that have a recuperative effect.

These are the cases where the *rational* aids of all psychotherapy may also be used: Verbalization of unclear worries alone brings relief, because an ego can face verbalized ideas better than unclear emotional sensations. The very fact that a doctor spends time, interest, and sympathy on a patient's worries may not only be "transference" of a past situation, but also an original and a very substantial relief for lonely people who have no friends to talk to, or for people who have been misunderstood or scolded for their difficulties up to now. Information about emotional and especially sexual matters may help to set at ease excited souls. Further, if a patient sees connections between hitherto unconnected symptoms, worries, or parts of his personality, if he is helped to detect general patterns of behavior behind concrete actions, and if he even detects the relationship of such patterns to one another, all this certainly makes his ego relatively stronger in its relation to the deeper forces within his personality. (Certain authors believe that rational help of this kind constitutes psychoanalysis; [3] actually, it is frequently a first step in psychoanalytic cures, as a necessary prerequisite for psychoanalytic work proper, which does not consist in detecting behavior patterns, but rather in bringing about a dynamic alteration in the conditions which created the pathological patterns.) There are also physiological "rational measures." Relaxation of tense muscles has, for *physiological* reasons, a mental cathartic effect. The relaxing effect of sedatives may be helpful; and the old advice of warm baths for nervous people is effective not only because such baths supply pleasurable stimulation to skin eroticism and represent atonement, but also because they create a peripheral vasodilatation and thus work counter to the central tension which all neurotics suffer from. The effectiveness of these rational methods can be further increased by advice which may lead the patient away from

[3] For instance, K. Horney. Cf. her books *New Ways in Psychoanalysis*, New York, Norton, 1939, and *Self-Analysis*, New York, Norton, 1942.

unnecessarily tempting or exciting situations, or may propel him toward some reassuring position.

But the effectiveness of all these rational methods is a very limited one. Psychoanalysts understand the irrational nature of neuroses, and how little can be achieved by rational suggestion. The more acute a difficulty is and the less it represents a real neurosis (being primarily a task of immediate adjustment), the greater is the probability of success through rational methods. If, however, the difficulty represents a remobilization of old conflicts and latent neurotic patterns, then the effectiveness of rational methods will to a greater or lesser degree be limited to the significance of inducement premiums which may be used to secure positive transference feelings.

This does not imply that under no circumstances may "brief psychotherapy" be attempted with psychoneurotics or patients with neurotic character disturbances. But here such therapy is more difficult and the outcome more doubtful. The most auspicious material is presented by immature, childlike personalities, whose repressing forces are not yet internalized, but are represented rather by anxiety about external danger. In such cases the reassuring conviction that the external world is not so bad after all may still be helpful. While acute difficulties of life present the first and foremost field of indication for brief psychotherapy, psychoneuroses in such immature and childlike personalities present the second important one. The "cure through love," however, is impossible for persons who are no longer capable of believing in love.

In all other types of psychoneurotics things become much more difficult. I shall try to sketch briefly which mechanisms nevertheless offer a certain chance of success for short methods.

The basis of every psychoneurosis is a conflict between warded-off impulses and warding-off anxieties or feelings of guilt. Thus it seems that only a change in the dynamic relations of the constituents of this conflict can change the neurosis. In principle, this could be done in two ways; either by an increase in the defense or by an annulment of it. An increase of the defense may lead to an endeavor to repress anew the whole neurosis as a derivative of what has been warded off previously; an annulment of the defense would, of course, end the whole conflict.

The first type of "therapy" is represented by the old-fashioned suggestion hypnosis in which the authority of the doctor prohibits the patient from producing symptoms. The same temporary effect may also be attempted in an indirect way, by techniques which increase the patient's anxiety and thereby his repressions, by threats, maltreatments, symbolic castrations, and reproaches. Measures of this kind try to induce the patient to "repress the whole neurosis."

A repression of symptoms, however, increases the pressure of the repressed, and sooner or later new symptoms will be formed. Yet it may happen that the new symptoms are limited to the patient's becoming more afraid, more introverted, more rigid, more dependent on his doctor (consciously or unconsciously); in short, he will produce a new "substitute neurosis" in the place of his original neurosis.

The second type, the treatment by means of complete annulment of the repression, is represented by psychoanalysis, in which the undoing of the repression enables the infantile sexual strivings to participate in the development of the personality and to turn into satisfiable adult sexuality.

Seemingly, these two methods are strictly contradictory. But actually many compromises exist between them, in the sense that an undoing of a repression might be used for the intensification of some other repression; or that an increase in a specific repression might result in the creation of some less distorted derivatives at some other place. Compromises of this kind can frequently be observed in the course of a psychoanalytic treatment, when improvements occur before a real psychoanalytically induced change is achieved. What then happens is that (1) the patient uses a new insight, acquired by a successful interpretation, for resistance purposes—that is, for a reinforcement of other repressions; (2) the patient's feeling relation toward his analyst (his "transference") changes the dynamic relation between repressed impulses and anxiety, the analyst being felt either as a threatening or as a forgiving and reassuring force.

Most psychotherapies offer the patient certain occasions for discharge, which are accepted as substitutes for the spontaneous symptoms, either because they really bring relief to the patient's conflicts, diminish his inner pressure, and give occasion for reinforcement of repression in other parts of his mind, or because he unconsciously fears measures of revenge on the part of the doctor or hopes for rewards from him.

Glover once wrote a very interesting paper in which he investigated the ways in which incomplete or inexact interpretations, and also other psychotherapeutic procedures, influence the patient's mind.[4] His answer was that these procedures offer artificial substitute symptoms, which may make the spontaneous symptoms superfluous. Actually, many of the psychotherapeutic measures have similarities with neurotic symptoms, and it may be stated—partly in reiteration of, partly as a supplement to, Glover's view—that exercises, baths, or other physical measures which are prescribed for neurotics may be looked upon as "artificial conversions"; that is, to the extent that they are successful, they actually now serve in the life of the patient as a conversion expression of his conflicts. Prohibitions of any kind, withdrawal of alcohol and tobacco, etc., represent "artificial phobias." Exact advice as to the conduct of life or prescribed diets represent "artificial compul-

---

[4] E. Glover, "The Therapeutic Effect of Inexact Interpretation," *Int. J. Psa.,* Vol. 12, 1931.

sions." This is still more true about prescribed curative rituals like the prayers of Christian Science, or about the penances dictated by a priest at confession, or about the magic formulae of "autosuggestion" which are an imitation of the word-magic which so many compulsion neurotics use spontaneously in their defense against their symptoms.[5] Many pieces of medical advice serve, if accepted by a compulsive patient, as compulsive symptoms with the significance of penitence. Baths, for example, have been used since ancient times as purgation and atonement by washing off the dirty substance of sin. In obeying the doctor, the patient purchases protection from his superego. Occupational therapy, in so far as the advised occupation, sport, hobby, etc., is pleasurable, may represent less an "artificial obsession" than an "artificial impulse neurosis," or even a kind of "artificial perversion." If the psychotherapist is either especially kind or especially strict, he creates an "artificial passive-receptive dependence," and under certain circumstances an "artificial masochism," which may even make a patient react favorably to a doctor's blaming his failure on the "unwillingness of the patient to be cured." The treatment itself may assume the significance of an atoning ritual which renders the neurosis superfluous. The extreme of "artificial-passive receptive dependence" is achieved in hypnosis, where the "rapport" between patient and doctor in itself forms a substitute neurosis, which might be called "artificial infantilism." [6] Prescriptions for drugs, in so far as the patient believes that "good stuffs" may neutralize "bad stuffs" within him, serve as a kind of "artificial paranoia."

The efficacy of therapeutic methods of this type depends on whether or not the substitute offered is suitable to the dynamic structure of the patient. This suitability depends first on the type of the patient; a hysteric cannot accept "artificial compulsions" nor a compulsion neurotic "artificial conversions." Besides this, the substitute must (a) be pleasurable, that is, either have a secret sexual significance or a secret "reassuring" significance, and therefore be more attractive than was the spontaneous symptom. A secret sexual meaning, for example, is obvious in sports, hobbies, hydrotherapy; it is a little less obvious if a pleasure, hitherto inaccessible, is permitted by the doctor and gives substitutive discharge, like games, play-acting, books, the special nature of which may be chosen in accordance with the patient's emotional needs. A secret reassurance may be hidden in permission of this kind or in other transference satisfactions. The effect will be better if circumstances make it possible for a patient who has looked upon his neurotic symptoms as a (deserved or undeserved) suffering, to accept this pleasure as a

[5] Cf. K. Abraham, "Psycho-Analytical Notes on Coué's Method of Self-Mastery," *Int. J. Psa.*, Vol. 7, 1926.

[6] Cf. S. Ferenczi, "Introjection and Transference," *Sex in Psychoanalysis*, New York, Brunner, 1950; and S. Freud, *Group Psychology and the Analysis of the Ego*, London, Hogarth, 1948.

"compensation" he feels entitled to, which is a sign of forgiveness and puts to an end his striving for revenge. But (b) the secret significance of the substitute must also be sufficiently far removed from the original instinctual meaning of the symptom to be acceptable. The substitute has to fulfill the same conditions which a suggestion given to a "bored" person must fulfill: it has to be near enough to the original objectionable idea to be attractive, and it must be far enough removed from it to avoid its recognition as a "derivative." [7]

A substitute will be more readily accepted when it is most likely at the same time to bring some relief on a rational basis. The "rational" measures, which may cure acute difficulties of life and which have been discussed above, may also bring relief in severe psychoneuroses and thus create positive feelings toward the analyst.

The establishment of a transference neurosis is the most frequent and important substitute for a spontaneous neurosis. By "establishment of a transference neurosis," Freud meant that the repressed infantile instinctual conflicts find their representation in the emotional relations toward the analyst, and therefore do not need as many other expressions as before. The doctor is looked upon as a reincarnation of the parents, and as such he may be thought of as providing love and protection, or as threatening with punishments. [8]

The doctor's very presence may influence the psychodynamics of the patient in the same way as the educational measures of the parents once did, because unconsciously the doctor's presence is misunderstood as a repetition (or correction) of what happened in childhood. Improvements achieved on this basis are called "transference improvements."

The mechanisms of transference improvements are identical with the mechanisms by which educators achieve their success. Either the idea of continuing the neurotic behavior becomes connected in the subject's mind with the idea of some danger, or the idea of improvement becomes associated with the hope for a specially attractive reward, or both these connections occur simultaneously.

Transference improvements of the threatening type work in the same way as castration threats which originally caused the child to repress certain impulses; now, the belief in new castration threats causes the patient to repress the symptoms which are derivatives of the original repressed impulses. The reassuring type of transference improvement works because the patient, giving up his neurosis "for the doctor's sake," hopes to get sexual satisfaction through the doctor's appreciation and love; and he mostly at the same time needs this appreciation and love for his own security and self-esteem. Many therapists have great skill in applying threats and reassurances one after the other, thus combining the two types of influence and treating patients with a "Turkish bath method," one day hot, the

[7] Cf. O. Fenichel, "On the Psychology of Boredom," No. 26, *First Series*.
[8] Cf. S. Freud, *A General Introduction to Psychoanalysis*, New York, Liveright, 1935, 1948.

next day cold. Ferenczi discussed the effectiveness of this method in observing a horse-tamer.[9]

Just as there are transference improvements, so are there also transference aggravations. They occur not only in cases in which "transference has become resistance," that is, in which the patient discontinues co-operation because he is interested in the fulfillment of his transference wishes only, but also in cases in which a negative transference brings an aggravation of the neurosis in the same way as a negative feeling toward the educator makes a child naughty. A neurotic may become worse just to spite the doctor. If the patient becomes aware of this fact, of its transference nature, and of the history and purpose of his original spite, the resistance will be overcome.

Analysts know that not only expectations of being loved and of being punished are transferred, but much more specific expectations, impulses, and emotions. In analysis, any transference, although it may provide the most important material and may be utilized for the purposes of the analysis, is in principle a resistance, because the wrong connection of past emotions with the present obscures the true connections, and because the patient, interested in the immediate satisfaction of his transference wishes, loses interest in overcoming his resistances. "Transference improvements" are likewise no exception to this rule, and the phrase "flight into health" is frequently justified.

The situation is different in psychotherapies which foster the "wrong connection" of the patient's unconscious wishes as the means of achieving their therapeutic success. They cannot let transferences develop spontaneously for the very purpose of studying their spontaneous features. They have to favor everything which provokes utilizable transference feelings, and to stop any negative transference which begins to develop. The difficulty is that this has to be done rather planlessly, because the dynamics of the patient's conflicts are unknown, at least in their details; knowledge of them can be gained only by letting the transference feelings develop spontaneously.

Everything which in analysis creates a transference resistance is capable of creating a "success" in a treatment where the transference is not analyzed. But the same factors are also capable of creating an unfavorable transference action, e.g. a cancellation of the treatment. And the therapist does not know which it will be.

The majority of therapists do not follow any conscious "system," but their intuition. The doctor guesses, acts parts, changes his behavior according to the patient's manifest reactions without understanding them. A good "born psychologist" will succeed, a bad one will fail.

A therapist who has studied psychoanalysis is in a somewhat better situation.

[9] S. Ferenczi, "Zaehmung eines wilden Pferdes," *Zentralbl. f. Psa.*, Vol. 3, 1913.

He will try to judge what might favor and what might hamper transference successes, in terms of his dynamic understanding of the patient's symptoms and utterances.

It is clear that transference improvements are not trustworthy. They do not undo the pathogenic conflicts of childhood, but simply displace or repeat them. Any change in the feeling relationship toward the doctor, or any external experience which motivates the patient to such a change, endangers the entire success. This was the reason why Freud gave up hypnosis as a means of treatment.[10] It turned out that the improved patients remained improved only as long as they continued on good terms with the doctor. They had become dependent on him, and this dependence was the condition of their being better. "The transference has not been analyzed."

Hypnosis reveals still more about the nature of transference improvements. In hypnosis, it is not only obviously the dependence of the patient on the doctor, the "rapport," which serves as the substitute neurosis; hypnosis also shows what kind of rapport is the most effective one. After Ferenczi and Freud first stated that what bound the hypnotized patient to his hypnotist was an infantile libidinal tie, later research made clear many more things about the question of which type of infantile sexuality is the decisive one. In "dependence" the hypnotized patient attains satisfaction of a sexuality which has not yet been differentiated from narcissistic needs. The patient reverts to the phase of passive-receptive mastery. The first two years of life, in which external "omnipotent" persons have taken care of us, protected and provided us with food, shelter, sexual satisfaction, and re-participation in the lost omnipotence, gave us a feeling of being secure in a greater unit while losing our own individuality. This memory establishes in every human being the tendency to experience a nostalgia for such a state, whenever his attempts at active mastery fail. It is this type of regressive longing which is satisfied in hypnosis.[11]

This regressive longing is not equally developed in all persons. The oral type of patients, those who are disposed to the development of depressions, addictions, and impulse neuroses, produce this longing most intensely.

It is the same longing which acquires social significance when, in states of general frustration, it is developed in the masses in a high degree, and threatens to take the place of the tendency toward active mastery of difficulties.

The same methods may be utilized in psychotherapy. It is an old technique of authorities and educators to reply to subjects or children, who are dependent

---

[10] Cf. S. Freud, "On the History of the Psycho-Analytic Movement," *Coll. Pap.*, Vol. I, London, Hogarth, 1948.

[11] Cf. S. Rado, "The Psychoanalysis of Pharmacothymia (Drug Addiction). I. The Clinical Picture," *Psa. Quart.*, Vol. 2, 1933; and P. Schilder and O. Kauders, *Hypnosis*, New York, Nerv. Ment. Dis. Pub. Co., 1927.

on them and who are begging for protection and "narcissistic supplies": "You will get what you need—but on conditions. If you obey, you will get the needed protection and love. If you don't obey, you will be destroyed." The initiation rites of primitive (and less primitive) peoples always combine frightening experiences with the solemn establishment of a permission.[12] The meaning is: "You may now enjoy the privilege of being adult and of participating in our society; but don't forget that you may do so only as long as you obey our rules; and the pains we inflict on you are to remind you that much greater pains will be inflicted upon you in case of disobedience." The participation in power is permitted—but in a restricted sense, *on conditions,* and the subjects and children, because they are in need of this participation, are ready to pay the price of this limitation.[13]

This is the way in which psychotherapeutic transference improvements are achieved: "If you are a good boy and don't behave neurotically, you get love, protection, participation from the omnipotent doctor; if you do not obey, you have to fear his revenge." In this respect, the psychotherapist is in good company; he uses the same means of influence which God uses.

And the psychotherapist of this type is actually near to God. Medicine in general, and psychotherapy in particular, has long been the realm of the priests. And it still often is today. The healing power of Lourdes or of a Catholic confession is still of a much higher order than that of the average psychotherapist. Neurotics, who are persons who have failed in actively mastering their surroundings, are always more or less looking out for passive-dependent protection, for a "magic helper."[14] The more a psychotherapist succeeds in giving the impression of having magic powers, of still being the representative of God as the priest-doctors once were, the more he meets the longing of his patients for magic help. Christian Science and other institutions or sects, which promise health and magic protection as rewards for faith and obedience, may, due to their history and the awe surrounding them, achieve better and quicker cures than many scientists.

This does not necessarily mean that the psychotherapist will be more successful the more he uses visible "magical instruments" and behaves like a sorcerer; for more modern patients, magic is not necessarily represented by large apparatuses, but rather by a certain unapproachability to the person in authority. Nevertheless, the importance of all the age-old instruments of impressive magic and the ancient magic power of "faith" should not be underestimated either.

The magic power, projected onto the doctor, does not necessarily need to be

[12] T. Reik, "The Puberty Rites of Savages," *The Psychological Problem of Religion.* Vol. I, *Ritual: Psycho-Analytic Studies,* New York, Farrar, Straus, 1946.
[13] Cf. O. Fenichel, "Trophy and Triumph," No. 10 in this volume.
[14] E. Fromm, *Escape From Freedom,* New York, Farrar and Rinehart, 1941.

used directly for a prohibition of neurotic symptoms. It may also, as in cathartic hypnosis, be used for an annulment of certain repressions. However, any recovery which is achieved in this way remains dependent on the patient's passive-dependent attitude toward the doctor. The patient's ego, instead of being enabled to mature, is definitely established as immature, and any attempt again to lose this new and artificial dependency will result in a re-establishment of the repression which had only been abandoned at the command of the authority.

This is the decisive limitation of cathartic treatment. If the patient's resistances are overcome by the short-circuit of a hypnotic command, he may achieve the ability to remember forgotten memories and so provide important material. But the therapeutic value of this knowledge is not very great. The dynamic changes brought about by the patient's working through the history which necessitated the ego's developing its defenses, the obligation of a mature ego to face and solve its conflicts, are missing. Resistances which have been overcome by "force" instead of having been analyzed will come back.

Recently new and very promising attempts have been made at "hypnoanalysis," that is, to use hypnosis or chemically induced states of semi-sleep not only to achieve "abreactions" but actually to overcome the drawbacks of the fact that the ego does not face its conflicts and remains dependent.[15] It is not yet possible to predict where such promising devices will lead. Of course, the therapeutic effectiveness of "hypnoanalysis" remains more or less limited to an analysis of symptoms.

Many psychotherapists try to achieve their effect by "augmenting the patient's self-confidence." Since self-confidence generally diminishes anxiety, this should actually be a good device. Unfortunately, increase in self-confidence is very difficult to achieve without analysis in neurotics who suffer from inferiority feelings. However, an attempt at "augmenting self-confidence" by suggestion is a two-edged sword. If a patient has self-confidence because a doctor has told him to have self-confidence, he has more confidence in the doctor than in himself. The self-confidence is a borrowed one and is once more lost when participation in the doctor's power is lost.

Psychotherapy, which makes the patient dependent for the purpose of telling him to be independent, is a situation similar to that of present-day education in general. Present-day education also sets up at one and the same time the contradictory ideals of active independence and obedient submission. How the poor child—or in the case of psychotherapy, the poor patient—is to extricate himself from the tangle is his affair.

15 Cf., for instance, M. Gill and M. Brenman, "Treatment of a Case of Anxiety Hysteria by an Hypnotic Technique Employing Psychoanalytic Principles," *Bull. Menninger Clin.,* Vol. 7, 1943; or L. S. Kubie, "The Use of Induced Hypnagogic Reveries in the Recovery of Repressed Amnesic Data," *Bull. Menninger Clin.,* Vol. 7, 1943.

When the circumstances are favorable, he usually does it in the following fashion: Under the mask of independence and activity (which he is consciously very proud of) the patient unconsciously enjoys passive-receptive dependence. The dependence may be thought of as being temporary only and preparatory to a later independence (a state which is anticipated in imagination). This is the mental situation of children and adolescents, and this makes so many neurotics tend to remain children or adolescents.

A climax of dependence masked as independent power is achieved by the methods of *autosuggestion,* where a weak and passive ego is controlled by an immense superego with magic powers. This power, however, is borrowed and even usurped.

In what way does "wild psychoanalysis" work—i.e., methods of psychotherapy which use a limited amount of interpretation, either "without going as deep as Freud, because that is not always necessary," or "by directly attacking the patient with deep interpretations"? It may work in different ways, and if a success is achieved at all, it may be ascribed to a combination of the following mechanisms: (a) Transference improvements, achieved by dynamic changes due to the feeling relation to the doctor and more or less independent of the specific content of what the doctor says. Improvements of this kind can frequently be observed in the beginning of an analysis. (b) Rational help by verbalizing of conflicts, showing of connections, giving advice in actual difficulties. (c) Unspecific help by directing the patient's attention to matters which he has not considered hitherto, that is, by giving him courage to think and talk about forbidden topics. (d) More specific help of the same kind, that is, real analytic influence—an influence which, because it is limited in depth, is used, it is true, as a resistance against further analysis. Frequently, an analytically gained new insight is misused for the purpose of increasing some other repression. The shifting of the emphasis from actuality to childhood, promoted by some psychotherapists, may mean further repression of, or illusions about, present worries. (e) All the artificial neuroses, created by non-analytic therapeutic measures, may also be inaugurated by limited and inexact interpretation.

There is no doubt that the psychoanalytic understanding of the ways in which non-analytic psychotherapies work can be utilized for a planned systematization of the procedure to be chosen. So long as every psychotherapeutic school had its own "theory," the results were unpredictable and dependent on chance, or rather entirely on the therapist's intuitive skill. The methods of psychotherapy, therefore, have remained the same since the times of the earliest witch doctors; the results were perhaps not bad, but they were not understood and were thus unreliable. You never could tell whether or not they would be achieved at all.

A brief psychotherapy, based on psychoanalytic knowledge, can change this state of affairs. An analyst is able to use the patient's symptoms, history, behavior, and utterances for the purpose of establishing a "dynamic diagnosis" about the patient's leading conflicts, the relative strength of repressing and repressed forces respectively, the defense system and its weak spots, the patient's rigidity or elasticity, and his general accessibility. This dynamic diagnosis will enable him to predict with a certain degree of probability what the patient's reaction to certain measures will be. Combinations of limited interpretations, provocations of certain types of transference, the providing of well-chosen substitutive outlets, alterations of the environment, suggestions or prohibitions of unconsciously tempting or reassuring situations or activities, a verbalizing of actual conflicts, mental-hygienic advice—all these can very well be arranged on a systematic basis.[16]

It is to be hoped that under the pressure of bitter practical necessity, a psychoanalytic theory of non-psychoanalytic influence will soon be advanced. This is the more necessary inasmuch as various resistances to psychoanalysis are already falsely enlisting under the banner of "brief psychotherapy."

Psychotherapy works in quite another way when it attempts to change, not the patient's mental structure, but his environment—that is, to use "situational therapy."

A change of environment is most effective in cases of children in whom the neurosis has not yet become definitely internalized. If a child is neurotic because he is afraid of unfriendly surroundings, a change in these surroundings will change his fear and therewith his repressions and his neurosis. Sometimes a change of environment may also be effective in the opposite way. The surroundings may mean to the child a constant excitement and temptation, and a cessation of this external stimulation may decrease the intensity of the instinctual demands sufficiently.

After the neurosis has become more internalized, simple cures of this type become impossible. Psychotherapy is often thought of as a re-education. But repression has made the consequences of the bad influence of the education inaccessible to new experiences. However, a re-education may be conceivable if the bad consequences of the education do not consist of something which this education has done, but of something which it has omitted. Then, what has been omitted may be inserted later on. This is to be seen, for example, in so-called "psychopaths," the deficiencies of whose superego are due to a disturbed childhood during which they never had occasion or time to identify themselves with any "good" parental figures. Aichhorn has given many examples of a very effective "psychotherapy"

[16] Cf. the discussion in F. Alexander, et al., *Proceedings of the Brief Psychotherapy Council,* Inst. f. Psa., Chicago, 1942.

in such cases, based on the idea of providing later on what had not been provided in childhood.[17]

However, in other types of neuroses too, a change of environment may be helpful. Then such an improvement is traceable less to a real undoing of the pathogenic anxieties than to an exclusion of precipitating factors which lead to an exacerbation either of anxieties or temptations. Relatively healthy original phobic or compulsive ceremonial conditions, which somehow had been lost in reality, may be found again in a new environment.

An improvement which is exclusively based on change of environment will remain dependent on this change. If the neurotic is forced to go back to his old milieu, he will fall sick again. A stay in a sanitarium as the sole curative element is therefore again a doubtful measure.

Nevertheless, a change of environment may be rendered very beneficial by applying psychotherapy while the patient is in the more favorable environment. If the case is studied in the sanitarium and the daily routine is arranged to meet his needs (abreactions, reassurance, transference), genuine improvement may occur. The sanitarium is certainly indicated when the task consists of getting over a certain period of emergency (attacks of depression) or when psychoanalysis or other psychotherapeutic measures cannot be performed in the usual environment (addicts, schizophrenia, depressions).[18] It also has to be admitted that sometimes if time is gained everything is gained. After a "nervous breakdown" a limited time under changed conditions may suffice to let the ego regain its lost equilibrium or a substitute for it. The old advice for nervous people "to have a vacation," that is, to leave the conditions which provoked the neurosis, certainly contains an element of truth.

The overwhelming number of patients needing treatment, as well as theoretical considerations, have induced certain psychiatrists to try *group psychotherapy*. Although the transference relations become much more complicated in a group (object relationships of members to each other such as love, hatred, jealousy, envy, as well as identifications and the influences of "good" and "bad" examples, complicating the picture), other psychological characteristics of a group seem to be favorable for psychotherapeutic purposes. The hypnotic situation has been called by Freud a "group of two," [19] indicating that the libidinal

[17] A. Aichhorn, *Wayward Youth*, New York, Viking, 1935.

[18] Cf., among other literature, D. M. Bullard, "The Organization of Psychoanalytic Procedure in the Hospital," *J. Nerv. Ment. Dis.*, Vol. 91, 1940; J. O. Chassell, "Psychoanalytic Therapy in a Mental Hospital," *Psychiatry*, Vol. 3, 1940; R. P. Knight, "Psychoanalysis of Hospitalized Patients," *Bull. Menninger Clin.*, Vol. 1, 1937; K. Menninger, "Psychoanalytic Psychiatry: Theory and Practice," *Bull. Menninger Clin.*, Vol. 4, 1940; E. Simmel, "Psycho-Analytic Treatment in a Sanatorium," *Int. J. Psa.*, Vol. 10, 1929.

[19] S. Freud, *Group Psychology and the Analysis of the Ego*, London, Hogarth, 1948, p. 100.

ties in a group are similar to hypnotic rapport. This similarity can be made use of for psychotherapeutic purposes. The examples of the others with whom the patient can identify himself, and the general tendency to undo instinctual derivatives and mental differentiations when in a group may help to overcome resistances. For an analytic working through, however, the situation of intimacy with the doctor alone seems indispensable. It is understandable, therefore, that Thomas, in summarizing all attempts at group psychotherapy hitherto made, states that "repressive inspirational" methods by far outweigh the analytic ones.[20] One may wonder whether authors like Schilder, who believed in the purely psychoanalytic effects of group therapy,[21] were not in error about what they themselves were doing. "Repressive inspirational" methods, however, may be of various kinds. All magical procedures are intensified in the presence of many believers with whom the novice may identify himself. Many attempts at group therapy have been made, ranging from those initiated by Pratt as far back as 1906 for tubercular patients,[22] to the practices of Christian Science and other sects, as well as those communities which are united by common public performances of a sacred or profane kind, and the work of Burrow who, by "phylo-analysis," tries to bring his patients to a reconsideration of their natural ways of functioning.[23]

A problem which is entirely different from "brief psychotherapy" is represented by "long psychotherapy" in cases where, for reasons inherent in the clinical pictures, psychoanalysis proper would not be possible. In psychotics or psychopaths, where no co-operative ego is at hand with which to conduct psychoanalysis, a co-operative ego must first be established. The clinical technique of psychoanalysis must be changed and adjusted to the object where it does not fit the subject. However, as long as the aims remain psychoanalytic, we think that a technique of this kind should be called "psychoanalysis" rather than "non-analytic psychotherapy," since what characterizes psychoanalysis is the ultimate aim of freeing the individual from his defensive struggles and not whether or not he lies down on the couch or tries to fulfill the "basic rule" immediately.

From the practical point of view, the author has had two years' experience of working in the Los Angeles Psychiatric Service and several years of conducting a social workers' seminar, in which an attempt was made to formulate dynamic diagnoses of non-analytic patients. As to the technique, the principles described above were applied. Any fuller discussion would have necessitated seminars

---

[20] G. W. Thomas, "Group Psychotherapy: A Review of the Recent Literature," *Psychosom. Med.*, Vol. 5, 1943.

[21] Cf. P. Schilder, *Psychotherapy*, New York, Norton, 1938.

[22] J. H. Pratt, "The Home Sanatorium Treatment of Consumption," *Johns Hopkins Hospital Bull.*, Vol. 17, 1906.

[23] T. Burrow, *The Structure of Insanity*, London, Kegan Paul, 1932.

dealing with case histories, with at least one entire evening devoted to every case. The successes were moderate—not quite as moderate, however, as had been anticipated. I should think that about half the cases were really helped. What was mostly effected was a kind of limited analysis in which limited analytic successes helped to bring about and continue transference successes—successes based on an increase in repression at other places. I was especially impressed by the intense gratitude of certain types of patients whose worries had never been taken seriously and discussed with them before. Some types of patients understood very easily an explanation of emotional connections which lead to the formation of symptoms, and reacted to this understanding by improvement. Other types had a special resistance to understanding at all what might be meant by "emotional connections"; and it was of course difficult to help these, since their resistance could not be attacked by proper psychoanalytic methods.

To summarize: The fields of indication for "brief psychotherapy" are in the following order:

(1) Traumatic neuroses and acute conflicts.

(2) Immature personalities who need re-education.

(3) Hysterical types who are ready for a dramatic transference and for easy "magical" influences.

I am very skeptical as to the possibility of changing deep-seated character structures (and most of the so-called "psychosomatic" disorders are based on pathological character structures) by means of a few interviews.

Two closing remarks must be added:

(1) All who are interested in brief psychotherapy had best reread Breuer and Freud's *Studies in Hysteria*.[24] They will be surprised how many of the problems of modern "brief psychotherapy" were already solved or at least seen and discussed before psychoanalysis was developed.

(2) Do not underestimate the advantage of pure gold.

[24] J. Breuer and S. Freud, *Studies in Hysteria,* New York, Nerv. Ment. Dis. Pub. Co., 1937.

NINETEEN

Psychoanalytic Remarks on Fromm's Book *Escape from Freedom* *

I

FREUD's *Group Psychology and Analysis of the Ego* is the starting point for all investigations concerning the psychology of leadership. The phenomenon of *hypnosis* is the model of all "authority," and hypnosis is a *regressive* phenomenon; an old pattern is remobilized: the relationship of the child to his parents whom he believes to be omnipotent (after having lost the belief in his own omnipotence). Through the feeling of being loved and protected by the parents, the child enjoys sexual and narcissistic (security) satisfaction simultaneously. The deep memory traces of this experience form in later situations of danger, anxiety, insecurity, or frustration, a temptation to long for a "hypnotist" who magically brings all that is missing, in the same unconditional and oral way as the mother once brought the food. This longing can be misused by different "hypnotists," under different conditions in very different ways. The hypnotist offers magical reparticipation in the lost and projected omnipotence. This narcissistic satisfaction had once been identical with an (archaic) sexual satisfaction; nor should it be forgotten that also mature sexual satisfaction brings an experience of undoing of individualization, of "flowing together," of "oceanic feelings." Hunger and satiety govern the rhythm of the infant's life; "sexual longing" and "sexual satisfaction" as well as "narcissistic need" and "narcissistic satisfaction" are two different derivatives of this very same root.[1] Normally those two types of deriva-

---

* First published in *Psa. Rev.*, Vol. 31, 1944, pp. 133–152.
[1] S. Rado, "The Psychic Effect of Intoxicants," *Int. J. Psa.*, Vol. 7, 1926.

tives have a different development. To get sexual satisfaction, an object is needed; contentedness with oneself can be achieved without any object by the feeling of having done the right thing. But often this differentiation is incomplete, and under certain cultural conditions it seems to be so regularly. People's self-esteem, then, is dependent on supplies from without, and for such persons the longing for being hypnotized remains the model for all their human relationships: they are ready to renounce not only the valuing functions of their superego but also their very ego functions, perception or judgment, if they can get magical protection, participation in omnipotence, and oceanic feeling instead.

All that is well known. It is not necessary to go into further detail; I only wish to add that these insights into the regulation of self-esteem make the effectiveness of education in general understandable. Educators have the power to influence children because children are so much in need of affection that they are ready to sacrifice other instinctual demands for its sake. The parents' attitude is: if you obey you get what you need; if you don't obey you do not get it, you will become or remain helpless and you will have to starve mentally. This attitude may be called *the promise of supplies on conditions.* The nature of the conditions and the way in which they were applied are later reflected in the superego. "Education" certainly differs enormously under different cultural conditions; but it is always a promise of supplies on conditions.

And something else is valid about every education: it reflects the cultural conditions which it attempts to reproduce. What the paterfamilias does with the children, all governments or ruling classes do with their subjects: they give promises of supplies on conditions. There is a great difference between a nursing mother and an industrial employer; nevertheless the employer makes use of the fact that once there was a nursing mother; because it is the memory of the pleasurable dependence of the infant upon the mother which makes people long for external supplies and ready to believe promises and to fulfill conditions.

The same circumstances are decisive in the psychology of religion. Religion, too, is a promise of conditioned protection.

Different papers have been published concerning the psychology of this "reparticipation in the projected omnipotence" and its social significance. It is sufficient to mention a few of them. Reich [2] showed how Fascism succeeds in directing the rebellious tendencies of discontented masses into another direction, making use of preceding culturally conditioned alterations in the individual mental structures. The individuals became unable to perform independent actions but instead longed for receptive substitute gratifications; instead of killing their real enemies, they gladly accepted the permission to kill scapegoats whose killing united them with the omnipotent leader or fatherland. Kardiner (at that time

[2] W. Reich, *The Mass Psychology of Fascism,* New York, Orgone Inst. Press, 1946.

still in accordance with Freud's libido theory) described how the ego first "masters" the environment passively and receptively, and later learns to master it actively; and that certain social conditions inhibit the activity and bring back the passive-oral type of mastery.[3] Fromm (also at that time still in accordance with Freud) published his paper on "Authority," in which he explained the projection, introjection, and reprojection of the idea of power, and how social circumstances enforce the development of what he called the "authoritative character," which again is the longing for participation in an external omnipotence.[4] And the author of this paper has said among other things: "The most effective way to participate again in the lost omnipotence seems to be represented not by the fantasy of devouring the powerful person but by the idea of being devoured by him. This is the model for all subsequent narcissistic pleasure feelings in which the subject in its smallness feels itself securely placed in something infinitely great which nevertheless has ego quality; like patriotism (one's nation is infinitely greater than one's ego, and nevertheless it is one's nation), religious ecstasy (God is infinitely greater than the ego, and nevertheless the believers are one in Him), hypnosis (the hypnotist is infinitely greater than the ego, and nevertheless it is he who performs functions which normally are those of the ego), the relationship to authority in general (the totalitarian leader is infinitely greater than any single individual of the nation, and nevertheless he is *the* single individual of the nation). And the differences of the methods which are applied to claim the power of the powerful—robbery, theft, permitted participation, and the magical substitutes for all that—are a basic subject for any social psychology." And: "Because magical participations may have the same effects of blocking the aggressions as real participations would have, magical participations in power are a means to make powerless people spontaneously accept their powerlessness. The illusion of being loved, supported by supplies of self-esteem and even exalted by the authority which actually had first deprived one of one's activity and then brought one into a masochistic receptive attitude, is a means by which class societies maintain themselves." [5]

It cannot be denied that religion and class antagonism as well as looking back for magical units and "promise of supplies on conditions" are ubiquitous and not at all specific. There are innumerable variations of these phenomena, and the investigation of the differences of these variations may be one of the main tasks of all social psychology. Variations in primitive societies have been

[3] A. Kardiner, "The Role of Economic Security in the Adaptation of the Individual," *Family,* Vol. 17, 1936; "Security, Cultural Restraints, Intra-Social Dependencies, and Hostilities," *Family,* Vol. 18, 1937; "Influence of Culture on Behavior," *Social Work Today.*

[4] E. Fromm, as cited on p. 155 of this volume.

[5] O. Fenichel, "Trophy and Triumph: *A Clinical Study,*" No. 10 in this volume.

especially investigated where the assignments of privileges "on conditions," submissions out of fear of being outcast, and ingratiations have very definite forms. But also the quoted papers did more than state the existence of the "participation" phenomena. They partially studied very specific forms of them: for example Reich, the modern German petit bourgeoisie; Kardiner compared different primitive societies; Fromm the possible forms of authority. Many more variations exist than have been investigated so far. The first main subdivision of the phenomena in question is probably that of their forms in "stable" and in "unstable" societies. In stable societies the individual may feel really as "belonging," as a part of a whole, getting the promised "protection" at least to a certain degree (slaves in ancient society, craftsmen in the Middle Ages). In unstable societies a greater or smaller tendency toward rebellion has to be mastered by changes of the individual mental structures by use of the regressive tendencies. An example of the different use of the same ideology under different conditions has been given by Fromm in his paper on the Christian dogma.[6]

Generally, satisfaction of any kind tends to give the feeling of being where one belongs and of needing no further "magical protection"; satisfactions make one conservative. But frustrations do not necessarily make one rebellious. They arouse two contradictory simultaneous reactions, a tendency to rebel, and a tendency to feel "lost" and, therefore, to long for the return of the omnipotent savior. The relative strength of the active tendency to do something about the situation and of the passive regressive longing depends on various circumstances. One among them is most obvious: the greater the hopes for a success, the greater the rebellious tendencies; the greater the hopelessness, the greater the regressive longing. The complications which these regressive tendencies toward passivity bring into the relation between frustration and aggression, which is of paramount practical social importance, could be seen and explained only by psychoanalysis. Freud's psychology of depressive states and melancholia explains the connections between oral frustrations and extreme passive behavior.[7] It seems that general frustrations—i.e., general decrease in the living standard—are reacted to in the same way as oral frustrations are reacted to by small children. We hasten to add that "social frustrations" do not work only in this direct way. They have also indirect effects by inducing the frustrated people to change their ways of child raising. And not only the active behavior of personally frustrated parents toward the children changes; also the social educational institutions are extremely and

---

[6] E. Fromm, "Die Entwicklung des Christusdogmas," *Imago,* Vol. 16, 1930. Cf. the papers by G. Zilboorg, "The Paradoxical Aspects of the Present-Day Crisis," *Ann. Amer. Acad. Pol. & Soc. Sc.,* Vol. 216, 1941, and "Paternalistic Aggression and Individual Freedom in the Present Crisis," *Amer. J. Orthopsychiat.,* Vol. 11, 1941.

[7] Cf. S. Freud, "Mourning and Melancholia," *Coll. Pap.,* Vol. IV, London, Hogarth, 1948.

directly dependent on present (and past) social conditions, blocking the direct outlet of aggressive tendencies and increasing the tendencies toward submission (which, increasing—in an unstable society and under frustrating conditions—will be the more effective, the more they may be combined with a permitted and commanded outlet of the dammed-up aggression into another direction). Frustrations on the one hand, and the way in which the children are directed to react to those frustrations on the other hand, are the two main sources for institutionalized character formation.

Concerning the factors which increase the regressive longing in modern times we know more: The breaking-through of the bourgeois society against the feudal chains brought much "freedom" to the individual; the antagonism of classes was denied, everybody had equal rights, and the general competition brought not only the overcoming of prejudices but also real possibilities of development of productive forces. This generally progressive nature of capitalism slowly began to be counterweighted by its inner contradictions. Two of them were psychologically of special importance:

(1) The bourgeoisie could develop only by producing the new class of proletarians whose means of satisfaction had to remain limited, which made the redevelopment of "limiting ideologies" necessary.

(2) The inner contradictions of capitalism have the effect that the production is more and more socialized, necessarily done more and more on a larger scale, whereas simultaneously the market for the "cheaper" products is ruined. The individual as a producer cannot exist outside of the great unity, as consumer he is alone and helpless. Certainly, it is true, the machines of monopolistic capitalism make the individual a powerless dwarf; but this circumstance alone does not necessarily mean that he must feel helpless and lonely; as a producer he "participates" in the "omnipotence" of the machine, and it may be possible for him to feel proudly: "We are the machines." However, the "appropriation had remained private"; the individual's helplessness is less rooted in the fact that the machines are bigger than he is and that he cannot produce anything alone, than in the fact that he has no power of disposal over the products. Not the immensity of the machine matters, but its use by monopolistic capitalism, the fact that the individuals conjointly produce, but individually are kept from consumption. And it is not only in respect to consumption that individual activity loses its possibilities. In a world which goes to pieces there is also no unifying ideology. People feel "alone" and feel that there is "nothing stable," because their life really is threatened, and really everything is destroyed which still a year ago was believed to be stable.

II

Is there any contradiction between these statements and Freud's libido theory? Kardiner [8] and Fromm [9] are of this opinion. I cannot agree with them. It is true that the problems discussed have not been discussed much by Freud. Nevertheless it seems to me that those problems not only are in accordance with Freud's conceptions but that only Freud's conceptions bring the full explanation of them. Man is governed by certain biological basic drives which are not at all rigid patterns but are formed and developed according to satisfying and frustrating experiences, which means through social forces. That, and how the social forces form the individual mind, become understandable in detail through our understanding of unconscious drives and their displaceability. Freud says: Man is an instinctual being, driven by innate forces. Fromm says: Man is first a social being. There is no contradiction between these two statements. A man is a social being because he cannot feel instinctively satisfied without other beings; because he exists only in so far as an individual, as he feels himself in need of contact with other individuals. But what does Fromm state? According to him Freud said that the human individual is, first of all, a secluded entity with certain instinctual demands, and only *secondarily* he asks for other individuals whom he needs as instruments for his satisfaction. Freud never said that. A human being is never "first of all a secluded entity." If we assume that there is something like a "primary narcissism," the embryo or infant in this stage is no human being yet. According to Freud the human being becomes a human being (an "ego") by entering into "interrelations" with other human beings.[10] Man being a "social animal," the social relations form the individual, not the biological need, states Fromm. That also is correct, but in no contradiction to Freud. What Fromm does not see, or tries to deny, is that social relations can only "form individuals" because of a certain biological structure of man; and that the study of this biological basis and of what happens to this basis under different social circumstances makes it understandable how social relations form individuals. It is true that changed social conditions also change the individual's needs. But it can be shown psychoanalytically that in the new needs old biologically based needs have found a new and changed expression, and this cannot only be proved but is also of an immense heuristic value: it explains many details of real facts which otherwise would remain unexplained. Fromm denies that sexuality is the basis of love. Such denial means not only, first, the denial of facts which psychoanalysis has shown, namely the facts of the genetic and

[8] A. Kardiner, *The Individual and His Society: The Psychodynamics of Primitive Social Organization*, New York, Columbia Univ. Press, 1939.

[9] E. Fromm, "Selfishness and Self-Love," *Psychiatry*, Vol. 2, 1939.

[10] Cf. S. Freud, "On Narcissism: An Introduction," *Coll. Pap.*, Vol. IV.

"correlative" and "substitute" relations of sexuality and love, but also, second, denial of many heuristic possibilities. (But psychoanalysis has never said that love *is* sexuality. Love is a certain attitude toward sexual objects which develops under certain social conditions.) Fromm ridicules the idea that pure "satisfactions" or "frustrations" of instincts might form a character; instead, he says, this is done by the "relationship of the individual to the world as a whole," of which relationship the different satisfactions and frustrations are merely special manifestations. But what else is "relationship to the world as a whole" than the memory of past experiences and the anticipation of experiences of satisfaction and frustrations in the future? Whereas Fromm thinks that he, in contrast to the "biologically oriented" Freud, is especially "real" and "concrete," this "relation to the world as a whole" is very abstract and in comparison with Freud's concrete analysis of the instinctual attitudes, extremely vague. Fromm agrees more or less with Horney that a character is a unit, which they think Freud has denied, and serves the purpose of adaptation; "of adaptation against anxiety," said Horney; [11] "of adaptation against loneliness" says Fromm. But adaptation of this kind is only one side of the character; there are two others: Some attitudes do not serve the purpose of security but of instinct satisfaction; and, partly, character traits, especially neurotic ones, are not at all adaptations made by the ego, but things which happen to the ego against its will by instinctual forces which return from the repressed.

Like Kardiner [12] also, Fromm is of the opinion that "oral" and "anal" character traits are not built by or against pregenital instinctual forces but are outcomes of social conflicts which "accidentally" took place in the oral or anal field. Like Kardiner, he thinks that an "attitude" could never be explained by an "instinct." But clinical facts are denied as well as heuristic possibilities abolished, if we state that "dependency" has nothing to do with "orality" and "stinginess" nothing with "anality." On the other hand, the statement that a biological substratum is molded by institutions, in no way implies an underestimation of the influence of the institutions.

III

What has been said up to now might be summarized as follows: The ways of production and distribution, and their contradictions, inflict severe frustrations upon individuals of all classes (though in different forms and to different degrees). Today they arouse especially feelings of being lost and of "not belonging." These feelings have various mental consequences; one of these consequences is a longing to have once more an omnipotent person in the external world to whom

[11] K. Horney, *The Neurotic Personality of Our Time,* New York, Norton, 1937.
[12] A. Kardiner, *op. cit.*

one may submit, losing one's helpless individuality in a magnificent oceanic feeling. This longing forms the psychological condition in the masses which meets the influence of Fascism halfway. At least that is the case in the times of Fascism's coming to power and in the period right afterward. The leaders make use of this longing; they give or promise its satisfaction, and they do so on conditions. So they are able to offer to the frustrated and longing individuals magical rewards, and so they are able to achieve a voluntary obedience and a general renunciation of independent judgment and feeling.

I do not know whether Fromm would concede that this summary of our own considerations is simultaneously a summary of his book *Escape from Freedom*. I suppose he would not. He probably would protest against two details in this formulation: against the "frustrations" and against the "conditions." But the above formulation is the way in which the reviewer would express Fromm's ideas. He tried to make them clear to himself and to bring them into agreement with what we knew and thought about these problems before Fromm's book.

Without any "interpretations" and additions Fromm's main theses are:

In the course of history revolutionary (and evolutionary) changes in economic conditions have often created deep changes in the position of (all or certain) individuals in society; they have brought liberation from old chains, prejudices, limitations, frustrations; people have become free from something which had bound them hitherto. But such liberations have always been bought at a high price; with their limitations the individuals also lost their feeling of belonging, their being a part of a whole—they became lonely. And always, in such situations, they became afraid of this loneliness. A mental conflict was aroused in them between the tendency to enjoy the new liberty and the anxiety created by the loss of the belonging and by their regressive longing. There are various possibilities of escape from this conflict. Which escape is chosen depends on the social and cultural conditions. The longing for a *"Fuehrer"* and sado-masochistic submission in Fascism is one modern escape of this kind. But there is not only a "freedom from . . ."; there is also a "freedom to. . . ." It is possible to strengthen the uniqueness and activity of the individual in such a way that he may find contact and "belonging" with other free individuals in "love and creative work" without any chains. To make this possible, mankind must rationalize their ways of production and distribution.

IV

This is not the place to review and discuss all details of Fromm's book. But I should like to pick out certain points which seem worth while, especially concerning Fromm's criticisms of Freud.

These criticisms begin in the first chapter: "Freud was so imbued with the spirit of his culture that he could not go beyond certain limits which were set by it." Freud's main mistake was that he took modern man's drives for "the biological drives of man." "The individual appears fully equipped with biologically given drives which need to be satisfied. In order to satisfy them, the individual enters into relation with objects." "Contrary to Freud's viewpoint, the analysis offered in this book is based on the assumption that the key problem of psychology is that of the specific kind of relatedness of the individual to the world, and not that of the satisfaction or frustration of this or that instinctual need." To the objection that the relatedness of the individual toward the world is nothing else than the sum of all his drives, Fromm probably would answer with the arguments of the Gestalt psychologists that the "whole" is not the "sum." In discussing this, he cannot avoid falsifying Freud: "Although there are certain needs, such as hunger, thirst, sexuality, which are common to man, those drives which make for the differences in man's character, like love and hatred, lust for power and yearning for submission, enjoyment of sensuous pleasure and the fear of it, are all products of the social process." And he thinks that that contradicts Freud; the truth is that this is just the opinion Freud holds. Freud never denied that all those strivings—love, hatred, love of power, yearning for submission, enjoyment of sensuous pleasure, and especially fear of sensuous pleasure—are products of experiences—i.e., of the social process. What else does psychoanalysis do than find out in which way those attitudes are formed in the individual by experiences during his childhood? Freud only added one thing which Fromm now tries to get rid of: He found out *how* the "social process" "produces" "those strivings": by transforming the aims, objects, and directions of "certain needs which are common to man such as hunger, thirst, sexuality"—especially "sexuality." And what is the "wholeness" of the "interpersonal relationships"? Fromm gives examples of drives which came into existence at certain points of the historic development and thinks this is an argument against Freud: the drives "to enjoy nature's beauty" and "the drive to work." Certainly nobody will deny the social origin of these "drives," but their social origin does not contradict the assumption that deeper biological needs have been transformed into these "new drives." [13]

As an example of the "ambiguity of freedom"—simultaneously with freedom, loneliness, and oceanic longing increase—Fromm discusses the sixteenth century, and these chapters are the most interesting ones of his book. The Italian Renaissance and the German and Swiss Reformations are discussed in this connection. "Protestantism and Calvinism, while giving expression to a new feeling of freedom, at the same time constituted an escape from the burden of freedom."

[13] Cf. O. Fenichel, "The Drive to Amass Wealth," No. 7 in this volume.

Fromm succeeds in showing that the development of a new feeling of time and of new ethics of "working" are the most important psychological changes which accompanied the economic development of capitalism. The new religions "gave expression to the new feeling of freedom and independence as well as to the feeling of powerlessness and anxiety by which their members were pervaded." And Fromm is of the opinion that the roots of many of today's escape mechanisms were developed at that time: the morals of being active at any cost (which is so characteristic of Calvinism), the absolute authority of certain words, and an all-pervading hidden hostility, especially against one's own ego, self-humiliation and the concept of "duty" as a substitute for external authority. How Freud is treated in this connection may be seen from the following quotation: "Freud has seen the hostility of man against himself which is contained in what he called the superego. He also saw that the superego was originally the internalization of an external dangerous authority. But he did not distinguish between spontaneous ideals which are part of the self, and internalized commands which rule the self." I wonder whether Fromm knew before Freud that the superego is an internalization of an external dangerous authority; actually Freud *did* distinguish between different types of "internalization," "ideals" which became a part of the ego, and "ideals" which rule the ego as the external authority did before.[14]

The new ideals of "work" and "duty" were useful as long as the capitalistic world was able to function economically; when its inner contradictions inhibited economic progress, the same conflicts and the "two aspects of freedom for modern man" came back. Growing freedom continued to show an exquisite dialectic character. More "freedom from" gave rise to more longing for belonging. The "freer" individuals became more "insignificant and powerless" because "capitalistic economy put the individual entirely on his own feet" (which, it seems, is quite true; but we mentioned before that two other sources of this "insignificance" seem more important: the contradictions between socialized production and private appropriation on the one hand, and the rising conflicts between bourgeoisie and proletariat on the other).

Fromm goes on: Capitalism brought not only increase in individualistic tendencies, but also an increase in the self-negation and asceticism which had begun with Protestantism.

Modern man does not do what he likes to do or what is advantageous for him; "the man-made world has become his master." He is isolated because his "interpersonal relationships" are not governed by "love" but by the rules of the market. "Man does not only sell commodities, he sells himself and feels himself to be a

---

[14] Cf. S. Freud, *The Ego and the Id,* London, Hogarth, 1947; *The Problem of Anxiety,* New York, Norton, 1936.

commodity. . . . If there is no use for the quality a person offers, he has none; just as an unsalable commodity is valueless though it might have its use-value." That explains the immense amounts of "social anxiety" in our society; "the self-confidence, the feeling of self, is merely an indication of what others think of a person." Monopolistic capitalism brings this development to a maximum. The individual becomes a nothing and the only counterbalance which society can offer to him is the fact that there are always people who are still more of a noth-ing (for example, wife and children for the proletarian man). Fromm gives a good description of the progredient cutting out of every individual tendency not only in production but also in consumption. The individual cannot do anything else than develop the "mechanisms of escape."

The first of these "escapes" is "authoritarianism." Fromm recapitulates the main thoughts of his paper about authority: Somebody outside of the subject determines his self. The subject renounces the functions of his ego and gets the feeling of being sheltered. There is no reference either to sexuality or to the historical development of the feeling of omnipotence.

Fromm adds an unsexual theory of sadism and masochism, which phenomena are "explained" as escapes from isolation: Freud's concept of a "death instinct" limits research about sado-masochism (with which we would agree). "In psycho-analytic literature a viewpoint different from Freud's has been presented by Wil-helm Reich and Karen Horney." "Although Reich's views are based on concepts of Freud's libido theory, he points out that the masochistic person ultimately seeks pleasure and that the pain incurred is a by-product, not an aim in itself." ("Although"?) "Horney was the first one to recognize the fundamental relation of masochistic strivings in the neurotic personality, to give a full and detailed description of the masochistic character traits and to account for them theoreti-cally as the outcome of a whole character structure." Horney stated that the masochist behaves masochistically because he has an oceanic longing for being united with a great unity; the unity with whom he unites seems the greater to him, the smaller he is himself, and that is the reason for the striving for self-humiliation.[15] It is not clear why the feeling of pain should give the conviction of being united with a greater unity; but it is to be admitted that this theory is very similar to that of Fromm. But certainly it cannot be admitted that Freud did not see "the fundamental relation of masochistic strivings in the neurotic per-sonality," [16] or that Reich's paper about the masochistic character did not give "a full and detailed description of the masochistic character-traits" and did not

---

[15] K. Horney, op. cit.

[16] S. Freud, "From the History of an Infantile Neurosis," and "Psychoanalytic Notes upon an Auto-biographical Account of a Case of Paranoia (Dementia Paranoides)," Coll. Pap., Vol. III, London, Hogarth, 1948; "The Economic Problem in Masochism," Coll. Pap., Vol. II, London, Hogarth, 1948.

"account for them as the outcome of a whole character structure." [17] However, Fromm is of the opinion that a masochistic person may behave masochistically also in sexual life, but that this connection is merely accidental. The aim of the masochist is only "to get rid of his individual self." Fromm quickly shows that he does not mean that the masochist just uses the mechanisms of the "lesser evil" or of doing "prophylactically actively" what would happen passively anyhow. He simply states that the person who is afraid of feeling insignificant and power- less can overcome this fear by making himself extremely insignificant and power- less. He saves himself from his conflict by "reducing the individual self to noth- ing," by overcoming "the awareness of the separateness as an individual." "The phantasy of suicide is the last hope if all other means have not succeeded in bring- ing relief of the burden of aloneness." But people who are pathologically striving for suicide usually are not called masochists but depressives; they mostly do not simply feel alone, but alone with an overwhelming conscience; they have no pleasure as the masochists have; and they have fantasies connected with the idea of "death" which, it is true, might mean overcoming "the awareness of separate- ness of an individual."

With certain remarks Fromm in this connection goes so far as to identify masochistic behavior and neurotic behavior: "In neurotic strivings one acts from a compulsion which has essentially a negative character: to escape an unbearable situation." That is the same idea as Horney had: neurosis as an active adaptation to a certain pathological condition—to anxiety, according to Horney, to isolation, according to Fromm. They do not see that there are neurotic phenomena which are not adaptations at all but the failure of any adaptation, something which happens to the ego from the part of the unconscious drives. If the masochist had no other aim than getting rid of himself, he would strive for an entire lack of feelings rather than for suffering. On the other hand, it is certainly correct to say that the sadist, too, is dependent on his object, and in a similar way as the mas- ochist is. Fromm calls sado-masochistic relations in which one person needs to be dependent on another person, "symbiosis." "Symbiosis" is often believed to be love; but it is a cover for inability to love. In a similar way Fascism is believed to be power; but actually it is a reaction-formation against the feeling of power- lessness. "In a psychological sense the lust for power is not rooted in strength but in weakness." The striving for domineering is not identical with potency; "these two qualities are mutually exclusive." Instead of a full sado-masochism some persons develop the longing for a "magic helper" who would be able to bring the necessary supplies. That becomes especially clear in the psychoanalytic cure, where the longing for the magic helper is called "transference." "The rela-

[17] W. Reich, "The Masochistic Character," Chap. XI in *Character-Analysis*, New York, Orgone Inst. Press, 1949.

tionship looks like love; it is often accompanied by sexual desires; yet it is essentially a relationship to the personified magic helper." And if transference is no longer sexual, the oedipus complex cannot be sexual either. "Although the phenomenon of sexual attraction between parents and children does exist and although conflicts arising from it sometimes constitute part of the neurotic development, neither the sexual attraction nor the resulting conflict are essential in the fixation of children on their parents. . . . When the parents, acting as the agents of society, start to suppress the child's spontaneity and independence, the growing child feels more and more unable to stand on its own feet; it, therefore, seeks for the magic helper, and often makes the parents the personification of him," which then is called oedipus complex. And if "oedipus complex" is interpreted in this sense, Fromm agrees that it is the nucleus of all neuroses: "The neurotic person is the one who has not given up fighting against complete submission but who at the same time has remained bound to the figure of the magic helper. . . . Neurosis is always to be understood as an attempt, and essentially an unsuccessful one, to solve the conflict between the basic dependency and the quest of freedom." It is regrettable that Fromm could not resist the temptation to write accessorily a theory of neurosis in a book with quite different aims. It seems that Freud's theory still is more in accordance with the facts.

The second escape mechanism is "destructiveness." One wonders whether sadism and masochism are not "destructive." But Fromm defines the difference which he has in mind: Sadism and masochism aim at "symbiosis," destructiveness at "elimination of the object."

The third escape mechanism is "automaton conformity." "This particular mechanism is the solution that the majority of normal individuals find in modern society. To put it briefly, the individual ceases to be himself; he adopts entirely the kind of personality offered to him by cultural patterns."

On this basis Fromm attempts to explain the "psychology of Nazism," the psychological ground being different in different classes but always based on the effectiveness of "mechanisms of escape." The next chapter shows that—mutatis mutandis—the same psychological dangers which brought about Nazism are also existent in individuals of democratic countries. People there have the right to express their thoughts. "The right to express our thoughts, however, means something only if we are able to have thoughts of our own." It is shown by instructive examples how we usually suppress our children's own thinking and feeling very early. Fromm acknowledges also that suppression of sexuality plays its part, but warns against an overestimation of this part.

The last chapter, "Freedom and Spontaneity," seems the weakest of the book. "Positive freedom consists in the spontaneous activity of the total integrated personality." But Fromm cannot say much more about this than that this spontaneous activity has to be achieved through love and creative work. The tendency toward his spontaneous activity (probably in contrast to Freud's "instincts") is innate to everybody and biologically determined. It is suppressed today, but it cannot be suppressed entirely. Even today there are many hopeful glimpses of originality and creative work, namely, in artists and in children. "Love is the foremost component of such spontaneity," love as distinguished from "symbiosis," and "spontaneous ideals" as distinguished from foreign and suppressive pseudo-ideals. Freud is reproached again for not having distinguished between the two in his conception of "superego." Love and spontaneous creative work are inclined to bring "human happiness," which is something else than "subjective experience of pleasure." Fromm's attempts to define the differences between "happiness" and "subjective experience of pleasure" remain absolutely insufficient: "The sensation of pleasure can be the result of a pathological perversion and proves as little about the objective meaning of the experience as the sweet taste of a poison would prove about its function for the organism." And actually Fromm remains consistent in this idea of an "objective happiness" by formulating a statement which is extremely strange in a so-called materialist: "Psychologists will only be helpful in this direction when they can see the relevance of moral problems for the understanding of a personality. In psychology, including Freud's, which treats such problems in terms of the pleasure principle, one fails to understand one important sector of personality." And only then, after having discussed the "psychological fight" in such a manner, Fromm states that "the psychological problems cannot be separated from the material basis of human existence, from the economic, social, and political structure of society." Not only do we need the Bill of Rights; but "the irrational and planless character of society must be replaced by planned economy. . . . Society must master the social problem as rationally as it has mastered nature."

A psychoanalytic appendix, "Character and Social Process," contains only repetitions of Fromm's criticisms against Freud. It starts the discussion of the relations of character and social process by stating that the same or similar experiences form the same or similar character structures. "Social character is a character structure which prevails under certain social conditions which means in a certain society or only in a certain class in a given society."

But "the ideology of a given society is the ideology of its ruling class." The individual has to adapt himself to given institutions, to given restrictions or to given possibilities of ways of expressing "love and creative work." The real dynamics are decisive, not mere "ideas." (Example: The socialistic parties in Germany in 1933 had "ideas" which were not effective because the dynamic

274 COLLECTED PAPERS OF OTTO FENICHEL: SECOND SERIES

character structure of the members of the parties was not in accordance with them.) "It is Freud's achievement to have shown this, even if his theoretical frame of reference is incorrect." Freud did not see that the individual is structured by social forces in such a way that he intends to act as given conditions force him to act. The "lagging behind" of the acquired social character complicates the picture. It remains psychologically effective even if the material basis has changed. Then the feelings of the individuals do not fit the social needs. Mental structuralization is brought about by *education*. And Fromm tries to discuss the conception of "education" in general. "The educational system of any society is determined by this function; therefore, we cannot explain the structure of society or the personality of its members by the educational process; we have to explain the educational system by the necessities resulting from the social and economic structure of a given society." The most important means of education is the family. Reich has called the family the "factory of ideologies"; Fromm calls it "the psychological agent of society." But innate biological needs cannot be put out of function. The most important of the "psychological qualities inherent in man that need to be satisfied" is "the tendency to grow, to develop and realize potentialities which man has developed in the course of history." (That, according to Fromm is "innate." But the erogeneity of certain organs is not!) If these tendencies are repressed, symbiotic and destructive escape mechanisms develop. In full contradiction (or do I only not understand it?) Fromm formulates: "Although there is no biologically fixed human nature, human nature has a dynamism of its own that constitutes an active factor in the evolution of the social process." As this dynamism he defines "a tendency to grow, to develop and to realize potentialities." This "dynamism" (but no "instincts") is innate, but "we are not yet able to state clearly in psychological terms what the exact nature of this human dynamism is." We have to acknowledge its existence to avoid the "sociological relativism in which man is nothing but a puppet on the strings of social circumstances." "Metaphysical and biological errors," which Fromm puts under the same heading, result, if these "innate forces" "are not correctly evaluated." The suppressed instincts come back with Fromm in a distorted form as a mystical "innate tendency to grow, to develop and to realize potentialities." Fromm summarizes his criticisms to Freud:

(1) Freud, according to Fromm, looks upon man as an instinctual entity formed by satisfactions and frustrations, who needs objects out of instinctual demands. "We believe that man is primarily a social being and not as Freud assumes primarily self-sufficient and only secondarily in need of others." "The key problem is that of the . . . relatedness of the individual towards the world, not that of satisfaction or frustration of single instinctual desires." We have already

had the opportunity to answer this pseudo-Gestalt criticism: The statement that the bonds between human beings are of an instinctual nature does not mean at all that the individual is a closed entity and develops interpersonal relationships only secondarily.

(2) Freud "mistook the causal relation between erogenous zones and character traits for the reverse of what they really are." The development and destiny of erogenous zones is dependent on the development of the "whole human relationship to the parents," and not *vice versa*. The behavior is "rooted in the whole of the character structure," but no character is to be explained by erogenous zones. Freud's assumption that instinctive energies might be turned into character attitudes, is called "mysterious" by Fromm. The clinical facts which prove Freud's assumptions are not even mentioned. Fromm is, like Kardiner, of the erroneous opinion that if he shows that an "anal" character is the result of conflicts with the parents, he has contradicted the statement that this character is "anal." Instead of studying the interrelation of erogenous zones and object relationships, they think statically and are of the opinion that the insight into the role of object relationships contradicts the importance of erogenous zones.

(3) Freud interprets "all ideal motives in man as a result of something mean." "We believe that ideals like truth, justice, freedom . . . can be genuine strivings." We believe that such a statement shows a misunderstanding of psychoanalysis and a rejection of the very materialistic advantages of psychoanalysis, which has shown that all these ideals are *not* "genuine strivings," but are formed out of biological needs by socially determined experiences.

(4) Freud neglects "the differentiation between psychological phenomena of want and those of abundance." He thinks that man is lazy and obeys a "nirvana principle"; only outer needs enforce actions. But Fromm states that "free and spontaneous acts are always phenomena of abundance." With which idea we return from a clear-cut materialistic basis again to an idealistic "vital force" which urges man to act and which is called by Fromm "need to growth and development." Freud has certainly not neglected the possibility of "acts of abundance"; he actually saw in the prolonged childhood of man, which gives the possibility of postponement of certain struggles for life, one of the prerequisites for the development of culture.[18] But he stated correctly that such phenomena are secondary, and that in the last analysis only tensions, i.e., needs and dissatisfactions, are the driving forces. Fromm is consistent enough to attack even the way in which psychoanalysis studies sex. "Not only did Freud omit phenomena of abundance, but he also had a limited understanding of the phenomena to which he paid so

---

[18] Cf. S. Freud, *The Problem of Anxiety* and *Civilization and Its Discontents*, London, Hogarth, 1946.

much attention, sex. . . . The sexual drive as a phenomenon of abundance, the sexual pleasure as spontaneous joy, the essence of which is not negative relief from tension" (what else?) "had no place in his psychology."

It is surprising that the summaries with which Fromm describes his point of view can be wholeheartedly accepted. He states: ". . . that man reacts to changed external situations by changes in himself, and that these psychological factors in their turn help in molding the economic and social process. Economic forces are effective but they must be understood not as psychological motivations but as objective conditions; psychological forces are effective, but they must be understood as historically conditioned themselves." And: "Social conditions influence ideological phenomena through the medium of character; character, on the other hand, is not the result of passive adaptation to social conditions but of a dynamic adaptation on the basis of elements that either are biologically inherent in human nature or have become inherent as a result of historic evolution."

It would have been advantageous for Fromm and his book if he had actually been guided by these principles and had not contradicted them so often. It is not to be understood why an idealistic tendency to grow and to develop should be regarded as "biological inherent in human nature," and sexual partial instincts should not.

V

The insight into the social importance of the "wish to belong" and the "fear of isolation"—in customary psychoanalytic terminology, of the "narcissistic need" and the "fear of loss of love"—would give opportunity for the discussion of important psychoanalytic problems which certainly cannot be solved here. I only want to give a hint of what they are:

(1) The relation of the fear of being isolated to castration fear. What Freud called "fear of loss of love," [19] and which would be better called "fear of losing necessary narcissistic supplies," is often used to hide a deeper repressed castration anxiety. But there is no doubt that this hiding distorts in a regressive way, and that an original "fear of being abandoned" is a fear of the infant, and a more archaic one than castration fear is. It makes its appearance again in all states of society which promote regressions.

(2) The relation between the "longing to belong" and the ideas of eating and of being eaten, of diffusion, of losing one's own self. Under certain circumstances the longing turns into anxiety. This is not investigated, not even mentioned by Fromm. It cannot be understood as long as the sexual nature of the involved phenomena is denied. Longing for and fear of fusion are related to each other in the same way as sexual longing and sexual fears are related to each other.

[19] S. Freud, *The Problem of Anxiety.*

VI

To return to Fromm's book: Does our review mean that everything which is good in it is not new, and everything which is new is not good? It seems we have to answer: Yes. We showed in sections I and II that the essential psychological theses of Fromm were known beforehand. And we hope to have shown that Fromm's criticisms of psychoanalysis, which are new, are not only incorrect but befog the issues, that is, deny just those aspects of psychoanalysis which would bring the most valuable applications to sociology. In this respect Fromm's book in general can be looked upon in the same way as Kardiner's and Horney's writings. For the purpose of avoiding and correcting mistakes which psychoanalysis admittedly has made, they abandon psychoanalysis altogether instead of applying it in a better way. On the other hand, we will not do injustice to certain values of Fromm's book. We have to admit: there is a difference between knowing something in principle, and the elaboration of the real and concrete effectiveness of these principles under certain cultural conditions, which Fromm has done for the sixteenth century and for the present. There are not many sociological books written from the point of view of psychoanalysis, and we have to be grateful for every contribution. But for the same reason we have to be strict and have to ask for an application of a correct psychoanalysis to a correct sociology. Fromm's psychoanalysis is certainly not correct. And even his sociology tends to glide into idealism and overlooks certain basic facts.

❊ ❊ ❊ ❊ ❊ ❊ ❊ ❊ ❊ ❊ ❊ ❊ ❊ ❊ ❊ ❊ ❊ ❊

TWENTY

Remarks on the Common Phobias*

I

PHOBIAS, as examples of neuroses as well as with reference to their specific mechanisms, have often been made the subject of psychoanalytic research. Freud showed that all psychoneuroses are the outcome of conflicts between infantile sexual strivings, remobilized by regression, and fears of the dangers unconsciously connected with these strivings; that neurotic symptoms are a compromise between the instinctual demands and the counterforces motivated by fears. Since the motivating anxiety becomes manifest in phobias, they seem to represent the simplest type of neurosis. In a situation which unconsciously represents an instinctual temptation, anxiety is felt instead of excitement, and subsequently the situation (and therewith the anxiety) is avoided. Most infantile neuroses follow this relatively simple phobic pattern. In all other types of neuroses, the anxiety manifest in the phobias has found further elaboration.

However, the phobic situation does not in every instance represent a sexual temptation. It may represent an aggressive impulse,[1] or it may be reminiscent of an early frustration, sometimes of an unconsciously feared punishment. Most frequently it combines an unconscious temptation with an anticipation of punishment.

This relatively simple explanation created many new problems, most of which have already been solved. For example, if the phobic situation unconsciously revives an infantile striving, and the anxiety functions as a "warning signal" against the danger, it might be expected that the warning would be only a slight one. But the anxiety which accompanies most phobias is overwhelming. Freud

---

* First published in *Psa. Quart.*, Vol. 13, 1944, pp. 313–326.
[1] This point was especially stressed by H. Deutsch in "The Genesis of Agoraphobia," *Int. J. Psa.*, Vol. 10, 1929; and by E. Hitschmann in "Bemerkungen ueber Platzangst und andere neurotische Angstzustaende," *Int. Z. Psa.*, Vol. 23, 1937.

distinguished the "traumatic situation"—in which the organism is so flooded with emotion that the normal mechanisms of mastering excitation (discharge and binding) are inadequate—from the "danger situation," in which the judging ego concludes: "The present situation is not the traumatic one but it might become so." [2] If it is the function of "anxiety as a danger signal" to avoid the development of a "traumatic situation," this function fails entirely in phobic anxiety and brings to pass precisely what it was intended to avert. The ego, which gives the signal of danger, starts something which it cannot control. This happens if the organism, through a series of previous repressions, has dammed up forces which are waiting for any opportunity for discharge. The ego, using what was intended to be the helpful "floodgate" of the "anxiety signal," loses control, releasing the flood.[3]

Another problem concerns the displacement of temptation or punishment to the phobic situation. Freud discovered that this displacement was a ruse to escape from greater dangers. Fear of horses was for little Hans less intolerable than fear of his father.[4] The Wolf-Man had to face the wolf only when his sister showed him the picture in the book, whereas he had to see his father every day.[5] It is possible to remain indoors to avoid the street; it is not possible to get outside one's own body whose excitement was originally feared. Whereas the displacement, "animal for father," substitutes one external object for another, the substitution, "street for excitement," is a projection because an inner danger has been externalized. The same is true for phobias in which feelings of guilt are replaced by external fears.[6] The connections between substitute and substituted are associative ones, and the paths of displacement are determined historically, somatically, and by the specific nature of the instincts involved. Sometimes the connections between the substitutes and the specific content of the unconscious are very transparent.[7]

A factor common to all phobias is regression. In childhood, dangers could be overcome by seeking the protection of seemingly omnipotent adults in the environment, and in a sense, all phobic patients behave like children whose anxieties are allayed by a comforting mother whose presence dispels fear. Such a demand for reassurance from parents or substitutes for them is especially evident in those cases of agoraphobia in which the presence of a companion is imperative. Since

[2] S. Freud, The Problem of Anxiety, New York, Psa. Quart. Press and Norton, 1936.

[3] The same point probably determines whether, in situations of real danger, fear activates purposeful defense, or paralyzes by anxiety.

[4] S. Freud, "Analysis of a Phobia in a Five-Year-Old Boy," Coll. Pap., Vol. III, London, Hogarth, 1948.

[5] S. Freud, "From the History of an Infantile Neurosis," Coll. Pap., Vol. III.

[6] S. Freud, "Repression," Coll. Pap., Vol. IV, London, Hogarth, 1948.

[7] The ways of these displacements are discussed by A. Katan-Angel in "Die Rolle der 'Verschiebung' bei der Strassenangst," Int. Z. Psa., Vol. 23, 1937.

this condition does not obtain in all agoraphobias, it is improbable that the libidinous conflict centering around the companion is an essential feature. Helene Deutsch correctly stated that in those phobias in which the presence of a companion is demanded, the companion not only represents the protecting parent, but additionally the unconsciously hated parent whose physical presence serves as a denial of unconscious destructive fantasies.[8]

That the gains of regression are secondary is often not recognized. The individual is not striving for the "helplessness" [9] of childhood but for the relative security of being protected by grown-ups. This neurotic helplessness which the patient feels as loneliness and lack of human contact is due to a remobilization of infantile instinctual conflicts.

II

Certain paths of displacement in phobias are determined directly by the specific nature of the warded-off instincts. A fear of being devoured serves the purpose of a defense against oral demands (even if these oral fears cover a more deeply repressed castration anxiety); anxiety aroused by going out onto the streets is a defense against exhibitionism; anxieties connected with high places are frequently associated with unconscious fantasies of erection, claustrophobias with fantasies of a return into the mother's body.

Not only exhibitionism and scoptophilia are warded off in agoraphobia. Abraham described "locomotor anxieties" in which the function of walking had unconsciously assumed a sexual significance. This is due to an increased erotic pleasure in walking, not necessarily identical with "muscle eroticism." [10]

A man with agoraphobia had the feeling that his legs were pulled from under him. His analysis revealed a close association between learning to walk and prohibitions against infantile masturbation. Losing his balance, losing his legs, and losing his penis were intimately interconnected. In a similar manner, many phobias are directly related to sensations of equilibrium: falling, heights, travel by automobile and by rail.

Surprisingly little attention has been given to the erogenous significance of sensations of equilibrium. In addition to Freud's comments,[11] there are few papers confined to this topic.[12] Sensations of equilibrium and position in space are important sources of sexual excitement to children and subsequently to adults.

---

[8] H. Deutsch, op. cit.

[9] F. Alexander, "Psychoanalysis Revised," Psa. Quart., Vol. 9, 1940.

[10] K. Abraham, "A Constitutional Basis of Locomotor Anxiety," Selected Papers, London, Hogarth, 1948.

[11] S. Freud, Three Essays on the Theory of Sexuality, London, Imago, 1949.

[12] T. M. French, "Psychogenic Material Related to the Function of the Semicircular Canals," Int. J. Psa., Vol. 10, 1929; P. Schilder, "Psychoanalyse des Raumes," Imago, Vol. 22, 1936, and "The Relations between Clinging and Equilibrium," Int. J. Psa., Vol. 20, 1939.

However, because the painful sensations of the affect of anxiety are partly experienced through the medium of the identical sensory apparatus which registers equilibrium, the connections between erotic pleasure and anxiety are closer in the case of "equilibrial eroticism" than in any other of the component instincts. This is confirmed by clinical experience. Conflicts emanating from the sexualization of infantile sensations of equilibrium give rise to equilibrial phobias. Furthermore, a phobia of another origin, through the association of sexual excitement with anxiety, may mobilize the infantile equilibrial eroticism.

Whoever wishes to study infantile sexuality should go to an amusement park where the concessions offer all such sensations except genital end-pleasure. Nearly all of these directly stimulate the sensory organs of equilibration and perception of the human body in space, calling forth a high degree of emotional response. Some people frankly enjoy them as sources of erotic pleasure. Others are afraid of them because they have repressed the pleasure which once was connected with these sensations. For some individuals, sensations of equilibrium and of bodily movement in space have become the sole representatives of infantile sexuality. Many who have no consciousness of infantile masturbation can recall a variety of games and fantasies about levitation, falling, floating in space, about changes in the size of the whole or parts of their bodies, of their beds being tipped or turned around, or of vaguer, similar sensations that "something is rotating." In some instances, no pleasure but only anxiety is connected with experiences of this kind, such feelings of "alienation" and fear having completely replaced the original sense of pleasure in them.

In falling asleep, archaic types of ego feeling are regressively gone through before consciousness is lost. A high percentage of these is felt as equilibrial and spatial sensations. A healthy person is usually not aware of them unless he directs his attention to them. A small number of persons whose infantile masturbation is represented by these sensations may enjoy them as a kind of masturbatory equivalent; the majority are afraid of them, and in extreme cases such fear may be the cause of severe sleep disturbances.[13] Isakower has studied sensations of this type, and has shown how they may be utilized for research in archaic phases of ego development.[14]

Narcosis (chloroform and ether) differs from normal sleep in so far as during narcosis the period of self-observation is retained longer, with the consequence that the archaic ego feelings are experienced more clearly; hence the number of neurotic reactions to narcosis. A certain number of people enjoy being anesthetized; by far the greater number develop a phobia of having to re-experience it.

---

[13] Cf. "Symposium on Neurotic Disturbances of Sleep," *Int. J. Psa.*, Vol. 23, 1942.

[14] O. Isakower, "A Contribution to the Patho-Psychology of Phenomena Associated with Falling Asleep," *Int. J. Psa.*, Vol. 19, 1938.

This type frequently develops fear of death which in analysis is found to be conceived as a consummation of these sensations. Certainly other factors are involved in the fear of death, but it can with certainty be stated that a high percentage of death phobias are phobias of sensations of equilibrium and space. Sometimes they are manifestly so, as when they are combined with fears of falling, floating, exploding, and the like.

Febrile states, too, remobilize physiologically archaic ego feelings. "Fever and Infantile Sexuality" is a clinically very important chapter still to be written. Certain children enjoy the sensations of fever; others are afraid of them. The fact that sensations which are enjoyed to a certain degree suddenly evoke extreme discomfort if this degree of intensity is exceeded is more easily observed in fever than in sleep or narcosis.

Elsewhere I have affirmed the validity of Freud's theory that sexual excitement which is blocked in its progredient genital concentration, and cannot find its natural outlet for physical or psychogenic reasons, causes anxiety and discomforting vegetative sensations.[15] These sensations consist partly of regressions to infantile equilibrial and spatial orientations. In psychoanalytic practice, when patients describe vague sensations of rotating objects, rhythmically approaching and retreating objects, sensations of crescendo and decrescendo, we often regard them as representations of a primal scene. Practically, this may well be true. But such sensations are not limited to a direct response of the psychic apparatus to an awareness of a sexual scene. They are less specifically the result of an overwhelming excitement which cannot be mastered because it transcends the capacity of the undeveloped apparatus of discharge of the tension. When, in the adult, endogenous blockings hinder the normal course and discharge of excitation, the effect is similar and fearful equilibrial and spatial sensations are reactivated.

Hence, fears of falling asleep, of being narcotized, or of having fever are expressions of underlying fears of being overwhelmed by psychologically painful sensations of disequilibrium in space. External phobic situations may represent internal sensations of which the patients were originally afraid. An inability to tolerate the sound of dripping water, the ticking of a clock, or other rhythmic sounds, is a projection of the individual's genital pulsations, emanating from repressed sexual excitement.

III

The basic role of the projection of sensations can best be demonstrated in claustrophobia.[16] These patients' dread of their own emotional excitation disturbs

---

[15] O. Fenichel, "The Concept of Trauma in Contemporary Psychoanalytical Theory," No. 4 in this volume. Here are surveyed also the causes for "neurotic fear of sexual excitation."
[16] Ibid.

its normal course, augments the original anxiety, and initiates a vicious circle.

One patient had the compulsion to leap from a moving subway train. Typically this was for her the avoidance and the simultaneous breaking through of sado-masochistic fantasies. It was her unconscious sexual aim to be beaten. Analysis showed clearly the combination of avoidance and achievement of her striving in the symptom: the motion of the subway car stimulated sexual excitement, to which the patient at first submitted with pleasurable feelings; but when the excitement reached a certain degree of intensity, she felt it imperative to escape from the subway car at any cost—that is, from the excitement itself. Further indulgence of the excitement would release the traumatic situation. The impulse to leap from the moving subway train naturally contained the idea of the vegetative sensations of the traumatic situation: loss of equilibrium, and falling in space. The neurotic fear of falling springs from the same source. To yield to the impulse to jump because of anxiety caused by sexual excitement is both an escape from the intolerable anxiety and the climax of this anxiety in the symbolic consummation of the forbidden wish.

Lewin's fine clinical study of claustrophobia [17] found, as a typical content, unconscious sexual strivings which had acquired a specific form due to infantile fantasies about intrauterine life. The development of the clinical picture of claustrophobia is facilitated by two physiological circumstances. Firstly, the imposition of any hindrance to bodily movements itself causes anxiety from a damming of drives (the fantasy of immobilization is as effective as literal restraint). Secondly, any state of anxiety is physiologically accompanied by feelings of being closed in; and thus, reversely, an external closeness (or the idea of it) facilitates the mobilization of the entire anxiety syndrome.

Being closed in is not experienced so oppressingly if one feels that it is possible to break out, and it increases to panic if all avenues of escape are closed. Persons who are afraid of trains, boats, and airplanes say that the impossibility of getting out in case of an emergency is unbearable, and that they figuratively rescue themselves from one station to the next while traveling on a train. Again, the endogenous excitement is projected onto the vehicle, and the urge to burst from the room or jump from the car is a need to escape from the intensity of this inner excitement, distorted into fearful equilibrial sensations.[18]

The close relationship between intense equilibrial stimulation and anxiety is also decisive for the psychological significance of the physical disease of seasickness. It may be that persons with repressed sexualization of body movements in space are more inclined to become seasick. It may also happen that an attack of

[17] B. D. Lewin, "Claustrophobia," *Psa. Quart.*, Vol. 4, 1935.

[18] Clinical experience shows that certain types of neurotic indecision are based on the same fear: a definite decision excludes the possibility of escape. Some forms of stubbornness, too, represent highly emotional rejections of commands which are felt to leave no loophole of escape.

seasickness activates repressed "equilibrium memories" and thus precipitates neurotic reactions.

What is feared by the patient in an enormous excitement of this kind is a breaking down of the ego. One patient felt anxiety only when someone other than himself was driving the automobile in which he was riding. "Why should I be afraid," he said, "when I can stop the car at any time?" It is the loss of voluntary decision which is feared, and it is this loss of control which is represented by a moving vehicle uninfluenced by the wish of the passenger, by a room which cannot be left at will, and also by the mounting sexual excitement approaching orgasm.

Wilhelm Reich, in his analysis of the normal and the pathological course of sexual excitement, observed that in sexual intercourse the first phase of voluntary movements is followed by an involuntary phase in which the act can no longer be interrupted voluntarily without intense displeasure.[19] This loss of ego control at the climax of sexual excitement is normally also the climax of sexual pleasure. "Orgastically impotent" egos, according to Reich, do not experience this pleasure; for them, it becomes anxiety at the loss of ego control.

IV

The majority of agoraphobics have a specific conditioning relative to the "narrowness" or "broadness" of the fearsome street. The sensation of "narrowness" is a basic element of the experience of anxiety. The first physiological symptom of fear is a feeling of constriction in the chest accompanied by difficulty in breathing. (The opposite feeling of spaciousness is physiologically coincident with mastery of fear. Nevertheless, since it represents a sudden change in the sphere of "broadness," it may also serve, through "representation by the opposite," as a symbol for "narrowness," i.e., fearfulness.) It is in an attempt to protect himself against unpleasant sensations that the patient feels the street, and not his own body, as narrow or broad. This may explain the projection in agoraphobia. There are patients who are afraid only of narrow streets, some who fear only open spaces, others who are fearful of both. Most of them fear a sudden change in the width of the street they are passing through. Many agoraphobics, like all claustrophobics, have to ensure the possibility of an escape from the fearsome environment which represents the wish for an escape from their own sensations. These conditions are more essential in agoraphobia than the demand for a companion.

V

Some phobias are allayed if the patient fulfills the phobic demand—for example, avoids the fearsome street. Another patient who avoids the streets may soon

[19] W. Reich, *Die Funktion des Orgasmus*, Vienna, Int. Psa. Verlag, 1927.

feel compelled to avoid certain rooms in his house. In the first instance, projection has succeeded; the patient now is afraid of the street *instead* of being afraid of his own excitement. In the second, the projection has failed; the dangerous instinct re-emerges from repression, and has to be projected each time. Whether or not the projection succeeds is dependent upon the economic equilibrium between instincts and anxiety, and that in turn upon the history of the personality.[20]

The projection especially of sensations of disequilibrium may succeed in relieving patients of certain anxieties, restlessness, and kinesthetic sensations, if the environment actually meets the projection halfway. External confusion and turmoil rids them of their inner confusion and anxiety. In addition to people with a thunderstorm phobia, who, by partially projecting their sensations onto the thunderstorm, externalize the condition of their anxiety, there are others who enjoy thunderstorms because the external din makes complete projection possible. Since the noise is outside and not inside they do not need to be afraid any more.[21]

In certain individuals who require "stimulation" or "distraction" to enable them to do their best work, analysis reveals neurotic disturbances of concentration which warrant systematic investigation. Their work is disturbed in these instances by an inner restlessness which is relieved in surroundings that provide external restlessness. The analysis of a man who was an excellent worker in coffeehouses (he preferred noisy ones) but was unable to work quietly at home disclosed that, while the café provided certain instinctual satisfactions (scoptophilic and homosexual), the noise and confusion served chiefly the need to relieve intrapsychic tensions in an environment that was a substitute representation of them in external reality. It would be worth while to study which types of personality, when suffering from neurotic disturbances of concentration, need absolute quiet around them, and which types need external noise. Probably this does not constitute an absolute either-or. What is comfortable and relaxing up to a certain intensity may suddenly become unpleasant and frightening beyond this intensity. Also, some timid, frightened individuals often reassure themselves by their ability to frighten others.[22] Some anxious people create an atmosphere of anxiety around them and feel better by creating the illusion that this anxiety is outside themselves. If this projection succeeds too well and they discover that people around

---

[20] Cf. S. Freud, "Repression," *Coll. Pap.,* Vol. IV.

[21] Cf. O. Fenichel, "The Counter-Phobic Attitude," No. 11 in this volume, for a discussion of the relation of phobias (in which the projective situations are avoided) to other neurotic conditions (in which the projective situations are sought after).

[22] Cf. A. Freud, "Identification with the Aggressor," *The Ego and the Mechanisms of Defence,* New York, Int. Univ. Press, 1946; T. Reik, "Aggression From Anxiety," *Int. J. Psa.,* Vol. 22, 1941; L. B. Hill, "The Use of Hostility as Defense," *Psa. Quart.,* Vol. 7, 1938; R. P. Knight, "Intimidation of Others as a Defense Against Anxiety," *Bull. Menninger Clinic,* Vol. 6, 1942.

them are really frightened, they may suddenly become excessively frightened themselves.

VI

The victim of a street phobia is not only fearful of the street, but, in interchanging the ideas, "the street is narrow" and "I feel narrow = afraid," behaves as if the street were afraid. The phobic mechanism makes use of the still effective animistic type of thinking that persists in the unconscious. There exists, moreover, one type of animistic misunderstanding of the world which is very similar to the mechanism of agoraphobia and which is commonly experienced in everyday life as well as in psychopathology. In an excellent paper published in 1912, Hanns Sachs [23] clarified the role of narcissistic projection in the feelings with which we react to nature. Consciousness of nature is less a process of becoming aware of the physical elements of nature than of becoming aware of feelings evoked in the individual by the contemplation of these elements. One's feelings are then consciously believed to be identical with these external realities. This is not to say that all emotional responses to nature are based on projections of one's feelings onto nature. An object in nature may also represent other external objects, and the emotions seemingly aroused by it may be displaced from them. A mountain, for example, may represent the father's penis, the endless ocean or desert, the mother's womb. But even if that is the case, the narcissistic element is never entirely missing. The person, experiencing himself in a landscape, does not simply feel love or hatred for the father-mountain or the mother-ocean, but undergoes a kind of identification with them. He feels the *unio mystica* with the nature-parents.

We may assume that projections are always operating in the consciousness of nature. The aesthetic categories in which landscapes are placed support this assumption. The landscape is "sublime" or "depressing" because the individual feels sublime or depressed in it. The same landscape has a different effect according to different moods of the observer.

The common observation that certain landscapes mobilize similar feelings in different people is also correct. The endless stretch of flat prairies makes many people melancholy; mountains usually make people more active and impulsive. This is due to the reflective effect of projections onto the ego.

There are innumerable preferences, prejudices, and anxieties associated with types of landscapes, changes of weather and season, light and darkness, times of the day, etc., which, if studied in detail, would teach much about the projective mechanism in question, and about the ontogenetic connections between infantile sexual excitement and the sensations which are later projected.

Projections of sensations, especially of equilibrial and spatial sensations, are

[23] H. Sachs, "Ueber Naturgefuehl," *Imago*, Vol. I, 1912.

not limited to the phobias and the "consciousness of nature." They also make their appearance in all kinds of ego regressions because the development of the reality principle not only means the abandonment of a primitive tendency to see the world as one would like it to be, but also of a primitive tendency to see the world not as it is, but as one is oneself. For instance, "animistic misunderstandings" of this kind in which proprioceptive sensations are involuntarily expressed manifest themselves in children's drawings of external objects,[24] in various schizophrenic phenomena,[25] and even in the child's simple castration fear.[26] These problems, however, are already beyond the scope of phobias.

VII

Observations are presented to supplement the theory of phobias—especially with reference to disturbances of the (eroticized) sense of equilibrium and of the body in space—in persons and in situations in which subjective excitations tend to be transformed into anxiety.

The fact that these anxiety-producing sensations are projected onto the phobically endowed objects is especially stressed. This fact, which has been marked by Freud and Abraham, is here presented in a somewhat different light.

In emphasizing the importance of the fear of overwhelming inner excitement as a source of anxiety in the phobias, little has been said here about the fear of castration and the fear of being abandoned. These are neither denied nor minimized. These deeper forms of infantile anxiety are the very root of the development of the fear that the ego will be flooded with its own excitement. The infant, not yet able to satisfy its demands, frequently experiences "traumatic situations." The memory of such frightening experiences certainly forms the basis for the tendency of the ego to anticipate and avoid them. In so far as this is the basis of all later fears, we may say that all anxieties are fears of being flooded by unmanageable quantities of excitement. When the ego has developed sufficiently to achieve adequate instinctual satisfaction and to master reality, instinctual temptations should not be avoided as dangerous but anticipated as pleasurable. In an adult ego the idea that excitement is necessarily dangerous emerges only when satisfaction is frustrated by endogenous obstacles, that is, by fears of castration or of loss of love, originating in animistic misinterpretations of the external world.

[24] S. Spielrein, "Kinderzeichnungen bei offenen und geschlossenen Augen," *Imago*, Vol. 17, 1931.

[25] For example, in the "Influencing Machine" (V. Tausk, "On the Origin of the 'Influencing Machine' in Schizophrenia," *Psa. Quart.*, Vol. 2, 1933) or in the projection of bowel sensations onto the object of a delusion of persecution (J. H. W. van Ophuijsen, "On the Origin of the Feeling of Persecution," *Int. J. Psa.*, Vol. 1, 1920; A. Staercke, "The Reversal of the Libido-Sign in Delusions of Persecution," *Int. J. Psa.*, Vol. 1, 1920). From a different point of view, the same phenomena are discussed by F. S. Cohn in "Practical Approach to the Problem of Narcissistic Neuroses," *Psa. Quart.*, Vol. 9, 1940.

[26] Cf. O. Fenichel, "Early Stages of Ego Development," No. 3 in this volume.

TWENTY-ONE

Anorexia *

I was doubtful whether to tell you in a more general way how psychoanalysis approaches the problem of anorexia, or whether to tell you about the material produced by this particular patient. This material, however, gained in but two interviews of about one hour's duration each, was so impressive that I prefer to do the latter. Let me make only two short theoretical remarks as an introduction:

(1) You know that a refusal to eat is a frequent symptom of the major psychoses. No depressive person is able to eat; and the withdrawal from the objective world in schizophrenia manifests itself sometimes as a refusal of active eating, which makes tube feeding necessary. It may occur that a depression or a schizophrenia starts with this symptom before any other symptom makes its appearance, and thus may mask itself as an anorexia. Some so-called anorexias are equivalents of depression. We have first to exclude the possibility that an "anorexia" may cover a major psychosis. Fortunately, we are able to do so in the case in question, for this patient showed no signs of either depression or schizophrenia.

(2) The psychoanalytic approach rejects from the beginning a question like: Is a given case hormonally determined or psychogenic? The hormonal state of an organism is the source of its instinctual demands and therefore determines the nature and intensity of its mental conflicts; and a mental experience, for instance when creating an "oral fixation," certainly changes the hormonal state secondarily. This patient doubtless had hormonal disturbances. Their detailed discussion is your field, not mine. I am going to talk only about the psychic material which the patient told me during two hours. Of course, the order in which I am going

* This paper was first presented at Los Angeles in August, 1945. Dr. Fenichel's manuscript has been translated into English, in conformity with the other papers, but no attempt has been made to give it the final form Dr. Fenichel might have given it if he had prepared it for publication.

to present the material is not the order in which it was given to me by the patient, but is due to my dynamic psychoanalytic thinking.

I. The patient, a woman, had an exaggerated interest in all matters related to food, and this interest was not only a negative but also a positive one. Recently she had read a lot of books about diet and vitamins, and she had started doing this not only in order to combat her loss of appetite, but even before the loss occurred. She liked to cook and to bake, to serve food to others, and to feed other people (things which are frequent in persons who have conflicts about their original wishes centered around being fed). The patient reported that throughout her life she had an inclination to become hungry whenever she felt angry. We shall see that she probably also felt hungry whenever she became sexually excited. In other words, eating was for her a general means of expressing emotional excitement. Conflicts around any kind of emotional excitement expressed themselves as conflicts around eating. She was "orally fixated."

It is true that the patient was not only interested in cooking but in all kinds of housework. As a young girl she had had the idea that she would not want to marry a rich man because then she would not be supposed to do her housework herself. She also liked to do things in strict order; she loved systems and schedules. From the analytic point of view, she was not only orally, but in general pregenitally fixated.

Let us go back to her oral fixations: In puberty, at the age of thirteen, the patient was obese and used to eat a lot. She had the feeling that she never could get enough. She had severe conflicts with her mother, who refused to let her eat as much as she wanted. It seems that there were also other times in which the situation was the other way round: the mother wanted her to eat and she refused. At least there are two points which make it probable that such periods existed: (a) at the age of seven the patient was so thin that this caused worry, and (b) when describing the Jewish surroundings in which she is living at present and which she does not like, she mentioned that she could not stand Jewish women coming to visit her and bringing her food, and asking her to eat more; and she could not stand the Jewish people around her having no other interests than "delicatessen."

II. The patient's not eating, which constituted her anorexia, started as a voluntary business. When she came back from Berkeley she was told that she looked so pretty since she was thin. She liked this and started a kind of diet. Somehow this dieting got out of control. While at first she did not want to eat much, she later became unable to eat.

III. Her conflicts around eating had—superficially—to do with the "wish to leave a given neighborhood." In Berkeley, where she was happy in the beginning, because for the first time she was alone with her husband, she could not find an apartment and was compelled to live in a store, where the baby hurt itself on the cement floor, and after a fall of rain the water stood on the floor several inches high. She wanted to get away and succeeded in inducing her husband to give up his good job at the shipyards and return to Los Angeles.

In Los Angeles there came a new disappointment. They did not find an apartment either and lived first together with the patient's mother (toward whom the patient's feelings were very ambivalent), and later only one block away from her mother, in a Jewish environment, represented to the patient by feeding Jewish women and "delicatessen." She wants to get away and her not eating has the significance of a protest against her living in this neighborhood. Actually all difficulties began at Passover. The patient does not like "matzoh" and did not eat bread. The Jewish question concerns her a lot; although not religious, she is still not capable at present of eating butter and meat together.

IV. The patient protests against her neighborhood. What does this neighborhood mean to her? Not only the mother, who, at one time—in adolescence—fed her too little, and at another time (supposedly) too much. Her relationship to her husband, too, is very problematic. He avoids the "happy home life" which the patient is craving for. He again has a job at the shipyards, but besides this he does night work at the prize fights and Sunday work at a golf course. He never has time for her. He comes home for dinner and eats with his eyes on his watch because he has to leave again. He does so because he wants to earn more money to give to his mother. Probably this circumstance is not important. (But it may be that it is important. In the beginning of their relationship there were arguments around questions of "your family," "my family." Perhaps also the patient's longing for an undisturbed dinner, that is, for a meal, was of importance.) More important was the fact that the husband was hasty and restless and the patient was longing for rest; also that he did not like order and systems, whereas she needed to have her systems obeyed. Since the patient has been in the hospital she has felt better and is able to eat.

A preliminary summary of the case shows us that the patient's refusal of food is a protest (a) against husband and mother; (b) against her own wish to eat much, which was manifest in adolescence and represents her emotional needs.

V. Behind the husband, the figure of the mother seems to be decisive. The mother is a dominant, strict person who always overshadowed the father; she taught the children to fulfill their duty and used to scold the father. The conflicts around eating in the patient's adolescence seem to have been a kind of equivalent of conflicts which other adolescent girls may have with their mothers around sexuality. The mother, by the way, according to the patient's description, changed very much after the father's death, four years ago. Her severe heart disease seems to have been overcome, she wants to be young again, and has several men friends. There seems to be a kind of rivalry between mother and daughter.

The patient's marriage, incidentally, started in an unhappy way. What she liked in this man was only the fact that he loved her. While they were engaged, she wanted to call off the whole thing but he began to cry and she was so moved that she called off the calling off. She calls her husband "selfish" and says that he showed his "real self" only after they were married. He has frequent temper tantrums.

VI. Concerning her own wish to eat much, which she has to repress, there are many facts which make it indirectly probable that her eating in adolescence stood in place of sexual urges. The most outstanding fact is that she did not feel sexual urges at that time at all. She had no sexual intercourse before her marriage, though she had not only boy friends with whom "she went" but went with her subsequent husband for two years before marrying him. When she started intercourse after marriage she was totally frigid. By the way, after about a year this frigidity was overcome spontaneously and the patient experienced orgasm; during the last year, that is, since the anorexia developed, she has been frigid once more. The patient did not know "the facts of life" until she married. She has no sexual childhood memories whatsoever. All this brings out how intense her sexual repression must have been.

The patient has two younger brothers, one seven years, one eleven years her junior. When the second brother was born, the mother's pregnancy was thought to be very dangerous because of her heart disease and she spent most of the time in a sanitarium away from home, so that the patient did not see her. Before the first brother was born, however, the mother lived together with her daughter at home. The latter has no memory about her mother's pregnancy, but I may remind you that it was exactly at the age of seven that the patient did not eat and became so thin that the family worried about it.

VII. Why does the patient's protest take the form of refusing food? She calls herself "very stubborn." It seems that she is right in this respect. Her own child, now two and a half years of age, who was already able to talk some time ago, gives trouble by not talking. He, too, seems to express a kind of "oral stubbornness." It may be speculated that the mother's stubbornness provoked a corresponding stubbornness in the child. It may be added that children who protest against their mothers by not eating are not necessarily always protesting against being given too much. They may have specific wishes about how or what to be fed, and their not eating may mean "if you don't give me exactly what I want, I won't eat anything."

VIII. The patient's protest against her mother was certainly not a whole-hearted one. She also loved her mother and therefore accepted her threats and punishments. Her mother used to put a great deal of emphasis on "fulfilling one's duties," and the patient is extremely conscientious and dutiful. She expects constantly to be criticized or rejected, and before making any "confession" she is used to saying, "And now you are going to despise me."

IX. The "rest" in the hospital, that is, the change of environment which sig-nifies an escape and enables the patient to give up her stubbornness, has a char-acteristic forerunner. As a young girl she had had a room of her own with many books in it. She used to retire into this room and read all day. She developed a high reading intellectuality, and it is probable that reading equaled eating in her unconscious. If we assume that her eating difficulties stand for sexual wants, it is interesting to what fields her reading interests turn. She used to read about psy-chology, astrology, palmistry—and in the last years, about dieting and vitamins.

X. The patient has the feeling that she could eat again if (a) her husband would give up his night work and spend more time with her; (b) she could move and leave the Jewish surroundings. It may be noted that in her longing for her husband to give up the many jobs there is no hidden jealousy. She knows that he does not spend his time with other women, but she wants to have "rest" together with him and to have "home life" and "home work" with him.

When I spoke with the patient for the second time she was very confident and obviously dissimulating. Her husband had actually given up one of the two side jobs and she had eaten well here in the hospital. These two circumstances gave her hope that she would now be able to eat well at home, too. Of course I reassured her and did not discourage her belief. However, for myself, I remained very skeptical about the possibility that so deep-seated a disturbance could really be overcome by two talks in combination with a mild physical treatment.

The second patient, a man, was of an extremely different type. If anorexia is defined as an extreme loss of appetite or even of the ability to eat, then he had no anorexia. He did not have the experience "I can't eat," but he rather felt a com-mand of "I must not eat." He did not lose the capacity to enjoy food, but rather he had two contradictory feelings in order to explain why he actually did not eat. On the one hand, he felt an ascetic pride of "I must not give in to a sensual enjoyment of this kind"; on the other hand, he ate extremely slowly in order to enjoy it as long as possible. In other words, he was a compulsion neurotic.

This patient impressed me immediately by his way of talking. He talked slowly, particularly, and in an especially ordered way, logically and not emo-tionally, explaining things and not expressing himself directly. This is characteristic for compulsive types. At the same time, the patient talked in a very child-ish and naïve way; he was immature in his behavior as well as in his opinions. He struck me as being like a boy of sixteen, rather than as a man of his real age of twenty-two. On the other hand, he was not like an average sixteen-year-old, because he was dry, theoretical, and intellectual, without immediate emo-tional contact. He was not capable of being simply happy, or unhappy, or afraid, or sad, like other people. His substitute for happiness was his slow way of eating. "I enjoy my food."

The patient's immaturity manifested itself in a positive and a negative way. In its positive sense, he had no other interests in this world than to play around with railroad timetables. Since he became an accountant, the accounting figures could fortunately substitute a little for the timetables. In its negative sense, he simply did not know any sexuality. He never had an ejaculation, did not know what "masturbation" meant, and was not sure whether or not he had ever had wet dreams: "Sometimes I feel a little moist in the morning, but I never re-member a dream." Asked about sexual matters, he only gave a detailed ac-count of where and when he had gotten knowledge about sexual facts; he dis-cussed the subject "scientifically" and insisted that it never disturbed him "emo-tionally." It did not make any difference for him—at least that is what he stated —whether he was together with girls or with boys. For instance, in his present office he was among a lot of girls, but that did not make any impression on him. In other words, the sex of the people around him did not interest him, because the people around him did not interest him, because he had no direct emotional contact with his fellow men. To summarize what has been said up to now, this patient was an obsessional neurotic and severely disturbed in his psychical mat-uration.

This diagnosis was confirmed by the fact that the patient had a lot of other obsessional symptoms, some to do with food and eating, some not.

His books had to stand in a very exact order and he could at times spend hours in putting the regular and the classified telephone books so exactly on top of each other that no edge stuck out. After his parents came home in the evening, he used to get up from bed to make sure that they had closed the door of the apartment properly. Historically, the oldest compulsion he knew of was a com-pulsive rubbing of the nose, a habit which he indulged in at the age of six or seven, and which was irritating to his parents: it also indicated to the interview-ing psychoanalyst that his sex disturbance must be connected with some early childhood conflict revolving around masturbation.

But the patient also had symptoms concerning food as a little child.

(a) His father used to come home from work in the afternoon and therefore the parents had American meal times, taking dinner in the afternoon. This was believed to be unhygienic for a boy and he got his dinner alone at noon. He rejected this system by simply not eating. At that time, this was conscious obstinacy with a conscious purpose: he did not want to eat in isolation but together with his parents. His clinging to his parents was characteristic for him and we shall come back to it later.

(b) Between the ages of six and twelve he was a problem child in respect to eating. His difficulties had already at that time the double nature of "you must not have pleasure" and "I want to prolong my pleasure." (In parenthesis I may add the theoretical remark that a combination of "you must not give way" and a prolongation of pleasure by not giving way is typically experienced by children in the anal sphere, where withholding of the feces is at the same time a "not yet" and a prolongation of a pleasurable stimulation.)

(c) The most interesting symptom was that all these compulsions concerning eating were preceded by a phobia concerning eating. As a little child, the patient could not eat eggs. He ran away when he saw eggs, he vomited when he was forced to stay, and he even vomited when he saw the egg cups out of which the eggs were eaten. I may add that we know that most compulsion neuroses are secondary elaborations of phobias of early childhood. Why eggs, we do not know. It is pure speculation if we think of the fact that eggs are things out of which chickens come.

We mentioned that the patient's clinging to his parents was characteristic. In school he was the "sissy," never had friends, was bad in gym and did not participate in athletics, whereas he was a good pupil in all intellectual disciplines; the boys on the street used to laugh at him and he was afraid of leaving the house.

What we know about the parents explains to us the character of the patient. He was a typically spoiled only child. He was quite a big boy when he still used the potty instead of going to the toilet. His mother still used to dress him when he had already been going to school for a long time. She used to warn him that strange children, other boys, gymnastics, and all physical activities were dangerous. He believed it and clung to the mother.

Both parents had obsessional characters themselves. The father was said to be very "nice" but from time to time he flew into a temper—for instance, if a spoon dropped to the floor; the patient added, not because his father was so orderly, but because clumsiness made him angry. His mother loved housework and order, though, it is true, not in so exaggerated a manner as the patient himself.

As a child the patient was constipated. He was told that he was trained to cleanliness already as a baby, that he never soiled, that he never gave difficulties in respect of cleanliness, but only in respect of food. His whole character make-up makes it probable that this training was too early and too intense and ended with the repression of unchanged wishes for disorder and dirt.

About the present prevalent trouble of "you must not eat," which the patient explained by the two contradictory feelings of "you must not have pleasure" and "it is better to prolong your pleasure," we only know that he always had the ideal of a very thin and ascetic-looking young man. We can assume that the patient, who had early in life successfully repressed his anal drives and who had probably, for that very reason, not developed his genital sexual drive at all and had always accepted the rule "any pleasure of the body is dangerous," felt the danger of a rebellion of his repressed bodily feelings in the way he enjoyed his food. He got into a conflict between the contradictory ideas of "I want to have at least my pleasure in food" and "I must be punished for this wish by not eating at all."

About precipitating factors, we only know that the idea "you must not eat" was a result of a period of obsessive brooding with which the patient filled out a vacation time, which he, unable to have a friend, spent quite alone. Vacation meant for him stopping of accounting, and accounting, continuing his earlier play with railroad timetables, was probably the only outlet he had. When this was taken away from him during a vacation, all his conflicts were intensified.

As to therapeutic results, we must be still more doubtful than in the first case. Obsessional neuroses which have resulted in so intense a loneliness and barring of free emotions are very difficult to treat. What I tried to do was to show the patient intellectually that something was missing in his life which made human life worth while; namely, direct experience of emotions in contact with one's fellow men. For the time being, he fights his compulsion by means of a counter-compulsion. "Since I had to come to a hospital, I see that it is not good not to eat; I must eat, whether I like it or not." He is confident that in this way he will overcome his so-called anorexia. I am not sure whether he has understood that in this way he still will be a sick boy.

TWENTY - TWO

Neurotic Acting Out [*]

IN MOST cases it is not very purposeful to start an analytic investigation with an exact definition of the phenomenon to be investigated. The exact definition should rather be the result of the research, not its starting point. But an inexact definition, as an approximative description, is necessary to make clear what one is going to talk about. Obviously, all "neurotic acting out" has the following in common: It is an acting which unconsciously relieves inner tension and brings a partial discharge to warded-off impulses (no matter whether these impulses express directly instinctual demands, or are reactions to original instinctual demands, e.g. guilt feelings); the present situation, somehow associatively connected with the repressed content, is used as an occasion for the discharge of repressed energies; the cathexis is displaced from the repressed memories to the present "derivative," and this displacement makes the discharge possible.

This definition is certainly correct; but it is insufficient. If a person who was unable to express an anger against his boss is in a general angry mood against everybody, or if a person, after having repressed an infantile sexual temptation, produces a neurotic symptom as a distorted expression of his repressed wish, or if a person develops feelings towards his analyst which he once had toward his father, all these phenomena are also in accordance with the above definition—but they are no "acting out." What is the relation of "acting out" to "displacement," "symptom formation," and "transference"?

All these phenomena have in common that the pressure of repressed forces toward discharge disturbs the function of reality testing and the ability of the ego to react adequately. But "acting out," as distinguished from the other phenomena, is an acting, not a mere feeling, not a mere thinking, not a mere mimic expression, not a mere single movement. This fact distinguishes it from symp-

[*] First published in *Psa. Rev.*, Vol. 32, 1945, pp. 197–206.

tom formation. It is true that there are also symptoms which involve a certain acting; but these symptoms actually could also be called "acting out." In general, compulsive acts, for example, are not included in the conception of "acting out," because they are limited in their extent, and because they are experienced as strange and not as ego-syntonic. If certain rituals are rationalized to such an extent that the subject identifies himself with them, they certainly can be included in the conception of "acting out." Concerning the relationship to "displacement" we may state: "Displacement" is the mechanism by which "acting out" is achieved; but not every displacement results in "acting out."

Upon what does it depend whether the displacement substitute for what has been warded off is expressed in mere thoughts or single movements—or whether it results in acting? It is not easy to give an answer to this question immediately. The first idea is that this might be due to the circumstance whether or not the ego found a possibility of rationalization. When the ego succeeds in pretending that it is purposeful or that some ideal is fulfilled in that way, acts may be performed which otherwise would have been blocked. But this cannot be the decisive factor. Neurotic acting out is not always well rationalized. There are people who act absolutely irrationally, who have no tolerance toward tensions whatsoever and give in to every neurotic impulse, without asking themselves why they are acting that way.

With "transference" mere acting out has in common an insufficient differentiation between the present and the past, an unwillingness to learn, a readiness to substitute certain rigid reactive patterns for adequate responses to actual stimuli. But these reactive patterns again are not necessarily real actions—sometimes they consist in mere emotional attitudes; and we rather call it "transference" if the attitude concerns certain definite persons, and "acting out" if something has to be done regardless toward whom.

Actually, there is no human action which is not influenced by the individual's past, and which would not, to a certain extent, give discharge to other impulses of the associative neighborhood. But the normal individual recognizes the differences between the present situation and the patterns he has acquired in his past, and is able to modify these patterns according to the present situation. The higher the pressure of repressed impulses toward motility, the more actuality is taken as a mere precipitating factor which brings occasion to let out something quite different. The analyst then has to show to the observing part of the patient's ego the irrationality of his actions, splitting the observing part of the ego from the actual acting part. This task is made difficult by the ego-syntonic character of the action in question. "Acting out" is more dangerous than mere transference feelings, because it may have more real consequences.

The analytic situation furthers transference as well as acting out in a twofold way: (a) The unemotional and steady attitude of the analyst diminishes the component of "actual adequate response" in the patient's utterances and increases relatively the "irrational" component; (b) the analytic process, by educating the patient to produce less and less distorted derivatives of his repressed impulses, mobilizes and provokes all repressed impulses. That is the reason why "acting out" is relatively more frequent in persons who undergo analytic treatment (therefore we ask our patients not to make decisions of vital importance during analysis); and therefore we will now have to distinguish between acting out outside and inside of psychoanalysis.

I. Acting out outside of psychoanalysis:

We usually distinguish between "symptom neuroses" and "character neuroses." You know that the relation between neurotic symptoms and neurotic character trends is a reciprocal one: Infantile symptom neuroses, mostly phobias, are reacted to by the development of certain attitudes or reaction patterns which represent changes in the realm of the ego of a relatively rigid nature; they impoverish the whole personality, but being done once and for all, they bring the advantage of sparing the individual subsequent acute conflicts. Subsequently, however, such neurotic character trends may or may not form the basis for the development of other secondary symptom neuroses. Today, character neuroses are much more frequent than symptom neuroses, certainly due to general changes in the usual educational attitudes; and these changes in their turn are socially determined. A subdivision of "character neurosis" is formed by people who not only develop rigid defense attitudes, but who arrange to meet certain experiences, corresponding to certain unconscious needs, again and again; they have been called "neuroses of fate." The patients may either actively provoke certain experiences, or the experiences seem to happen to them passively. Alexander, in first describing "neurotic character" as a nosological unit,[1] had those persons in mind (whereas we classify them today as a subtype of "neurotic character"). He was of the opinion that their analytic treatment is easier than that of symptom neurotics, because they are ready to act, whereas the "autoplastic" neurotics, during their analysis, have to learn to develop the courage to take the decisive step to alloplastic action. Is it not rather the other way round? Such persons are not really "alloplastic"; they have no object relationships, but only pseudorelationships; they misuse objects for attempts to solve their intrapsychic conflicts; to cure them, it is necessary to make them understand this, to bring them back to their conflicts, to make them autoplastic first, and then to treat them like average neurotics. The higher the pressure from the repressed, the more compulsive and the more ir-

[1] F. Alexander, "The Neurotic Character," *Int. J. Psa.,* Vol. 11, 1930.

resistible their impulses to neurotic action become. Nevertheless, not all persons under high mental tension "act out."

Certain forms of pathological reaction, often described as "impulse neuroses," are characterized by intense irresistible impulses, which are experienced more like drives than as compulsions. The insight into the structure of these neuroses probably will be of great help for an understanding also of less stereotyped "acting out." In summarizing the psychoanalytical insights into the structure of these impulse neuroses, we can say: The "irresistible impulses" serve the purpose either to escape from a (real or imaginative) danger, or to deny a danger, or to reassure against a danger. We have to add that this formula is valid only if we include the possibility of depression into the conception of "danger." This defensive purpose of the pathological impulses does not exclude that they may bring simultaneously a distorted instinct satisfaction of a sexual or aggressive nature. But only the fact that this satisfaction is condensed with a defensive purpose (or: made possible again by a successful defense against a supposed danger) explains the irresistible nature of the impulse. The defensive aims may or may not be achieved. Compulsive running away, for example, means either a running away from punishment or temptation, or a running toward reassurance (and satisfaction, becoming accessible again by reassurance). Kleptomania means in principle to take possession of things which give the strength or the power to fight supposed dangers. This is not the place to discuss the relation of these impulses to the psychogenesis of the perversions. But the impulse neuroses are certainly rooted in an early phase of development in which striving for security and striving for sexual satisfaction were not yet differentiated from each other.[2] The infant is dependent on the mother's care in physical, sexual, and self-esteem respects simultaneously. Just as there are persons with oral fixations, there are also persons with fixations on oral types of the regulation of their self-esteem, dependent on external supplies, on being loved, on getting. Being fixated to the oral phase of development, they tend to react to frustrations with violence, and their main conflict is a conflict between a tendency to take by violence what was not given to them, and a tendency to repress all aggressiveness, out of fear of loss of love, that is, fear of getting still less in the future. It does not make much difference which person gives the necessary supply; the objects are not yet persons —only the deliverers of supply, and therefore interchangeable. And actually such a relative unimportance of the partner's personality is characteristic of all "acting out" too. The same oral type of regulation of self-esteem forms the dispositional basis for depression; it may even be permissible to state that depression is the

[2] Cf. O. Fenichel, "Neuroses Related to Perversions," *Outline of Clinical Psychoanalysis,* New York, Norton, 1934.

state into which such persons fall, if the necessary supplies are missing.[3] The identity of the basic disposition for pathological impulses and for depression corresponds to the fact that most impulsive acts serve the purpose of avoiding depressions. Naturally it makes a great difference whether the supply is demanded from a real object, or whether the subject is regressed to narcissism and directs his demands to the own superego only. All this is best studied in addicts, in whom structure and clinical pictures are similar, but more complicated by the chemical effect of the drugs; this complication is absent in the "acting out-neurotic characters," who otherwise are comparable to addicts.

The spontaneous "acting out" is not only comparable to addiction. It is also similar to the characteristic "repetitions" of the traumatic neurotic. Often the actions which are repeated have a very impressive and dramatic character; we may speak of "traumatophilic" persons. The repetition symptoms of traumatic neurotics serve the purpose of achieving a belated mastery of experiences which brought too great an amount of excitement to be mastered in a normal way. Children also usually repeat impressive experiences in their play, often without being aware of the repetitious character; the event which once was experienced passively in too intense a manner is now repeated actively while the ego may determine the dosage of the excitement on a bearable level.[4] Certain types of "acting out" serve the same purpose. The attitude "I have to bring about a certain experience to ward off a certain danger, or to enforce the necessary protective supplies" does not exclude the attitude "I have to bring about a certain experience to get rid of a disturbing overwhelming impression." We have to remember that there are combinations of traumatic neuroses and psychoneuroses, people who are impressed by some overwhelming infantile trauma, for instance a primal scene, whose life is overshadowed by both the compulsion to repeat the traumatic experience again and again (for the sake of a belated mastery), and the fear of repetition of the trauma. Whereas a simple traumatic neurosis, for instance after an automobile accident, is cured spontaneously in the course of time—the high amounts of excitement gradually finding their discharge—these people are in a worse situation: Experiencing their own sexual excitement as a danger signal, they try to stop it, which results in certain displeasurable sensations; thus they are in the same situation as if the man with the automobile accident would have a new accident every time he is trying to drive a car again.[5]

Now we can try to formulate the preconditions for "acting out" (as contrasted to mere "transference" of feelings): (a) A (perhaps constitutional) "al-

---

[3] Cf. S. Rado, "The Problem of Melancholia," *Int. J. Psa.,* Vol. 9, 1928; and G. Gero, "Construction of Depression," *Int. J. Psa.,* Vol. 17, 1936.

[4] Cf. S. Freud, *Beyond the Pleasure Principle,* London, Hogarth, 1948.

[5] Cf. O. Fenichel, "The Concept of Trauma in Contemporary Psychoanalytical Theory," No. 4 in this volume.

loplastic readiness"; (b) fixations on orality, high narcissistic need, and intolerance toward tensions; (c) early traumata.

II. *Acting out inside of psychoanalysis:*

If persons of the "acting out" type undergo psychoanalytic treatment, they certainly will produce the "acting out" also in their analysis. People who have the same psychic structure, but who have not produced a spontaneous acting out because these tendencies were not strong enough or were counterweighted by opposite tendencies, may be induced by the psychoanalytic mobilization of unconscious tendencies to begin to "act out" during their cure. But even people with other psychic structures may begin to "act out" while in analysis—as a form of "transference." The acting out can be done during the analytic session ("transference actions") or outside of the session. As a simple example of the latter we may think of persons who discuss their analysis in detail with a friend —carrying away a part of the material from the analysis, but also getting satisfaction or frustration from the reacting friend, which the unresponsive analyst refuses. It is clear that persons who need certain reactions from their environment, without much taking into consideration the special personality of their objects, are more inclined to actions of this kind—and these are again the "oral characters."

From the standpoint of the cure, all these actions have to be looked upon as resistances. It is true that the unconscious content which the analyst is looking for unveils itself, but it does so in the wrong place and in a distorted connection; and it does so in a way which makes more difficult the main task of psychoanalysis: to force the patient's ego to face his impulses and their true nature. "The patient acts out his memories instead of recalling them" means that he avoids facing them and keeping them at the necessary distance—by means of the "short circuit" of acting.

It is true that acting out may also have advantages. (a) It is a source for the gaining of material; the analyst may be enabled directly to observe the patient's past (supposing the patient does not keep silent about what he is "acting out" outside of his sessions). (b) Acting out increases the demonstrability of the actuality of the material. After having felt the impulse to act out, the patient certainly will no longer be able to believe that certain childhood influences are far away from his present state.

But both advantages can only be used as such if the actions are, as soon as possible, followed by interpretation and understanding. If the ego-syntonic character of the acting makes such an interpretation impossible, the acting out is, for the analysis, a loss, because material which has been mobilized by the analytic process finds an outlet without any insight into its true nature. Acting out which is not immediately followed by interpretation is "simply a mishap," Freud stated once. It is perhaps necessary to stress this resistance aspect of "acting out" especially, because there are certain analysts who overestimate the therapeutic effectiveness of "abreaction" and underestimate a slow "working through," and who therefore like dramatic scenes in their analyses. Just as a "counter-transference" of the analyst may correspond to the "transference" of the patient, so also a tendency for "acting out" on the part of the analyst may endanger his work as much as such a tendency on the part of the patient. I would like to add that long experience in training and control analyses showed that individualized "counter-transference" of analysts toward certain patients are very rarely any hindrance of analytic work; but a tendency on the part of the analyst to "act out" some unconscious inner conflicts of his by means of "the patients" in general, is a much greater danger.

In general we can say: When a patient who was very rigid and introverted and who never dared to feel his emotions as real and actual, in the course of his psychoanalysis begins for the first time to "act out"—this is a progress to be welcomed. When a person has a general tendency to "act out," using the speed of his acting for befogging the true nature of his impulses, this is a resistance which has to be checked.

In technical respect, acting out gives us but one, though a very decisive, specific problem: How can we induce the patient to substitute studying of his impulses for following them, or at least to observe and to judge first critically what he is intending to do. If the patient's ego is reasonable enough to admit that his actions have not been rational and adequate, and to become curious about their real nature, the interpretation of acting out does not give any specific problem. But what can be done if such a reasonable ego is missing, and the action is accepted as ego-syntonic and unproblematic? I hope that a number of case histories in the following symposium will bring the answer to this question. Certainly in different cases, various things might be done. But looked upon theoretically, I think that all these various things eventually are based on the same principle: Where there is no reasonable ego, ready to see and to acknowledge its true motives, it has to be created. That is best done by utilizing the healthy remnants of the ego, in order to enlarge it gradually to proportions suitable for analytic work—if necessary by variations in technique suited to the ego remnants.

There is one thing which is of special help in this respect, and which simultaneously is the best prophylactic against "acting out as a resistance": well-timed interpretation of the transference. If persons who did not spontaneously act out, begin to act out as a resistance during an analytic cure, this is mostly due to a mistake in timing of transference interpretations. It is true that a transference attitude might be interpreted too early; it should not be interpreted before it has developed enough to show clearly its specific nature and meaning. But a transference attitude might also be interpreted too late. The connection between the repressed contents and the actuality becomes closer and the demonstrability of its transference character decreases, if the attitude is not attacked analytically at the right time. Some types of acting out are reminiscent of inoperable malignant tumors whose operation was omitted.

A special question is the carrying away of the transference from the analysis. This may become dangerous for the whole analysis and has to be stopped. But how can this be done? In principle, there are only three possibilities: It may be stopped by analytic interpretation, by an especially inviting behavior on the part of the analyst, or by active prohibitions given by the analyst.

The analytic interpretation is certainly the method of choice. But unfortunately, the simple demonstration of the resistance purpose of the behavior will not work if the patient is seduced by his strong impulses. The analyst first has to establish the conditions in which analytic interpretation of the resistance may become possible. As we said before, this may sometimes be done simply by proper timing of transference interpretations. In other cases, especially in those "traumatophilic" character cases, whose whole life history is a history of "acting out," no interpretation seems to be "properly timed."

An especially inviting behavior on the part of the analyst is out of the question, because the transference would become still less transparent, if the analyst reacted to the patient's actions with specific and artificial counter actions.

So it seems as if in certain cases a direct prohibition of the patient's acting would become necessary. As you know, one-half of Ferenczi's suggestions about an "active technique" [6] consisted in such prohibitions. Their danger lies in the following fact: The impulses of the patient have once before met with prohibitions, which was the cause of his pathogenic repressions. An analyst who actively prohibits his patient's impulses might be perceived as a replica of the parents, who once forbade the utterances of infantile sexuality. In general, the analyst has every reason to encourage and not to discourage instinctive expressions, and certainly he has to avoid being looked upon as a threatening castrator. That is the reason why prohibitions should be avoided as long as possible; if they cannot be avoided, they have to be given in a way which tries to avoid any possibility of their being perceived as castration threats. If possible, it is best if the prohibition can be combined with the first method, the analytic interpretation. This means: if it is possible, it should be shown to the patient why the prohibition has become necessary; it is still better if the situation can be explained in such a way

[6] S. Ferenczi, *Further Contributions to the Theory and Technique of Psycho-Analysis,* London, Hogarth, 1950.

that the patient himself decides to impose the prohibition upon himself. You can "prohibit" in such a way that it looks more like a mere advice or suggestion. And if all that does not succeed, it is necessary to analyze as soon as possible the castration threat which has been involved in the prohibition.

I am sure that if the ways of successful handling of "acting out" as a resistance are studied theoretically, they will turn out as attempts of the analyst to re-establish the patient's reasonable ego—if possible by means of interpretation; if not, by means of prohibitions or promised premiums. There is no other way. Case histories will show us how that is done *in concreto*.

TWENTY-THREE

Nature and Classification of the
So-called Psychosomatic Phenomena *

Not long ago, in a paper published in *Psychiatry*,[1] Judah Marmor asserted—as an argument against Freud's instinct theory—that it can be proved that the goals and characteristics of a child's impulsive strivings are formed through the influence of experience stemming from environmental factors. That this fact would contradict Freud's theories is absurd. The demonstration of the ways in which experience forms desires and fears in a child's mind is the very essence of Freud's psychoanalytic method. The misunderstanding is based partly on a terminological error. Freud's concept of *Trieb* does not include the idea of absolute unchangeability and rigidity—otherwise he could not have examined the *Triebschicksale* [2]—but the English word "instinct" does carry these implications. The error, of course, was not only one of mistranslation. So-called "culturalism" generally misjudged Freud when it considered him solely "biologically oriented." Other authors of like bias, while correctly stressing the fact that social institutions shape the character structure of the people living under them, have given little or no consideration to the nature of the raw material out of which character structures are formed.[3] This shaping is done through gratifications and frustrations of relatively uniform biological needs, through the blocking of certain reactions to gratifications and frustrations, and through the favoring of others. In short, it has been forgotten that man is an animal, a biological unit, and that "the influence of experience" signifies the shaping of biological needs.

* First published in *Psa. Quart.*, Vol. 14, 1945, pp. 287–312.
[1] J. Marmor, "The Role of Instinct in Human Behavior," *Psychiatry*, Vol. 5, 1942.
[2] S. Freud, "Instincts and Their Vicissitudes," *Coll. Pap.*, Vol. IV, London, Hogarth, 1948.
[3] This was shown by G. Zilboorg, in "Psychology and Culture," *Psa. Quart.*, Vol. 11, 1942.

It can of course be admitted that such one-sidedness was a reaction to the opposite extreme, to a "biologizing" of psychoanalysis which denied that neuroses are social evils and maintained that they are due to the unfortunate fact that nature has given man an id and an ego which may come in conflict. We have even seen attempts to explain the institution of the family on the basis of man's oedipus complex, instead of accounting for the oedipus complex through the institution of the family. This, however, does not alter the fact that "culturalism" was one-sided.

Coming after the predominance of "culturalism," the "psychosomatic" tendency in psychoanalytic theory seems almost a relief. We are again reminded of the fact that the mind is never independent of physical-chemical processes and that emotions as well as instinctual gratifications and frustrations do not consist of mere "thoughts" but—as Freud has explained in his "Three Contributions" [4] —of physical alterations. It is true that under the heading "psychosomatics" new resistances to psychoanalysis are again developing—a circumstance to be discussed later. In general, however, the stressing of the connections between physiological processes on the one hand and the structure of personality and neuroses on the other, combined with research in this direction, must be welcome to every follower of Freud, just as they were welcome to Freud himself, who described analytic theory as a superstructure which will one day have to be set on a physiological basis.

Approaching the question of psychosomatics from the point of view of psychoanalytic theory, I must first admit that I cannot present any new research findings. A short time ago it was stated in the journal *Psychosomatic Medicine* that "Psychosomatic medicine is in the limelight at present. Its importance is daily being better understood. However, the pictures presented are still indistinct and the part played by psychic factors lacks definition. Better focusing and clearer ideas as to sequence and serial arrangements of events are desirable." [5]

This, I think, is correct. The nature and classification of psychosomatics need clarification. My task is the ordering of well-known phenomena, not the description of new ones, and even in my attempt at classification I am not, of course, entirely original. What I intend to give is rather a classified summary using all the research findings up to the present time. To anyone who knows this literature it will be clear that Alexander has frequently expressed very similar thoughts, but that there are also decisive differences between Alexander's position and mine.[6]

[4] S. Freud, *Three Essays on the Theory of Sexuality*, London, Imago, 1949.

[5] L. G. Rowntree, "Psychosomatic Disorders as Revealed by Thirteen Million Examinations of Selective Service Registrants," *Psychosom. Med.*, Vol. 7, 1945, p. 30.

[6] Cf. F. Alexander, *The Medical Value of Psychoanalysis*, New York, Norton, 1932; "Functional Disturbances of Psychogenic Nature," *J. Amer. Med. Assoc.*, Vol. 100, 1933; "Addenda to 'The Medi-

First of all, the word "so-called" in the title of this paper needs an explanation —and even here I am not original. I do not like the expression "psychosomatic" because it suggests a dualism which does not exist. Every disease is "psychosomatic," for no "somatic" disease is entirely free from "psychic" influence. Not only resistance to infection but all vital functions are continually influenced by the mental state of the organism, and the most "psychic" conversion may be based on a "physical" compliance. Even an accident may occur for psychogenic reasons. Thus when we say that between the realm of organic disease arising from purely physical and chemical causes, and the field of conversion, there lies a large field of problematic functional and even anatomical alterations, all three fields are, for all that, "psychosomatic." It is the in-between field, however, which we want to study.

Psychoanalysis is generally looked upon as one approach through which these in-between phenomena can be examined—one among many possible approaches. Analysts, however, think differently. When we consider psychoanalysis as a therapy, we gladly concede that it would not be indicated in all types of psychosomatic disorders; in some of them it is expressly contraindicated. Psychoanalysis as a theory, however, is for us the theory of the dynamics governing the human organism. If the theory is correct it is the *only* means of explaining what actually takes place. It is not one possibility of explanation among many; where psychoanalytic theory fails to provide an explanation, there is no explanation yet at hand.

The field to be studied is bounded on one side by purely organic diseases and on the other by conversions. We may assume that what is meant by organic disease is self-explanatory, but the concept of "conversion" needs perhaps a little comment because too frequently everything that is psychogenic is incorrectly designated "conversion." In hysteria, functional changes occur within the body which are distorted expressions of wishful thoughts and fantasies. They represent returning repressed instinctual impulses. These symptoms can be interpreted like dreams; the functional changes can be retranslated from their body language into the verbal language of the basic wishful thoughts and fancies. Vomiting may mean, "I am pregnant"; a convulsion, "I have an orgasm"; blindness, "I do not wish to see"; an abasia, "I want to go to forbidden places and in order to avoid doing so I do not go anywhere"; or the opposite, "I refuse to go because staying where I am has a hidden sexual significance for me," or even "because the function of walking as such ["stamping one's feet on Mother Earth," as Freud said [7]] has a hidden sexual significance."

cal Value of Psychoanalysis,'" *Psa. Quart.,* Vol. 5, 1936; "Psychological Aspects of Medicine," *Psychosom. Med.,* Vol. 1, 1939; "Fundamental Concepts of Psychosomatic Research: Psychogenesis, Conversion, Specificity," *Psychosom. Med.,* Vol. 5, 1943.

[7] S. Freud, *The Problem of Anxiety,* New York, Psa. Quart. Press and Norton, 1936.

Not all somatic changes of a psychogenic nature are of this kind. Unconscious instinctual attitudes may influence organic functions in a physiological way without the changes having any definite psychic *meaning*. This difference was defined long ago by Freud in his paper on psychogenic disturbances of vision in which he says:

"Psychoanalysis is fully prepared to grant, indeed to postulate, that not every functional visual disturbance is necessarily psychogenic. . . . When an organ which serves two purposes overplays its erotogenic part, it is generally to be expected that this will not occur without alterations in its response to stimulation and in innervation, which will be manifested as disturbances of the organ in its function as servant of the ego. And indeed, when we observe an organ which ordinarily serves the purpose of sensorial perception presenting as a result of the exaggeration of its erotogenic rôle precisely the behavior of a genital, we shall even expect that there are toxic modifications as well in that organ. For both kinds of functional disturbances . . . we are obliged to retain, for want of a better, the time-honored, inapposite name of neurotic disturbances. Neurotic disturbances of vision are related to psychogenic as, in general, are the actual neuroses to the psychoneuroses; psychogenic visual disturbances can hardly occur without neurotic disturbances, though the latter surely can without the former. Unfortunately, these neurotic symptoms are as yet little appreciated and understood, for they are not directly accessible to psychoanalysis." [8]

The sentences quoted are of basic importance, although the terminology is rather confusing. There are two categories of functional disturbances. One of them is physical in nature and consists of physiological changes caused by the inappropriate use of the function in question. The other has a specific unconscious meaning, is an expression of a fantasy in a "body language," and is directly accessible to psychoanalysis just as is a dream. Freud calls both categories "neurotic" and does not suggest any special term for the first category, whereas the second category he calls "psychogenic." This is rather confusing, because any misuse of an organ is "psychogenic" too. The second category is, of course, "conversion." The first has frequently been called "organ-neurotic," lately, "psychosomatic."

Alexander, who is to be credited with having constantly stressed and clarified this difference, attempted to simplify matters by stating that conversion symptoms occur regularly in the realm of skeletal muscles, whereas psychogenic vegetative disturbances would be of the other category.[9] Unfortunately, things are not as simple as that. Both types of symptoms occur in both realms. No one who

[8] S. Freud, "Psychogenic Visual Disturbance According to Psycho-Analytical Conceptions," *Coll. Pap.*, Vol. II, London, Hogarth, 1948.
[9] F. Alexander, "Fundamental Concepts of Psychosomatic Research."

has ever analyzed a hysterical vomiting or a disturbance of menstruation, for instance, can doubt their function of expressing the idea "I am pregnant" and thus being of the nature of a conversion. Nonconversion "organ-neurotic" disturbances in the functions of skeletal muscles will be taken up later.

The above quotation from Freud contains the key to a classification of organ-neurotic or psychosomatic phenomena. These sentences actually allude to two different things. Functional changes due to what Freud calls "toxic" influences—that is, to changes in the chemistry of the unsatisfied and dammed-up individual—are not necessarily identical with changes caused by an unconscious use of these functions for a libidinal purpose. Moreover, a third and simpler possibility must first be considered, that of "affect equivalents," in which the physical expressions of an affect are experienced even though the individual succeeds in warding off the recognition of their significance. Thus we propose to distinguish four classes of organ-neurotic symptoms: (1) affect equivalents; (2) results of changes in the chemistry of the unsatisfied and dammed-up person (expressions of "unconscious affects"); (3) physical results of unconscious attitudes or of unconsciously determined behavior patterns; (4) all kinds of combinations of these three possibilities.

Affect equivalents

All affects (archaic discharge syndromes which replace voluntary actions) are carried out by motor or secretory means. The specific physical expressions of any given affect may occur without the corresponding specific mental experiences, that is, without the person being aware of their affective significance. This blocking of awareness is the simplest form of defense against affects. Freud collated "anxiety equivalents" in his earliest paper on anxiety neurosis; [10] Landauer collated "equivalents of mourning." [11] Sexual excitement as well as anxiety may be supplanted by sensations in the intestinal, respiratory, or circulatory apparatus. A certain percentage of what are called "organ neuroses" are actually affect equivalents. In particular, so-called "cardiac neuroses" (which may also be conversion hysterias) are frequently anxiety equivalents. The same holds true for those vegetative neuroses which occur when the relative rigidity of a compulsion neurotic or a reactive neurotic character is disturbed.

There are also "subjective affect equivalents." Once an emotion has become associated in childhood with a certain physical attitude, this attitude may be used in later life as a distorted expression of the emotion in question.[12]

The fact that affect equivalents have a diminished discharge value as com-

[10] S. Freud, "On the Right to Separate from Neurasthenia a Definite Symptom Complex as 'Anxiety Neurosis,'" *Coll. Pap.*, Vol. I, London, Hogarth, 1948.
[11] K. Landauer, "Aequivalente der Trauer," *Int. Z. Psa.*, Vol. 11, 1925.
[12] F. Deutsch, "The Choice of Organ in Organ Neuroses," *Int. J. Psa.*, Vol. 20, 1939.

pared with fully experienced affects may result in the affective attitude becoming chronic (Freud and Breuer called it "strangulated affects").[13] Symptoms created by chronic affective attitudes without adequate discharge may cease to be pure affect equivalents and actually belong rather in the following (second) category.

The disturbed chemistry of the unsatisfied person

The very terms which we use to describe the events at the basis of the neuroses, like "source of an instinct," "satisfaction," "frustration," "state of being dammed up," refer of course to chemical as well as to nervous alterations. It is the hormonal state of the organism which is the source of its instinctual demands. The way in which external stimuli are perceived and reacted to depends upon the hormonal state, and the instinctual action which brings about the cessation of the drive does so by altering the disturbing chemical condition. The omission of such action, whether determined by external circumstances or, as in the neuroses, by internal inhibitions, necessarily interferes with the natural chemistry of the processes of excitation and gratification.

Here we must, first of all, remember Freud's concept of "actual neurotic" symptoms.[14] When a neurotic conflict is established, the relative insufficiency of the controlling ego in the state of being dammed up manifests itself in certain symptoms. The decrease in discharge resulting from the neurotic conflict creates a condition which is identical with that brought about by the heightened influx of stimuli from a trauma. There are negative symptoms, consisting of general inhibitions of ego functions, traceable to a decrease in available energy due to the consumption of energy in the defensive struggle. There are positive symptoms, consisting of painful feelings of tension as well as of emergency discharges including outbursts of anxiety and rage which represent attempts to get rid of the tension.

The negative symptoms are less interesting from the standpoint of "psychosomatics." It will suffice to say that any defensive mechanism using counter-cathexis necessarily creates a certain impoverishment of the personality, the awareness of which constitutes a portion of the well-known inferiority feelings of neurotics.

The positive symptoms are more interesting. The neurotic, engaged in an acute inner defense struggle, becomes restless and agitated. He feels that he needs some change but does not know what it should be. He develops emergency discharges such as apparently unmotivated emotional attacks, chiefly anxiety spells. These positive actual neurotic symptoms, representing vegetative "nevertheless discharges" after other avenues of discharge have been blocked, are the simplest

[13] J. Breuer and S. Freud, *Studies in Hysteria*, New York, Nerv. Ment. Dis. Pub. Co., 1937.
[14] S. Freud, *A General Introduction to Psychoanalysis*, New York, Liveright, 1935, 1948.

example of the organic alterations under discussion. Where the instinctual need is not adequately satisfied, the chemical alteration connected with the gratification of the drive is lacking and disturbances in the chemistry of the organism result. Undischarged excitement results in an abnormal quality and quantity of hormones and thus in alterations in physiological functions.

Whereas "actual neurotic" symptoms are generally unspecific expressions of the state of being dammed up, symptoms due to the changed chemistry of a person with a disturbed instinctual economy may also be of a more specific nature. Furthermore, other intermediary factors may be interpolated between the original drive and the final symptoms.

Those states which have been called "unconscious affects" are of special importance in this connection. In affect equivalents the mental content of an affect has been warded off, whereas the physical concomitants of the affect do take place. But there are also states in which even the physical discharge is warded off. This may be achieved by various defense mechanisms which I once tried to tabulate.

As everybody knows, a "latent rage" or a "latent anxiety" is a state in which neither rage nor anxiety is felt but where there is a readiness to react with exaggerated rage or exaggerated anxiety to stimuli which would normally provoke a slight response of rage or anxiety. Certainly the qualities of feelings come into being only by their being felt, but there are states of tension in the organism which, were they not hindered in their discharge and development, would result in specific emotions. These are unconscious "dispositions" toward these emotions, unconscious "readinesses for affects," strivings for their development, which are held in check by opposing forces even while the individual is unaware of such a readiness. "Unconscious anxiety" and "unconscious sexual excitement" in this sense are paramount in the psychology of the neuroses. The unconscious dispositions toward affects are not theoretical constructions but may be observed clinically by the same methods by which unconscious ideas may be observed: they, too, develop "derivatives," betray themselves in dreams, symptoms, and other substitute formations, through the rigidity of the opposing behavior or merely by general weariness.[15]

In considering the relationship between actual neuroses and psychoneurosis, we may add that theoretically all psychoneuroses could be described as a subcategory of symptoms due to the disturbed chemistry of the dammed-up individual. Freud always stressed the fact that all neuroses would turn out in the last analysis to be organic diseases. However, this organic basis of the average psychoneurosis is entirely hypothetical, whereas certain physical symptoms of "unconscious" or "strangulated" affects are now accessible to research. "Un-

15 Cf. S. Freud, *The Ego and the Id*, London, Hogarth, 1947.

conscious affects" apparently cause quantitatively and qualitatively different hormonal secretions and in this way influence the vegetative nervous system and the physical functions. Alexander is of the opinion that the difference in the hormonal state in conscious and in unconscious affects is due only to the chronicity of the so-called unconscious affective attitudes. It is more probable, however, that the physical concomitants of unconscious affects are also qualitatively different from those of conscious ones. It is even possible that these secretions may be as specific as the physical syndromes of conscious affects, but this has as yet been insufficiently investigated.

Physical results of unconscious attitudes

The behavior of a person is continually influenced by his conscious and unconscious instinctual needs. Whereas the oscillations of conscious drives are automatically regulated through instinctual actions, unconscious warded-off impulses which cannot find an adequate outlet but seek again and again to find discharge and to produce derivatives have less obvious and more lasting effects. Continued or repeated attempts at substitute outlets may eventually produce physical alterations.

Simple examples of this kind were given by French [16] and Saul.[17] Habitual forced clearing of the throat, kept up over weeks and months, has a drying effect upon the throat and may eventually result in a pharyngitis. The habit of sleeping with the mouth open also dries the throat and may cause a pharyngitis. Both habits may at times have organic causes; at other times they are certainly an expression of unconscious wishes. There are many kinds of behavior which may induce common colds.

To summarize: an unusual attitude which is rooted in unconscious instinctual conflicts causes a certain behavior. This behavior in turn causes somatic changes in the tissues. The changes are not directly psychogenic, but the person's behavior which initiated the changes was psychogenic; the attitude was intended to relieve the internal pressure; the somatic symptom which was the consequence of the attitude was not sought by the person either consciously or unconsciously.

A good example of an organ neurosis psychoanalytically understood as the physical result of an unconscious attitude is peptic ulcer as seen through the research of the Chicago Institute for Psychoanalysis.[18] People with a chronically frustrated oral-receptive demanding attitude, who repress this attitude and

[16] T. M. French, "Physiology of Behavior and Choice of Neurosis," *Psa. Quart.*, Vol. 10, 1941; "Some Psychoanalytic Applications of the Psychological Field Concept," *Psa. Quart.*, Vol. 11, 1942.

[17] L. J. Saul, "A Note on the Psychogenesis of Organic Symptoms," *Psa. Quart.*, Vol. 4, 1935; "Psychogenic Factors in the Etiology of the Common Cold and Related Symptoms," *Int. J. Psa.*, Vol. 19, 1938; "A Clinical Note on a Mechanism of Psychogenic Back Pain," *Psychosom. Med.*, Vol. 3, 1941.

[18] F. Alexander, *et al.*, "The Influence of Psychologic Factors upon Gastro-Intestinal Disturbances," *Psa. Quart.*, Vol. 3, 1934.

often manifest very active behavior of the reaction-formation type, are, unconsciously, permanently "hungry for love." It would be more exact to state that they are "hungry for necessary narcissistic supplies"—the word "hungry" to be taken literally. Their permanent hunger makes them act like an actually hungry person. The mucous membrane of the stomach begins to secret just as does that of a person who anticipates food, the secretion having no other specific psychic meaning. This chronic hypersecretion is the more immediate cause of the ulcer. The ulcer is the incidental physiological consequence of a psychogenic attitude; it is not a distorted satisfaction of a repressed instinct.

It may be asked whether this etiology is valid for all cases of ulcer. It is possible that the functional changes which in some cases are brought about by repressed oral eroticism may in others be determined by purely somatic causes.

Belonging to the same category are certain functional changes in the striated muscles which are not conversions (and therefore contradict Alexander's idea that all disturbances in the muscular functions are conversions, whereas disturbances in the vegetative functions are organ neuroses). I described these changes in 1927,[19] and because not much attention has been paid to them since I shall say a few words about them here.

Pathogenic defenses generally aim at barring the warded-off impulses from motility (the barring from consciousness is only a means of achieving this). Thus pathogenic defense always means the blocking of certain movements. This inhibition of movement indicates a partial weakening of the conscious ego's mastery of motility. The struggle of the defense is reflected in functional disturbances of the voluntary muscle system. When people with localized or general muscular spasms that hinder their motility try to relax their spastic muscles, either they are totally unable to do so or they may develop emotional states as do patients in a psychocathartic treatment when their thoughts approach their "complexes." This shows that the spasm was a means of keeping the repressed in repression. Observation of a patient during an *acute* struggle over repression likewise demonstrates this. A patient in psychoanalysis who can no longer avoid seeing that an interpretation is correct but nevertheless tries to, frequently shows a cramping of his entire muscular system or of certain parts of it. It is as if he wanted to counterpoise an external muscular pressure to the internal pressure of the repressed impulses seeking an outlet in motility.

The muscular expression of an instinctual conflict is not always a hypertonic one. Hypertonic, lax, flabby muscular attitudes also block or hinder muscular readiness. Hyper- and hypotonic states may alternate and therefore the whole field is better designated as "psychogenic dystonia."

Dystonia and intensity of repression are not necessarily proportionate to each

[19] O. Fenichel, "Organ Libidinization Accompanying the Defense against Drives," No. 14, *First Series.*

other. Not only the question whether and to what extent mental conflicts find expression in alterations of muscular functions, but also the type and location of these alterations is very different in individual cases. The location of the symptoms depends on physiological as well as psychological factors. One of these factors is easily recognizable; it is the specificity of the defense mechanism used. In the case of compulsion neurotics the mechanism of displacement of spasms of the sphincters will play a more important part; in hysterics the blocking of inner perceptions will be more predominant.

Spasms paralyzing skeletal muscles are one of the physical signs of anxiety; they may appear as an anxiety equivalent. Not only fear but also spite and, in particular, suppressed rage may be physically expressed as muscular spasm.

Psychogenic dystonia seems to be decisive in certain "organ-neurotic" gynecological conditions in which a hypotonus of the pelvic muscles may have unfavorable consequences which were not unconsciously intended as such.[20] Psychogenic dystonia may also be the decisive etiological factor in conditions like torticollis.[21]

It is very interesting that these disturbances of muscular functions are mainly co-ordinated with disturbances of inner sensitivity and of body feeling.

A continuous misuse of the muscles for neurotic spasms has necessarily a tiring effect. Actually the fatigue characteristic of so many neurotic states is probably due to the dystonic innervation of muscles. This fatigue is most outspoken in cases of inhibited aggressiveness; often it can be directly called an equivalent of depression. In this connection, if we were to try to discuss the problems of the psychodynamics of rheumatic muscular disorders—which are not at all clear as yet—we would probably see that they are not due to specific unconscious attitudes but rather to a combination of alterations through attitudes and through "changed chemistry." And this is true of most of the organic disturbances of a psychogenic nature.

Combinations

The three categories of organ-neurotic symptoms—viz., affect equivalents, physical expressions of a disturbed chemistry and physical expressions of unconscious attitudes—appear as a rule in a combined form. Often the symptoms remain limited to a given organ or a system of organs, the choice depending primarily on physical and constitutional factors, but also on all the other factors

[20] M. J. Eisler, "Ueber hysterische Erscheinungen am Uterus," *Int. Z. Psa.,* Vol. 9, 1923; E. Jones, "Psychology and Childbirth," *Papers on Psycho-Analysis,* 5th ed., Baltimore, Williams and Wilkins, 1948; K. A. Menninger, "Emotional Factors in Organic Gynecological Conditions," *Bull. Menninger Clin.,* Vol. 7, 1943; J. Rickman, "A Psychological Factor in the Aetiology of Descensus Uteri, Laceration of the Perineum and Vaginismus," *Int. J. Psa.,* Vol. 7, 1926.

[21] J. Westerman-Holstijn, "From the Analysis of a Patient with Cramp of the Spinal Accessory," *Int. J. Psa.,* Vol. 3, 1922.

which may determine the somatic compliance also in the case of conversion symptoms. Briefly the choice of organ depends upon the following factors: (1) the nature of the instinctual demands which are warded off, (2) fixations due to the earlier experiences of the individual, (3) the ability of the organs in question to express certain needs symbolically, (4) which organs had just been used or were specifically cathected at the moment when the decisive repression occurred, (5) the previous *physical* history of the individual. A discussion of the various organ systems one after the other will best illustrate the combination type of psychosomatic symptoms.

The hormonal vegetative system cannot be simply classified as one of the various organ systems, for it is through hormonal vegetative pathways that the greater part of functional disturbances in the other systems is created; the symptoms due to "distorted chemistry" are exclusively determined in this way. Of course, unconscious attitudes may also influence the hormonal functions. Such desires as an unconscious identification with the opposite sex may have the same kind of influence on the production of hormones as an unconscious oral desire has on the production of gastric juice in cases of peptic ulcer.

Pregenital fixations not only produce certain unconscious attitudes but necessarily also change the hormonal state of the individual. However, not all orally fixated patients become either obese or extremely thin. This probably happens when an oral fixation coincides with a certain hormonal constitution.

Wulff has described a psychoneurosis, not infrequent in women, which is related to hysteria, cyclothymia, and addiction.[22] It is characterized by the individual's fight against her sexuality, which, through previous repression, has become especially greedy and insatiable. This sexuality is pregenitally oriented and sexual satisfaction is perceived as a "dirty meal." Periods of depression in which the patients stuff themselves (or drink) and feel "fat," "bloated," "dirty," "untidy," or "pregnant," while at the same time keeping their surroundings untidy too, alternate with "good" periods in which they behave ascetically, feel slim, and conduct themselves either normally or in a somewhat elated manner. The body feeling in the "fat" periods turns out to be a repetition of the way the girl felt at puberty before her first menstruation, and the spells often actually coincide with the premenstrual period. The menstrual flow then usually brings a feeling of relief: "The fat-making dirt is pouring out; now I am slim again and will be a good girl and not eat too much." The alternating feelings of ugliness and beauty connected with these periods show that exhibitionistic conflicts are also of basic importance in this syndrome. Psychoanalysis discloses that the unconscious content is a pre-oedipal mother conflict which may be covered by an

[22] M. Wulff, "Ueber einen interessanten oralen Symptomenkomplex und seine Beziehung zur Sucht," *Int. Z. Psa.*, Vol. 18, 1932.

oral-sadistic oedipus complex. The patients have an intense unconscious hatred toward their mothers and toward femininity. To be fat means getting breasts; being uncontrolled, incontinent or pregnant. The urge to eat has the unconscious aim of incorporating something which may relax the disagreeable inner "feminine" tension. Eating means a reincorporation of the object whose loss has caused the patient to feel hungry, constipated, castrated, feminine, fat. Thus, food means milk, penis, child, and narcissistic supplies which soothe anxieties. The exhibitionistic behavior signifies a tendency to compel the giving of these supplies and also the fear of not getting them because of repulsive ugliness. The depression signifies the recurrent failure to regain the lost stability, a failure that occurs because of the forbidden oral-sadistic means by which this re-establishment is attempted. The ascetic periods, by pacifying the superego, achieve a greater degree of relaxation.

In some cases this neurosis is nothing but a kind of food addiction. In others, however, not only body feelings but actual body changes dominate the picture. Certain cases of obesity, especially of cyclical obesity, correspond in structure with Wulff's description.[23]

Vegetative alterations in the gastrointestinal, respiratory, and circulatory systems are also mostly combinations of the three categories of organ-neurotic symptoms. It is easily understandable that a colitis may be brought about by unconscious anal impulses which are continuously effective. It may be the result of the organism being chronically under eliminative and retentive pressure, just as an ulcer may be the result of a chronic receptive pressure. The conflict between eliminative and retentive tendencies may itself be determined in different ways. It may represent a simple conflict between (anal) sexual excitement and fear; or the feces may represent introjected objects which the person wishes to preserve as well as to eliminate.

Children who like to postpone defecation (either for the sake of retention pleasure or because of fear) later often develop "obstipation." The retention, which was once voluntary, has become an "organ-neurotic" symptom. The prolonged continuance of an "obstipation" must influence the smooth muscles of the intestinal tract. A spastic colon—that is, a readiness to react to various stimuli with constipation or diarrhea—is either an anxiety equivalent or a sign of the patient's fixation on the anal phase of his libidinal development. No matter what stimulus started the excitation, the execution is an intestinal one. It may also be a symptom of a continuous and repressed aggressiveness, sometimes as a revenge for oral frustrations. In a deeper layer, then, diarrhea may express generosity or it may reflect fantasies concerning internalized objects.

[23] H. Bruch, "Obesity in Childhood and Personality Development," *Amer. J. Orthopsychiat.*, Vol. II 1941.

In actual neurotic states, constipation is one of the characteristic symptoms. Retention generally characterizes the state of being dammed up, and retention symptoms are frequent among organ-neurotic symptoms in general. However, organ-neurotic symptoms are also "emergency discharges." Some symptoms are compromises between retention and elimination. Certain types of pathological defecation betray a castration anxiety displaced to the anal sphere.

Breathing, like other muscular functions, has its characteristic dystonia. Variations of respiratory rhythm, especially transitory cessation of breathing, and variable and irregular participation of the individual parts of the thorax in the act of breathing, are the ways in which continuous small psychological alterations exert their influence on the process of respiration. These phenomena become particularly evident when a new action or motion is initiated, and whenever there is any change in direction of attention. The intimate connection between anxiety and respiration makes it probable that these constant variations in the respiratory function express slight degrees of anxiety. The "normal" respiratory dystonia may be considered an anxiety signal of low intensity. It is as if the ego were cautiously testing the path whenever a new thing is perceived, a new action undertaken, or attention redirected—wondering, so to speak, whether or not it should be afraid.

The role played by respiratory sensations in anxiety explains the fact that to a certain extent every anxiety is felt as a kind of suffocation. Therefore, neurotic anxiety manifesting itself in respiratory symptoms is not necessarily a sign that the warded-off impulses concern respiratory eroticism. The reverse, rather, may be true: respiration may acquire an erotic quality only after and because anxiety has become connected with sexual excitement. However, the respiratory function may also become "sexualized" and fantasies of a "respiratory introjection" [24] may form the basis of complicating conversion mechanisms.

It is well known that in bronchial asthma it is particularly a passive-receptive longing for the mother which is expressed in pathological changes of the breathing function. The asthmatic seizure is, first of all, an anxiety equivalent. It is a cry for help directed toward the mother whom the patient tries to introject by respiration in order to be permanently protected. This intended incorporation as well as the instinctual dangers against which it is directed are characteristically of a pregenital, especially anal, nature; in fact, the whole character of the typical asthma patient shows pregenital features. It must be added that in asthma, conversion mechanisms as well as purely somatic factors of an allergic nature likewise play a role.[25]

[24] O. Fenichel, "Respiratory Introjection," No. 23, *First Series*.
[25] Cf. T. M. French and F. Alexander, *Psychogenic Factors in Bronchial Asthma*, Psychosomatic Med. Monographs, No. 3 and 4, 1941.

Rage and sexual excitation as well as anxiety manifest themselves physiologically in functional circulatory alterations. The heart is considered the organ of love, the heart beats fast in rage and fear, the heart is heavy if one feels sad. Vagotonic and sympathicotonic reactions are the very essence of the physical components of affect syndromes. These components may always serve as affect equivalents if a person wards off awareness of his emotions. Any kind of "unconscious emotion" may express itself in acceleration of the pulse.

However, certain personalities are apparently especially predisposed to the development of just this type of expression. Whereas sexual excitement may certainly disguise itself as palpitation, a chronic irritability of heart and circulatory system is more typically due to aggressiveness and fear of retaliatory aggressiveness. Characteristically, such patients suffer from an inhibited hate toward the parent of the same sex and simultaneously from a fear of losing parental love should this hate be openly expressed. The fear of being abandoned, carried over from infantile experiences, takes the form of a fear of death. An identification with a cardiac sufferer in the patient's environment is frequently in the foreground, especially if the patient has wished for the death of this person and now fears retaliation. Attacks are frequently precipitated when circumstances necessitate competition with the parent of the same sex; the patient then tries unconsciously to escape into a passive-dependent attitude.[26]

There seems to be a correspondence between the fact that people who entirely block external discharge of their emotions are more disposed toward reaction within the circulatory system, and the fact that the circulatory system is closed and not capable of intake or discharge.

General vasomotor reactions such as blushing, turning pale, fainting, and dizzy spells are very common in neuroses. This is due to the fact that vasomotor expressions are in the foreground of the physical manifestations of all affects and that vasomotor reactions are ready channels for emergency discharge whenever muscular discharge is blocked.

Vasomotor alterations, probably in combination with certain dystonic muscular phenomena, are also the cause of the majority of nervous headaches. The physiology of nervous headaches still presents many unsolved problems. Psychologically it is important to distinguish actual neurotic headaches expressing a state of inner tension, organ-neurotic headaches due to a more specific behavior caused by an unconscious conflict (for example, specific muscular tensions dur-

---

[26] Cf., for example, W. H. Dunn, "Emotional Factors in Neurocirculatory Asthenia," *Psychosom. Med.*, Vol. 4, 1942; K. A. Menninger and W. C. Menninger, "Psychoanalytic Observations in Cardiac Disorders," *Amer. Heart J.*, Vol. 11, 1936; M. L. Miller and H. V. McLean, "The Status of the Emotions in Palpitation and Extrasystoles with a Note on 'Effort Syndrome,'" *Psa. Quart.*, Vol. 10, 1941; E. Weiss, "Neurocirculatory Asthenia," *Psychosom. Med.*, Vol. 5, 1943; E. Wittkower, "The Psychological Factor in Cardiac Pain," *Lancet*, Vol. 233, 1937.

ing sleep), and conversion headaches (such as those expressing pregnancy fantasies).

Even in cases where it is not yet known by exactly which physiological pathways an organ-neurotic symptom has been brought about, it is possible to see what the underlying psychological attitude is. An example of this is essential hypertension, which has recently been made the subject of psychoanalytic research, first at the Chicago Institute for Psychoanalysis,[27] later by other authors.[28] Cases of essential hypertension are characterized by an extreme, unconscious instinct tension, a general readiness to aggressiveness as well as a passive-receptive longing to get rid of the aggressiveness. Both tendencies are absolutely unconscious and are effective in people who seem superficially to be very calm and permit themselves no outlets for their impulses. This unrealized inner tension probably becomes effective through hormonal influence via vasomotor responses and the kidneys; further physiological research is needed to show exactly in which ways.

For physiological reasons, skin manifestations often become expressions of irritations in the endocrine-vegetative system. The simple symptom of nervous sweating and the symptom of dermographia are examples of the general vegetative irritability of the skin in response to conscious and unconscious emotional stimuli. These symptoms may be chronic as a sign of the patient's state of inner tension, or they may appear as temporary symptoms during actual neuroses, or they may appear in the form of "spells" whenever an event touches upon unconscious conflicts, or they may have become elaborated into conversion symptoms.[29] There is no doubt that cutaneous irritability reflects vasomotor instability.

The tendency of the skin to be influenced by vasomotor reactions, which in their turn are evoked by unconscious impulses, has to be understood from the point of view of the general physiological functions of the skin.[30] Four characteristics of the skin as the external cover of the organism, representing the boundary between it and the external world, are of general importance:

The skin as the covering layer has, first of all, a general protecting function.

[27] F. Alexander, "Emotional Factors in Essential Hypertension," *Psychosom. Med.*, Vol. 1, 1939; L. J. Saul, "Hostility in Cases of Essential Hypertension," *Psychosom. Med.*, Vol. 1, 1939.

[28] L. B. Hill, "A Psychoanalytic Observation on Essential Hypertension," *Psa. Rev.*, Vol. 22, 1935; K. A. Menninger, "Emotional Factors in Hypertension," *Bull. Menninger Clin.*, Vol. 2, 1938; L. A. Schwartz, "An Analyzed Case of Essential Hypertension," *Psychosom. Med.*, Vol. 2, 1940; E. Weiss, "Cardiovascular Lesions of Probable Psychosomatic Origin in Arterial Hypertension," *Psychosom. Med.*, Vol. 2, 1940.

[29] R. D. Gillespie, "Psychological Aspects of Skin Diseases," *Brit. J. Dermatology*, Vol. 50, 1938; W. J. O'Donovan, *Dermatological Neuroses*, London, Kegan Paul, 1927; P. Schilder, "Remarks on the Psychophysiology of the Skin," *Psa. Rev.*, Vol. 23, 1936; J. H. Stokes, "Masochism and Other Sex Complexes in the Background of Neurogenous Dermatitis," *Arch. Derm. Syph.*, Vol. 22, 1930.

[30] M. Barinbaum, "Zur Problem des psychophysischen Zusammenhangs mit besonderer Beruecksichtigung der Dermatologie," *Int. Z. Psa.*, Vol. 20, 1934.

It examines incoming stimuli and, if necessary, blunts them or even wards them off. For the purpose of applying the same protective measures against internal stimuli, the organism has a general tendency to treat disturbing internal stimuli as if they were external ones.

Second, the skin is an important erogenous zone. If the drive to use it as such is repressed, the recurrent tendencies for and against cutaneous stimulation find somatic expression in cutaneous alterations.

Third, the skin as the surface of the organism is the part which is externally visible. This makes it a site for the expression of conflicts around exhibitionism. These conflicts in their turn concern not only a sexual component instinct and opposing fear or shame, but also various narcissistic needs for reassurance.

Fourth, anxiety equivalents, too, may be localized as reactions of the skin. Anxiety is physiologically a sympathicotonic state, and sympathicotonic reactions of vessels in the skin may represent anxiety.

These examples are very insufficient and specialists in pathological physiology have much more to say, but it must be remembered that they are only quoted as examples for the "nature and classification" of these phenomena.

Problems of psychogenesis of organic diseases, and pathoneuroses

In order to mark the boundaries of the "psychosomatic" field, we started with a few remarks about conversion. We have now to add a few remarks about the opposite border, the field of organic diseases.

Not every organic symptom in which analysis can demonstrate a correlation with mental connotations is necessarily of an organ-neurotic nature. Nothing happens in the organism that is not drawn secondarily into the mental conflicts of the individual. The mere existence of such a connection does not prove anything about the genesis.

The coexistence in a patient of a tumor and of unconscious ideas of pregnancy, or even the analytic proof of the coincidence of the development of a tumor and an intensification of the wish for pregnancy, must not lead to unwarranted etiological conclusions. If the patient dreams of being pregnant at a time preceding the diagnosis of the tumor it would perhaps show that he was unconsciously aware of the tumor before he knew of it consciously, but it does not indicate that the wish to be pregnant caused the development of the tumor.

A further complication in the relation between organic symptom and mental conflicts is brought about by the fact that somatically determined conditions may secondarily change the psychic attitudes of the individual. Adaptation to pain or to changes of body functions is not always easy. The ways in which this adaptation is attempted, and whether or not it succeeds, depends of course on the total structure of the personality, on its history and its latent defense struggles. First of all, the somatic process in the organ consumes much of the libido and the mental attention of the person; his other interests and object relationships are relatively impoverished, which explains why in general being sick makes a person narcissistic.[31] Besides, the disease or physical change may unconsciously represent something to the patient which disturbs the existing equilibrium between repressed and repressing forces. A disease may, like a trauma, be taken as a castration or as an abandonment by fate, or at least as a threat of castration or abandonment. It may also be perceived as a masochistic temptation or mobilize some other latent infantile longing and in this way provoke a neurosis.

The narcissistic withdrawal of the sick person, as well as his unconscious misinterpretations of the disease in terms of instinctual conflicts, underlie the fact that neuroses sometimes develop as a consequence rather than as a cause of somatic diseases. Ferenczi called neuroses which are consequences of somatic diseases "pathoneuroses." [32]

A special category of pathoneuroses, appearing mostly in combination with disturbances due to changed chemistry, are the hormonal pathoneuroses.

A quantitative or qualitative change at the source of the instincts must necessarily influence the intensity and nature of the instinctual conflicts and their mental outcome. The authors who have worked in this field stress the *interrelation* of hormonal and mental data, that is, the fact that neurotic symptoms or attitudes in hormonally sick persons also influence the hormonal state.

The opposite of a pathoneurosis would be a "pathocure": the disappearance of a neurosis with the outbreak of an organic disease. This happens with "moral masochists" whose neuroses represent first of all a suffering by which they pacify their superego. Neuroses of this type become superfluous when replaced by another kind of suffering.

Whenever a connection between an organic symptom and a mental conflict is encountered, the first question must be, "Has the conflict produced the symptom, or the symptom the conflict?" No doubt there is sometimes a vicious circle, symptom and conflict perpetuating each other.

Space does not permit a discussion of hypochondriasis, which we hypothetically believe to be a specific changed chemistry. As a matter of fact, the physiological basis of hypochondriasis is still entirely unknown and the whole subject must be treated at length elsewhere.

Psychoanalytic therapy in organ neuroses

A few words, in conclusion, about the applicability of psychoanalysis as a therapy in the states discussed.

The great variety of the phenomena here examined makes any general state-

---

[31] S. Freud, "On Narcissism: An Introduction," *Coll. Pap.,* Vol. IV.

[32] S. Ferenczi, "Disease—or Pathoneuroses," *Further Contributions to the Theory and Technique of Psycho-Analysis,* London, Hogarth, 1950.

ment impossible. There are states which have become "organic" to such an extent that immediate physical treatment is necessary. But whenever symptoms are the outcome of chronic or unconscious attitudes, psychoanalysis is indicated for the purpose of making this attitude conscious and thus overcoming it.

Freud stated that organ-neurotic symptoms are not "directly accessible" to psychoanalysis.[33] Indirectly, they are. If the anxiety or other obstacles which hinder the adequate discharge of a person's impulses are removed by analysis, the indirect symptoms disappear without having been made a specific object of psychoanalysis. The change in the function cannot be "analyzed" because it has no unconscious meaning; however, the attitude which produced it *can* be analyzed and if the attitude is given up, or the state of being dammed up is overcome, involuntary consequences likewise disappear.

It is clear that the attitude or the blocking of discharge and not the symptom itself is the object of the analysis. A trial analysis will, as usual, first have to estimate the relative etiological importance of the unconscious factors and establish a "dynamic diagnosis." Monosymptomatic conversions are, of course, no more difficult to analyze than any other hysteria; the closer an organ neurosis is to a psychosis, the more doubtful is the prognosis.

As to the treatment of pathoneuroses, a number of them, as would be expected from the nature of the disturbance, run an acute course and recover spontaneously when the basic somatic disease disappears. If the disease served as a precipitating factor of a genuine neurosis or psychosis, the treatment depends on the nature of the neurosis or psychosis provoked.

How much can be achieved through shorter nonanalytic methods of psychotherapy is a question not to be answered without a detailed discussion as to what the really effective mechanisms of these nonanalytic psychotherapies are, a question which can be answered only by means of psychoanalytic theory. Again there is not sufficient space for such a discussion. I only want to say that, from my experience and scientific conviction, the nonanalytic methods are more applicable in neurotic disturbances related to traumatic neuroses or in acute external difficulties. Superficial methods offer less probability of success, the more a disturbance is an expression of a distorted character structure. Unfortunately, many of the "psychosomatic" disturbances are so based. Certainly it is progress if the connection between symptoms and the person's emotional state becomes at all apparent, and it may be of some help if the patient is enabled to see and to verbalize some of his main conflicts.

I am also rather skeptical about attempts to relate definite psychosomatic pictures to definite personality structures.[34] This procedure may be valid for some

---

[33] S. Freud, "Psychogenic Visual Disturbance According to Psycho-Analytical Conceptions," *Coll. Pap.*, Vol. II.

[34] F. Dunbar, *Psychosomatic Diagnosis,* New York, Hoeber, 1943.

cases. In other cases, as Alexander has pointed out,[35] a disorder may be characteristic for a certain emotional state rather than for a personality type, and such a state may occur in various types. Relations between symptoms, emotional state, and personality type are complicated, and I am afraid that they cannot be cleared up without the use of the psychoanalytic method of research. Psychoanalytic characterology and typology are still in their infancy, but they are sufficient to make one skeptical about a "dynamic personality research" not based on psychoanalysis.

The greater our fund of information, the more obvious it becomes that the solution of every problem creates other new problems. In contrast to certain psychosomatic publications in which the word "psychosomatic" seems to have become a slogan, used to demonstrate that "the psychoanalytic viewpoint is but one among many viewpoints" and that "we have to study physiology too" and that "we can do what psychoanalysts do in a much shorter time," I have the feeling that the insights thus far gained show that the necessary physiological and chemical research in laboratories will bring real progress in our understanding of human nature only if combined with a genuinely psychoanalytic understanding of the psychodynamics.

[35] F. Alexander, Review of *Psychosomatic Diagnosis,* by F. Dunbar, *Psychosom. Med.,* Vol. 7, 1945.

TWENTY-FOUR

The Means of Education[*]

IN CONSIDERING any educational influence, it is necessary to distinguish three factors:

(1) that which is being influenced, i.e., the mental structure of the child;

(2) the influencing stimuli, which converge upon this structure;

(3) the influencing process, i.e., the alterations that occur in the child's mind in response to these stimuli.

The first of these factors is, in the final analysis, determined by human biology, the second by the cultural environment in which the child is reared. Hence, it is appropriate to assume that the first factor is a subject for study by biologists, the second for sociologists, whereas the third would be in the realm of psychoanalytic research. In a science of education all three disciplines would have to be employed.

Any such schematic division is, to be sure, only relatively valid. The mental structure, to begin with, is not identical with the hereditary biological constitution which can be investigated by biology; it is actually composed of both this constitution and all previous external influences. It is not possible to disregard these external influences in any single respect. Already in utero, environmental formative influences are at work, and even developmental tendencies, which are certainly innate, need precipitating external stimuli to materialize. Strangely enough, even in the realm of the biological needs—which in their relative force and specific form are necessarily influenced by environment—the decisive contribution was not made by a biologist, but rather by psychoanalysts. Certain primitive needs, such as hunger and the need for warmth or for excretion have, of course, been studied thoroughly by biologists. But for a considerable number

[*] First published in *The Psychoanalytic Study of the Child*, Vol. 1, 1945, pp. 281–292. A modified version of a paper published in *Z. psa. Paedag.*, Vol. 9, 1935.

of other needs and impulses—and precisely for those whose modification through education forms character—it is not a biological treatise, but rather Freud's *Three Contributions to the Theory of Sex,* that is the basic textbook; in other words, the very existence and operation of infantile sexuality had to be reconstructed from the psychoanalyses of adults.

The influencing stimuli are of course manifold. Those of interest in a discussion of "education" are the systematic and institutionalized ones. They are not quite so varied as other external stimuli, inasmuch as traditional ways of child rearing are usually relatively characteristic for a given cultural sphere, or for a given society, or a given sector of a society. The study of the history and social function of these traditional ways certainly belongs in the field of sociology. Both history and social function are very complicated. All educational procedures contain conservative elements reflecting the history of the society in question, as well as tendencies toward reform, corresponding to current social ideology which, for its part, is determined by social and political conditions and changes.

In any event, the objective social function of educational institutions differs greatly from the thoughts entertained by individual educators as to their educational goals. The institutions aim at the production of certain character structures which not only induce "sociality" within the next generation, but also the development of certain ways of thinking, feeling, and reacting in general, which effect adjustment to the existing order. Those individuals whose mental structure has been molded by traditional educational procedures to conformity with the existing order present the chief obstacles to necessary changes within this order; on the other hand, attempts to reform educational systems will be unsuccessful, or at least greatly limited in their effectiveness, as long as the existing social order requires maintenance of the old educational institution in its own interest.

In spite of the divergence of educational stimuli, certain general, basic educational tasks connected with the small child are identical in all societies, namely the furtherance of certain developments in the mind of the child. Before we consider the third factor, the processes within the child's mind, let us first examine these general developmental tendencies. Infants and small children live mainly according to the so-called "pleasure principle." They obey every impulse, have no interest except that of getting rid of their tensions; their continual attempt to do whatever they feel like doing at the moment is restricted only by the inhibiting force of their physical limitations. Unquestionably it would be impossible to have a society composed of individuals who live according to the pleasure principle. Uncontrolled instinctual impulses are uncontrolled natural forces.

However, no two-year-old child, even without the benefit of "education," would retain his original, primitive kind of behavior. Cumulative experience forces him to take into consideration the prospective reaction of his surroundings to his actions. "Reason" develops, and opposes unreasonable behavior. He who eats as many sweets as he pleases may expect a tummy ache. He who grabs at the beautiful fire gets burned. He who tortures his environment will be tortured in return. Life governed by the impulse of the moment is gradually (although never completely) transformed into life governed by the "reality principle," a situation wherein reality and the probable consequence of intended actions is subjected to judgment. Pleasure is renounced in order to avoid subsequent pain, or to attain subsequent, more intense pleasure. As the ego of the child gains in strength, it learns to bear tensions by postponing the reaction, and to interpolate between stimulus and reaction a kind of "trial action" in fantasy, which affords insight into the prospective consequences.

Education certainly can and should help in this development. It is not necessary for every child to burn himself; education can anticipate the pain of burning through warning or threatening. This holds true especially for the experience: "He who tortures his environment will be tortured in return."

We do not know how a child would behave without any "education." We do not know to what extent the natural encounters with reality would suffice in the development of reasonableness. But we do know that in actual practice more is demanded of every child than pure reasonableness, that educational procedure everywhere is not merely help in the development of the "reality principle," but frankly of an emphasized and exaggerated reality principle. How the parents react to instinctual acts becomes the child's main "encounter with reality," and serves as the motivating force for the child to change his instinctual behavior.

This affords a key to the basic principles of all education, principles which are obvious in the training of small children, but which become more involved as the problems of the more subtle guidance of older children arise.

The development of judgment is created by the production of instinctual conflicts brought about by external forces, that is, a remodeling of certain instincts in such manner as to connect their goal with the repression of other instinctual impulses. In the case of the burned child this is obvious. It is the instinct of self-preservation that, after the experience, appears to be stronger than the original desire to play with fire. Crude child training works in the same manner. It connects pain with certain pleasures, until the fear of pain becomes stronger than the desire for pleasure. The underlying principle in more subtle education is no different. Only, however, the pain that becomes connected with the pleasure to be suppressed is a more subtle one.

It is characteristic of children that they very deeply need love and affection from the persons of their environment. This is a psychic component of the biological helplessness of the human infant. The infant is wholly dependent on external care and would perish without it. Its concepts of objects and of reality are formed in connection with experiences of hunger and satiety (attained through external supplies), or, to state it more generally, through the alternation of states of need and satisfaction. In the course of this process, the child becomes aware of his actual weakness and is obliged to relinquish what is probably the initial feeling state, omnipotence. Instead he now develops the feeling that grown-ups, who can either give or withhold satisfaction, are omnipotent. The child's longing for love and affection from these persons is simultaneously a longing for participation in their omnipotence. The self-esteem of the child is dependent on the flow of these supplies. When the child is loved, he feels powerful; when neglected, he feels helpless and in danger of becoming "nothing at all." This dependence of self-esteem on external supplies (food or love) can be understood through observation in later life of the type of person who has remained fixated on this level. For many persons, their fellow-beings are mere instruments for obtaining supplies of approbation; if they fail to receive such external supplies, they have no adequate sense of identity. The normal person gradually learns to achieve relative independence of the environment in the matter of self-esteem, which is measured rather by comparison between his actual behavior and his ideals; however, the primitive type of external regulation of self-esteem remains operative in everyone to some extent. It is this emotional dependence of self-esteem that becomes the vehicle of all "more subtle" ways of education. If the possibility of receiving this vitally needed affection becomes dependent, because of educational measures, upon the suppression of certain original instinctual demands, the situation is similar to that of the child who grabs at the fire. Again a conflict arises between the impulse in question and the interest of self-preservation, the latter here making its appearance in the form of the need to be loved. The child acquires a readiness to sacrifice certain of his interests in order to secure the supply of necessary affection. In general, this is the psychology of sacrifice which is always a lesser evil accepted voluntarily in order to avoid a greater one.

And now it seems clear we have identified the three basic means of all education, namely, direct threat, mobilization of the fear of losing love, and the promise of special rewards. The second means can be applied effectively only if the child has previously experienced the fear of losing love.

Fear of punishment and fear of losing the parents' affection differ from other frightening experiences that impel the child to defend himself against the demands of his primitive pleasure principle. Other dangers require unconditional cessation of the dangerous activity, but in the case of these fears the activity may be continued in secret, or the child may pretend he feels "bad" in circumstances where he actually feels "good." (Ferenczi once remarked in a lecture on this subject: "Out of this lie, morality came into existence.")

Objection will probably be taken to the statement that threats and rewards are the sole tools of education. The application of these principles, it may be said, can perhaps achieve some sort of training, but not that which education fundamentally desires: good behavior not only through fear of opposition to the grown-ups (who can, after all, be deceived), but good behavior for its own sake.

Actually, an internal acceptance of suggested ideals or anti-instinctual standards is developed only after a period during which the child has a twofold ethics, one operative when he feels himself watched by grown-ups, and another one effective when he is alone or with other children.

It is an important step in maturation when prohibitions set up by the parents remain effective even in their absence. There has then been instituted in the mind a constant watchman who signals the approach of possible situations or behavior that might result in the loss of the mother's affection, or the approach of an occasion to earn the reward of mother's affection. This "watchman" completely fulfills the essential function of reason described earlier: the anticipation of the probable reactions of the external world to one's behavior. A part of the child's ego has become an "inner mother," threatening potential withdrawal of affection.

The fact that the need for the parents' affection arises as a longing to be united with their omnipotence makes it understandable that every child wants to be like his parents, to "identify" himself with them. Of course the original wish is to identify with the parents' activities, not with their prohibitions. The ideals established by the parents are, of course, an essential part of their personality, and the child in striving for rewards does not want merely to suppress certain undesired impulses, but also to fulfill positive ideals. This general striving to be like the parents may make it easier for the child to accept prohibitions also. The actual identification with the parents' prohibitions is rather a displaced substitute for the intended identification with their activities, forced upon the child by external necessity.

The first "internalized parental prohibitions" are very strong in so far as they are connected with the threat of terrible punishments, whose origin will be discussed later. But they are weak in so far as they may be easily disobeyed or circumvented when no one is looking, or when other circumstances seem to permit something previously forbidden. The internalization of the prohibitions is not yet a final one; it is still easy to shift them back to persons in the external world, like policemen or bogeymen. The child still fluctuates between yielding to his impulses and suppressing them; there is, as yet, no unified, organized character in the prohibitions. It is a situation where, under educational influence, one part of the child's own instinctual interests is utilized for suppressing other instinctual interests.

A next step in development is taken when such a "unified organized character" enters into the prohibitions, ideals, and standards acquired through education. Under our cultural conditions, this occurs between the child's fourth and seventh year, and in the following way:

The child loves his parents, and he does so with a real, that is, sexual love. The parents do not satisfy these sexual desires. The child remains unsatisfied and tends to look for compensation. People who are disappointed in their wishes react by fleeing into the past, by reactivating earlier wishes that once did find satisfaction. The disappointed child, too, reactivates a very archaic aim, the very oldest form of love, if it is permissible to call such a thing love at all: the aim of incorporation of the loved object, of taking it into one's own body, of becoming fully united with it. We can also put it in the following way: "If I cannot love my parents, I want to be like my parents." The early wish for identification with the parents, which has been mentioned before and which was present before any other kind of love, is remobilized when the child realizes that certain sexual longings of his have no hope of fulfillment. When the parents forbid the child expression of his sexual desires, he psychically takes the parents into his own person. A part of his ego, changed through this incorporation, then speaks in his mind in the same way as the parents have hitherto spoken. The fact that this change within the ego, which promotes the final incorporation of both parental ideals and prohibitions, is the successor of and the substitute for the child's sexual interest in his parents, the so-called oedipus complex, accounts for the fact that anti-instinctual attitudes often have attributes characteristic of instincts: they are impulsive and irrational. Think, for instance, of the ascetic passion of an ascetic. The reason for this is that through educational influences, instinctual impulses have been transformed into anti-instinctual impulses. Many a modern person has some of the attributes of an ascetic, that is, he represses instinctual demands not because reason requires it, but rigidly, instinctively, blindly. The incorporation of the parents' standards and prohibitions is called the "superego" because, though it is a part of the ego, it has a power over the rest of the ego similar to the earlier power of the parents over the child. The mode of mastering impulses by a rigid and instinct-like superego is, in a normal person, subsequently replaced by the mastering of impulses by a reasonable ego.

The erection of the superego creates a multiplicity of new problems, some of which are extremely complicated, others of which still remain unsolved. They need not be considered in this discussion.

The principal change brought about by the creation of a superego is that the child has become emotionally more independent of external affection, because his superego now decides whether or not he is worthy of being loved. Anxiety as a regulator of the primitive impulses has been partly supplanted by guilt feeling. However, conflicts may arise between the child's ego and superego, which again make him seek the helping intervention of the adults around him. Often the child is seeking external "forgivers" or "condemners" to defend himself against an unreasonable superego. Such needs, again, are used by educators who in the last analysis have no other means at their disposal than threats and rewards—although threats and rewards become more and more subtle, the more highly developed the child's ego becomes, and the more lofty the ideas that are at stake. However, educational influences after the sixth or seventh year are by no means limited to the child's superego. It is not only the superego that is influenced by satisfying and frustrating experiences, and more particularly by suggestions as to how to react to satisfactions and frustrations (presenting examples of different ways of reaction, or blocking other possibilities of reaction). What is commonly called "ego" or a person's "character," i.e., his habitual ways of reacting to external as well as to internal demands, is created by experiences of this kind. Even the so-called "id," i.e., the instinctual impulses, is dependent on educational influences to the extent that external experiences determine the relative strength of the various impulses—in other words, the distribution of the available energy among them. Thus we see that "education" not only induces a person, by means of threat and reward, to suppress his original pleasure-seeking impulses. It does much more in a positive sense by determining what happens to the energy of the repressed impulses, through changing the ego by the very act of suppression, as shown in the example of the creation of the superego. Blocking off certain types of reaction to frustrating experiences, facilitating others, especially through direct examples or through the creation of ideals, are ways of achieving such change within the ego. Examples and ideals are, of course, socially prescribed and limited.

And now a formulation of the hidden dangers of "bad" education can be undertaken. Whereas the reality principle says: "Do not yield to your impulses where such impulses are dangerous," a given education may artificially picture too many impulses as "dangerous." The child may be forced to repress his impulses to such a degree that severe damage may result. That is to say, the repressed instincts still exist in his unconscious, a circumstance that has a twofold consequence: first, they may reappear in an undesired form as neurotic symptoms or character disturbances; second, the energies needed in the constant struggle of repression are not available for other purposes.

There are two characteristic features of childhood that augment this danger. The first is the child's magical orientation, which causes the child to feel that everybody and everything, including the inanimate, feels and acts as he himself does. The fantastic nature of some of his impulses gives rise to fantastic expectations of punishment. This "retaliation fear" makes him overestimate slight threats and regard them as severe ones, and thus makes him the readier to accept educational prohibitions. As the carrier of the retaliative power, the superego is not only as strict toward the ego as the parents previously were, but it also endangers the child's ego in the manner in which he had earlier wished to endanger his parents.

A second consequence of the biological helplessness of the human infant is that every man takes into his later life a memory of the time when omnipotent outsiders set everything right when he himself was too weak to do so. This memory becomes the basis for a yearning which may be mobilized whenever the individual encounters a situation of helplessness. An active and independent attempt to master the world will be adopted when there is a possibility of succeeding. A frustrating and suppressing "authoritative" upbringing, inducing a lack of self-confidence, creates a passive longing for external omnipotent helpers. There are many ways in which various societies have abused this "yearning back."

What, then, causes education in some circumstances too relentlessly to hammer into children the conception, "Your impulses are dangerous," and where is the borderline between that which is necessary and that which is harmful?

To be sure, it is not necessary for every child to burn himself; education can and should anticipate the pain of burning by warning or threat. It is necessary to teach a child to take into consideration the interests of other people, because this taking-into-consideration is objectively the condition that governs the supply of love needed by the child. But it is also true that occasional satisfaction facilitates the relinquishment of perpetual satisfaction; definitive repression, however, results in the disturbance of all activities through the return from repression of the unsatisfied impulses.

One sometimes hears the statement that infantile sexuality might become dangerous if it were not repressed. Precisely the psychoanalyst, it is said, knows best that man is an instinct-driven being, that "the beast in man" is still alive, and that man would only kill and seek sexual enjoyment had he not learned to control himself. Actually this danger is not so grave. Experience shows that unsatisfied instincts are much more difficult to master than occasionally satisfied instincts. Sexual instincts are periodic phenomena that disappear after being satisfied and reappear only after a lapse of time. Economic instinct regulation by means of periodic discharge is possible. If the analyst today so often finds sexuality asocial and therefore dangerous, analysis shows that this is the consequence of a previous sexual repression, which hinders full periodic psychological discharge. Some people fear that unless a child represses his sexuality, he may become useless to society; he will expend all his energy in the sexual field, and nothing will be left for sublimation. Such a deduction is not justified. Sublimations are, it is true, produced by sexual energy (without explaining in detail, it may be added, by pregenital and not genital energy), but a voluntary suppression of sexuality does not bring about sublimation, but rather repression. The result is that the unsatisfied sexual impulse remains in the unconscious unchanged, and, from there, disturbs the intended sublimated activity.

If one remembers that prior to Freud science did not even know of the existence of infantile sexuality, one realizes how intensely mankind must have wished that it actually did not exist. Awareness of this wish should warn us against subscribing to the idea that infantile sexuality is dangerous, since this idea may be the product of the same tendency.

Thus the question arises as to the source of this tendency against accepting the existence of infantile sexuality. Of course, the anti-instinctual orientation of traditional education is an outgrowth of both present and past social situations, and must be criticized in the light of these social situations. The social limitations are perhaps best seen in the failure of too quick and simple attempts at reform. "Progressive education," in trying to avoid the errors of the preceding period and in order to prevent frustrations, has sometimes gone to the opposite extreme. It has, thereby, become no less dependent on social forces than "authoritarian" education. "Avoidance of frustration" is certainly impossible. Reality necessarily brings frustrations, and an artificially protected childhood is therefore a very poor preparation for it; the avoidance of early frustrations has the same effect as intense ones on persons brought up normally. The tendency of educators "always to be lenient" has the further consequence that (1) the child gains the impression that aggressiveness is terribly forbidden; when he feels aggression, he must repress it; the external leniency makes the superego (at least in its attitude toward aggressiveness) stricter, until the child may even long for an external strict authority as a relief; (2) the parents have to repress their own aggressiveness, which certainly will eventually make its involuntary appearance in an undesired manner and to an undesired degree.

There is no doubt that an artificial change in the education of a few individual children cannot spare these children severe conflicts. Actually, it is just the opposite. Sooner or later such children will be driven into even more severe conflict, because they will hear on all sides the contrary of what they are taught at home or at their special school.

The temptation is great to digress, to investigate the present-day situation in the light of a critical sociology of education. However, not much is yet known about this. The way to do it would be to compare the relations between educational procedures and prevalent character structures (and their social functions) in different societies. Modern anthropology has just begun to attack these questions; its work is, of course, seriously hampered by the lack of recorded history of most primitive societies. To return to modern conditions, I want to present two examples to give a general glimpse of the complexity of the problem.

A person's self-esteem, as well as the content and extent of his defenses, depends upon his "ideals." Ideals are developed less by direct teaching than by the general spirit that surrounds the growing child.

An authoritarian society must promote readiness for subsequent submission in its members by drumming into them the idea of all authority: conditional promises. "If you obey and submit, you will attain (real or imaginary) participation in power and protection." A democratic society favors the ideals of independence, self-reliance, and active mastery. Societies in which "authoritarian" and "democratic" elements are engaged in active struggle will be contradictory in their ideals as well. The child learns that he must submit and obey in order to get the supplies he needs; and at the same time he learns: "Stand on your own feet." Historically the "authoritarian" type of ideal was unopposed in feudalism; the subjects actually were provided for if they renounced their independence, and the psychic readiness of the majority of the people to accept such dependence was necessary to preserve society. Rising capitalism brought the opposite ideal. Free competition required the new ideals of equality and fraternity. The subsequent development of capitalism, however, not only created anew a majority of people who had to be kept contented in relative frustration and dependence, but economic contradictions gave rise to such instability in the social structure that, with the disappearance of free competition, there was a resurgence of authoritarian necessities. Simultaneously every member of society feels endangered in any attempt to become solidly established, and even in his very existence; hence the individual's activities are hopeless, and thus regressive longings for passive-receptive regulation come to the fore again. Old feudalistic ideals are revived and even intensified; and the result is a mixture of ideals, conflicts, and, later, neuroses. Differences in economic conditions as well as in the history are responsible for the enormous variations in the mixture of "authority" and "democracy" encountered today in different countries. In general, all capitalistic society, by preparing the children for the role that money and competition will play in their life, favors the intensification of anal-sadistic strivings. This is the more unfavorable because, simultaneously, genital sexuality is discouraged and thwarted.

A second, even more general example: It is characteristic of present-day society that many people are unable to satisfy their needs, despite the fact that the means of satisfaction are present. Textbooks of psychopathology discuss at length the deficiencies of the superego in persons who steal. But actually it seems that the problem should be formulated in another way: Why is it that so many people do *not* steal? It is true that in the first place they abstain because they are prevented by force. But the majority are not prevented merely by force and fear of punishment. Social reality has succeeded in awakening, in a special kind of conscience, an intrapsychic force that opposes the needs that ask for satisfaction. One does not steal because "it is not right." Thus special social institutions bring about the development of special counter-instinctual forces in the members of that society. This same necessity must likewise be the decisive factor in the anti-sexual orientation of certain civilizations.

These problems cannot, of course, be discussed in detail here. I shall be content if I have succeeded in making it clear that science (psychoanalysis among others) cannot do more than study the psychic characteristics of human beings, the mechanisms of pedagogical influences, and the actual use that has been made of these influences in various societies. It cannot set goals. What actually will be done with the knowledge compiled by science is dependent on social factors. Lest these conclusions sound too pessimistic, I hasten to add that latent within all scientific knowledge is the possibility of practical application and improvement.

TWENTY-FIVE

Elements of a Psychoanalytic Theory of Anti-Semitism*

SINCE psychoanalysis is a method of treating or investigating individual minds, there can be, strictly speaking, only a psychoanalysis of the anti-Semite, not of anti-Semitism. The question is, what can the comparison of *psychoanalyses of many anti-Semites* contribute to an understanding of the social phenomenon of anti-Semitism?

The motives of human action are determined not only by the biological structure, on the one hand, and actual external stimuli, on the other; but also by the history of the individual, i.e., by the influence of past external stimuli on the biological structure, which have formed and modified patterns of reaction; it is early gratifications and frustrations, permitted or prohibited discharges of instinctual energies in infancy, which created fears, hopes, and desires, and formed individual patterns of reaction. The irrational and rigid ones among the reaction patterns stem from influences which have met with a defense and have therefore remained unconscious, not participating in the maturation of the personality. Hence, irrational social reaction patterns have been designated "mass neuroses," because they actually are motivated by previous unconscious structure-forming conflicts of the individuals—like neuroses. They differ, however, from neuroses in two points: in regard to the social sanctions they receive, and to the social functions they fulfill.

In other words: The psychoanalysis of anti-Semites is indispensable if anti-Semitism is to be understood. But it is in no way sufficient to explain it. After a study of the influences determining the structure of the anti-Semitic personality

---

* First published in *Anti-Semitism: A Social Disease*, Ernst Simmel, ed., New York, Int. Univ. Press, 1946, pp. 11–32. A modified version of a paper published in *The American Imago*, Vol. I, 1940.

and of how this structure functions, the questions of the genesis of these influences and of the social function of the anti-Semitic reaction still remain unanswered. Although both individual neurotic phenomena and "mass neurotic" phenomena of political and historical significance have their origin in individual structure as well as in external influences, they are diametrically opposite in one respect. The individual neurotic does not react to current experiences in an appropriate way but with a definite pattern developed in childhood; this relative importance of the individual structure and comparative insignificance of current experiences may lead analysts—preoccupied with the treatment of neurotics—to underestimate the significance of current experiences and to overestimate structure. In the case of historically important mass-psychological phenomena, the contrary is true. The human instinctual structure has remained relatively unchanged in the course of historical times. It cannot be the chief factor requisite for an understanding of changes within these times. Of importance here are the current, external stimuli which affect the relatively constant human structure very differently in different eras and societies, particularly those current situations that affect whole groups in the same, or in a similar, way. The instinctual structure of the average man in Germany was no different in 1935 from what it was in 1925. The psychological mass basis for anti-Semitism, whatever it may be, existed in 1925 too, but anti-Semitism was not a political force then. If an understanding of its origin and development in that ten-year period in Germany is sought, then the investigation must be focused on what happened there during those years, and not on the comparatively unaltered unconscious. In order completely to understand the reaction of the masses to these happenings, however, it is essential also to understand *that which* is reacting, that which is roused or inhibited or displaced in the human structure; and for this psychoanalysis is needed.

In order to gain this understanding let us therefore begin at the surface and descend gradually to the depths. The principal thing which changed during those ten years was the amount of anti-Semitic mass propaganda. The effectiveness of this propaganda was the chief thing which altered the attitude of the masses. But why did this propaganda arise, and how did it work? What was present in the masses which made them believe what they were told? The first thought is that people are most ready to accept suggestions which bring some advantage to them. What advantage does anti-Semitism bring to the average man? Well, for instance, the prospect of obtaining a job which has been taken from a Jew. This should not be underestimated, but one sees at first glance that such an explanation is not sufficient, that it is too superficial because it is too unspecific. What purpose, then, does the spreading of anti-Semitic propaganda serve? Here we can perhaps learn more from Czarist Russia than from Germany. The Protocols of the Wise Men of Zion were forged by the Czarist police, who knew for what purpose they forged them. As a result of the general misery extant, there was a rebellious tendency directed against the ruling powers. The police surmised that, if the propaganda succeeded, the Jews would be thought to be the cause of conditions, and not the authorities, and the revolutionary tendency would be redirected against them. The terrible pogroms showed that this intention succeeded. The advantage that anti-Semitism gave to the average person, then, was different from that of the prospect of a job. The people were in a conflict between a rebellious tendency and the respect for authority to which they had been trained. Anti-Semitism gave them the means of satisfying these two contradictory tendencies at the same time; the rebellious tendency through destructive actions against defenseless people, and the respectful tendency through obedient action in response to the command of the ruling powers. The police plot achieved its goal: the people believed that their enemies were likewise the enemies of the ruling powers.

This undoubtedly correct, but neither sufficiently deep nor sufficiently specific, theory of anti-Semitism we shall call the "scapegoat theory." As is well known, the Jews used to load all their sins onto a goat and then drive it out into the desert in order to purify themselves. In the same way the ruling classes laid their sins onto the Jews. Just here, I should like to mention an excellent article by Arnold Zweig, which shows how deeply this conception of the Jews as scapegoats is anchored in the soul of the German people.[1] Zweig analyzes a folk tale by Grimm, the story of "The Jew in the Thorn," which tells of a man-servant who, having been swindled out of his wages, manages to get the money from a Jew instead of from his master; the chief point being that he feels himself to be absolutely right in cheating the Jew—after all, he himself had served his seven years honestly. Zweig correctly points out that all the features of modern anti-Semitism are strongly marked in this ancient folk tale, which dates at least from the time of the Bauernkrieg (Peasants' War), 1500 A.D. At that time, too, there was a ruling class that needed to deflect the mass-discontent directed against itself; then, too, apart from this mass-displeasure, there was a mass-preparedness for submission, a change in the structure of the masses brought about by education; their conscience troubled them when they dared to think of proceeding against the authorities. They were therefore grateful that they could vent their rage without anything happening to their masters or without rousing their anger, and against an opponent who dared not defend himself.

But we must go further. This explanation applies to the persecution of all minorities. It needs specifications on such questions as: What kind of people tend to

[1] A. Zweig, "Der Jude im Dorn," *Die Weltbuehne,* Berlin, 1936.

accept suggested "scapegoats"; what kind of people tend to reject the suggestion; how do the members of the minority react to their role as scapegoats? Moreover, it is in itself not specific enough as a theory. The next problem that presents itself, a problem not neglected by Zweig either, is Why are the Jews especially suitable as displacement substitutes? Is it mere chance that in a given situation anti-Semitic propaganda is instituted and not, for instance, propaganda against redheads? Surely not. There must be something in the mass mind which meets anti-Semitism halfway; the Jew must be the "born scapegoat" for his hosts. That he is preferred to redheads is due to his history, which shows how often he has proved his suitability as a scapegoat.

Why is this role so fatally suited to him?

The first answer to this question is a rational one. The Jew has always been more defenseless than the redhead. Secondly, when the social order, or rather, disorder, produces undue misery, then the victim of this misery rarely is in a position to discover its origin, partly because the underlying causes are too complicated, and partly because the existing ruling class does everything in its power to obscure the true connections. The point is then to find someone in the environment who appears to the victim to be the cause of his misery. For centuries it has been the Jew, in his role as money lender, and as tradesman, who has appeared to those confronted with financial need as the representative of money, regardless of how much Jewish poverty prevailed at the same time. This point must not be underestimated, either. It must be remembered that the Armenians, too, who were persecuted by the Turks, just as the Jews had been persecuted by the Russians and Germans, were the commercial people among their Turkish hosts. Still the impression persists that too much importance should not be placed on this situation, that it only serves to strengthen other factors which come from more unconscious depths, and which are not yet known. It must also be pointed out that the persecution of minorities for their commercial activities does not hold with respect to other social phenomena analogous to anti-Semitism, for instance the persecution of Negroes in America. The American Negroes were slaves, and in order to understand their ostracism, the history and social function of slavery, and of the fights for and against it, have to be studied. But the Negroes have another trait that makes them suitable as scapegoats: they are black. Jews have also been reviled by anti-Semites because of their cultural or physical "racial" peculiarities. Their hair frequently is black, even if their skin is not; moreover, they are foreign in their customs and habits, in their language, in their divine service, and in their everyday life which is so interwoven with their divine service. This foreignness they share with the Armenians, the Negroes, and the gypsies; and herein is to be found the secret which has made others believe them to be wicked evil-doers. People of one's own kind and the ruling powers one does not suspect of evil, but people who look different and speak and behave differently—they may be capable of anything. In this sense, there is some truth in the frequent anti-Semitic assertion: "Anti-Semitism is the Jews' own doing, because their behavior is provocative." However, it must be added that it is not the "bad manners" of the Jew which are provocative, but his specific strangeness, which we will now try to study.

At this point the question of anti-Semitism moves away from the psychology of the anti-Semitic people, and goes over to the psychology of the Jews. The obstinacy with which the Jews have resisted assimilation through the ages, although other people in similar situations have, during the course of history, been absorbed by their hosts, represents a problem too complex for thorough examination here. It is obviously due (1) to the ghetto system, which excluded the Jews artificially from full participation in the cultural life of the host nations, the origin and function of this system presenting a problem of its own, and (2) to a stubborn acceptance of the ghetto system by the Jews themselves. The Jews retained their peculiarities, and their hosts did not understand them. These peculiarities, however, were conspicuous. They stem partly from the time when the Jews had an independent state, and were adhered to because of their never-ending hope of regaining that state—and partly from much later times. Cult and holy literature stem from that very ancient past, and have an oriental stamp. In their clothes and everyday language, however, they were fixated at an entirely different period. The Jewish language as well as traditional Jewish clothing resemble the language and clothing used by the Germans during those centuries when the Jews, driven from Spain, passed through and temporarily settled in Germany on their way to the East. The Jews retained peculiarities of their hosts, which these hosts themselves had given up long since. Subsequently, their strangeness gave the impression of something archaic, of something left over from ancient times—which the non-Jew himself had overcome—similar to the strangeness with which the nomadism of the gypsies impressed the settled peoples.

What does all this mean psychologically? What underlies the equation of primitive thinking: Foreign = Hostile? Even today we meet every foreigner in a contradictory or, as we say, ambivalent manner. Some nations, like the British, do this to a large extent, others, like the Americans, to a lesser. The essential quality of foreigners is that one does not know them yet and therefore does not know what to expect from them. Perhaps it would be as well to be on good terms with them, or perhaps it would be better to render them harmless as quickly as possible. How different it must have been in ancient times, when nations had less frequent contact with one another, when the cultural peculiarities of each nation were much more strongly marked. Foreigners might bring advantages through inventions they had made or be a danger if they were more advanced in the technique of arms. In the ancient world foreigners were *sacer,* an interesting word, which meant both holy and accursed. The strangeness of the Jews was of a special kind because of its archaic character, which often was combined with an indisputable mental superiority in certain spheres, which, in turn, perhaps was made use of by the commercial Jews, to take advantage of other people. The Jews were clever, and at the same time appeared to be connected with old primeval powers with which the others had lost touch. When the authorities said that these "uncanny" people were evil, the others readily believed the authorities because of their own obvious misery.

Therefore, what could one expect from the Jews? What fantastic evils were they capable of? We may begin here with ritual murder and the poisoning of wells, but we must also specify other things. Let us look at any kind of anti-Semitic literature. We read, again and again, that the Jews are murderers, are filthy, are debauched.

The first problem again must be to find the rational part of these accusations. Actually there is none. The Jew is a merchant and as such may be a swindler, but criminal statistics show that Jewish murderers are fewer than those of any other race. The religious laws of the Jews prescribe particular cleanliness; and although the impoverished Jewish towns are undoubtedly very dirty, they are no more and probably less so than the Polish, White Russian, and Russian peasant villages; with regard to sexuality the Jews do not tend to excesses more than any other group. The accusations made against the Jews are creations of the peoples' imagination and these charges must be investigated in connection with the archaic foreignness that the Jews possess in the eyes of other races.

In psychoanalysis, we are in the habit of saying: "The patient is always right" —i.e., even the most senseless neurotic phenomenon has a hidden meaning. In reality, the Jews are not murderous, dirty, or debauched to a greater extent than other groups. The latent meaning in the assertion that they are implies that murderous, dirty, and voluptuous tendencies are really concealed somewhere, and that once again the Jew is a scapegoat, a displacement substitute. Where are these tendencies to be found? Who is the real sinner?

Freud has taught us that everybody struggles all his life with repressed instincts which continue to exist in the unconscious; that among these original instincts, murderous tendencies and sexual impulses play the chief part, especially those sexual impulses which are considered objectionable, low, and dirty. The lust to kill, love of dirt, and low voluptuousness—these are the things which people try painstakingly to keep hidden in their unconscious. One means of defense against strivings of one's unconscious is projection, that is, seeing in others that which one does not wish to become conscious of in oneself. This is a manifestation most marked in certain mental diseases, but it is also present in normal people, as for example, in the crusader against homosexuality, who is really fighting against his own repressed homosexual impulses. To the anti-Semite, the Jew appears to be murderous, dirty, and debauched; thus the former can avoid becoming aware of these tendencies in himself. To him the Jew is the incarnation of the lust to kill, of low sexuality. It will shortly become clear how this projection is facilitated. But it is already comprehensible why riotous impulses are so easily deflected against the Jews. For the unconscious of the rioters, the Jew represents not only the authorities whom they do not dare to attack, but also their own repressed instincts which they hate and which are forbidden by the very authorities against whom they are directed. Anti-Semitism is indeed a condensation of the most contradictory tendencies: instinctual rebellion directed against the authorities, and the cruel suppression and punishment of this instinctual rebellion, directed against oneself. Unconsciously for the anti-Semite, the Jew is simultaneously the one against whom he would like to rebel, and the rebellious tendencies within himself. And a racial minority such as the Jew is especially suited to act as the carrier of this kind of projection because of its archaic and emphatic foreignness.

It can be expressed in one sentence: One's own unconscious is also foreign. Foreignness is the quality which the Jews and one's own instincts have in common. This is a particular case of Freud's explanation of the general phenomenon of that which is "uncanny" psychologically.[2] The feeling of uncanniness comes over us whenever something, that we once believed to be true and then rejected, proves to be true after all. All happenings are uncanny which seem to prove the existence of magical connections in the world, because we once thought magically, and later renounced this way of thinking in favor of the logical one. To the average person a murderer, in particular a parricide, or someone guilty of incest is uncanny, because each of us has felt such impulses—and later repressed them. Conversely, a person or race which is in any way uncanny, is capable of murder and incest. The Jew with his unintelligible language and incomprehensible God appears uncanny to non-Jews, not only because they cannot understand him and therefore can imagine him capable of all sorts of sins, but even more so because, somewhere in the depths, they can understand him very well, for his customs are archaic, that is, they exhibit elements which the non-Jews once had, but lost later. The average German regards Jewish language and dress not only as "strange," but a caricature, a ridiculing of his own language and dress. The Jewish language is, to him, "German in an ugly disguise."

There is also a rational reaction which helps to strengthen the irrational side. The Jews as a racial minority have been oppressed everywhere. It is clear that

[2] S. Freud, "The Uncanny," *Coll. Pap.*, Vol. II, London, Hogarth, 1948.

the ruling people must fear the possible revenge of the oppressed people, particularly when the oppression appears to be unsuccessful, with the oppressed rising again and again, in the belief that they themselves are a chosen people, and refusing to give up their peculiarity despite all torture. Jehovah is held to be a revengeful God; and there is no doubt that he is described in many places in the Old Testament as a very revengeful old gentleman. But there is also no doubt that the command: "Love thy neighbor as thyself" does not come from the Christian religion but from the Jewish, that the Jewish God showed many loving and merciful traits, too. Why have these traits been forgotten by other races, and why do they imagine Jehovah, like the abstract concept of the Jew and of the Jewish people, to be malicious and revengeful? This concept, being of an irrational nature, cannot be changed by any real experiences with Jews. It is well known that every anti-Semite is acquainted with one Jew who is free of all abominable Jewish qualities, yet this does not make any difference in his anti-Semitism.

The endless vengefulness of the wicked Jews is again a projection. The ruling people cannot imagine that the oppressed are not revengeful. They recognize archaic-deep features in their behavior, and they know how revengeful they themselves would be. Rejected instincts and rejected ancient times are revived for them in these incomprehensible people who live as strangers in their midst. That which they had believed to be overcome appears to rise again and again like a hydra, and they try to cut off its heads. At the same time, they despise it in the same way in which they despise their own disavowed instincts. Contempt and disregard are intended to help them overcome their fear. They try to refute their fear by proving to themselves how easy it is to attack the defenseless. But the proof is never definitive. With a curious pride, even with arrogance, the defenseless rise again and again. The fear is not dispelled, and therefore they must go on despising and humiliating over and over again to refute this irrefutable fear. And yet they never succeed.

Apart from all this, there are still other circumstances which make the position clearer. One is the fact that Jewish peculiarities and culture center almost exclusively around a common faith, the Jewish religion.

When the Romans conquered a nation, they erected a temple in Rome to the gods of the conquered people—to be on the safe side. This god might be powerful, then they would have to fear his revenge for oppressing his people; in any case, it was better to be reconciled with him. The revenge of the gods of the oppressed nation is a dangerous thing.

Now there is a strange thing about the gods. The religions of all peoples and all times work with the fear which stems from the "uncanny." Both the image of the god himself and the cult contain many "archaic" features reanimating elements that are old and have been overcome, in order to fill the believers with fear or awe, and thus keep a hold on them. The gods have always had not only supernatural traits but besides also "low" animal and instinctual traits which evoke fear. One thing seemed to rouse their particular wrath: namely, to be looked at. In the Jewish religion, too, the sight of the Holy of Holies was reserved for the High Priest once a year, and the congregation had to turn away at Yom Kippur when the priest threw himself on his knees before God. The sight of God (among primitive people the sight of the king, his representative) means death.

Instead of discussing the significance and genesis of this prohibition against looking, it may suffice here to state that it is universal. From this prohibition against looking it is only one step to the idea that God is a terrible, horror-inspiring—an ugly sight. And, as is well known, many of the gods of primitive people are incredibly ugly. In the higher religions, there are concealed allusions of a similar kind understandable as such through psychoanalysis. It is interesting that the uncanniness of the ugly God is based on his reanimating something which had been overcome. For the ugly features of a god are always animal features, and the first incarnation of the dead chief, the great ancestor, who was later made a god, was the totem animal, and totemism preceded religion. This awe-inspiring part of the cult, where a dreadful being threatened to show himself, exercised a strange charm. Today we see a degenerated residue in the side-shows at fairs. The fairs originated in connection with the worship of God, and were connected with it (much as a satyr play is connected with the seriousness of the tragedy) and are still called "Messe" in German, which has the meaning of "mass." Here people are offered dreadful sights which are otherwise forbidden or inaccessible. And what is there to be seen? Rare animals, deformities, waxen images of criminals, sexual secrets. It may seem like blasphemy to relate this to the worship of God, but there is a connection which does not rouse this feeling and which leads us back to anti-Semitism. At the fair one does not see native, but exotic, animals; and one does not see native, but exotic, gods. This double character of wonder and fear, of highest beauty and terrifying ugliness, attributes of God, merges with the double character of wonder and fear, inherent in foreigners—both are *sacer*—in terms of the feeling one has for strange gods, and which caused the Romans to erect temples to the conquered gods. It is unbearable, in the long run, to have contradictory feelings for one and the same object. And in the same way that the fairy tale makes it possible for the child to manage the contradictory feelings it has for its mother, by introducing two mothers, a wholly good mother and a wholly wicked stepmother, thereby dividing between two people the love and hate felt toward the same person, so the perception of a strange god has been used by all people in all ages to divide the love and hate felt for God between two objects: their own God, who is good and beautiful, and the strange one who is wicked and ugly.

Many religious systems are dualistic. They have a good and a bad principle, an Ahriman and an Ormuzd, separate from God—a devil. Reik has shown that the devil is the degenerate strange god, the god of the strange, of the conquered people, whose revenge is feared.[3] The devil is always more uncanny than God, always has more archaic characteristics, namely animal qualities—goats' feet, horns, tail, and ugliness. Therefore, he is always suitable as a carrier of the projection of one's own instinctual impulses; he is murderous, dirty, debauched, a tempter, and a deceiver. It is clear to the anti-Semite that the Jewish God, and thus the Jew, is the devil, the anti-Christ, the wicked principle directed against God, which crucified God. The devil, too, characteristically is despised and dreaded at the same time. One thing more: this "degraded" strange God is not only animal and ugly—he is usually crippled. The deformed, blind, lame, and hunchbacked are *sacer* to primitive people; they are regarded as beings near to God, as seers, but also as dangerous; altogether, they are uncanny to the ordinary mortal. Interesting, though outside the theme of this paper, is the fact that ordinary man entertains similar feelings toward the artist; he, too, has retained a more archaic character. Frequently, we see that people who have longer noses and darker hair than others are therefore regarded as practically deformed. What is the rational essence of the special position of deformed people? The deaf, hunchbacks, and, in particular, red-haired people are regarded as malicious and ill-natured. Why? Because they are really at a disadvantage compared with average people, and because the average people tend to despise and laugh at them, and they, in turn, tend to protect themselves by aggressiveness. The physically inferior are a badly treated minority, and therefore their revenge is feared. This fear is condensed with the deep feelings of uncanniness entertained toward the devil and the cripple-god, and increases when any physical disadvantage or dissimilarity is combined with superiority in certain mental spheres (think of the uncanny, skillful, lame blacksmith of the sagas). Such a combination is considered proof of a magic alliance with supernatural powers (particularly so if the bearers of such marks regard themselves as the "chosen people"). Like the Jewish language, the typical Jewish physical appearance is felt and cartooned as diabolically ugly.

But the sight of a cripple not only rouses the fear of strangeness and revenge, but also the special fear that he will want to transform others into cripples. It would lead too far to undertake a psychoanalysis of the burial and death customs of the various peoples. But we know that they are all based on the tendency to prevent an unconsciously feared return of the dead, who could revenge them-

[3] T. Reik, *Der eigene und aer fremde Gott,* Vienna, Int. Psa. Verlag, 1920.

selves for their dying by fetching the living and causing them also to die. Is there any reason to suppose that other people fear that Jews may want to change them into Jews, too?

Reference is often made to the opinion once expressed by Freud that anti-Semitism is connected with the Jewish custom of circumcision.[4] It is, of course, not my intention to maintain that anti-Semitism consists only of the uncircumcised despising the circumcised as unmanly, and fearing that the circumcised will want to circumcise them in revenge. The matter is somewhat more complicated, and circumcision is only one of many customs which are felt to be uncanny. But I should like to elaborate what Freud meant by this remark.

Circumcision is not a purely Jewish custom. Many other races have this archaic custom, too; the problem here is why the Jews have remained conservative in this respect, as in so many others. Apart from the oriental peoples, circumcision is practiced among many primitive races—proof of the age-old nature of this custom. Some primitive races which do not practice circumcision have other analogous customs, more or less sanguinary injuries to the genitals or other parts of the body which have become substitutes for the genitals. To be sure, such injuries are usually perpetrated on young people at puberty and not soon after birth. This is the essence of the so-called "initiation ceremonies" whereby the young people are accepted into the adult community. It is certain that this is the older form of the custom, and that in the case of the Jews, for some unknown reason, the ceremony was transposed from puberty to infancy. It is not easy to determine the meaning of such holy practices.[5] Perhaps it can be guessed by their effect. The youth who has now become a man will be proud of his initiation into the adult community, and this feeling will be increased by his now being allowed the right of sexual intercourse—among others; but the price he has had to pay for this admittance, that of having to endure pain, shows him drastically that he can enjoy the protection of this community only as long as he obeys it, and that he may expect unpleasant things if he does not adhere to certain conditions. And in fact, this and analogous social measures have worked. Even today, we find deep in the unconscious of man the fear that his penis may be cut off if he sins, a fear which acts as the chief motor for the instinct-suppression desired by the patriarchal society.

The drastic reminder of the sanguinary puberty rites of the primitives has been replaced by less drastic measures during the course of history.[6] The Jewish circumcision, although practiced on the infant, is still comparatively drastic. It

[4] S. Freud, "Analysis of a Phobia in a Five-Year-Old Boy," *Coll. Pap.*, Vol. III, London, Hogarth, 1948.

[5] T. Reik, "The Puberty Rites of Savages," *The Psychological Problems of Religion.* Vol. I, *Ritual: Psychoanalytic Studies*, New York, Farrar, Straus, 1946.

[6] O. Fenichel, "Trophy and Triumph," No. 10 this volume.

has remained a really sanguinary operation on the genitals. The knowledge of this fact on the part of the uncircumcised has undoubtedly increased the feeling of uncanniness which the Jew gives them. It has helped to lend a more precise form to the indefinite fear that a retaliation on the part of these curious people is imminent; this retaliation assumes a sexual form. The Jews will do something to the little girls of other races in the same way that they do something sanguinary-sexual to the little boys of their own race. Psychoanalysts are of the opinion, therefore, that circumcision, which is strange—yet familiar in unconscious depths—operates in the same way as the other customs which make the Jew appropriate as a devil-projection.

In addition to stubbornly retaining archaic features and rejecting occasional opportunities for assimilation—or rather accepting the external denials of opportunities for assimilation with a kind of Gueux pride—and centering all this around his religion, the Jew does this in a manner which makes him still more apposite as a scapegoat for others.

We assume that what is called "national character" is created historically through actual conditions of living which, reflecting traditional ways of child raising, are perpetuated through the impress of one generation upon the succeeding one. Among the traits of the Jewish national character, there is one which is especially striking. It seems as if less direct aggression is permissible to the Jew than to other nations (which may be connected with the fact that the use of arms was prohibited to them for centuries). Instead, they develop many forms of indirect aggression. One of these indirect aggressions is their traditional belief in their being the chosen people, superior to the "barbarians." Jewish tradition is extremely patriarchal. The son is not permitted in any way to rebel directly against the father. The father, however, is proud of his son when he himself is surpassed by his son in some intellectual or spiritual accomplishment. Analysts know similar pictures from the study of compulsion neurotics with severe and ambivalent father complexes. Their masochism and guilt feeling is obvious, their latent sadism and rebellion is masked by Gueux pride and intellect. This Jewish patriarchal tradition determined the way in which the Jews, through the centuries, became accustomed to react to the anti-Semitism of their environment: (a) Superficially: "The more others exclude us, the nearer we are to our God." (b) On a deeper level: "By participating in the power of our God, we are magically superior to our enemies to whom we are physically inferior." This attitude increased the uncanny magical fear the host peoples felt toward the Jews, which, in turn, gave rise to increased "attack" by the belief in magical superiority on the part of the Jews and increased attack gave rise to increased fear and anti-Semitism.

What caused Jewish national character to evolve in this way is a problem in itself. Here again, the ghetto system may offer a partial explanation. However, extreme patriarchism is in no way limited to people who have lived in ghettos, but is rather generally a sign that in the given culture the idea of murdering the father is more definitely repressed than in others, which must be due to the social history of the nation in question. Freud, in his book on Moses,[7] suggested a hypothesis as to why the Christian religion has admitted the idea of "killing God" to consciousness, whereas the Jews have repressed it. (This is the reason why the Christians, projectively, tend to accuse the Jews of this very crime of being the "murderers of God.") For our purpose, it is enough to understand that the ancient history of a people forms and determines the structure of the character of subsequent generations by means of tradition and education.

To sum up: The anti-Semite arrives at his hate of the Jews by a process of displacement, stimulated from without. He sees in the Jew everything which brings him misery—not only his social oppressor but also his own unconscious instincts, which have gained a bloody, dirty, dreadful character from their socially induced repression. He can project onto the Jews, because the actual peculiarities of Jewish life, the strangeness of their mental culture, their bodily (black) and religious (God of the oppressed peoples) peculiarities, and their old customs make them suitable for such a projection.

Perhaps there will be one objection to this formula: If it is true, two premises must be fulfilled before anti-Semitism can become a mass movement. First, a revolutionary mood, or at least an intense discontent of the masses with the existing state of affairs, a discontent that may be channeled in the direction of the Jews as scapegoats; second, a Jewish cultural life and tradition in the midst of the host culture, without there being much connection between the two. Both of these conditions were present in Czarist Russia, which therefore provided the ideal conditions for the development of anti-Semitism. The situation was probably similar in the anti-Semitic movement of the Middle Ages. However, the conditions do not seem to be fulfilled in modern anti-Semitism, either in National Socialist Germany or in the United States. In Germany, the emancipation of the Jews had made considerable progress. The majority of the Berlin Jews had little or no Jewish life or tradition, a fact which the Prague and Viennese Jews, who were nearer to the Eastern Jews, often used to ridicule. The Berlin Jews considered themselves Germans. There was no archaic foreignness appropriate for purposes of projection. However, the success of using the Jews and not redheads as scapegoats proves that the foreignness, or at least the memory of it, was still there. We may assume that discontent of the masses and Jewish separateness form a complementary series in order to produce anti-Semitism. In Germany prior to National Socialism, the discontent of the masses

---

[7] S. Freud, *Moses and Monotheism*, New York, Knopf, 1939.

was so enormous that little Jewish separateness was needed. Jewish emancipation was young, and the Middle Ages had been long. Historical changes occur slowly, and memories of "Jewish separateness" were, in spite of the relative actual absence of this separateness, strong enough to permit the development of anti-Semitism when mass discontent became acute.

But what about the United States? At first glance, one may perhaps assume that here the complementary series is reverse in structure. There is no general revolutionary mood, and at least in some parts of the United States, traditional Jewish life is practiced by many. However, Jewish peculiarities have certainly not increased recently, whereas anti-Semitism has. Does this mean that there is actually a mass discontent comparable to the discontent in pre-Hitler Germany? It seems as if our theory of anti-Semitism compels us to assume something of the kind. In a certain sense, something of "mass discontent" must be present; the question is, in what sense? Probably the answer has to be sought in two directions: (1) The suffering of the American people in the last war certainly did not stand any comparison with the enormous suffering of the European peoples. But if we do not compare Americans and Europeans, but rather measure the present conditions in America against the past, we must admit that relatively Americans *are* suffering. (2) In all fields we hear complaints about lack of enthusiasm among Americans for our democracy and for their rights, which they take too much for granted. Their intellectual insight into their advantages and into the necessity of fighting for them, as well as the readiness to act according to this insight, exist; nevertheless, an emotional enthusiasm for it is generally and strikingly lacking. Probably this is due to the feeling that the hope for a more positive emotional gain, for a reliable end of the insecurities of the present world situation is lacking, and cannot be achieved through any amount of enthusiasm. To understand this, however, one would have to analyze the sociology of democracy, and of the factual possibilities, the successes and failures of democracy.

And so we have come back to where we began, to an admission of the limitations of the psychological explanation. The full utilization of the psychological facts which we have studied so that they become a real and politically effective power is only possible under certain economic and political circumstances. To discuss these is beyond the scope of this paper. However, this does not mean that they are of secondary importance.

TWENTY - SIX

On Acting*

I

ADVERSARIES of psychoanalysis sometimes state that psychoanalysis, in investigating a psychological field, cannot do anything but name the instincts which are supposed to be at the basis of the field in question. That is certainly not true. No analyst was ever of the opinion that the significance of a given phenomenon, for example as "oral" or "anal," suffices to explain the phenomenon; and psychoanalysis does not study instincts only, but the dynamic interrelations between instincts and the outer world, or between instincts and counterforces from the outer world.

Nevertheless the question of what instincts (erogenous zones, or partial instincts) form the basis of a given phenomenon actually is a good starting point for a psychoanalytic investigation. Sometimes the "counterforces" and the ways in which they work can be better directly approached with the help of an understanding of the nature of the instincts against which they are directed.

Concerning *acting*, there is no doubt about the nature of the underlying basic partial instinct: it is *exhibitionism*. Therefore, let us start with a few remarks about exhibitionism.

Exhibitionism is a sexual partial instinct. It is normally present in all children, and it forms a characteristic part of sexual forepleasure. Its aim is to present the body, or especially the excited erogenous zones and their functions, to onlookers.[1] With the establishment of infantile genital primacy, the wish to show the genitals is certainly in the foreground in the exhibitionism of children of both sexes. Later the differences in the development of the castration complex in the two sexes determines a corresponding difference in the development of

* First published in *Psa. Quart.*, Vol. 15, 1946, pp. 144–160.
[1] S. Freud, *Three Essays on the Theory of Sexuality*, London, Imago, 1949.

exhibitionism. Male exhibitionism remains concentrated on the genitals; therefore it is apt to give reassurance against castration fear. In this way, the partial instinct of exhibitionism is used in the *perversion* "exhibitionism," in which unconsciously the spectator is either expected to confirm the presence of a penis, or to show his own penis, for the purpose of contradicting the existence of persons without a penis.

In the female, the idea of being castrated inhibits genital exhibitionism. Women who have a perverse wish to show their genitals are rare, and their analysis reveals unusual circumstances which make them believe that they still possess a penis. Instead, the exhibitionism of women is *displaced* from the genitals to other parts of the body and to the body in general. This nongenital exhibitionism of women is not apt to form a definite perversion; it is rather socially tolerated and encouraged.[2] This displacement of female exhibitionism is the source of all conceptions of "female beauty." It justifies the feeling that all "sublimation" of exhibitionism is somehow feminine, whereas the exhibitionistic man remains with his exhibitionism in the direct and unsublimated sexual sphere. This basic characteristic of exhibitionism makes it understandable that the art of acting is generally looked upon as a feminine art, and—although one should be careful of making hasty generalizations—that the percentage of homosexuals seems to be higher among actors than in most other professions.

Also other characteristics which are generally ascribed to actors may be connected with the specific characteristics of exhibitionism. In discussing acting, a follower of Adler took special occasion to polemize against the idea of connecting acting with sexual exhibitionism: actors are more or less *vain;* they need *applause* and *glory;* they need the approbation of an audience; the will for power is obvious. The theory of organ inferiority can often be confirmed. Demosthenes is not the only stammerer who later became a public speaker. Is there any reason to connect all this with sexuality?

We know that all these needs, which we call narcissistic needs, are not exclusive of sex. It is true that, in a normal adult person, narcissistic and erotic needs are differentiated from each other to a certain degree, but that was not always so. The infant in its original primary narcissism feels omnipotent, and does not need any object. Later, as is well known, the child loses confidence in its own omnipotence, and instead believes that the adults around it are omnipotent. When that occurs, it has only one tendency: to participate again in the omnipotence which it has lost, and which is now represented in persons around it. It wants to be reunited with these persons, to eat them, to be eaten by them, to rob them of their power, to ingratiate itself with them; any means to influence the powerful persons to give the necessary gratifications is tried. To be reunited

[2] Cf. J. Harnik, "The Various Developments Undergone by Narcissism in Men and Women," *Int. J. Psa.,* Vol. 5, 1924.

with them, or to obtain these gratifications, is narcissistic and sexual satisfaction simultaneously. Still later, the regulation of self-esteem becomes relatively independent of outer gratifications, and is controlled by the superego. But this independence is never a complete one, and certain persons remain fixated on the phase of development where sexual and narcissistic needs were identical, and where outer gratifications were needed.

The so-called "neurotic need for affection" achieves its highest degree in certain perversions of submissiveness (*Hörigkeit*), in addicts, and in persons with manic-depressive predisposition. Persons of this type do not know any sexual longing except this need of "being fed" or of "being reunited." Often this need is reinforced by regression after some decisive anxiety has been experienced, the regression to the receptive longing being a means of being protected against the supposed dangers by magic, supplied by the omnipotent adults. These "oral" persons—like perverts—are fixated on this sexual component of their childhood which promises to give instinctual pleasure and, simultaneously, *security*. Security is denial of the danger that had caused the anxiety which had blocked their further development. People with a strong "will for power" are always persons who are unconsciously afraid, and who need "power" to counteract their anxiety.[3]

What does all this have to do with exhibitionism? Exhibitionism is a partial instinct which, by its very nature, is especially apt to give narcissistic reassurance and erogenous pleasure simultaneously. The "characteristic role" which exhibitionism plays in normal sexual forepleasure, which we mentioned before, consists in the fact that it attracts and influences the onlooker; in the perversion it is a means of inducing the spectator to give the needed reassurance against castration anxiety. In exhibitionism, erogenous pleasure and the narcissistic satisfaction of having an audience are not condensed, they are *one and the same*. The sexual pleasure of the exhibitionist consists in using the spectator to satisfy his narcissistic needs. Persons who are fixated on this partial instinct are regularly persons who need this specific type of pleasure for the purpose of counteracting inner fears. In sublimated and desexualized exhibitionism, erogenous pleasure is absent; narcissistic pleasure remains. Actors—that is, persons who supply their dependent needs by a sublimated and desexualized exhibitionism—are persons with specific anxieties; or rather, with specific ways of handling their anxieties by influencing an audience.

The use of exhibitionism for magic is millenniums old. Freud devoted a paper, published after his death, to the apotropaic use of exhibitionism.[4] The man shows his penis as his weapon, to frighten the demons; the woman shows her genitals, which means: "remember the possibility of castration, and be afraid"—which also

---

[3] For a more detailed discussion of these points and for the literature, cf. O. Fenichel, "Early Stages of Ego Development," No. 3 in this volume.

[4] S. Freud, "Medusa's Head," *Coll. Pap.*, Vol. V, London, Hogarth, 1950.

frightens the demons. (The figure of the frightening phallic woman is a secondary one; the phallus attributed to her originally served the purpose of denying the fact that it is absent; but this attempt fails, and the woman remains frightening nevertheless.)

The magic threat of a display or a "show" also determines the origin of the theater. When priests, in sacred acts, imitated the gods, they certainly did so for the purpose of influencing the believers, and probably the idea of frightening them was not the least among the aims of that influence. We do not know much about the psychology of ancient priests, but we assume that the aim of magically influencing an audience, or especially of magically threatening an audience, plays a part in the unconscious of actors.

Summary of the unconscious aims of "acting"

1. It affords a certain erogenous satisfaction of an exhibitionistic nature. (This satisfaction has to remain at a minimum. If it is more intense, it will disturb the actor's performance.)

2. Direct narcissistic satisfaction from applause, an outwardly provided increase of self-esteem. Success on the stage is needed in the same way as milk and affection are needed by the infant.

3. Narcissistic satisfaction from a sense of magical influence on the audience. This influence may be directed toward compelling the audience to applaud, toward threatening the audience, or at least toward showing the actor's own superiority and power, which—as can generally be said wherever the "will to power" is strong—is needed for soothing anxiety, probably in an apotropaic way. From our general knowledge about exhibitionism, we may assume that this anxiety is mostly castration fear.

II

How are these aims of acting approached? By *playing parts*. What is "playing"? What is a "part"?

All languages state that the actor "plays." There must be a deep connection between actors acting on the stage and children playing games. The playing of "parts" certainly also assumes a dominant role in children's games.[5] Thanks to Freud,[6] we know what the psychology of children's play is. Playing is a process of learning while developing the ability to master the outer world. The primitive game is repetitive. It serves the purpose of achieving a belated mastery of highly cathected impressions. What was endured passively is done over again in play

---

[5] Cf. M. Klein, "Personification in the Play of Children," *Int. J. Psa.*, Vol. 10, 1929.

[6] S. Freud, *Beyond the Pleasure Principle*, London, Hogarth, 1948. Cf. also the summary by R. Waelder, "The Psychoanalytic Theory of Play," *Psa. Quart.*, Vol. 2, 1933.

in an active manner, until the child has become familiar with the qualities and quantities involved. The more highly developed game is anticipatory. It creates tensions which *might* occur, but, at a time and in a degree which is determined by the participant himself, and which therefore is under control. Such playing is an anti-surprise measure. Both these types of "playing" are also represented in acting on the stage. More frequently the actor acts by assuming emotions which he does not have but which he might have; or he displaces tensions, which he once experienced in his past, onto imaginary persons and abreacts "unmastered" tensions in identification with them. "Abreaction" is a term which originated in the world of the theater (Aristotle). Thus acting provides for the actor either a belated getting-rid of anxieties, or a defensive anticipation of possible future anxieties.

An actress-patient who was very much afraid of all her emotions, frigid also in her sexual life, always tense and on guard, changed immediately on the stage. Identified with her part, she could permit herself to give in to emotions.

In his "part" the actor shows himself, but not as he really is. Indeed in pretending to be somebody else, he does not show himself; he conceals himself. The importance of this point is demonstrated by the actress-patient described. Her exhibitionism, usually inhibited, was permitted to express itself under the conditions that she actually did not show herself, but some other character created by an author.

But that cannot be entirely true. A good actor actually reveals himself. He cannot play an emotion he has not experienced. The good actor *believes* that he plays his parts; actually he plays himself.

Something very similar may be observed in certain neurotic characters. People of this type sometimes give an ungenuine, affected impression. Analysis of what they are pretending reveals that they actively play at what they are afraid of experiencing passively and in an overwhelming manner. There are many variations of such pretending, the extreme represented by those habitual liars whose lies in the analysis turn out to be confessions of what they have actually experienced.[7]

Certainly the actor does not play himself as he actually is, but rather as he might have developed under different circumstances. Wittels has described "phantoms," fantasied personalities, which in everybody's mind play a certain role as ideals or possibilities for their own development, and which influence their actual behavior.[8] Although objection may be made to describing these "phan-

---

[7] Cf. H. Deutsch, "Ueber die pathologische Luege (Pseudologia phantastica)," *Int. Z. Psa.,* Vol. 8, 1922; and O. Fenichel, "The Economics of Pseudologia Phantastica," No. 9 in this volume.

[8] The "phantoms" are developed under the influence of real experiences and represent earlier identifications, not necessarily identifications with real objects but also with objects as the child saw

toms" as if they were independent intrapsychic personalities, it cannot be denied that everybody has fantasies and daydreams about how he would like to be, about roles which he would or would not like to assume under certain circumstances. If an actor's "phantom" fits his part, we say: "The part suits him." The good actor is characterized by the high multiplicity of his "phantoms."

To my knowledge, there are two schools of acting. One school believes only in "intuition," with the actor so in sympathy with his part that he feels the suitable emotions, and also in this way the correct expression of his emotions. The Stanislavski school, on the contrary, stresses extremely detailed study of the actor's expressions. Nothing can be improvised, and the effect is achieved by an exact knowledge of how any detail of intonation or movement influences the audience. According to our clinical studies, the truth lies in between these two extremes. The first school is right in so far as the actor's emotions have to be really felt by him in order to be impressive. The second school has in its favor the view not only that "having emotions" is not identical with being able to express them in an impressive way, but that acting technique has to be learned like any other technique. There may be a drop of truth in the old James-Lange theory that mimicry of an affective expression may secondarily produce the affect itself.

Playing, like thinking, is a test action: repeating the overwhelming past, and anticipating the possible future. The emotions of the actor are test emotions. It has often been stressed that the pleasure of the spectator in a tragedy is based on the fact that he knows that the cruelty he witnesses is "but a play." This is much truer of the actor himself. He may welcome the opportunity to act as if he were cruel because he knows that in reality he is not cruel. What he does not know, and what he should not know if he is to be a good actor, is that in a sense it is real and genuine cruelty that he feels in this role. Playing a part is making test identifications. The earliest test identification was probably the priests' identification with God. This identification too (like the identification of the believer with the priest who imitates God) was possible because the imitator felt simultaneously the infinite distance between himself and what he imitated, in the same way that the playing child imitates the serious actions of adults.[9]

---

them, or as the child would have liked them to be. Cf. F. Wittels, "Unconscious Phantoms in Neurotics," *Psa. Quart.,* Vol. 8, 1939.

[9] The imitation of idealized persons often represents an attempt to "try out" their ways of feeling, without losing the knowledge of the "trial" character. The "test" character of such limited "identifications" in the service of some purpose of the ego, differentiates imitation from full identification, which takes place unconsciously and independently of the ego's wishes.

Does this mean that the best actor would be a character who has not developed an actual marked personality, but who is ready to play any part given him, who has no ego, but is rather a bundle of identification possibilities? Some great actors have been of this type, and did on the stage what Caligula did in life.[10] But it is not all necessarily so. Certainly there are actors who have well-integrated personalities. They are not well integrated only in those parts of their personalities involved in their work. They are Caligulas on the stage, but not in life.

We can now better understand some types of failure on the stage. If a part somehow comes too close to painful emotions in the actor's unconscious, if he tends to become aware that the pretended emotions of his role also have reality values to him, then he can no longer successfully act the part. He is faced with the immediate necessity of further repression of the emotions, and becomes incapable of acting.

If the magic influence of the audience, which the actor unconsciously strives for, threatens to become too real so that the whole performance loses its "play" character, the actor will fail. Certainly the average actor does not use his playing directly to affect his audience as Hamlet uses the players. His only conscious aim is applause. His wish for reassurances against castration fear, or of "charming" the audience, remains unconscious.

Acting on the stage is endangered by the same two dangers which threaten the "double-edged character" of children's play. The pleasure in playing turns into displeasure if the intended "mastery" fails and the playing gets out of control. The fearsome loss of control may involve the player himself (he might become for good the animal he pretended to be), or the audience (he might charm or destroy it in an irreparable way).

III

Let us consider the "magic influence" upon the audience to which reference has been made and ask of what this influence actually consists.

Sachs, following Freud, developed a well-known general theory about the unconscious processes within the artist.[11] By presenting his work, which unconsciously represents an expression of repressed instinctual wishes, derivations of the oedipus complex, the artist induces in his public a participation in the forbidden wishes through acceptance and praise of his work. To see that the public accepts the artistic expressions of his unconscious guilt-laden impulses is for him a belated approval of them and removes or decreases his feelings of guilt

---

[10] H. Sachs, *Caligula*, London, Elkin Mathews & Marrot, 1931.
[11] H. Sachs, *The Creative Unconscious; Studies in the Psychoanalysis of Art*, Cambridge, Sci-Art, 1942.

about them. After having withdrawn from reality into daydreaming, the artist finds his way back from daydreaming to society by *inducing* an audience to participate in his guilt.

While this applies to all artists, it is especially true for the actor. It is the unconscious aim of all acting to make the audience feel the same emotions that the actor displays. The spectators go to the theater with the tacitly·acknowledged intention of identifying themselves with the actors' portrayals. The theater remains the realm of the infantile "ocular identification." [12] The actor seeks to induce the audience's participation and approval of the commission of the deeds which he, under the guise of pretense, would like to commit. If he succeeds, he feels less guilty.

That the audience is compelled to give up its spontaneity to accept hypnotically what the actor suggests (possibly through the "omnipotence of gestures"),[13] gives the actor a satisfying feeling of superiority and of having the audience dependent on him. Actually, he is dependent upon the audience. He has become an actor because he feels guilty unless he can draw the reassuring applause his narcissism requires. The actor needs the audience for the same reason that the audience needs the actor: both get reassurances against guilt feelings which make possible otherwise forbidden discharges of instinctual tension by mutual participation. In a good theatrical performance (as in ancient worship) actor and audience feel, "We do it together." The audience, knowing it is "only a play," loses its fear of the deed, and the actor (and likewise the author), secure in the same knowledge, loses his feeling of guilt through the approval of the brothers (audience), which releases him, the hero, of his loneliness. The magic induction is in the last analysis a *seduction* to participation in a repetition of the oedipus.

In a variation of "charming" the audience by his acting, the actor seduces the audience not only in order to win approval of his deed. His self-esteem, reestablished by approval, immediately increases by stressing the difference and distance between him and the audience: "You are but my puppets; I am God and you are nothing." By this feeling of power over the audience, he feels the unconscious temptation to reassure himself by destroying and castrating the audience, against any future possibility of reproach from it. Many actors are afraid not only of a lack of response from the audience, but also of too great an effect on it by evoking a response they can no longer control, and threatening the retaliation of the audience.

An actress-patient felt on the stage an impulse to make grimaces which was very disturbing to her work. It was relatively easy to understand that this meant:

---

[12] Cf. O. Fenichel, "The Scoptophilic Instinct and Identification," No. 33, *First Series.*
[13] S. Ferenczi, "Stages in the Development of the Sense of Reality," *Sex in Psychoanalysis,* New York, Brunner, 1950.

"I am afraid that just those characteristics of mine which I am trying to hide by acting might come out against my will. I am afraid that I shall not act what I intend to act, but what is really in my unconscious." But why were the "guilt-laden impulses" or the "lack of a penis" represented just by making faces? In the deepest layer of the unconscious they were chewing movements, and represented the impulse to devour the dismembered audience.

IV

The actor prepares by long preliminary work for the night when he will charm everybody. If he succeeds, a pleasure which has been forbidden to him hitherto will become accessible again. The work of the actor may be compared to the mechanisms of sexual forepleasure and end-pleasure. Rehearsals are usually very strenuous and painful and arduous. They are nevertheless pleasurable by reason of a mounting anticipatory tension straining toward the end-pleasure of the opening night for release.

The movie actor is cheated of this end-pleasure, but acting for the films gives the actor an exceptional narcissistic satisfaction. The actor cannot feel with his audience, but he can actually be a spectator of his own performance. But other pleasures, and especially the specific end-pleasure, are denied him. He feels frustrated. He is deprived of the unique experience of a *unio mystica* with the audience, and of the satisfaction of performing a complete part from the beginning to the end of the plot. The endless repetition of incoherent scenes is all rehearsal, and the only pleasure is anticipation of the satisfaction not of an actor, but at most of a spectator. The essential pleasure of the actor to bring "disjected membra" together, and to present them as a whole, is partly shifted to the director.[14] I was not surprised to find that those few motion picture actors I had the opportunity to analyze were longing to return to the stage. The films have many possibilities for the expression of modern needs and for providing the abreaction of the audience, which the stage never had. The actor is worse off. The knowledge that millions will see him is no reparation for the direct applause of hundreds.

V

If the actor succeeds, he has fewer guilt feelings, and if he has fewer feelings of guilt, he feels privileged to indulge more freely his instinctual pleasure and seeks greater sexual freedom. That society actually grants him such privileges, more or less, is connected with the peculiar position of the artist in bourgeois society. The artist is still regarded as nearer to God, and enjoys the privileges of

---

[14] It would be interesting to compare the psychology of the scenario writer, who is furnished the complete plot of a story and prepares the script from it, with the psychology of the playwright.

the priest. As is well known, the privileges accorded the artist are very ambivalent in intent. The actor is privileged, but he remains somewhat beyond the pale of "honest" society. He sins publicly and thereby exculpates the others (though he, subjectively, has also the striving of being himself exculpated). Like the whore, he is held in contempt but secretly envied.[15]

Since the times of totem festivals society has developed institutions to give an outlet to dammed-up instincts. At rare festival occasions deeds were permitted which normally were forbidden. They were permitted, however, only as long as the "deeds" were done in a manner of play entirely prescribed and according to ritual. The participants in these institutions were subject to taboos designed to insure the maintenance of the prescribed and institutionalized rituals. Within the restrictions of the taboos, and outside their contacts with their employers, they were granted certain privileges.[16]

In the classic bourgeois society, the actor had sexual privileges, if often only a pseudo-sexuality. We have described why those who are disposed easily to develop identifications, and who are in need of external oral gratifications, are those who are especially inclined to become actors. These individuals are frequently inhibited in their object relations because they see in the persons around them only objects for identification or sources of narcissistic gratification. It may have been that the majority of actors *acted* in a manner more sexual than other people, but perhaps experienced less satisfaction; or that at times they were able to indulge and achieve satisfaction only after their expiating success on the stage.

VI

The unconscious aims of the magic influence, which the actor tries to convey to his audience, and which has the value of exculpating him, are mainly two: seduction to participate in the actor's guilt, and the craving to gratify passive oral needs by any means, including if necessary, destruction or "castration" of the audience.

In the plots in which theater is used to wring an actual confession of guilt from a spectator, as in Hamlet, or in Schiller's "Cranes of Ibicus," not a repressed instinct but a suppressed feeling of guilt and expectation of punishment is mobilized. This, too, to a certain extent, seems to be a component of all theater. Pity and fear have to be provoked, and the evocation of fear—the fear of

---

[15] Cf. E. Kris and O. Kurz, *Die Legende vom Kuenstler,* Vienna, Krystallyerlag, 1934.

[16] There are many reasons why this position of the artist is especially marked for the actor. The theater has retained certain archaic features which, by their very archaic nature, are apt to mobilize repressed impulses and to arouse ambivalent feelings. The actors were, for long periods, nomads—like the gypsies—while all others had long settled. Actors are also looked upon like gypsies, and gypsies were often performers. Cf. O. Fenichel, "Elements of a Psychoanalytic Theory of Anti-Semitism," No. 25 in this volume.

God who was imitated by the acting priests—was certainly one of the main aims of the primeval theater. Not alone fear, but certainly also hope of salvation was aroused; otherwise the audience would have fled in panic and would not have remained true to God. Seduction and intimidation were both achieved by means of magical gestures. This combination of seduction and intimidation is the essential content of all totem festivals, initiation rites, religious rites, and theatrical performances. It states in effect: "You are given permission for instinctual satisfactions (or you are given your narcissistic indulgence), but only if you fulfill our conditions. And do not forget that you will be dreadfully punished if you transgress these conditions."

Not only has the spectator to be given protective reassurances ("it is only a play") if the attempted seduction is to succeed, but the actor, too, has to deny dangers which are believed to be connected with his seducing and imitating activity. He wants to seduce, or charm, or even to destroy the spectator, but not in such a manner or to a degree that might provoke the spectator to turn against him. The actor has to make sure that the audience remains dependent on him. The more he doubts inwardly its dependence on him, the more urgent his need for outer proofs of it. Seeking applause, as the actor invariably does, he denies to himself and others that he actually is dependent on the spectators.

An actress-patient, who had a deep oral fixation and whose object relationships consisted almost exclusively in trying to make people *give* to her, had, since her childhood, always had several dogs. Her later relationships included a number of men, all temperamentally depressive, who needed her sympathy but who actually tyrannized her. She had the illusion that the dogs and the men were dependent on her, whereas actually she was entirely dependent on them, even to the point of submissiveness (*Hörigkeit*). Her acting was (a) consciously the expression of the fantasy, "Look how rich I am; how much I am able to give away"; (b) unconsciously the expression of the fantasy, "You have to give me something, namely, the stuff which I in turn will give away again." "I feed you," was the surface. "If I act well, you will have to feed me," was the depth. Her words and gestures on the stage had for her the unconscious significance of food, and were "magical gestures" to demonstrate to the audience what she expected the audience to give to her. The narcissistic pleasure consisted in the fact that the playwright's "food" had passed through the actor's personality. This was the same patient who was sometimes disturbed while acting by the compulsion to make faces, which turned out to be chewing movements, expressing an unconscious impulse to devour the audience.

Exhibitionism in general, and acting in particular, has a deep connection with the castration complex. There are many ways in which the "charm" of acting may serve the purpose of denying castration or any possibility of it, or of denying that castration is a danger, and influencing the audience to give some equivalent reassurance.

I have had opportunity to observe a strange urethral way of gaining such reassurance. An actress who spoke very quickly, was often afraid of "losing control" over the words which gushed from her mouth, and was sometimes inhibited to the point of speechlessness or forgetting her lines. Her magic means of avoiding that was, between scenes, to drink one or several glasses of water whereby she filled herself with the substance which then came out in the form of her words. Unconsciously her copious urination was identical with having a penis.

The most drastic idea of forcing the audience to give such reassurance is the unconscious fantasy of castrating the audience. Such a castrating attitude was decisive in the structure of the neurosis of a patient who loved to act.[17] Analysis of her acting provided the opportunity to analyze grotesque-comic acting in general. This patient's acting had the unconscious aim of stating by magic gestures: "None of you has a penis. I, acting the part of a castrated person [in a deeper layer: acting the part of a penis which has been cut off], am showing you how you are supposed to look." The comic character of the acting concealed and denied the real aim of the grotesqueness to achieve a frightening effect. The neurosis of this patient expressed the failure of this defense, owing to its double-edged character. Her symptoms expressed the fear that the play might become real and she might lose both her audience and her penis for good.[18]

It is tempting to study the same influences from the standpoint of the spectator. The social function of the theater is fulfilled today by the movies and with greater effectiveness than the medium which served narcissistic needs of individual actors. To discover in this new medium the old elements which, since ancient times, have been the constituents of all theater, would be very interesting. But we shall limit our discussion to the actor.

A discussion of the psychology of the actor should not fail to include comment about the typical actor's neurosis, stage fright.[19]

---

[17] A. Reich, "The Structure of the Grotesque-Comic Sublimation," *Bull. Menninger Clin.*, Vol. 13, 1949.

[18] The same mechanism can often be observed in people who like to "perform" by telling jokes. An unconscious aggression may be given expression if hidden in the form of a joke, particularly if one succeeds in inducing the audience to participate in the aggression. But this too may have a "double-edged character." The fear is that a real magical effect of the joke might destroy its character as a joke. Cf. S. Freud, "Wit and Its Relation to the Unconscious," *The Basic Writings*, New York, 1938.

I once analyzed the traditional figure of the "clown" as the exhibition of a phallic figure, which has been regressively debased to the pregenital level for the purpose of denying the seriousness of castration. The many stories of the uncanny tragic clown represent the failure of these attempts. Cf. O. Fenichel, "The Symbolic Equation: Girl = Phallus," No. 1 in this volume.

[19] I do not remember any published case of the psychoanalysis of stage fright. There is a great

The general cause of stage fright is to be found in the double-edged character of all the psychological mechanisms we have discussed. The reassurance which theatrical performance unconsciously promises the actor is not always achieved. Stage fright occurs when the unconscious motives of the actor threaten to become conscious (when the "play" threatens to become "real"). Instead of participating in the actor's guilty misdeeds, the audience may turn against him and become the representative of the punishing superego. And stage fright has a special quality; it is the specific fright of an exhibitionist: shame. Unconsciously, it is the shame of an inferiority (being castrated), to cover which has been the chief motivation in the choice of acting as a profession. The shame may derive in addition from the threat of display of unconscious intentions hidden in the acting, of sexual tendencies (oedipus), and of primitive destructive impulses to obtain, by deception, gratification of the narcissistic demands. Shame and anxiety arise from the dread of being exposed as a sham, of having expropriated something, of adorning oneself with borrowed plumes. The playing of a part on the stage is moreover a source of potential shame because of the real dependency of the actor who tries to make believe that the others are dependent on him.[20]

---

deal of literature about the related symptoms such as fear of examinations and erythrophobia: E. Blum, "The Psychology of Study and Examinations," *Int. J. Psa.,* Vol. 7, 1926; J. C. Flugel, "The Examination as Initiation Rite and Anxiety Situation," *Int. J. Psa.,* Vol. 20, 1939; E. Stengel, "Pruefungsangst und Pruefungsneurose," *Z. Psa. Paed.,* Vol. 10, 1936; E. Jones, "Pathology of Morbid Anxiety," *Papers on Psychoanalysis,* 4th ed., Baltimore, Wood, 1938; S. Feldmann, "Ueber das Erroeten. Beitrag zur Psychologie der Scham," *Int. Z. Psa.,* Vol. 8, 1922.

[20] Compulsive mechanisms of actors have unconsciously the meaning of ensuring that acting is only "playing" to overcome stage fright. "Getting stuck" may express the resistance against any tendency which was supposed to find an outlet in the acting. It may also have the much more specific meaning of "getting stuck" before the castrated state, which one had intended to play, is achieved; and/or "getting stuck" *in* the castrated state.

TWENTY-SEVEN

Some Remarks on Freud's Place
in the History of Science *

In 1917 Freud published a short paper entitled "One of the Difficulties of Psycho-Analysis." In it he wrote that psychoanalysis tends to arouse an affective prejudice, with the result that whoever hears about it is "less inclined to believe in it or take an interest in it." [1] After explaining the force of narcissism in human beings, he discussed how the discoveries of psychoanalysis wounded narcissistic self-esteem. The discovery of the unconscious revealed "that the ego is not master in its own house"; [2] moreover, the statement that mental life is primarily unconscious was "not affirmed [by psychoanalysis] on an abstract basis, but has been demonstrated in matters that touch every individual personally and force him to take up some attitude towards these problems." [3] Freud compares this narcissistic humiliation to two other similar humiliations man has suffered as a result of the development of scientific knowledge: the cosmological humiliation for which Copernicus was responsible when he proved that the earth is not the center of the universe, and the biological humiliation caused by Darwin when he showed that man is an animal like all other animals.

When one who has devoted his life to the practice and the further development of Freud's ideas attempts to evaluate what among his contributions is essential to human knowledge, he is so overwhelmed by the abundance of new concepts Freud introduced that he is at first inclined to give up the task. It is at this point that Freud's "One of the Difficulties of Psycho-Analysis" comes to

---

* First published in *Psa. Quart.*, Vol. 15, 1946, pp. 279–284.

[1] S. Freud, "One of the Difficulties of Psycho-Analysis," *Coll. Pap.*, Vol. IV, London, Hogarth, 1948, p. 347.

[2] *Ibid.*, p. 355.

[3] *Ibid.*, p. 356.

one's assistance. It describes a special "difficulty" of psychoanalysis. It must be the principal merit of psychoanalysis to have overcome this difficulty. This is a consequence not alone of the discovery of the unconscious but more, the mode of thinking that made this discovery possible—the decisive step beyond those narcissistic prejudices which sober research into reality has taken. Psychoanalysis has made possible nothing less than this: to see a half of reality—the data of mental life—not more or less as we should like to see it, but with the same objectivity with which physics, chemistry, and biology have long since viewed phenomena in their respective fields. An attitude that has long been accepted as a matter of course in these sciences has been attained in the field of psychology. A certain displeasure in the individual ("science grays the many-colored pattern of life") is overcome, and the practical advantages offered by scientific knowledge —the potentialities of prognosis and technique—gained.

Psychoanalysis as a dynamic science takes its point of departure from the description of mental phenomena, and views the observed phenomena as the result of a hidden play of forces. Its interpretative aspect is no different from other sciences which aim to discover hidden structural connections. As a genetic psychology, it seeks also to determine their historical development so that the structure may be viewed as the finished product of such development. Consequently, "morphological" and "historical" points of view play a fundamental role in psychoanalysis, but they do not delimit the scope of psychoanalytic knowledge. Psychoanalysis is not only concerned with life histories; its aim is, in addition, to compare the course of many life histories and many mental phenomena in an attempt to discover the *general laws* governing mental life. It seeks to comprehend laws governing mental functions as a special case of the function of life in general, just as the biological sciences comprehend other life functions. Although Freud's metapsychology may in time be supplemented or altered, the insight psychoanalysis has given us into such general laws is, indeed, considerable.

Freud was not the first to consider the field of psychology from a scientific point of view. There were scientific psychologies before him, and others exist today. But compared to "philosophical" psychologies, scientific psychologies have always been in the minority and have been able only to consider disparate functions and action. An understanding of the multiplicity of everyday human mental life based on natural science really only began with psychoanalysis.

For centuries psychology was considered a special field of speculative philosophy, far removed from sober empiricism. If one considers the more or less metaphysical questions that were held to be of paramount importance, one easily recognizes that the problems discussed originated in theology. They reflected the antitheses "body" and "soul," "human" and "divine," "natural" and "supernatural." Psychoanalysis, which overcame these prejudices, gave us also the means to understand them. It explained not only the narcissism which is humiliated because man realizes he is not master in his own house, but also "magical thinking," which is closely related to this narcissism. Magical thinking, it is true, has played in the remote history of human thought a significant role in furthering adaptation to reality. Nevertheless, we know that it later tended entirely to replace realistic thinking wherever such thinking would have led to consequences painful to man's self-esteem.

Gradually, scientific thinking has gained ground over religio-magical thinking. The natural sciences, originating and evolving at definite periods in the development of human society (from technical necessity), have had to overcome the most violent and stubborn resistances in their striving to describe and to explain natural phenomena. These resistances in different sciences find varying degrees of intensity of expression. One need only compare any issue of a clinical journal with one devoted to chemistry or physics to find evidences of this variation. The influence of magic is everywhere more in evidence in medicine than in the so-called pure sciences. The traditions of medicine stem from the activity of medicine men and priests; further, psychiatry is not only the youngest branch of the magic-imbued science of medicine, but also the one most saturated with magic. It deals with facts which until recently were closed to the scientist and accessible only to the priest. The resistance to science increases in proportion to the approach of the subject matter of the science to the intimate concerns of men. Not so long ago the pathologist was forbidden to dissect the human body. Human pathology and physiology finally freed, magic nevertheless persisted in the realm of mental research. Here causality and quantity were not conceded to exist; one was supposed to meditate and to feel reverent. In all such psychologies there is a remnant of belief in the immortality of the soul.

A glance at the history of science teaches us that the process of overcoming magic has been a devious one. There have been advances and retreats. The fluctuations in the struggle between the reality principle and magic seem to have been dependent upon other historical conditions that are far more complicated. They can only be understood through sociology, by a study of conflicting groups and interests in society.

In scientific and historical evaluations of psychoanalysis, one often hears two opposite opinions. Some say that Freud is a confirmed materialist who strives to shut off the living stream of mental phenomena in rigid categories. There are also those who say that, at a period when the natural sciences were at the height of their development, his contribution consisted of once again forcing recognition of the irrational, the psychogenic, against the prevalent overestimation of rationalism, that he thereby revealed the limitations of "materialistic medicine," which, for example, had been baffled by the phenomenon of hysteria. How can this contradiction be explained?

The golden days of medicine, epitomized by the name of Virchow, simply did not include the total human being in its researches. The neglect of psychology indicates nothing other than that progress in scientific thinking was purchased at the price of letting one entire realm of nature—the mind—remain a reservation for religion and magical thinking. The physical scientists were unconscious mystics in the mental sphere.

The contradiction in the scientific historical evaluation of Freud's work is resolved by recognizing that he accomplished two things at the same time: by opposing pseudomaterialism and by strongly emphasizing the existence of a mental sphere and the inadequacy of the physical sciences in dealing with psychopathology and the psychological aspects of life, he won this terrain for science. It is agreed too that Freud gave the "subjective factor," the "irrational," its just due. I believe that Freud's discovery clearly reveals the spirit of that broad cultural trend which proclaimed as its ideal the primacy of reason over religious prejudice, and the unbiased investigation of reality. What had previously been considered sacred and untouchable might now be touched because the very validity of such taboos had been denied. The absolute "ideals" made known to us through revelation were likewise brought down to earth and examined as manifestations of the workings of men's minds. Despite the distance between Freud and Virchow, they had much in common. Freud investigated the mental world with the same scientific courage that Virchow applied to the physical. That meant rebellion against the prejudices that had prevailed up to that time. It represents the same spirit of liberal thinking in science that in ethics proclaimed "the rights of man."

The objection may be raised that such a statement is a one-sided presentation of psychoanalysis. Does not this science contain a great deal of mysticism, or at least of the mystic tradition? Did it not develop from hypnotism, derived in turn from Mesmerism? Is not, furthermore, "mental healing" a variety of magic? Certainly it has descended directly from magical methods. But psychoanalysis, despite its background of magical thinking, has transformed magic into a natural science. Its object, not its method, is irrational. We know that in every phase of mental development rudiments of earlier phases persist, and it would not be difficult to find many echoes of magic in the theory and the practice of psychoanalysis. This would not be difficult in any branch of medicine. Psychoanalysis will always retain certain historical traces of magical thinking. And wherever in psychoanalysis there is encountered a resurgence of recessive theorizing, one can be sure that mystical rudiments are pushing to the surface at the expense of the scientific elements.

To what extent this holds true depends upon social conditions. There is no doubt that despite the great resistance to his discoveries that Freud encountered, his daring nevertheless accorded with the current trend of the preponderance of reason in thinking which was a general trend fifty years ago. No doubt today, contrariwise, there is a swing away from the "rational" to the "ideal." Such a tendency comes to expression in psychoanalysis early in its history because this science was delivered from magical thinking far later than any other science.

Scientific psychology explains mental phenomena as the result of primitive bodily needs developed in the course of biological development and therefore changeable (the instincts), and, in addition, as the operation of environment on these instincts. There is no place for a third factor such as an immanent principle of perfection. To psychoanalysis, therefore, all "ideals" are human ideas whose origin can be explained by the interplay of instincts and environment. Every trend of thought which required ideals that savor of the beyond, the absolute, and that exclude all criticism, must be inimical to scientific psychology and must lead to a reversion to magical thinking.

In seeking to implement his practical needs as a physician treating hysterics, Freud discovered and developed the science of psychology. Compared to this fact the therapeutic application of psychoanalysis pales into insignificance. Social conditions make the direct therapeutic efforts of psychoanalysis inadequate in comparison with the extent of neurotic misery in our day.

Psychoanalysts can do no better than to follow Freud's example.

Index of Names

367

Index of Subjects

Abreaction, 302, 353

Acting, 349; abreaction in, 353; and castration anxiety, 352, 359f; forepleasure and end-pleasure, 357; instinctual impulses in, 360f; magic aims of, 356, 358; and pretending, 353; relation to playing, 352f; thinking as, 50

Acting out: inside of psychoanalysis, 301ff; neurotic, 296ff; and object relationships, 299; outside of psychoanalysis, 298ff; and resistance, 301ff; and technique, 302f

Active: and passive, 165, 168f, 263, 300

Active technique, 303

Actor: and audience, 355f; ego of, 355; movie versus theater, 357; narcissism of, 356; sexuality of, 358

"Actual neurotic" state, 310

Adaptation, 266, 271

Addicts, 300

Affects, 118; blocking, 221; defense against, 219f, 221ff; derivatives of, 221; as discharge phenomenon, 215f; and ego, 75; and ego control, 216; equivalents, 223f, 309f, 318; taming of, 118, 217, 219; unconscious, 221, 311ff; vicissitudes of, 221

Aggression, 62f, 75, 158, 172; and trophy, 162

Aggressor: identification with, 147, 169

Agoraphobia, 280, 284

Aim: of instinct, 4

Alloplastic, 115, 300; and autoplastic, 298

Ambition, 14f

Ambivalence, 32f

Amnesia, 233

Anal character, 208

Anal conflicts, 316

Anal erotism, 148; and possession, 98

Anal sadism, 12f

Analysis: acting out in, 301ff; prohibitions in, 303 (See also Character analysis, Ego analysis, Id analysis, etc.)

Analytic process: and acting out, 298ff; and counter-phobic attitude, 172f

Animistic thinking, 55, 229, 235, 286, 364f

Anorexia, 288ff

Anticathexis, 20, 37, 51, 52, 172, 187; for binding, 165

Anticipation, 165

Anti-instinctual forces: instinctual character of, 329

Anti-Semitism, 335ff; displacement in, 338, 347; projection in, 340f

Anxiety, 20, 28, 204f; bodily sensations in, 283, 284, 317; and child's play, 165, 168; and counter-phobic attitude, 164ff; and defense, 50, 64; defense against, 163, 164, 219f; denial of, 171; economics of, 166; and ego, 39, 49, 62, 164f, 218; and equilibrium-eroticism, 58, 59; equivalents, 320; and fixations, 170; and functional pleasure, 166; genetic series of, 55, 63; hysteria, 56; and infantile sexuality, 84f, 167; and laughter, 161; libidinization, 170; mastery of, 164, 165f; masturbation and, 84f; model of, 38; in phobias, 278; pleasure in, 66, 166; pregenital, 97f; and primitive ego, 39; projection of, 172; and quantity of excitation, 56, 287; search for, 170; signal, 38, 49, 50, 279; as source of sexual excitation, 170; in traumatic states, 50, 56; triple stratification of, 218; and triumph and trophy, 171

Apprentice, 147

Art: and counter-phobic attitude, 172

Attitudes, 114; defensive, 114, 187, 203, 210; genesis of, 204

Audience, function of, 355ff

Authoritarian ideals, 333

Books That Live

THE NORTON IMPRINT ON A BOOK
MEANS THAT IN THE PUBLISHER'S
ESTIMATION IT IS A BOOK NOT FOR A
SINGLE SEASON BUT FOR THE YEARS

W · W · NORTON & COMPANY · INC ·